# I'm *Common Sense* & I'm Running for Office!

*Common Sense Solutions for America's Most Pressing Problems!*

**Join the *Common Sense* Revolution at: www.ThatsCommonSense.com**

**James Daniels**

Unless otherwise noted, quotations from the Holy Bible are taken from, The Holy Bible, New King James Version, copyright © 1979, 1980, 1982 by Thomas Nelson, Inc. Used by permission.

Unless otherwise noted, quotations from the Quran are taken from the Yusuf Ali English text, originally published in 1934, under the title, The Holy Qur-an, Text, Translation and Commentary, (published in Lahore, Cairo and Riyadh). This version is widely used by English-speaking Muslims because it is a clear, modern and eloquent translation by a well-respected Muslim scholar. The English text was revised in 2009-10 to more closely match the source book. This newly-revised improved text is the text quoted in this book. You may access the text online at: http://www.sacred-texts.com/isl/yaq/index.htm

On occasion, in order to gain a better understanding of the meaning of a Quranic text, quotations are also taken from two other highly regarded English translations of the Quran which are noted as: Pickthall and Shakir.

Underlining of any Biblical or Quranic Text has been added by this Author for emphasis.

# Dedication

This book is dedicated to the proposition that all men are created equal, and endowed by their Creator with a good and healthy dose of *Common Sense*, which, if and when applied to one's individual life and the overall governance of the people, will provide a fertile field from which may spring the fruit of abundant life, watered by liberty, thus enabling each of us to pursue happiness to the extent we desire.

I can assure you that you will not agree with every *Common Sense* solution offered in this book; but these are written to challenge you to think about the said topics and to apply your own *Common Sense* to each of these areas of your personal life, as well as to our nation's policies.

My hope is to inspire you, challenge you, and yes in some areas even anger you; but when all is read and done, my desire is for you to feel fulfilled, yet with a sense of urgency to help spread the message to others who are in desperate need of the message of *Common Sense!*

Contents

## The Amendments To The Constitution Of The United States...409

# Introduction

America, I'm *Common Sense* & I'm Running for Office! Elect me, *Common Sense*, as your President, Congressman, Governor, State Legislator and Mayor and together we will take back America from the Communist ignoramuses who are presently destroying our great nation! Spend a little time with me in the pages of this book and get to know me, *Common Sense*, for I'm the solution for America's most pressing problems!

What is *"Common Sense?"* Merriam Webster defines *Common Sense* as: sound and prudent judgment based on a simple perception of the situation or facts.

I agree that *Common Sense* is indeed "sound and prudent judgment," and would add—sound and prudent judgment based upon the simple facts and plain truths which are "commonly" held and believed by all or at least most of humanity. In other words, the sense of right and wrong, of what is true and what isn't, that is common among us. *Common Sense* is that awareness of what works and what doesn't work, not based upon book learning, but based upon simple life experience. *Common Sense* recognizes the truthfulness and reality of that which is obvious—obvious even to the casual observer.

I believe that every one of us is born with a healthy God-given dose of *Common Sense*. Unfortunately, some among us, usually through "higher learning," suppress that God-given *Common Sense* and choose to believe the ranting and ramblings of men who, *"Professing themselves to be wise, became fools!"* (Romans 1:22). You know what you call somebody who professes himself to be wise? A professor! That was not meant to disparage all professors, just most. Education is great and very important for one's success in life, as long as you don't abandon your *Common Sense* and believe a lie. We've all known people who possessed "book smarts," but had little or no *Common Sense*. Unfortunately, in America today many, if not most, of our political leaders have abandoned *Common Sense!* It is time for America to return to the *Common Sense* principles of our Founding Fathers!

America's fifty-five Founding Fathers who signed the Declaration of Independence were men who possessed *Common Sense*. We behold their *Common Sense* declaration when they, as one man, with a firm reliance upon Divine Providence and pledging to one another their lives, fortunes and sacred honor, did then put with pen their signatures of unanimous agreement to the words penned by Thomas Jefferson in the Declaration of Independence, that,

*We hold these truths to be self-evident, that all men are created equal, that they are endowed by their Creator with certain unalienable rights, that among these are life, liberty and the pursuit of happiness. That to secure these rights, governments are instituted among men, deriving their just powers from the consent of the governed. That whenever any form of government becomes destructive to these ends, it is the right of the people to alter or to abolish it, and to institute new government, laying its foundation on such principles and organizing its powers in such form, as to them shall seem most likely to effect their safety and happiness.* (The Declaration of Independence, July 4, 1776, paragraph 2)

Now, that's *Common Sense!* It is *Common Sense* that:

A) We are *"created"* by a Creator! Even the most simple among us has the *Common Sense*, upon opening his eyes to behold the vastness and absolute mathematical perfection of the universe, from its magnificent galaxies down to the structure and unimaginable power resident within every atom; when even a moron looks at the beauty, complexity and diversity of life, from the immense diversity of the animal kingdom, to the unfathomable complexity of the molecular machines operating within every single cell of every living thing, to man himself, created in the likeness and image of God, possessing intelligence, free-will and the innate ability to know right from wrong, one comes to the *Common Sense* conclusion that all things were created and not the result of a God-less accident—which by the way is physically and mathematically impossible! But he who believes that the universe and life are an accident and believes in evolution has, of necessity, abandoned *Common Sense*, and has believed a lie, jumping into the realm of "faith" to believe such nonsense; but the evolutionist's faith is not founded upon any evidence whatsoever—faith not founded upon infallible proof is not faith, but folly! Whereas, the Christian's faith in God as Creator of all things and the Lord Jesus Christ as God manifest in human flesh who died for our sins and rose from the dead as our Lord and Savior, is founded upon absolute infallible proofs: e.g., the Bible's "proof of prophecy," wherein the Bible foretold of major events in human history hundreds and even thousands of years before they occurred and they indeed happened exactly as the Bible foretold, thus scientifically proving the Bible to be Divinely inspired by God Who "knows the end from the beginning!" (See Deuteronomy 18:9-22; Isaiah 42:1-9, 43:8-13, 44:6-8, 45:1-22, 46:5-13; Amos 3:7-8; John 16:13); also the proof of Jesus Christ's many miracles which prove He is God as He claimed to be (See John 5:36, 10:22-33, 14:10-11); and the proof of Jesus Christ's glorious resurrection from the dead (See John 20:1-31; Acts 1:1-3; Romans 1:1-4; 1 Corinthians 15:1-11; 2 Peter 1:16-21; 1 John 1:1-4). A Christian's faith in God, Jesus Christ and the Holy Bible is founded upon historical fact and infallible proofs! In light of these irrefutable proofs, believing in God, Jesus and the Bible is just *Common Sense!*

B) All men are created *"equal"* for "God is not a respecter of persons." Therefore, no man, by his politics, has the right to favor one man or group of men over any other, favoring them with special benefits and privileges, as is the common and perpetual practice of the Democratic Party with their anti-family, pro-homosexual policies. Neither does any man, by his politics, have the right to mistreat another man because of his race or Christian faith, as is the common and perpetual practice of the Democratic Party by their anti-Christian, anti-Black, pro-slavery policies from the Civil War until this day! Such unlawful favoritisms and mistreatments must be stopped!

C) We *"are endowed by [our] Creator with certain unalienable rights, that among these are life, liberty and the pursuit of happiness."*

One of our most beloved Founding Fathers, Benjamin Franklin, in commenting on the U.S. Constitution's construction to provide the rights declared in the Declaration, makes this humorous yet poignant observation:

*The U.S. Constitution doesn't guarantee happiness, only the pursuit of it. You have to catch up with it yourself.*

Many today think it's the government's job to make you happy. Hate to break it to you, but that's wrong. The government's job is to protect your life and grant you the freedom to pursue happiness on your own—that is if you want to, you don't have to pursue happiness if you don't wish to. We will discuss this further in Chapter 2, The God-given *Common Sense* Role of Government.

D) And finally, *"That to secure these rights, governments are instituted among men, deriving their just powers from the consent of the governed. That whenever any form of government becomes destructive to these ends, it is the right of the people to alter or to abolish it, and to institute new government, laying its foundation on such principles and organizing its powers in such form, as to them shall seem most likely to affect their safety and happiness.*

Seeing as this Declaration is referring to the British form of government, and predates the writing of our U.S. Constitution, which we trust and believe our Founding Fathers to have penned very wisely and prudently, we in this book are not advocating, with regard to the current government which has become *"destructive to these ends to abolish it, and to institute new government.*

But, we are indeed declaring, that We The People of these United States of America are coming, not by the power of the bullet but by the power of the ballot, to the polls to exercise our "right to altar" the current form of government by the *Common Sense* provisions our Founding Fathers instituted of general elections for members of the House of Representatives every 2 years, the Presidency every 4 years, and the Senate every 6 years.

And we hereby pledge our lives, our fortunes and our sacred honor to never again allow the enemies of America to gain Office!

After being "inspired" to write this book and having begun this undertaking, as I was conducting some research, I discovered something that heretofore was unknown to me, that a book of similar title, *"Common Sense,"* was published on February 14, 1776, and distributed among the 13 Colonies, becoming the best-selling book in America at that time. The author of that book is Thomas Paine, who, because of the impact of his book *Common Sense* upon the thinking and discourse of his day, was bestowed the title "Father of the American Revolution." Like I intend to do in this book, Thomas Paine referred to the Holy Scriptures contained in the Holy Bible to support and substantiate his arguments. Upon discovering this fact of similarity of titles and source of inspiration, I was quite honestly shaken just a bit, but also encouraged to press forward. I have therefore included the entire text of Thomas Paine's book *Common Sense* within the confines of this book as Appendix A. I have further included the entire text of the Declaration of Independence as Appendix B; and the entire text of the U.S. Constitution including all Amendments as Appendix C. Please take special note of Amendments 13, 14 and 15, known as the Civil War Amendments, which were written and ratified by the Republican Party to grant to all former Black slaves, whom the "anti-slavery" Republican Party had fought and died for to set free from slavery, equal rights with all Whites in America. Also note Amendment 16, written and ratified by the Democratic Party in 1913 to create the "Income Tax" whereby the Democratic Party has been violating our Founding Fathers principle of *"not taking from the mouth of labor the bread it has earned."* (See Chapter 6, *Common Sense* Solutions For Getting America's Economy Back On The Road To Prosperity! for a full discussion of the income tax issue; the 16th Amendment needs to be repealed and replaced with a 10% Federal Sales Tax.

Unlike Thomas Paine, however, I am not a significant figure or force for freedom, but simply a servant of Jesus Christ, serving His people as a minister, and humbly sharing the Common Sense concepts in this book in the hope of helping in some small way to restore righteousness—right thinking and actions—to our great Republic. My prayer is that, by God's grace, as Thomas Paine's book of *Common Sense* sparked the first American Revolution, bringing freedom and prosperity to America, may this book likewise fuel the fire of the new American *Common Sense* Revolution known as the Tea Party Movement, propelling the Tea party Revolution to the next level—for this book of *Common Sense* solutions for America's most pressing problems is the Tea Party Revolution ON STEROIDS!

The shame of the matter is that this book need be written at all. But as one looks at the current state of national affairs, one must ask the question,

"Has America Gone Mad?" *Fasten your seatbelts, America, here we go!*

# Chapter 1: Has America Gone Mad?

Seriously, has America gone mad? As American's we pride ourselves in knowing that even if the rest of the world goes to Hell in a hand-basket, at least America will still retain some semblance of sanity. But sadly, I have to report the news that most American's have lost their mind; America has gone mad!

And I can prove it!

## America, You Elected An Environmental Nut-Job As Your President—Have You Gone Mad?

Here's the proof. In the Presidential Election held on November 4, 2008, a majority of American's who voted elected a man to the Presidency who had publically declared in January, 2008, in an interview that was widely disseminated through social media channels (though tragically under-reported in the mainstream media), that,

*"Under my plan of a cap and trade system, **electricity** rates would necessarily **skyrocket.**"* —Presidential Candidate Barack Hussein Obama (To see, search YouTube.com, "Obama my plan makes electricity rates skyrocket").

Since Obama's *plan of a cap and trade system* is an assault on all so-called fossil-fuels, not just coal, but also oil, then Barack Obama's cap and trade plan will also cause heating oil and gasoline prices to *"necessarily **skyrocket!**"*

So let's get this straight: In 2008, then Presidential Candidate Barack Hussein Obama promised the American people that if we elected him, he would do everything in his power to make our electric, heating oil and gasoline costs *skyrocket,* yet a majority of you still voted for him! Are you out of your mind? America, have you gone mad?

Mr. Bill O'Reilly, if I may *opine* for a moment on this subject, and I'll be careful not to bloviate: Barack Obama's, and for that matter the vast majority of Democrats', policy of Cap-and-Trade is purely a *climate-change policy* based upon a false belief, first, in global warming, and second, that global warming is caused by man's use of so-called fossil-fuels, which the leftist environmentalists refer to as *dirty-energy*, in contrast to the energy sources they prefer of wind and solar, which they refer to as *clean energy*, supposing that fossil-fuels are harmful to the environment and responsible for global warming.

First of all, anyone with an ounce of *Common Sense* knows that global warming is a complete hoax concocted by the leftist environmentalists to further their anti-Biblical, anti-God world view of Earth over Man, verses the correct Biblical world view of God's command for Man to fill, subdue and dominate the Earth. As it is written:

**Genesis 1:26-28**

[26]*Then God said, "Let Us make man in Our image, according to Our likeness; let them have <u>dominion over the fish of the sea, over the birds of the air, and over the cattle, over all the earth and over every creeping thing that creeps on the earth</u>."*

[27]*So God created man in His own image; in the image of God He created him; male and female He created them.*

[28]*Then God blessed them, and God said to them, "Be fruitful and multiply; <u>fill</u> the earth and <u>subdue</u> it; have <u>dominion</u> over the fish of the sea, over the birds of the air, and over every living thing that moves on the earth."*

Definition of "fill": to be fenced, (go) fill fully, over-flow, possess wholly.

Definition of "Subdue"**:** to *tread* down; to *conquer, subjugate, violate,* bring into bondage, force, keep under, subdue, bring into subjection.

Definition of "Dominion": to *tread* down, that is, *subjugate,* (come to) have dominion, prevail against, reign, rule over, take.

The above is what God has commanded Mankind regarding the Planet He has placed us in charge of, to be the stewards over!

But getting back to the global warming hoax, all one needs to do is simply watch his local evening news weather-cast to know for a scientific fact that global warming is not occurring! You know what I'm talking about, right? Whenever your city does hit a new record high temperature occasionally, the weather-caster always tells you when the previous record was set, and isn't it almost always something like, 1907 or 1918?...which scientifically proves that the Earth was just as hot one-hundred years ago! Think about it; record high temperatures were being set a hundred years ago when there were no or very few automobiles, plus back then we did not have the mammoth sprawling cement and glass jungles we call cities that now dominate the local landscape, which are scientifically proven to retain heat much more than earth does, yet without the heat-retention of our cities and no automobiles *spewing fossil-fuel pollutants into the atmosphere* to create a *green-house effect,* still record high temperatures were set which held for a century or longer! This fact proves that global warming is not occurring or at least is simply the cyclical trends that occur every century or so.

Second, the leftist environmentalist's assertion (note that the word *assertion* begins with the word *ass*), that Man's use of so-called fossil-fuels to power our automobiles is responsible for spewing pollutants into the atmosphere that in-turn create a green-house effect is ludicrous! Come on folks, use your *Common Sense!* Have the millions of automobiles driving daily all over Europe for the past hundred years ever caused enough pollutants in the atmosphere to shut down all the airports in Europe? Of course not! But one little volcano in Iceland in just one week belched enough pollutant matter to cause a cloud over Europe that shut down Europe's airports! A single volcano can spew more toxic pollutants into the atmosphere in one week than all the automobiles in a hundred years! And scores of volcanos have been erupting all over the planet for the past 6,000 years, and yet our atmosphere is still clean and clear! Of course it is! The Earth is a bad mother humper! You can't hurt this girl! Planet Earth will take several hundred-thousand of us out in a heart-beat with a tsunami, volcano, earthquake or hurricane; but she is designed to cleanse and recycle herself; you can't hurt Mother Earth!

So, the next time you hear one of those leftist environmentalists lying sacks of bull-dung mention their fabricated hoax of global warming as if it were true, scream at your TV, *Hey moron, watch the weather report on your local news!*

Or better yet, elect me, *Common Sense*, to Office, and I'll implement a *Common Sense* view of the environment that balances our God-given right to use our planet's bountiful resources with good stewardship of those resources. I'll close the Environmental Protection Agency (EPA)—a government agency whose very name is an abomination—declaring by its name that the environment needs "Protection" from Man; as mentioned above, such a world view elevates the Earth over Man—but the Earth was created for Man, not Man for the Earth. This anti-Man world view held by President Obama and the Democratic Party is not merely anti-Man, but also anti-God, because Man was made in the image and likeness of God, and because such policies are in direct disobedience to God's command for Man to fill, subdue and dominate the Earth.

God gave the resources of the planet for us to use for our benefit! Look at these few passages from the Bible that show God intends for Man to use the natural resources He has placed here for our benefit:

### Genesis 2:11-12
*[11]The name of the first is Pishon; it is the one which skirts the whole land of Havilah, where there is <u>gold</u>. [12]And the <u>gold of that land is good. Bdellium and the onyx stone</u> are there.*

### Genesis 4:22
*[22]And as for Zillah, she also bore Tubal-Cain, an instructor of every craftsman in <u>bronze and iron</u>.*

### Haggai 1:8
*[8]Go up to the mountains and bring <u>wood</u> and build the temple, that I may take pleasure in it and be glorified," says the LORD.*

As you can see, God intends for us to utilize the natural resources of the planet to the benefit of Mankind.

But the Democrats have an exactly opposite view of Mankind's use of our planet's natural resources.

By the way, I'm getting pretty sick of Republicans, including the Republican National Committee's Chairman, Reince Priebus, declaring that the reason America needs to remove President Obama from the White House in the 2012 Election is because he has *failed to deliver on his promises!* —Now I agree with Reince Priebus that Obama promised to cut the deficit in half in his first term, but instead increased the deficit and added $6-trillion in National Debt! And that is indeed reason enough to remove this debt-producing, economy destroying monster named Barack Obama from the White House!

But anybody with the intelligence of a watermelon knew when Obama made that promise that he was lying through his teeth! Obama is a Democrat, for God's sake! Everybody knows that Democrats could care less about America's security and economic prosperity—the ONLY thing Democrats care about is taking money from people who worked for it and promising to give it to another person who did not work for it as a "government benefit" in order to "buy" that other person's vote so they may stay in power—regardless of their policies' negative effect on our nation's economy!

So Republicans need to stop talking about Obama's broken promises—which as I stated anybody with the intelligence of a fruit fly already knew were a bunch of bull-dung! What Republicans need to be addressing is the real reason why America needs to remove President Obama from the White House in the 2012 Election—Not for the promises he failed to keep, but for those promises that he is successfully and systematically fulfilling—his promises to *Fundamentally Transform America* into a Communist, Muslim-bowing, European-style economically bankrupt nation!

Candidate Obama promised to make your electric, heating oil and gasoline prices skyrocket, and to fulfill his promise he has appointed as his Secretary of Energy Steven Chu, who prior to being appointed stated publically,

*Somehow we have to figure out how to boost the price of gasoline to the levels in Europe.*

The gasoline prices in Europe are $8.00 to $9.00 per gallon!

When President Obama took Office the price of gasoline was $1.84 per gallon; as I edit this manuscript in Late February, early March 2012, I just paid $4.09 for Premium Unleaded! Under President Obama's Administration the price of gasoline has more than doubled! Though there is always an annual increase due to supply and demand as summer approaches, never in the history of the United States has gasoline hit these prices in the winter months of February and March!

On February 28, 2012, while President Obama's Secretary of Energy Steven Chu was testifying before the House Appropriations Sub-Committee on Energy, Congressman Alan Nunnelee, expressing concerns on behalf of his constituents' over the rising price of gasoline, asked Secretary Chu the following direct question about the Obama Administrations policy regarding *skyrocketing* gasoline prices,

*Is the overall goal [of the Obama Administration] to get our price [that we have to pay at the pump for gasoline down]?*

To which, speaking on behalf of President Obama, Energy Secretary Chu responded,

*No. The overall goal is to decrease our dependency on oil.* (View for yourselves at: http://c-spanvideo.org/program/EnergyDepartmen).

What's the best way to *decrease our dependency on oil*? As Candidate Obama promised and as Energy Secretary Chu had formerly declared, to make gasoline so damn expensive we can't afford it!

But the big question is, why? What's wrong with oil? The answer is NOTHING! There is nothing wrong or harmful about being *dependent on oil!*

*Oh, but it makes us dependent on foreign oil from the Middle East,* I hear some of you saying. No it doesn't! We have more oil reserves right here in the good old USA than the Middle East ever dreamed of having! The only reason we have to import oil from the Middle East now is because the anti-America environmentalist Democratic Party nut-jobs have blocked every attempt to access those God-given oil reserves!

In February, 2012, President Obama had the audacity to give a speech claiming that *Drilling for More Oil* was only a *Bumper-sticker and not a solution* and that those who called for more drilling simply *didn't know what they were talking about.* Mr. President, you have got to be the stupidest human being to ever grace the face of the Earth! Every 5$^{th}$-grader knows that all economics are driven by the basic principle of supply vs. demand. *Drill Baby Drill* is not only a solution, it is the ONLY solution to reducing gasoline prices and to ending our dependence on Middle East oil!

I agree that we need to decrease, even entirely eliminate, our dependence on Middle East oil, but there is no reason whatsoever why we need to decrease our dependency on oil—oil is awesome baby!

I'm *Common Sense*, and I'm running for Office! Elect me and I will appoint as my Energy Secretary Sarah Palin, and I'll have her tour the country wearing a T-shirt that says, *"Drill Baby Drill!"* Well, that should secure for me the male vote in America anyway.

What about wind and solar energy? Though there is nothing wrong with the free-market—note I said the *free market*—exploring and developing such avenues of generating electricity, wind and solar won't power our automobiles! The only thing that powers our automobiles is gasoline, i.e., oil!

*Oh*, you say, *that's why we're developing battery-powered electric cars!* Why are you wasting your time and my tax dollars developing electric cars? They don't help the environment in any way…they use electricity which is mostly generated by burning coal! I thought you environmentalist nut-jobs didn't like coal; so why do you want everyone to drive cars that increase coal burning?

And who wants to drive an electric car anyway? I sure don't! I want my Corvette with her big gas-guzzling V-8! And I love my SUV with its big V-8 which is great for pulling my boat. And I love driving my big V-8 Cadillac!

I have a message from America for you Democratic-Party environmentalist global-warming hoax believing nut-jobs: You can take your electric cars and shove them up your A.-double-S! We the American People don't want them! Take the electric cars with you to France when you move there! Good-bye and good riddance!

OK, Mr. O'Reilly, I'm done opining, and I kept my promise not to bloviate.

## America, You Elected A Communist As Your President— Have You Gone Mad?

But America's insanity in electing Barack Hussein Obama as President becomes even more evident when you look back at then Presidential Candidate Obama's economic world view!

In 2008, then Presidential candidate Barack Hussein Obama, while canvassing and campaigning in a middle class neighborhood in Holland, Ohio, was asked by "Joe the Plumber" (Joe Wissenbacker),

*Your new tax plan is going to tax me more, isn't it?*

Candidate Obama responds,

*It's not that I want to punish your success, I just want to make sure that everybody who is behind you, that they've got a chance at success too....I think that when you spread the wealth around, it's good for everybody.*

What the flip!

First, note that Obama didn't make this mind-bobbling statement to some wealthy Wall Street Executive or high-flying millionaire, but to an ordinary, everyday hard-working plumber! And unlike Candidate Obama's declaration that his energy plan was to skyrocket your energy costs, which was not widely publicized by the media, this jaw-dropping encounter with Joe the Plumber was seen by everyone in America!

So, let's get this straight. Obama wants to take money from an average hard-working American and give it to someone who didn't work for it, whom Obama views as *behind*, so they too may have a chance at success, because Obama believes that, *"when you spread the wealth around, it's good for everybody."*

Taking from one man's labor to benefit the whole society…hmmm…guess what you call that my friends, COMMUNISM! That's right, Communism!

*From each according to his ability, to each according to his need.*—Carl Marx, Father of Communism.

In other words, in the mind of a Communist, *"when you spread the wealth around, it's good for everybody."*—Barack Obama.

Candidate Obama admitted to Joe the Plumber, in front of the TV cameras for all the world to see, that he is a Communist, which by the way was not the first time Obama admitted publically to being a Communist. It is no wonder, therefore, on the night of Obama's election victory, as a celebratory crowd gathered in front of the White House, there it was, a large Communist flag being waved proudly and defiantly back-and-forth in the midst of that crowd and right in the face of all America!

Yet, after seeing for yourselves Barack Obama's admission to being a Communist, the majority of you still voted for him to be President! Are you out of your mind? America, have you gone mad?

*Wait a minute!* you say, *Obama is not a Communist, he's a Socialist!*

Oh, that's great! Good defense, Num-nuts. Like being a Socialist is any better than being a Communist. It's not! The basic difference between Communism and Socialism is that Communism comes about by way of a populous revolt in which a group of people agree together that they want to "share the wealth" with one another, and so they kill all the leaders and take over a country and establish Communism—nobody owns anything for themselves, but everyone works together for the "common good" of all. The problem with Communism is that it doesn't work! We'll discuss that in Chapter 6, *Common Sense* Solutions To Getting America's Economy Back On The Road To Prosperity!

But my point here is, at least at first, the initial group of Communists voluntarily agrees to that system, except of course for the poor bastards they murdered.

But a Socialist is a Communist at heart, who is too pussyfooted to kill all the leaders and take over by force of arms, so the Socialist weasels his way into a position of prominence, and enacts policies that force the Communist ideal upon the unsuspecting masses by *spreading the wealth around* through taxation and redistribution of wealth from the "haves" to the "have-nots."

So Communism is voluntary, but Socialism is forced upon the masses by a few in power; that makes Socialism even more evil and sinister than Communism. In its philosophy, Socialism is exactly the same as Communism, just more deceptive in its implementation. However, since the term *Socialist* sounds more benign than Communist, and therefore clouds the truth, we call it like it really is: Barack Obama is a Communist, pure and simple, and we do not abide Communists in America!

I'm *Common Sense* and I'm running for Office! Elect me and I will declare a clear, constant and consistent message from my Presidential Bully Pulpit that Communists and Socialists are not welcome in America! I will explain why Communism and Socialism are failed social experiments, un-American, ungodly and frankly idiotic! I will make it clear that those who hold such views are free to leave the shores of our beloved USA, for the shores of those Communist Socialist Paradise's these morons long for, such as Cuba, North Korea, China, Greece or any other Communist Socialist state they wish to flee to; but I will make it clear that they are not welcome here in the Land of the Free and the Home of the Brave! We do not abide Communists in America!

## America, You Elected A Muslim-Born Man As Your President—Have You Gone Mad?

America's madness doesn't stop with electing an environmental nut-job and Communist as its President, but America's madness grows even darker and more sinister when you consider the fact that the majority of Americans who voted in the 2008 Presidential Election voted for a man who was born a Muslim, bears a Muslim name, attended Muslim schools as a child in Indonesia, Madras's, where hatred for Jews & Christians is part of the curriculum; and though while living here in America, Obama attended a non-Muslim "church," it is one which nonetheless believes and espouses the same hatred as does Islam of America & Israel! Not to mention that the "Church" Obama and his family attended for 20-years was a Black Racist Cult that espoused hatred of all White people, but welcomed the White-hating, Jew-hating Muslim and Founder of the Nation of Islam, Louis Farrakhan to preach his vile satanic ideology in that "Church's" pulpit!

You that voted for Obama, are you out of your mind? Have you gone mad! Indeed you have!

Why is that madness? Because America has been declared war on and attacked by Muslims, the followers of Islam, as the Quran commands all Muslims to do:

**Quran 9:5**
*But when the forbidden months Are past, then fight and slay The Pagans wherever ye find them, And seize them, beleaguer them, And lie in wait for them In every stratagem (of war); But if they repent, And establish regular prayers And practise regular charity, Then open the way for them: For God [Allah] is Oft-forgiving, Most Merciful.*

The above passage from the Quran commands all Muslims worldwide to cause every person on planet Earth, every Christian, every Jew, every person regardless of their religious affiliation, to submit and convert to Islam—if they refuse, kill them! I repeat, this is a command from Allah that every Muslim must obey or he will go to Hell!

Yet, in light of 9-11, a majority of Americans elected as their President a Muslim-born man, who bears his Muslim father's name, who attended Muslim Madras's in Indonesia where he was taught the Quran, and to this day has not denounced the Muslim religion in which he was born! In fact he celebrates and promotes the anti-Israel, anti-Christ Muslim false religion!

All I can say is that America has absolutely gone mad! I will show you how to win the war against Islam in Chapters 3, 4 and 5.

## Black America, You Elected A Pro-Slavery Democrat—Have You Gone Mad?

Perhaps the saddest fact of the 2008 Election is that Black Americans turned out in record numbers to vote for a man because he is half-black, but who is a Democrat! How in God's name could any black American ever vote for a Democrat? It was the Democrats who fought the Civil War to keep slavery legal in their States! Thank God the "anti-slavery" Republican Party won the Civil War and the Democrats lost! But having lost the Civil War, the Democratic Party has from that day to this, constructed economic policies to keep Black Americans in economic-slavery, dependent on their "Washington Masters!"

I implore every Black American to read Chapter 9, Why Blacks Should Never Vote Democrat!

## America, You Elected A Pro-Homosexual As Your President—Have You Gone Mad?

Finally, America, you elected a man as your President who is pro-homosexual-sin and who is himself a practicing homosexual, who likes to engage in the practice while smoking Crack! You knew this about Obama, America, before the 2008 Election, because you saw the video testimony of Larry Sinclair! (To view on YouTube.com, search: "Larry Sinclair Obama Drug and Sex Party Limousine" or "Larry Sinclair Obama Steamy Love Affair").

And now, elected President, Obama appoints as the Director of the Office of Home Land Security—a department created after September 11, for the purpose of protecting us from Muslim terrorists—a woman who is an avowed Lesbian! Would anyone appoint an avowed Adulterer to such a high position? Of course not! And homosexuality is a far greater and more destructive sin than adultery. But the worst part is that, shortly after the openly Gay Janet Napolitano takes charge of the department dedicated to securing our Home Land against Islamic terrorists, she releases a memo declaring that the greatest risk to America's security is not Muslims, but Pro-Life Christians and military veterans!

Has America gone mad? The woman is obviously insane! And yet President Obama doesn't immediately fire her! Is President Obama insane too?

Even worse, the people who elected Obama to the Presidency, upon hearing of this threat by the Director of Home Land Security upon the very people that make America great—our Christian Churches and our military veterans—did not immediately demand that Janet Napolitano resign or be fired.

Let it be now declared, that We The People of the United States of America demand the immediate resignation or firing of Janet Napolitano for her insane abuse and misuse of her position and authority!

One of the most important chapters in this book with regard to saving America and restoring *Common Sense* to our culture is Chapter 8, Why It's Not OK To Be Gay!

For now, we can declare with certainty that, yes indeed my friends, America has gone mad! But I pray that this book will help restore some sanity to humanity. It all begins with a Common Sense understanding of the God-given role of government.

# Chapter 2: The God-given *Common Sense* Role Of Government

Having established in the previous chapter that America has gone mad, America's return to sanity must begin by reestablishing the proper understanding of what the God-given common sense role of human government is; for, from the proper understanding of government's role shall spring all else that government does; i.e., what government should and should not do.

## Thomas Paine's Common Sense Role Of Government!

The Father of the American Revolution, Thomas Paine, in his pamphlet titled, *Common Sense*, states the role of government this way:

*Here then is the origin and rise of government; namely, a mode rendered necessary by the inability of moral virtue to govern the world; here too is the design and end of government, i.e., freedom and security.* —Thomas Paine, Common Sense, Philadelphia, February 14, 1776.

First, Thomas Paine correctly states a fundamental truth regarding the moral condition of humanity when he declares,

*Here then is the origin and rise of government; namely, a mode rendered necessary by the inability of moral virtue to govern the world;*

Paine is simply stating the fundamental truth that government is necessary because the moral character of Man is corrupt, selfish and sinful, and when left unrestrained, Man will cause harm to his fellow Man in his quest to satisfy his own selfish base desires. Man's moral corruption occurred at the very beginning of Mankind in the Garden of Eden, when Man willfully chose to disobey the loving, life-giving command of his Creator and thus descend into a state of selfish, sinful rebellion against God (Genesis 3). The truth is that Man is inherently evil, not inherently good.

Regarding this moral depravity of Mankind, God declares in the opening chapters of His Holy Word:

**Genesis 6:5-6**

*Then the LORD saw that the wickedness of man was great in the earth, and that every intent of the thoughts of his heart was only evil continually. And the LORD was sorry that He had made man on the earth, and He was grieved in His heart.*

Thousands of years later, the Old Testament Prophet Jeremiah declares that Mankind's fallen state of moral depravity has not improved:

**Jeremiah 17:9**

*The heart is deceitful above all things, And desperately wicked;*

Again, many centuries after Jeremiah, the New Testament Apostle Paul delivers a scathing indictment of Mankind:

**Romans 1:18-32**

*For the wrath of God is revealed from heaven against all ungodliness and unrighteousness of men, who suppress the truth in unrighteousness, because what may be known of God is manifest in them, for God has shown it to them. For since the creation of the world His invisible attributes are clearly seen, being understood by the things that are made, even His eternal power and Godhead, so that they are without excuse, because, although they knew God, they did not glorify Him as God, nor were thankful, but became futile in their thoughts, and their foolish hearts were darkened. Professing to be wise, they became fools, and changed the glory of the incorruptible God into an image made like corruptible man—and birds and four-footed animals and creeping things.*

*Therefore God also gave them up to uncleanness, in the lusts of their hearts, to dishonor their bodies among themselves, who exchanged the truth of God for the lie, and worshiped and served the creature rather than the Creator, who is blessed forever. Amen.*

*For this reason God gave them up to vile passions. For even their women exchanged the natural use for what is against nature. Likewise also the men, leaving the natural use of the woman, burned in their lust for one another, men with men committing what is shameful, and receiving in themselves the penalty of their error which was due.*

*And even as they did not like to retain God in their knowledge, God gave them over to a debased mind, to do those things which are not fitting; being filled with all unrighteousness, sexual immorality, wickedness, covetousness, maliciousness; full of envy, murder, strife, deceit, evil-mindedness; they are whisperers, backbiters, haters of God, violent, proud, boasters, inventors of evil things, disobedient to parents, undiscerning, untrustworthy, unloving, unforgiving, unmerciful; who, knowing the righteous judgment of God, that those who practice such things are deserving of death, not only do the same but also approve of those who practice them*

Boy, does that describe a Democrat to the tee!

By the way, do you know what you call people who, *Professing to be wise, they became fools*? "Professors." No wonder many of our young people today are bereft of any *Common Sense*, for our college students are being instructed by a bunch of babbling buffoons who don't even know the most basic and simplest of all truths: that Jesus Christ is Lord, Creator of the universe and Only Savior of Mankind! Any person who does not understand this most fundamental fact is not qualified to shovel shit, let alone educate our children!

Just one more quote from the Apostle Paul declaring the moral sinfulness of Mankind:

**Romans 3:9-18**

*What then? Are we better than they? Not at all. For we have previously charged both Jews and Greeks that they are all under sin.*

*As it is written:*
> *"There is none righteous, no, not one;*
> *There is none who understands;*
> *There is none who seeks after God.*
> *They have all turned aside;*
> *They have together become unprofitable;*
> *There is none who does good, no, not one."*
> *Their throat is an open tomb;*
> *With their tongues they have practiced deceit";*
> *The poison of asps is under their lips";*
> *Whose mouth is full of cursing and bitterness."*
> *Their feet are swift to shed blood;*
> *Destruction and misery are in their ways;*
> *And the way of peace they have not known."*

*There is no fear of God before their eyes."*

As you can see from just a few passages from the Holy Bible, God's indictment of man's lost and sinful condition is clear and severe. By the way, that's why Jesus Christ, the Son of God, came into the world—to save sinners like you and me! If you'll acknowledge your sinful condition by turning to God and seeking His forgiveness, i.e., repent, and place your faith, hope, trust in Jesus Christ—who died in your place to pay the penalty for your sins, and who on the third day rose from the dead, conquering death, the consequence of sin—and call upon the name of Jesus Christ the Lord to save you from your sins, then Jesus will forgive your sins and save you from Hell—the due consequence of your sins, freely giving you His gift of eternal life to live forever with Him and the Father in Heaven! If you haven't called on the name of the Lord Jesus Christ to save you from your sins, then I strongly encourage you to stop and do so right here and now! The alternative is to remain lost in your rebellious sinful condition, and upon your death be separated from God forever and receive the due punishment for your rebellion and sin—the eternal fire and torments of Hell!

Hmmm…let's see…being saved or remaining lost…being forgiven of my sins or receiving the due punishment for my sins…living forever in the Paradise of Heaven or enduring the eternal torments of Hell…hmmm…which one should I choose…seems like *Common Sense* to me—Choose life! Choose Jesus!

We now turn back to our discussion of the God-given *Common Sense* role of government. Since therefore, mankind is unable to govern himself, i.e., for everyone to just get along, there must be an authoritative restraining structure put into place to create an atmosphere of "security and freedom"—this is what Thomas Paine calls: *"government; namely, a mode rendered necessary by the inability of moral virtue to govern the world;"*

Then, Thomas Paine, having acknowledged the necessity of some mode of government, defines what the role of that government should be in this way,

*…here too is the design and end of government, i.e., freedom and security.*

Wow! Talk about keeping it simple, that's about as clear and simple as you can get. And it is also a very limited view of the role of government. This very limited view of the role of government is what our Founding Fathers gave us in the Declaration of Independence and the U.S. Constitution; therefore the government of the United States of America must not expand its power and influence beyond this limited view; to do so is "unconstitutional."

If you want a more expansive government, then you need to get your ass on a boat or plane and get out of America; go to Cuba or China or North Korea or wherever the heck you want to go, but you are not welcome in America! America is the land of the free and the home of the brave! America is not the home of Communist cowards! We must get over the notion that everyone is welcome in America. No, everyone is not welcome in America! Only freedom loving, God-fearing, Free-Market Capitalists are welcome in America!

And by, "God-fearing," we mean those who love and believe in the One True God Jesus Christ.

Let's ponder for a moment the meaning of the above clear and simple words from the "Father of the American Revolution." Think about what Thomas Paine is saying. The *"design,"* i.e., the purpose of and reason for government, and the *"end,"* i.e., the limit of government's role, is *"freedom and security."* That's it! Just those two things.

So the function of government is to provide an atmosphere of security and freedom for its citizens. Security and liberty. Safety and freedom.

## Protecting & Defending The Constitution From All Enemies Foreign & Domestic!

The government's role in providing security for its citizens is perhaps best stated in the military Oath of Enlistment which every member of the U.S. Armed Forces must raise his or her right hand and swear to:

*The Oath of Enlistment (for enlistees):*

*I, _____, do solemnly swear (or affirm) that I will support and defend the Constitution of the United States against all enemies, foreign and domestic; that I will bear true faith and allegiance to the same; and that I will obey the orders of the President of the United States and the orders of the officers appointed over me, according to regulations and the Uniform Code of Military Justice. So help me God.*

Of course, when Thomas Paine penned his words we did not yet have a U.S. Constitution, but upon its creation, the meaning of the government providing "security" has come to mean that the government, by the powers vested in it, shall, *support and defend the Constitution of the United States against all enemies, foreign and domestic.*

The Presidential Oath of Office declares the same,

Each president recites the following oath, in accordance with Article II, Section I of the U.S. Constitution:

*I do solemnly swear (or affirm) that I will faithfully execute the office of President of the United States, and will to the best of my ability, preserve, protect and defend the Constitution of the United States.*

It has become tradition for the President to place his left hand on the Holy bible and raise his right hand while swearing the Oath, and to conclude with the words, indeed the prayer, *So help me God!*

First, note that both the Military and Presidential Oath's conclude with, *so help me God.* This same prayer is also uttered thousands of times every day all across America as witnesses take the stand in civil and criminal courtroom proceedings, calling upon the God of the Bible to help them to tell the truth. Contrary to the Muslim born President Barack Hussein Obama's declaration that America is not a Christian nation, America from its inception and throughout her history has always been a God-fearing Christian nation, and by God shall continue to be!

You see, the First Amendment of the Constitution provides for the freedom of the Christian religion. But the Demon-cratic Party has deceived you into thinking that the First Amendment guarantees the "separation of Church and State." The truth is that the First Amendment guarantees the exact opposite of "separation of Church and State,"—it provides for the unhindered freedom of the Christian religion to permeate every aspect of American culture and society! For God's sake, the Title of the First Amendment is, "The Freedom *of* Religion," not, "The Freedom *from* Religion!" This demonic lie that the First Amendment provides for the "separation of Church and State" has been perpetrated and perpetuated by the Democratic Party, and every Democrat who has echoed this lie will have to answer to Almighty God on the Day of Judgment. Unfortunately, most Americans have come to believe the lie. Repent America! Return to your Christian roots!

Second, notice that in both the Presidential Oath and military Oath that they, as representatives of and in their service to our government are swearing to, *preserve, protect and defend the Constitution of the United States...,* and, *support and defend the Constitution of the United States against all enemies, foreign and domestic;* (underlining added).

Thus, we discover that the means by which the government fulfills its rightful role of providing *security and freedom* is by *preserving, protecting, supporting and defending the Constitution of the United States from all enemies, foreign and domestic.*

*Common Sense* tells us that to *preserve, protect and defend the Constitution* does not mean to preserve, protect and defend the literal historic paper document upon which the Constitution is written, which is a simple enough task, but rather, and much more importantly, it means to *preserve, protect, support and defend* the precepts and principles laid down by our Founding Fathers in that historic document.

## *But President Obama Believes The Constitution To Be A "Deeply Fundamentally Flawed" Document!*

If I might interject at this point in our discussion of the God-given *Common Sense* role of government, herein resides one of the monumental problems with our current President, Barack Hussein Obama, who has sworn the Presidential Oath ascribed above to, *preserve, protect and defend the Constitution of the United States,* yet he has clearly stated that he does not believe in our Constitution!

During a Chicago interview on WBEZ radio station in September, 2001, while serving as Senator of Illinois, then Senator Obama made these telling remarks about his thoughts toward our Constitution:

Radio interviewer: *Barack Obama, what are your thoughts on the original Constitution?*

Barack Obama's answer: *I think it's a remarkable document,*
Interviewer: *Which one?*

Barack Obama: *The original Constitution as well as the Civil War amendments, but I think it's an imperfect document and I think it is a document that reflects some deep flaws in American culture, the Colonial culture, ...the Constitution reflected an enormous blind spot in this culture that carries on until this day, and that the framers had that same blind spot; I don't think the two views are contradictory, to say that it was a remarkable political document that paved the way for where we are now, and to say that it also reflected the fundamental flaw of this country that continues to this day.* (You may hear this and his full answer by searching YouTube.com: "Barack Obama the US Constitution is imperfect").

Whoa, wait a minute; we have a major problem here!

You morons elected a man to be the President of the United States who stated publicly that he believes that the U.S. Constitution *is a document that reflects some deep flaws in American culture,* and that the U.S. Constitution *reflected the fundamental flaw of this country that continues to this day.*

In other words, Barack Hussein Obama harbors the belief deep in his heart that not only the U.S. Constitution, but the United States itself is *fundamentally deeply flawed!*

Now you understand why Barack Hussein Obama promised to *fundamentally transform America!*

This presents a serious problem. How can a man, who believes that the U.S. Constitution is a document which is fundamentally deeply flawed, swear to the Presidential Oath to, *preserve, protect and defend the Constitution of the United States*? He cannot swear to such an Oath and truly mean it.

In fact, in light of his above comments which reveal his deeply held views regarding the U.S. Constitution, is not his campaign promise to *Fundamentally transform America* a direct declaration of his intention to usurp and overthrow the U.S. Constitution? Of course it is.

Barack Hussein Obama is not alone in his animosity toward the U.S. Constitution, and indeed toward the U.S.A. generally; most Democrats hold this same animosity toward our great nation.

Anyone who is a democrat or who votes Democrat will have to answer to Almighty God on Judgment Day for the animosity they held toward the nation which God raised up in these last days to be the End-Time Lighthouse for the Gospel of Jesus Christ and the Friend of Israel among the nations. If you are a Democrat or voted for Barack Hussein Obama, I sincerely urge you to repent of your ungodly alliance with the Democratic Party and their Head, Barack Hussein Obama, and turn toward God and the Republican Party, the one political Party in America that stands for God's Biblical principles of Life, Liberty, and one's personal pursuit of happiness.

But I'm not through yet with our discussion of the God-given *Common Sense* Role of Government.

## Our Founding Fathers' Belief In Liberty Via Limited Government!

Was Thomas Paine the only Founding Father who believes that government's role should be limited to providing and protecting *freedom and security?*

Approximately four months after Thomas Paine published his pamphlet titled, *Common Sense*, it is recorded in the *Journals of the Continental Congress* that, on June 11, 1776, the coalition of patriots we refer to as our Founding Fathers, appointed a committee comprised of Thomas Jefferson, John Adams, Benjamin Franklin, Roger Sherman, and Robert R. Livingston, with the purpose of drafting a Declaration of Independence from the British Crown. (Thomas Jefferson is held to be the main contributor and final drafter of that historic, world-changing document.)

From the First of July through the Fourth, 1776, Congress debated and revised the Declaration of Independence, adopting the final draft on July 4, 1776, and ordering that same day that the Declaration be printed. (You may find this information online at the Library of Congress website: http://www.loc.gov/rr/program/bib/ourdocs/DeclarInd.html)

Let us look at how similarly the Declaration of Independence states the simple and limited role of government to that of Thomas Paine's; below is the second paragraph of the Declaration of Independence (See Appendix B for the full document):

*We hold these truths to be self-evident, that all men are created equal, that they are endowed by their Creator with certain unalienable rights, that among these are life, liberty and the pursuit of happiness. That to secure these rights, governments are instituted among men, deriving their just powers from the consent of the governed. That whenever any form of government becomes destructive to these ends, it is the right of the people to alter or to abolish it, and to institute new government, laying its foundation on such principles and organizing its powers in such form, as to them shall seem most likely to effect their safety and happiness.*

This second paragraph of the Declaration of Independence begins with the phrase,

*We hold these truths to be self-evident,* in other words, these *truths* are obvious to all Mankind—*We hold these truths to be "Common Sense!"* Of course, the gift from God of *Common Sense* is a gift that Democrats are bereft of, because Democrats have turned their backs on God, and He has turned them over to a depraved mind (See Romans 1:18-32 above).

The *Common Sense* truth that we are focused on in this chapter is our Founding Fathers' definition of the role and scope of government; which we ourselves must hold to if we wish to be considered American.

In the above second paragraph of the Declaration of Independence, our Founding Fathers recognize that all Mankind, *are endowed by their Creator with certain unalienable rights, that among these are life, liberty and the pursuit of happiness.*

First, note the above *Common Sense* truth proclaimed in our Declaration of Independence that our *rights* as human beings are not bestowed upon us by government, but by God!

Second, note that these God-given rights are *unalienable,* which means these rights are: incapable of being alienated, surrendered, or transferred; in other words, god bestowed these rights upon us as human beings made in His image and likeness (Genesis 1:26-27), and government cannot take these rights away from us! Only our own unlawful actions may cause us to forfeit these God-given rights, but government may not under any circumstances take away our rights to *life, liberty, and the pursuit of happiness!*

But stripping us of our God-given rights to *life, liberty, and the pursuit of happiness* is exactly what President Barack Obama and the Democratic Party do on a daily basis to each and every American citizen, as the remainder of this book will prove.

Our Founding Fathers then continue by wisely stating, in order for Mankind to enjoy these God-given *unalienable rights* to, *life, liberty, and the pursuit of happiness,*

*That to secure these rights, governments are instituted among men,*

Our Founding Fathers then state that the design and end of that government is,

*...to effect their safety and happiness.*

Let us be clear here that it is not the role of government to make us happy, for no Earthly government can *cause* any person's happiness; but rather, government's role is simply to provide a secure environment whereby each citizen may pursue happiness to whatever extent and degree each citizen chooses.

As the wise Benjamin Franklin stated:

*The U.S. Constitution doesn't guarantee happiness, only the pursuit of it. You have to catch up with it yourself.*

This definition of the role of government wisely limits and focuses governments' scope of endeavor and involvement in the lives of its citizens. We may outline these limitations by observing the closing paragraph from the Declaration of Independence—the founding document or "Birth Certificate" of these United States of America:

*We, therefore, the representatives of the United States of America, in General Congress, assembled, appealing to the Supreme Judge of the world for the rectitude of our intentions, do, in the name, and by the authority of the good people of these colonies, solemnly publish and declare, that these united colonies are, and of right ought to be free and independent states; that they are absolved from all allegiance to the British Crown, and that all political connection between them and the state of Great Britain, is and ought to be totally dissolved; and that as free and independent states, they have full power to levy war, conclude peace, contract alliances, establish commerce, and to do all other acts and things which independent states may of right do. And for the support of this declaration, with a firm reliance on the protection of Divine Providence, we mutually pledge to each other our lives, our fortunes and our sacred honor.*

Note in the above concluding paragraph of our nation's founding document these words:

*...as free and independent states, they have full power to levy war, conclude peace, contract alliances, establish commerce, and to do all other acts and things which independent states may of right do.*

Herein we note three defined rights and a fourth less specific, not so much of each individual citizen, but of the whole as a union:

1) *...they have full power to levy war, conclude peace,*

Government's power to levy war and conclude peace could well be stated as the government's primary role and responsibility, i.e., to protect and defend the citizens of the United States, *against all enemies, foreign and domestic.*

Protecting and defending *we the people of the United States* against all enemies foreign would be the role of the U.S. military—which means it's the Federal government's responsibility to ensure with our tax dollars that they provide the largest, best equipped, best trained, most lethal military force on the planet, capable of overwhelming and annihilating every possible threat, even multiple threats simultaneously if necessary! And the civilian leadership, meaning the President, who bears the title of "Commander-In-Chief" and the Congress must by their actions give full support to our defense. This means that when the military commanders which the civilians have placed in charge of the military operations ask their civilian leaders for an additional 50,000 troops, as was recently done with the war in Afghanistan, *Common Sense* dictates that you as the "Commander-In-Chief" give them everything they ask for plus more. Personally, if the military commanders asked me, *Common Sense,* for 50,000 troops, I'd give them everything they asked for plus an additional 20%; I'd give them 60,000. That's just simple *Common sense!* Unlike President Obama who denied their request and only authorized 30,000, only about half of the troops the military commanders in the field requested. This is dereliction of duty on the part of the President! But even worse than being a dereliction of duty by the Commander-In-Chief, Obama's actions probably cost American lives, because any moron knows that an overwhelming military force ensures victory and protects and preserves the lives of our military men and women; but a weaker reduced military force costs lives and ensures defeat.

The government's obligation to protect and defend us, *"against all enemies...domestic,"* would fall under the responsibilities of State, County and City governments. This of course includes providing State, County and City law enforcement.

However, I must state here that the government's role in providing us *security* is so that we the people may enjoy the God-given right to liberty, i.e., freedom. Law enforcement does not have the right to kill us, unless we are immanently and directly threatening their life. In other words, no law enforcement officer has the right to shoot someone just because they are fleeing the scene of a crime; trying to run from law enforcement is not a Capital Offense! Yet law enforcement officers regularly murder American citizens just because they are running from them; this must immediately cease! Also, ramming your automobile into a law enforcement officer's vehicle in most cases is not directly and immanently threatening the life of the law enforcement officer and does not warrant the killing of the citizen. Come on folks! You've seen this kind of story on TV: The cop is sitting in his parked vehicle, and the moron in the vehicle in front of the cop decides to put his car in reverse and ram into the officers vehicle, probably at no more than 10 m.p.h., though the citizen ramming the rear of his car into the front of the police officer's car is a moron, his actions do not threaten the life of the officer; it damages the bumper of the officers patrol car and bounces him around a little, but it does not threaten his life, and does not give the officer the right to kill that citizen just because he is a moron. Another thing that law enforcement officers DO NOT have the right to do is "electrocute" American citizens who have not been found guilty of any crime; even those found guilty of crimes and sentenced to prison do not experience electrocution, unless it is a death penalty case in a State where electrocution is that States means of obeying God's commandment that those who murder another Man shall be put to death by Man:

**Genesis 9:6**

*Whoever sheds man's blood, By man his blood shall be shed; For in the image of God He made man.*

No State, nor the Federal Government, has the right to decide whether or not they wish to have and enforce the death penalty for crimes of capital murder; the death penalty for deliberately murdering another Man has been commanded by God our Creator to be enforced by human government. No human government has the right to disobey God.

Getting back to my point about cops not having the right to electrocute citizens, this practice of using a Taser by law enforcement and thereby electrocuting American citizens goes on every day in America. This practice must immediately cease! Cops are not God! And cops do not have the right to inflict punishment on you or even arrest you for simply disobeying their "commands." Not to mention that this practice of using Tasers has resulted in the deaths of citizens who had not been found guilty of any crime. Law Enforcement only has the right to place you under arrest if they have evidence that you have committed a crime worthy of being brought to trial before a jury of your peers. And even when the officer believes he or she has proper authority to place you under arrest, they do not have the right to inflict bodily harm upon you during the process of arrest. Now, if you choose to resist arrest, the officer certainly has the right as any citizen does to protect himself from bodily injury from your attempts to resist; but his efforts to subdue you must be measured and metered out in accordance with basic human decency; a suspect who is laying on the ground, and therefore incapable of further resistance, must not be kicked or beaten with batons or tazed or any other such uncivilized act.

Though our security is the government's number one responsibility, law enforcement must remember who they serve and not overstep their authority as is so often the case.

2) ...*contract alliances,*

Our government does and should enter into beneficial alliances with other nations such as N.A.T.O., to ensure global stability which enhances our national security. However, *Common Sense* dictates that our government should never enter into any alliance that subjugates our sovereignty to any other single or group of nations. Yet today, many, if not most, Democrats, especially within the Obama Administration, believe that the United States should subjugate our sovereignty and our Constitution to international law and the United Nations. Let me say this loud and clear, anyone who believes the U.S. should bow to any other nation, like, for example, to the Muslim King of Saudi Arabia, isn't fit to shovel shit, let alone hold political Office in the United States of America!

We therefore call upon every citizen of the United States to perform their duty as citizens of this great Land and to rise up on November 6, 2012, and remove, not by the power of the bullet but by the power of the ballot, Muslim-king-bowing Barack Hussein Obama and his Administration from the Office of the Presidency. And while we are at the Polls on November 6, 2012, We The People of the United States have an obligation to also remove all Democrats from the House of Representatives, plus all Democrats in the Senate whose seats are up for reelection, for Democrats are by nature and by their Official Democratic Platform not qualified to shovel shit, let alone hold political Office!

3) ...*establish commerce,*

This refers to trade agreements between the U.S. and other countries which must always be entered into with the best interests in mind of both our consumers and our businesses who would be engaging in import and export of goods and services. However, the government should not regulate or dictate to business within our borders. We will expand this in more detail in Chapter 6, *Common Sense* Solutions For Getting America's Economy Back On The Road To Prosperity! But here let me insert the wise and *Common Sense* words of Thomas Jefferson, the same who penned the words in the Declaration of Independence above, when he stated,

*A wise and frugal Government, which shall restrain men from injuring one another, shall leave them otherwise free to regulate their own pursuits of industry and improvement, and shall not take from the mouth of labor the bread it has earned. This is the sum of good government.*—President Thomas Jefferson, Inaugural Address, March 4, 1801.

Since, however, we are fifty United States, the federal government does have a beneficial role in assisting the free-flow of commerce between States by such means as the building of Federal Interstate Highways and providing air-traffic control. And for our general enjoyment and happiness of traveling and enjoying the beauty of this great land, I don't have a problem with the Federal government maintaining a few national parks and monuments. But that's pretty much about the entire scope of the role of government—1) to protect us from enemies foreign and domestic and, 2) to build and maintain federal highways and provide air-traffic control. Just about everything else the government does these days is an overstepping of government's role and a usurpation and violation of our rights and freedoms.

4) *"...and to do all other acts and things which independent states may of right do."*

This is, of course, just a general statement inserted by the Founding Fathers that is appropriate in such a document as the Declaration of Independence, but is in no wise a license for Government to do anything and everything that it may wish to do. Remember Thomas Paine's declaration regarding the limited role of government, which is, *"the design and end of government...freedom and security."* And that the Declaration declares the same limitations that government is established by God upon the earth to protect our God-given rights to *"life, liberty and the pursuit of happiness."*

Not only does the *Father of the American Revolution,* Thomas Paine state clearly his very limited view of the role and responsibility of government, and not only does the Declaration of Independence state the same very limited view, but so also does the U.S. Constitution. We clearly see this same very limited view of the role and responsibility of government in the opening words, the Preamble, of the U.S. Constitution:

*WE, the PEOPLE of the UNITED STATES, in order to form a more perfect union, establish justice, ensure domestic tranquility, provide for the common defense, promote the general welfare, and secure the blessings of liberty to ourselves and our posterity, do ordain and establish this Constitution for the United States of America.*

Some 236 years have passed since our Founding Fathers gave birth to this great nation, and as with all things, time has a way fading original intent and diverting from initial purpose. Like many great God-sent revival movements wherein multitudes were converted to Christ and thus to true religion, resulting in these masses organizing for common fellowship into a group which became a denomination, which over time loses its initial fire and diverts from its original purpose; so likewise, our government today has gotten away from what the Founding Fathers envisioned and intended—and if by some greater wisdom that diversion had been to the betterment and increase of securing our rights to life, freedom and the pursuit of happiness, then perhaps one could argue that the diversion from original vision and intent resulted in a more perfect union. But just the opposite is true. Our current diversions from our Founding Fathers' original vision and intent for these United States of America has decreased, not increased, our right to life, liberty and the pursuit of happiness.

## Government Is Not Giver-ment! Redistribution Of Tax Revenues Is Communism & Must Immediately Cease!

A portion of the blame must fall upon the citizenry of this great nation who have become complacent and been deceived into thinking that the government's role is to take care of them. Such individuals think of government as a giver-ment! Let me state here in no uncertain terms—it is not government's job to give you ANYTHING! Because, the government cannot give anyone anything without first taking it away from someone else.

I'm sorry to break this to you, but my tax dollars are not to take care of your lazy ass! Get up off your butt and take care of yourself!

God commands: *"we commanded you this: If anyone will not work, neither shall he eat."*—2 Thessalonians 3:10

And this verse refers to the charity of the Church! If the Church is not to feed anyone who does not work, how much less is that the role of the government! The government does not have the right to disobey the commandment of God!

This is where President Obama's belief that *"when you spread the wealth around, it's good for everybody"* flies right in the face of everything that is America—this is the Land of the Free and the Home of the Brave—not a communist country! Hey everybody...Communism FAILED! Where were you, President Obama...did you miss that? Why are you and most other Democrats trying to turn America into a communist country? Well, guess what: We are not going to allow you to do it! We The People of the United States of America are coming! We are coming to the polls this November 6, 2012, just like we did in the mid-term elections on November 2, 2010, and taking our country back from the hands of you Islam-loving, freedom-hating, America-destroying Communist Democrats!

Thomas Jefferson, Author of the Declaration of Independence, Third President of the United States and Founder of the University of Virginia, declared:

*The democracy will cease to exist when you take away from those who are willing to work and give to those who would not."*

A great modern-day Pastor and Statesman, a personal favorite preacher of mine, who has since gone on to his Heavenly reward, Adrian Rogers, is credited with these following profound words of *Common Sense* wisdom:

*You cannot legislate the poor into prosperity by legislating the wealthy out of prosperity. What one person receives without working for, another person must work for without receiving. The government cannot give to anybody anything that the government does not first take from somebody else. When half of the people get the idea that they do not have to work because the other half is going to take care of them, and when the other half gets the idea that it does no good to work because somebody else is going to get what they work for, that my dear friend, is the beginning of the end of any nation. You cannot multiply wealth by dividing it.*—Adrian Pierce Rogers, September 12, 1931—November 15, 2005, was an American pastor, conservative, author, and a three-term president of the Southern Baptist Convention (1979-1980 and 1986-1988.

America's Founding Fathers and our nation's founding documents, along with *Common Sense*, declare that the Federal government's role then is to provide and maintain a military force superior to all others, that is capable of protecting us from all enemies foreign—therefore our military must be the largest, strongest, best trained, best equipped military on the planet able to defend against any and all threats. The Federal government may also maintain the CIA to assist the Defense Department in defending and protecting us; and the FBI to investigate Federal crimes. State, County and City governments must maintain law enforcement, as well as other beneficial protective services such as Fire Departments and 911 emergency services, to maintain our security at the local level from all domestic enemies.

In addition to providing safety and security for its citizenry, Federal, State, County and City governments may and should use our tax dollars for other beneficial services that directly benefit each tax payer, such as Federal Interstate highways and a national air-traffic control system; plus State, County and City roads and highways, with street lights to light the night and traffic lights to control traffic flow in an orderly manner; along with funding of our children's education from Kindergarten through the 12th grade; but other than this very limited scope of tax-dollar funded services, there really isn't much else that God nor the Declaration of Independence nor the U.S. Constitution nor *Common Sense* declare to be the role and purview of government.

Again, I repeat, every dollar of my hard-earned money that I give to the government by way of taxes may only be spent on government programs and services that directly benefit me and my family!

Having provided "security" for me and my family, along with good roads to travel on, safe skies to fly in, and good schools for my children to attend, the remaining obligation of the government is to give me "liberty," in other words—stay the hell out of my life!

What government should not do is become a giver-ment! Government does not have the right to take money from me that I worked for by way of taxes, and give that money to someone else who did not work for it! That's Communism! And we will not tolerate Communism nor Communists in America!

Every dollar that I have worked for that is taken away from me by the government through taxation *MUST,* and I repeat, *MUST,* be spent by the government on services that directly benefit me the taxpayer!

To take my tax dollars and spend them to the benefit of someone else is plain and simply stealing! It is misappropriation of tax dollars! And we the American people will no longer tolerate the theft of our hard-earned money by Communist politicians!

The government does not have the right to give my hard-earned money to someone else; in other words, the government does not have the right to give money to anyone for any reason!

Nor does the government have the right to take my hard-earned money and give it to a business. President Obama is going around the Country giving speech after speech stating that the government must "invest" money into this lunatic idea or that idiotic project. No, the government does not have the right to take my money and give it to someone else! Who the hell does the government think it is to pick one person or one company over any other person or company and give them money! Is Barack Obama insane? Is the giver-ment under his leadership out of their minds? Hell no you can't give my hard-earned money to some a-hole who owns Solyndra or any other company!

*The democracy will cease to exist when you take away from those who are willing to work and give to those who would not.—*
Thomas Jefferson

Thomas Jefferson believed that if the government played Robin Hood, taking from the rich (those who have worked and sacrificed for their success) and give it to the poor (those who refuse to work hard enough to succeed), that it would literally be the end of the nation!

Listen again to the words of Pastor Adrian Rogers:

*You cannot legislate the poor into prosperity by legislating the wealthy out of prosperity. What one person receives without working for, another person must work for without receiving. The government cannot give to anybody anything that the government does not first take from somebody else. When half of the people get the idea that they do not have to work because the other half is going to take care of them, and when the other half gets the idea that it does no good to work because somebody else is going to get what they work for, that my dear friend, is the beginning of the end of any nation. You cannot multiply wealth by dividing it.*—Adrian Pierce Rogers

It's obvious that Pastor Adrian Rogers agrees with Thomas Jefferson's assessment of the danger to our nation of using tax revenue from one citizen to benefit some other citizen—in other words, redistribution of wealth, to *"spread the wealth around!"*

Therefore, all government programs which redistribute tax revenue from one citizen and give it to another must be stopped immediately! That is pure and simply Communism! Each citizen must pay his or her fair share of taxes—this means every citizen must pay the same percentage of their income as every other citizen. Yet today in America we have nearly 50% of Americans paying zero in Federal taxes! And President Obama has the audacity to go around giving speeches claiming that more successful American's "aren't paying their fair share!" Hey President Obama, you freaking imbecile, successful American's are the only Americans paying "their fair share," in fact they are paying more than their fair share! It is the less successful 50% of Americans who must immediately begin paying their fair, equal share of taxes—otherwise get your car off the roads I'm paying for, and get your kids out of the schools I'm paying for, and don't expect the Fire Department that I'm paying for to show up when your house is on fire! In fact, get your non-tax-paying ass out of the United States of America where you enjoy the protection of the greatest military force on Earth which my taxes are paying for!

Only when every citizen pays an equal portion of their income in Federal taxes, combined with the expenditure of those tax dollars going to services that are directly benefitting that taxpayer and not someone else, will we then have a just, fair and equitable tax system. And we will have a government that can balance its budget, get out of debt and even have a surplus! See my 10% Federal Sales Tax proposal in Chapter 6, *Common Sense* Solutions For Getting America's Economy Back On The Road To Prosperity!

## A New Declaration For The New American Revolution Of Common Sense!

In conclusion:

Because President Barack Obama and the Democratic Minority in the House of Representatives and Democratic Majority in the Senate are guilty of usurping the limits of their Constitutional rights and responsibilities,

First by violating our God-given right to life by slaughtering tens-of-millions of our citizens in the Democratic Party's abortion murder-mills;

And because the Democrats have further corrupted the moral fabric of our nation by appointing homosexuals to high office and to the Supreme Court;

And because the Democrats are destroying our right to pursue happiness by destroying our economy with insurmountable and likely irreversible debt;

And because the Democrats are attempting to overthrow America's Free-Market Free-Enterprise Republic by their attempts to convert our economy into a Communistic system with their "redistribution of wealth;"

And because the Democrats have violated the First Amendment of the U.S. Constitution by stripping us of our right to Freedom of Religion by barring prayer and Bible reading from our public schools and government venues;

And because the Democrats have jeopardized our security by refusing to acknowledge the existence of the very enemy who is waging war against our nation, the religion of Islam, and have further endangered our lives by calling for and inviting these enemies to conduct further acts of war against us by calling for their "right" to "practice their religion" which is the slaying of all who are not converted to Islam;

And because President Barack Hussein Obama himself has further violated his sworn Oath to protect and defend the Constitution of the United States by giving speeches, both at home and abroad, with the purpose of making friendly alliances with those who are waging war against us, the Muslims—leaving only one conclusion, that he the President, is in conspiracy together with them, either that, or he is ignorant of the basic teachings of the religion of Islam into which he was born, and whose madras schools he attended in Indonesia, which defies *Common Sense* that he would therefore be "ignorant" of their doctrine.

Therefore, We The People of these United States of America, do hereby resolve that it is time once again for a new American Revolution of *Common Sense*:

*"That whenever any form of government becomes destructive to these ends, it is the right of the people to alter or to abolish it, and to institute new government, laying its foundation on such principles and organizing its powers in such form, as to them shall seem most likely to effect their safety and happiness."*—Declaration of Independence.

Only, in this present cause, we shall not effect governmental change by the power of the bullet, but by the power of the ballot, as We The People did on November 2, 2010, and shall again on November 6, 2012, and on every election thereafter, by electing *Common Sense* Constitutionalists to Office! That, of course, means that no Democrat will ever again be elected to any Office!

Now, it's time for *Common Sense* Solutions for winning the war against Islamic terrorism!

# Chapter 3: *Common Sense* Solutions For Winning The War Against Islamic Terrorism—It's As Easy As: A, B, C! Step A: Acknowledge The Fact That Every Muslim Is A Potential Terrorist!

There are 3 easy, *Common Sense* steps that we must take in order to win the war against Islamic terrorism in which we are now engaged. If we do not take all 3 of these steps we will not win the war against Islamic terrorism. These 3 steps are as simple and *Common Sense* as A, B, C.

Step A: Acknowledge the fact that every Muslim is a potential terrorist.

Step B: Ban the vile, violent false religion of Islam from America's shores.

Step C: Counter Islam on foreign soil by mandating the freedom of Christianity in the Middle East.

Step A: Acknowledge the fact that every Muslim is a potential terrorist!

## The Ostrich Syndrome

America's leaders, and in fact many Americans, need to get their head out of the sand and stop pretending that we are not "at war with the religion of Islam,' when in fact it is the religion of Islam that has declared war against the United States, and in fact against all non-Muslims worldwide from Islam's very inception.

Islam's military war against all non-Muslims began at the very inception of Islam when Muhammad, the Founder of Islam, wrote the Quran in c.a. 610--630 A.D., in which every twelfth verse of Islam's holiest book either speaks to Allah's hatred for non-Muslims or calls for their death, forced conversion, or subjugation. In fact, the name "Islam" means "submission," i.e., submission to Allah, the moon god of the ancient Meccans.

Muhammad formed an army and proceeded to spread his new religion by the power of the sword; literally going town to town and demanding that the inhabitants convert to Islam. If the towns people resisted, Muhammad attacked, beheading the men, raping the women (what Islam calls same day marriage), seizing the property as their own and subjecting the women and children to slavery. After Muhammad's death in c.a. 632 A.D., his followers continued Muhammad's bloody rampage, inspired by the "divine command" of the Quran to "jihad," which means to "fight in the cause of Allah," which is the central theme of the Quran.

Oh, I guess President Obama forgot to tell you the truth about Islam when each year he invites these Muslim monsters to the White House to celebrate the Islamic Festival of Ramadan. This one act alone by President Barack Hussein Obama is so blatantly anti-American that it demands every U.S. citizen rise up on November 6, 2012, and vote this Muslim-loving monster out of the White House! Every soul who votes for President Obama to be reelected will have to answer to the Lord Jesus Christ on the Day of Judgment for why they voted for a man who honors the anti-Christ cult of Islam.

## *September 11 Was Merely Muslims "Practicing Their Religion!"*

All American's agree, at least all American's who possess *Common Sense*, that the government's number one priority and responsibility is our security. Without security, there can be no liberty. Our God-given rights to life, liberty and the pursuit of happiness all collapse when airliners are purposely flown into our most prestigious and iconic buildings, killing thousands of our citizens.

We all remember where we were that terrifying morning of September 11, 2001. After the first plane had crashed into the first Tower, we were glued to our television sets, staring in unbelief at the smoke and fire that was pouring from that Tower. The news commentators were speculating whether it was a small private plane, but could a small private plane cause such a gaping hole?...Could it have been a commercial airliner?

I had the privilege on numerous prior occasions while on business in New York City to enjoy lunch at the Windows On The World restaurant located at the top of one of the World Trade Center Twin Towers. I knew that, on any given day, nearly fifty-thousand people worked in those two magnificent Towers. Each Tower had its own Postal Zip Code. CNN used to broadcast from the First Floor of one of the Towers.

As we all watched, we were thinking, "What a horrible accident." There must be hundreds of people who were killed by the impact...and what about all those people who may be trapped in the floors above the burning crash site.

Then, as we watched on live television, suddenly a second large commercial airliner came into view, angled and banking, and then purposely flew directly into the back-side of the Second Tower, with the explosive impact causing a massive fireball to explode out of the other side of the building toward the cameras!

In that instant, every American knew immediately that we were under attack! We didn't know by whom, but we knew that we were now at war! We sensed that this event was our 21st-Century generation's Pearl Harbor.

It wasn't long before the report came in that the Pentagon too had been attacked, followed by the camera footage and reports of the carnage there.

Then we heard of the airliner crashing into a field in Pennsylvania. And subsequently the grounding of all air traffic nationwide.

By that evening, when President Bush addressed the nation, it had become clear that we had been attacked by Muslims, by followers of the religion of Islam.

As a Christian, I knew that Islam was a false religion, which meant that it was a "lie," and therefore that it had been satanically inspired, since satan is "the Father of lies" (John 8:44).

However, I knew little more than that. I had never read any verses from the Quran, Islam's "Holy Book." In fact, all of us were about to learn a whole lot more about this religion called Islam and its adherents called Muslims.

I want to interject a comment here before I continue: The information contained in this chapter, and indeed throughout this book, may upset you or even make you angry. But I simply ask you to consider one thing—is what is being stated true? If what is being said is true, then even though you may disagree with it or even though it may anger you, because it is true, you cannot reject it or deny it. $2 + 2 = 4$. You may want $2 + 2$ to $= 5$, or if $2 + 2$ would $= 3$, perhaps you would be happier. But the truth is that $2 + 2 = 4$. If you can demonstrate that anything I have stated in this book is not true, I will happily retract that error and make a public apology. But if these statements are true, I strongly encourage you to take them to heart and ponder their implications.

In the days that followed 911, we learned that all nineteen of the 911 hijackers were Muslims, devout followers of Islam who pre-recorded videos declaring their intentions to die as martyrs in the cause of Allah, i.e., "jihad," in obedience to the commands of the Quran, by hijacking those airliners and using them as weapons of mass destruction to murder as many innocent Americans as possible, actions which resulted in the diabolical murder of nearly 3,000 American citizens, as well as the destruction of two of America's most significant structural icons and the near destruction of a third; and we heard with our own ears from the flight recorders their voices screaming, "Allah Ak Bar!" which means "Allah is the Greatest!" which of course is a demonic declaration that the Moon-god of Saudi Arabia is greater than the One True God Jesus Christ, who is God in Unity with God the Father and God the Holy Spirit.

### The U.S. Is Not At War With Islam! Oh Really?
### Wake Up America!

Yet, in spite of all this startling evidence, President Bush went out of his way to make it clear that we were not at war with the religion of Islam, but rather with a group of "radical Muslims" who, just as they had hijacked those airliners on 911, had also "hijacked the religion of Islam."

President Obama has subsequently reaffirmed that the United States is not, never was and never will be at war with Islam.

Are the above statements of Presidents Bush and Obama true? No! Their statements are not true! I'm not saying that President's Bush and Obama are deliberately lying; they both may sincerely believe that the United States is not at war with the religion of Islam, but rather just an unhappy band of radicals who have hijacked that religion in violation of its clear teachings.

Although, since President Barack Hussein Obama was born a Muslim, given a Muslim name by a Father who was a practicing Muslim, and as a child lived in the Islamic nation of Indonesia and attended official Islamic religious indoctrination schools known as Madras's, it is a lot harder to believe that President Barack Hussein Obama does not know the clear and blatant teachings of the Quran.

But, in reproof of the statements of President's Bush and Obama that the United States "is not at war with Islam," I will now prove that it is indeed the religion of Islam and the commands of its holy book, the Quran, that the Islamic "terrorists" are obeying and from which they are receiving their "marching orders;" therefore, *Common Sense* dictates that it is the religion of Islam and its true followers who have declared war against the United States, and the whole world for that matter; and if Islam has declared war on us, then we are indeed at war with Islam.

Let's quit hiding our heads in the sand and pretending. Come on, folks! Let's stop playing childish games here. Our lives and very existence as a nation are at stake! How can you win a war if you won't even acknowledge who your enemy is! To refuse to state that the false-religion of Islam is the enemy is simply utter nonsense!

There are scores of verses in the Quran that directly command Muslims to kill Christians and Jews, and all other non-Muslims for that matter. In this chapter I will prove that the "terrorists" are not "radical Muslims" perverting the religion of Islam, but rather are true, good Muslims! In other words, any Muslim who is not a "terrorist," simply isn't a good Muslim. Islam is a vile, violent religion. Shortly, as you read the verses below from the Quran for yourself, you will come to realize this statement is true. But first, let me entertain you!

## It's Show Time! Watch Attorney General Eric Holder Tap Dance Around Islam!

One of the most shocking events in American history occurred on May 13, 2010, when Obama appointee, U.S. Attorney General Eric Holder, was questioned by Congressman Darrell Issa, California Republican, regarding the possible influence that the religion of Islam had upon the actions of terrorists. The number one Law Enforcement Officer of the United States could not even say the words, "radical Islam!" What is even more shocking than the fact that AG Holder could not even bring himself to name America's Number One Enemy, is the fact that he wasn't immediately fired! Here is the text of that on camera exchange (get ready to both laugh your ass off and have your blood boil!):

Congressman Issa: *In the case of all three attempts in the last year, the terrorists' attempts, one of which was successful, those individuals have had ties to radical Islam. Do you feel that these individuals might have been incited to take the actions that they did because of radical Islam?*

AG Holder: *Because of?*

Congressman Issa: *Radical Islam.*

AG Holder: *There are a variety of reasons why I think people have taken these actions, uhm, it's hard, one I think you have to look at each individual case, I mean we're in the process now of talking to Mr. Shahzad, to try to understand what it is that drove him to take the action he did.*

Congressman Issa: *But radical Islam could have been one of the reasons?*

AG Holder: *There are a variety of reasons why people*

Congressman Issa: *But was radical Islam one of them?*

AG Holder: *There are a variety of reasons why people do these things; some of them are potentially religious based.*

Congressman Issa: *OK, but all I'm asking is if you think among those variety of reasons, radical Islam might have been one of the reasons that the individuals took the steps that they did?*

AG Holder: *You see, you say radical Islam, I mean, I think those people who espouse a version of Islam that is not consistent*

Congressman Issa: *Are you uncomfortable attributing any of their actions to radical Islam? It sounds like you are.*

AG Holder: *No I don't want to say anything negative about a religion that is not...*

Congressman Issa: *No no, I'm not talking about a religion, I'm talking about radical Islam, I'm not talking about the general religion.*

AG Holder: *Right, and I'm saying that a person like Anwar al-Awlaki, for instance, who has a version of Islam that is not consistent with the teachings of it and who espouses a radical version*

Congressman Issa: *Again, could radical Islam have motivated these individuals to take the steps that they did?*

AG Holder: *I certainly think that it's possible that people who espouse a radical version of Islam have had an ability to have an impact on people like Mr. Shahzad.*

Congressman Issa: *OK, and could it have been the case in one of these three instances?*

AG Holder: *Could that have been the case?*

Congressman Issa: *Yep, again, could one of these three individuals have been incited by radical Islam? Apparently you feel that they could have been.*

AG Holder: *Well, I think potentially incited by a view of Islam that is inconsistent with the history of it.* [Note: this final sentence by Holder breaks up on all versions of the video I can find, so I cannot verify the exactness of this final quote; but the essence is accurate].

Congressman Issa: *It's hard to get an answer yes or no.* (You may watch this exchange by searching YouTube: Eric Holder Refuses To Say "Radical Islam").

What a contorted refusal by U.S. Attorney General Eric Holder to acknowledge that it is indeed the religion of Islam—and the religion of Islam alone—that is the motivating factor in each and every Islamic terrorist attack on the United States and everywhere else in the world.

First, we must applaud California Congressman, Darrell Issa, for having the balls to hold Attorney General Eric Holder's feet to the fire. This attitude on the part of the Obama administration toward our Islamic enemies revealed by this exchange is not only puzzling and disturbing, but it is downright dangerous to our national security.

There are two very important points, however, in the above Q&A between the Congressman and the Attorney General that are more than just disturbing and dangerous, but are essential to understand if we ever wish to have even a hope of winning the war against Islamic terrorism.

The first point is the ignorance, and might I add arrogance, of Mr. Holder to declare that the religious Muslims who are committing all of the terrorist attacks upon the United States and around the world, are each a Muslim...

*"who has a version of Islam that is not consistent with the teachings of it and who espouses a radical version."*

The second, is the ignorance of our noble Congressman Issa, when he makes the statement:

*"No no, I'm not talking about a religion, I'm talking about radical Islam, I'm not talking about the general religion."*

The point of these two errors are one and the same, and may be combined into one simple yet critical response: The belief that the Islamic terrorists are motivated by a religious belief that is contrary to the teachings of Islam and the Quran comes simply from a lack of knowledge of Islam and the Quran.

In fact, the lack of *Common Sense* on this issue by Attorney General Eric Holder is simply mind-boggling! Look again at this statement by Mr. Holder from the above exchange:

*"There are a variety of reasons why I think people have taken these actions, uhm, it's hard, one I think you have to look at each individual case, I mean we're in the process now of talking to Mr. Shahzad, to try to understand what it is that drove him to take the action he did."*

Since all these Muslim names are so hard to keep track of, just so we know who we're talking about here, Mr. Shahzad is the Muslim American who attempted to set off a car bomb in Times Square, New York City, on May 1, 2010.

So, Mr. Eric Holder, let me get this straight, you are really talking to Mr. Shahzad, *"to try to understand what it is that drove him to take the action he did?"*

Mr. Holder, are you really that clueless?

## NYC Mayor Michael Bloomberg Condones The Attacks Of 9-11 & Calls For More Of The Same!

Well, certainly New York City Mayor Michael Bloomberg could be looked to for leadership and some *Common Sense* on this issue, right? Wrong! Immediately after the attempted Time Square bombing, Mayor Bloomberg held a press conference stating what he believed would drive someone to do something like that—it was obvious to him that it was probably somebody who was upset about the HealthCare Bill passing! Mayor Bloomberg's comments implied that obviously it was one of those Tea Party people who were mad about Obama's Communistic Health Care system passing…and he was probably white, either Republican or Independent, probably a military veteran and for sure a Christian! After all, those are the people that Director of Homeland Security, Lesbian Janet Napolitano, sent out a memo warning law enforcement to keep a look out for, because those are the people who pose the greatest threat to our national security according to the Obama Administration!

My God! With statements like those above by top Obama Administration Officials, why aren't Americans rioting in the streets demanding the immediate resignation of President Obama and his entire Administration? With moronic statements like the one Mayor Bloomberg made, why aren't New Yorkers rioting in the streets demanding his immediate resignation! With leaders like these, who needs enemies? God help us!

Mayor Bloomberg, you of all people—a man who is Jewish and therefore the number one enemy and target of the religion of Islam, and who is the Mayor of where Ground Zero was for the 9-11 attacks—should have known immediately that this was most probably an act of Islamic terrorism!

How dare you, Mayor Bloomberg, accuse true American everyday citizens of such a cowardly act! You are right, we are mad as hell that Obama and the Democrats are turning our great freedom-loving country into a communist country—but because we are American Christians, we are neither cowards nor murderers! We are coming to remove you from office—but not by the power of the bullet, but by the power of the ballot!

And, Mayor Bloomberg, if you had any balls at all, you would immediately resign from office for your asinine comment! Your ignorant comment has disqualified you from being Mayor of the great city of New York—the City which took the brunt of the Muslim attack of 9-11! Then to put the cherry on top of your ignorance, with regard to the building of a Muslim Terrorist Training Center (I will prove shortly that every mosque is a terrorist training center)—a Mosque in the shadow of Ground Zero—you make the statement that Muslims:

*"Have the right to practice their religion!"*

Sir, are you really that ignorant? Or are you just out of your mind!

Mayor Bloomberg, your statement is a declaration of your approval of the attacks of 9-11, and a call for more of the same! Don't you realize, Mayor Bloomberg, that the nineteen hijackers on 9-11, *WERE PRACTICING THEIR RELIGION!* (YES, I'M YELLING! AREN'T YOU?).

For the sake of the safety of New York City, Mayor Bloomberg, We The People of the United States of America demand your resignation!

## *Every Muslim Who Is Not A Terrorist Is Simply Not A "Good Muslim!"*

But getting back to AG Holder's comment that he and the United States Department of Justice are interviewing the Time Square bomber, Faisal Shahzad, in an attempt to, *"try to understand what it is that drove him to take the action he did?"*

AG Holder, let me save you and the U.S. Department of Justice a whole lot of time and money—The naturalized American citizen, Faisal Shahzad, did what he did *because he is a Muslim!* His religion, Islam, *"drove him to take the action he did!"* The naturalized American citizen Faisal Shahzad did what he did to his country because his "holy book' the Quran, *"drove him to take the action he did!"* The American citizen, Faisal Shahzad, did what he did because his god, Allah, is the one who by his command, *"drove him to take the action he did!"*

May I remind you that attempted Times Square bomber, Faisal Shahzad, the 30-year-old naturalized American citizen working as a financial analyst with an MBA—yes, that's right, an American citizen with a college degree!—who was born in Pakistan and lived in Connecticut, did not even try to fight the charges levied against him, but pleaded guilty before Judge Miriam Cedarbaum to ten different terror-related federal charges, two of which carry a mandatory life sentence, including attempted use of a weapon of mass destruction. In fact, Mr. Shahzad declared that he wished he could plead guilty *"one-hundred times more!"*

Shahzad admitted he had received 40-days of terror training in Waziristan, Pakistan, from the Pakistani Taliban and warned that further attacks on the U.S. were coming!

Shahzad also confirmed to Judge Cedarbaum that he had driven the Nissan Pathfinder packed with explosives into midtown Manhattan and parked it in Times Square on Saturday evening, May 1, 2010, at its busiest time when the city's theater district was packed with tourists in order to do the maximum damage.

And Mayor Bloomberg, it wasn't because he was upset about the HealthCare Bill passing, but Faisal Shahzad—again I want to remind you that he is a naturalized American citizen with a college degree—stated to Judge Cedarbaum that what "drove him" to commit this heinous act (thank God he failed!) was because, *"I consider myself a Muslim soldier,"* he said.

And this gets to the heart of our discussion on how to win the war against terrorism—it's simple *Common Sense*, we must wake up and realize the fundamental fact that every Muslim is a potential terrorist. That is simply a fact which is irrefutable and undeniable. And anyone who wishes to continue to deny this fact is unfit to serve in a leadership role in our government. That's just a fact jack.

You see, people are now "shocked" that we are experiencing "home grown terrorism."

Don't you remember the incident when our military first began assembling in the Middle East in preparation for invading Iraq, and an American soldier threw a hand-grenade into an officer's tent where a meeting was being held and killed a number of his fellow American soldiers? Of course, he was pissed off about Obama's HealthCare Bill, right? No, he was a Muslim!

Do you remember a little incident on November 5, 2009, when U.S. Army Major Nidal Hasan, stationed at the Army base in Fort Hood, Texas, an Army Officer who was college educated, earning a six-figure salary, a "psychiatrist" for that matter, jumped up on top of a table and began massacring dozens of his fellow soldiers, shouting as he murdered his fellow soldiers, *"Allah Akbar!"* (Allah is greatest!). With the final toll of 13 dead and 30 wounded—Hasan had fired over 100 rounds and therefore was clearly trying to murder all 43 fellow soldiers he shot.

AG Holder, are you also interviewing Major Nidal Hasan in an attempt to, *"try to understand what it is that drove him to take the action he did?"*

Mayor Bloomberg, do you think this American citizen, a Major in the U.S. Army, massacred 13 and wounded 30 of his fellow American soldiers because he was pissed off over the Health Care debate?

Above, we applauded California Republican Congressman Darrell Issa, in his grilling of Attorney General Eric Holder, for demonstrating that he understands that what is driving these terrorists is their religious views, which Congressman Issa characterized as *"radical Islam."*

But Congressman Issa also makes a serious, and potentially very dangerous, mistake when he separates radical Islam from the "general religion of Islam." Remember, Congressman Issa made this comment:

*No no, I'm not talking about a religion, I'm talking about radical Islam, I'm not talking about the general religion.*

So, we have our noble Congressman Issa believing that there is a difference between the general religion of Islam and "radical Islam." And we have Attorney general Eric Holder actually claiming to know for a fact that, with regard to what is potentially driving these Muslim terrorists is a version of Islam which he claims,

*who has a version of Islam that is not consistent with the teachings of it and who espouses a radical version.*

Both Holder and Issa are wrong. There is no such thing as "radical Islam," just as there is no such thing as "radical Christianity."

There is "true" Christianity—those who are "Born Again" Christians and therefore have a personal relationship with Jesus Christ as their Lord and Savior and thus believe that the Bible is the inspired, infallible Word of God, and are therefore true followers of the Lord Jesus Christ (John 3:1-36); and then you have what I call "Church-ianity,' people who go to Church but don't have a personal relationship with Jesus Christ as their Lord and Savior. The first group are not "radical Christians," but just simply true Christians. The second group may attend Christian Churches, but they are not really Christians. Attending a Christian Church no more makes you a Christian than standing in a garage makes you a car!

But, those of us who are true Christians, who believe that the Bible is the Divinely inspired, infallible Word of God, endeavor to obey the New Testament's teachings. Of course we fall short every day, but at least we realize that we are supposed to be trying to follow the teachings of our Lord Jesus Christ and His Word which He spoke by the Holy Spirit through His Apostles recorded in the New Testament. (See, Matthew 4:4, 5:18, 24:35; Luke 1:1-4, 24:25-27, 44-45; John 6:63, 10:34-35, 17:17; 1 Corinthians 15:1-11; 1 Thessalonians 2:13; 2 Timothy 3:15-17; Hebrews 4:12-13; 1 Peter 1:10-12, 23-25; 2 Peter 1:16-21, 3:15-16; 1 John 1:1-4; Revelation 1:1-3, 9-11, 22:18-20; etc.).

Therefore, as true Christians, when Jesus commands us to:

**Luke 6:28**

*"bless those who curse you, pray for those who mistreat you"*

Then, the reality is, that every Christian has the potential to obey—and indeed should obey—those commandments. For example, every Christian while driving in heavy traffic, if he or she inadvertently cuts somebody off, and that somebody pulls up alongside, gestures with their hand and hollers, "F-you!," there is the potential for each and every Christian to holler back, "God bless you!" I can hear my Christian friends thinking…"Why did you pick that example! I don't do so well at obeying in such instances."

Therefore, because of the commands contained in the New Testament, it is an irrefutable and undeniable fact that every Christian is a potential "blesser!"

This is a critical point—Every Christian has the potential to obey the commandments of the New Testament. And those Christians who do obey are counted as good Christians; and those who fail to obey are counted as not such good Christians.

So it is with Islam. To be a 'good" Muslim, one must strive to obey the teachings of the Quran. And those Muslims who do obey the teachings of the Quran are counted to be good Muslims; and those Muslims who fail to obey the teachings of the Quran are considered to be not such good Muslims.

However, there is one very important point of contrast between Christian obedience and Islamic obedience that must be made here. A Christians "salvation," his winning Heaven and escaping the eternal flames of hell, is not dependent upon his obedience, but rather upon his faith. The Bible says:

**Ephesians 2:8, 9**

*"For it is by grace you have been saved, through faith—and this not from yourselves, it is the gift of God—[9]not by works, so that no one can boast."*

What the Bible is stating here, is that a Christian's salvation is by "grace," that means God's free gift; and one receives God's free gift of salvation (which includes the forgiveness of one's sins and eternal life in Heaven) "through faith" in Jesus Christ the Son of God as the One God sent to die in man's place for man's sins and on the third day to rise from the dead defeating death on behalf of man. And as you see in the passage above, this salvation is specifically 'not by works." So a Christian's salvation is not dependent upon the degree of his obedience or lack thereof. Christianity's salvation is dependent upon one's faith in Jesus Christ, not one's works.

However, in Islam, one's salvation—winning of Heaven and escaping of the eternal flames of Hell—is directly dependent upon the degree of one's obedience. It is a salvation dependent upon works.

The point here is that if a Muslim does not obey the teachings and commands of the Quran, he shall not enter Heaven, but shall be damned to Hell. Sort of gives a Muslim a real incentive to obey the Quran, doesn't it?

So, only one question remains. Have the Muslim terrorists "hijacked" their religion? Or as Eric Holder states, are Muslim terrorists basing their actions on *"a version of Islam that is not consistent with the teachings of it and who espouses a radical version"*?

Or, are Muslim terrorists simply obeying what the Quran teaches and commands them to do? If Muslim terrorists are simply obeying the Quran, then they are good Muslims; and conversely, the Muslims who are not obeying what the Quran commands are to be counted as not such good Muslims; in fact, the Quran declares that Muslims who do not practice "jihad" will be damned to Hell!

## Quoting the Quran—The Quran Really Says That? OMG!

Have you ever read any of the Quran? Grab a fresh cup of coffee, and let's see what the Quran teaches and commands all Muslims to do.

The Quran contains scores and scores of verses that directly command Muslims to go to war against nonbelievers, i.e., non-Muslims. Some are quite graphic, with commands to chop off heads and fingers and kill infidels wherever they may be found, and for these nonbelievers to be fought and subdued until they either convert to Islam, or are killed. Muslims who do not join the fight are called 'hypocrites' and warned that Allah will send them to Hell if they do not join the slaughter. Muslims believe these commands in the Quran to be the eternal, unchanging divine word of Allah. Unfortunately, today most people, like Eric Holder and even Congressman Issa, are not only ignorant of the teachings of the Quran, but also of the violent and bloody history of the spread of Islam. Because of the Quran's proclivity toward violence and Muhammad's own legacy of spreading Islam by way of the sword and military conquest, Islam has left a trail of blood, tears and terrorism across 15-Centuries of world history.

Attention: Attorney General Eric Holder, Congressman Darrell Issa, NYC Mayor Michael Bloomberg, and all American's...Read and weep! But more importantly, read, understand and WAKE UP AMERICA!

Let's begin right with Chapter 2 of the Quran. Note: words in (parentheses like this) are contained in the original text as such, and were not added by me). I have occasionally added words in [brackets like this] for clarification which are not contained in the original text; except in each case where after the word "God" I have inserted the Arabic name [Allah,] and after the phrase "fight/strive in the cause/way" I have inserted the Arabic word [jihad,] which words are in the original Arabic text. All underlining of words is my addition for the purpose of emphasis.

## *Jihad & Global Domination By Islam Are The Central Theme Of The Quran!*

**Quran 2:190-193**
*190. Fight in the cause [jihad] of Allah those who fight you,*
*191. And slay them wherever ye catch them, and turn them out from where they have Turned you out; for tumult and oppression [of Muslims] are worse than slaughter [of non-Muslims]; but fight them not at the Sacred Mosque, unless they (first) fight you there; but if they fight you, slay them. Such is the reward of those who suppress faith [in Allah].*
*193. And fight them on until there is no more Tumult or oppression, and there prevail justice and faith in Allah; but if they cease [submit to Islam], Let there be no hostility except to those who practise oppression.*
**SHAKIR:** *193. And fight with them until there is no persecution [of Muslims], and religion should be only for Allah,*

Wow! Right off the bat here in just 4 verses of chapter 2 of the Quran we learn at least four mind-boggling truths about the "religion" of Islam:

1) The command to Jihad, *"Fight in the cause of Allah,"* is commanded toward everyone and anyone who even merely "oppresses" Muslims! This is why Muslim "clerics" have no problem issuing an order to murder innocent people who dare to poke fun at Islam in a cartoon or dare to call Islam's beliefs into question. No "freedom of speech" in Islam, that's for sure! In fact, to merely oppose Islam makes one worthy of death! This theme of jihad is a continuous theme of warfare against non-Muslims and non-jihadist Muslims that runs throughout the Quran.

2) The Quran commands Muslims to take no prisoners and spare no one's life unless they submit to Islam: *"slay them wherever ye catch*

them…but if they cease [submit to Islam], Let there be no hostility except to those who practise oppression."

3) Here in Chapter 2 is the Islamic theological basis for using mosques to stock-pile weapons and even use their mosques as "fortresses" from which to fight: *"fight them not at the Sacred Mosque, unless they (first) fight you there; but if they fight you, slay them. Such is the reward of those who suppress faith [in Allah]."*

4) Perhaps most important of all for Americans to understand is the Quran's command that "jihad"—warfare against non-Muslims and non-jihadist Muslims—is to continue until the entire world—every man, woman and child—has submitted to the "religion" of Islam: *"fight with them until there is no persecution [of Muslims], and religion should be only for Allah,"*

Having fun boys and girls? Let's hang right here in Chapter 2 for a few more verses.

### Quran 2:216-218
216. *Fighting is prescribed For you, and ye dislike it. But it is possible That ye dislike a thing Which is good for you, And that ye love a thing Which is bad for you. But God [Allah] knoweth, And ye know not.*

Here in Quran 2:216, we discover that whether the Muslim likes it or not, *"Fighting is prescribed for you."* Are you getting this? Allah has commanded that every Muslim practice jihad, fight and slay all non-Muslims until the whole world is under the rule of the religion of Islam, whether they like it or not!

Check out this next verse!

217. *They ask thee Concerning fighting In the Prohibited Month. Say: "Fighting therein Is a grave (offence); But graver is it In the sight of God [Allah] To prevent access To the path of God [Allah], To deny Him, To prevent access To the Sacred Mosque, And drive out its members. Tumult and oppression [of Muslims] Are worse than slaughter [of non-Muslims]. Nor will they cease Fighting you until They turn you back From your faith If they can. And if any of you Turn back from their faith And die in unbelief, Their works will bear no fruit In this life And in the Hereafter; They will be Companions of the Fire And will abide therein.*

## *I Pray For All Muslims To Turn From The Darkness & Lies Of Islam & Come To The Light & Glorious Truth Of The Gospel Of Jesus Christ!*

Here in Quran 2:217, we learn that, even though there are certain "holy months" in Islam, like Ramadan, in which even though they should not fight, fighting is nevertheless sanctioned if a Muslim feels they are experiencing *"oppression"*—which is open to broad interpretation, because it is better to fight and *"slaughter"* the non-Muslims even during the *"Prohibited Month"* than to allow them to oppress you. Allah also warns here that, *"if any of you Turn back from their faith And die in unbelief, Their works will bear no fruit In this life And in the Hereafter; They will be Companions of the Fire And will abide therein."* This of course is a diabolical lie straight from Hell! The truth is that it's not failing to have faith in Allah that sends one to Hell, but it is failing to have faith in the crucified-for-sins and risen-again Lord Jesus Christ that sends a soul to Hell (Mark 16:15-16; John 3:14-18, 36, 5:21-28, 14:6, 20:24-31; Acts 4:10-12, 16:30-31, 15:11, 20:21; Romans 1:16-17, 3:20-28; 1 John 1:1--2:2, 5:1-13, 19-20; Revelation 1:5-6, 20:21; etc., etc.). Remember, the Quran was not written by Muhammad until 600 years after the time of Christ; so the truth of the Gospel of Jesus Christ was widely known by Muhammad's time—therefore, the Quran not only tells Muslims that fighting against the Christians is prescribed for them--which is the same as fighting against the Lord Jesus Christ Himself (See Acts 9:1-6), but the Quran also lies to them about what sends a soul to Hell.

Muslims in America and around the world, I pray for you, in the Name of Jesus Christ the Lord, the Only Begotten Son of God and Only Savior of the world, that your eyes be opened to the Truth of the Gospel of Jesus Christ, so that you turn from the darkness of Islam and come into the glorious Light of the Crucified and Risen Lord Jesus Christ, in Whom alone is forgiveness of sins and Eternal Life, Amen!

## *Muslims Who Practice Jihad Are Promised Heaven; Muslims Who Do Not Are Promised Hell!*

Let's continue with Quran 2:218.

218. *Those who believed And those who suffered exile And fought (and strove and struggled) In the path [jihad] of God [Allah],—They have the hope Of the Mercy of God [Allah]; And God [Allah] is Oft-forgiving, Most Merciful.*

Here in Quran 2:218, in direct contrast to those in the previous verse who, instead of fighting, *"Turn back from their faith"* and thus go to Hell, it is instead *"those who suffered exile and fought (and strove and struggled) in the path [jihad] of God [Allah],—They have the hope*
*Of the Mercy of God."*

So, right in the beginning of the Quran, the second chapter, in verses 216-218, we discover the Quranic teaching that those Muslims who practice jihad, i.e., fight *"In the path of God [Allah],"* are the ones who are rewarded by the Quran with the promise of Heaven, and those who do not are promised Hell. Quite a motivator to be a "Soldier of Islam," as the American citizen with a Masters Degree in Business, Faisal Shahzad, so boldly proclaimed without any fear before the American Court. Faisal Shahzad's only regret was that his bomb did not explode and murder massive amounts of innocent Americans.

Now do you understand "what motivates Muslims to do such things?" It is because the religion of Islam guarantees them Paradise if they do, and promises Hell if they don't!

Hold on, there is more! Next Chapter please.

## Allah Commands Muslims To Be "Terrorists" & Denies The Trinity & That Jesus Is The Son Of God!

Quran 3:151
*Soon shall We cast <u>terror</u> Into the hearts of the Unbelievers For that they joined companions With God [Allah], for which He had sew No authority: their abode Will be the Fire: and evil Is the home of the wrong-doers!*

The above is an extremely important passage for it is a direct reference to Christians who believe in the Trinity—God the Father, God the Son Jesus Christ who eternally existed prior to becoming a human, and God the Holy Spirit—this belief by Christians in the Trinity is what Muhammad incorrectly believed to be *"they joined companions with Allah."* Note that these Trinitarian Christians are declared to be *"the Unbelievers"* and *"their abode Will be the Fire:"* and that *"Soon shall We cast terror Into the hearts of the Unbelievers."*

So here in Quran 3:151, Allah commands his followers, Muslims, to *cast terror Into the hearts of the [Christians].*

Therefore, labeling Muslims as "terrorists" is Quranically correct.

Quran Chapter 4 also, not only directly attacks the Truth of the Trinity, but directly attacks both the Divinity of Jesus Christ and the fact that Jesus is the Son of God.

### Quran 4.171
*O People of the Book [Bible]! Commit no excesses in your religion: Nor say of Allah aught but the truth. Christ Jesus the son of Mary was (no more than) a messenger of Allah, and His Word, which He bestowed on Mary, and a spirit proceeding from Him: so believe in Allah and His messengers. Say not "Trinity": desist: it will be better for you: for Allah is one Allah: Glory be to Him: (far exalted is He) above having a son. To Him belong all things in the heavens and on earth. And enough is Allah as a Disposer of affairs.*

## Allah Curses The Jews, Who Are Of Course The "Chosen People" Of God, Proving That Allah Is Not God!

Also right here in Quran 4 is one of the many places where "Allah" curses the Jewish people, which is why Muslims hate Jews. When Muhammad presented himself to the Jewish people as a "prophet" he was rejected by the Jews because, of course, his teachings did not align with the True Word of God, the Holy Bible. Therefore Muhammad wrote that since the Jews did not accept him, Allah had cursed and rejected the Jews. Of course, anyone with the intelligence of a fruit-fly knows that the Jewish People are the true Chosen People of God, proving that "Allah" is not God!

### Quran 4:46

*Of the Jews there are those who displace words from their (right) places, and say: "We hear and we disobey"; and "Hear what is not Heard"; and "Ra'ina"; with a twist of their tongues and a slander to Faith [Islam]. If only they had said: "What hear and we obey" [obey Islam]; and "Do hear"; and "Do look at us"; it would have been better for them, and more proper; but Allah hath cursed them for their Unbelief; and but few of them will believe.*

So by Chapter 4 of the Quran Allah's hatred toward the true people of God, Christians and Jews, is declared loud and clear!

## The Quran Promises Paradise To Suicide-Homicide Bombers!

Chapter 4 is also where Muslims find their inspiration to become suicide-homicide bombers, for if they die while fighting, they are guaranteed Paradise.

**Quran 4:74-77**

74. Let those fight In the cause [jihad] of God [Allah] Who sell the life of this world For the Hereafter. To him who fighteth In the cause [jihad] of God [Allah],—Whether he is slain Or gets victory Soon shall We give him A reward of great (value).

Here in Quran 4:74, and in the verses below, we have the Islamic theology that motivates today's suicide-homicide bombers, because they are promised *"A reward of great (value)"* if they *"sell the life of this world For the Hereafter."*

75. And why should ye not Fight in the cause [jihad] of God [Allah] And of those who, being weak, Are ill-treated (and oppressed)?—Men, women, and children, Whose cry is: "Our Lord! Rescue us from this town, Whose people are oppressors; And raise for us from Thee One who will protect; And raise for us from Thee One who will help!"

Here in Quran 4:75, Muslims are chided and derided if they do not *"Fight in the cause [jihad] of God [Allah]"* simply for the *"cause"* that Muslims feel that they are being *"ill-treated (and oppressed"* by the people of the town in which they live. Can you imagine if the New Testament commanded Christians' to kill everyone who mistreated or oppressed them over the past 2,000 years! If that were the case, our Founding Fathers would have come to the New World not to spread Christianity as was the case, but to flee from it! And not only would they have fled such a vile religion, but they also would have banned it from their shores. It is now time to ban the vile and violent false religion of Islam from America's shores! Need further proof? Let's continue quoting the Quran—the religious motivation behind every Islamic terrorist.

## The Quran Teaches That Any Military Force Not Fighting Under The Islamic Flag Is An Army Of Satan & That Christians & Jews Are Servants Of Satan! Of Course, Just The Opposite Is True!

76. Those who believe [Muslims] Fight in the cause [jihad] of God [Allah], And those who reject Faith [in Allah] Fight in the cause of Evil: So fight ye against the Friends of Satan: feeble indeed Is the cunning of Satan.

Here in Quran 4:76, you now understand why Muslims call America the "Great Satan," because they believe, according to the verse above, that any military force that is not fighting under the Islamic flag is fighting on behalf of Satan. I will have more to say on this in just a moment.

77. Hast thou not turned Thy vision to those Who were told to hold back Their hands (from fight) But establish regular prayers And spend in regular Charity? When (at length) the order For fighting was issued to them, Behold! a section of them Feared men as Or even more than They should have feared God [Allah]: They said: "Our Lord! Why hast Thou ordered us To fight? Wouldst Thou not Grant us respite To our (natural) term, Near (enough)?" Say [to those desiring a respite from fighting]: "Short Is the enjoyment of this world: The Hereafter is the best For those who do right: Never will ye be Dealt with unjustly In the very least!

Here in Quran 4:77, the Quran rebukes Muslims who grow weary of war and fighting and who desire a "respite," and commands the other Muslims to remind them it is better to do what is right by fighting now in this world so they may receive a good inheritance in the next world by saying to them, *"Short is the enjoyment of this world: The Hereafter is the best."* This, of course, again proves that the Quran teaches an eternal reward to those Muslims who practice jihad.

Are you starting to get a little pissed-off yet at Islam? You better wake up America!

But let me get back for a minute to Quran 4:76, one of the Quranic verses that Muslims get their belief from that Christians and Jews are serving satan, and therefore, by killing Christians and Jews they are killing or defeating satan. Here is an example ripped from recent headlines. In what was another in a string of recent murders by Muslims of Christians in Turkey, on June 3, 2010, the Catholic Bishop of Turkey, Padovese, was murdered by his Muslim driver, Murat Altun. Here is a portion of an article about that murder posted on www.JihadWatch.org (you may also obtain the general information about this murder by conducting a Google search for: Catholic Bishop in Turkey murdered by his Muslim driver):

*The doctors who performed the autopsy reveal that Mgr. Padovese had knife wounds all over his body, but especially in the heart (at least 8). His head was almost completely detached from his neck, attached to his body by only the skin of the back of the neck.*

*Even the dynamics of the killing is clearer: the Bishop was stabbed in his house. He had the strength to go out the door of the house, bleeding and crying for help and there he was killed. Perhaps only when he fell to the ground, was his head cut off.*

*Witnesses said they heard the bishop cry out for help. But more importantly, is that they heard screams of Murat immediately after the murder. According to these sources, he climbed on the roof of the house shouted: "I killed the great Satan! Allah Akbar! [Allah is Greatest!] ".*

*This call coincides perfectly with the idea of beheading, making sense that it is like a ritual sacrifice against evil. This correlates with the murders [recently conducted by several] ultranationalist groups and Islamic fundamentalists who apparently want to eliminate Christians from Turkey.*

*Moreover, according to a Turkish newspaper, Milliyet on June 4, the murderer had told police that he his actions were the result of a "divine revelation."...*

*Muhammad had one of those, too, interestingly: "Therefore, when ye meet the Unbelievers (in fight), smite at their necks..." (Qur'an 47:4). Does Muhammad get an insanity defense?*

*Posted by Marisol on June 8, 2010,*

*http://www.jihadwatch.org/2010/06/turkey-bishops-assassin-shouted-allah-akbar-and-later-said-i-killed-the-great-satan.html*

Chilling, isn't it? What kind of "god" commands his followers to murder other human beings in his name simply because they are *"Unbelievers"*? And what manner of god commands his followers not just to murder those who don't believe, but to do so in such a vile manner as beheading?

# The Quran Commands Beheading Of Non-Muslims!

In the article above you now see in the Quran where Allah commands Muslims to behead the *"Unbelievers,"* a Muslim practice that we have become all too familiar with, unfortunately; e.g., Daniel Pearl, the Wall Street Journal reporter, who true and devout Muslims beheaded in Pakistan in 2002, for no other reason except that he was Jewish, slowly sawing off his head while Daniel was fully conscious, recording the beheading on video and posting it online for all the world to see.

The monsters who beheaded Daniel Pearl were not "radical Muslims" but good, obedient Muslims who were simply obeying what the Quran, the religion of Islam and Islam's god commanded them to do.

By the way, the Jews, Israelites, the descendants of Abraham, Isaac and Jacob (Israel), are the true Chosen People of God through whom God gave the Holy Bible to Mankind, and through whom God sent His Son Jesus Christ/Messiah into the world to Save the world from their sins, thereby defeating satan and satan's plan for Mankind to join in his rebellion against God. This is why satan and his false religion of Islam hate the Jewish people.

Let us look at the full verse of Quran 47:4, plus verse 47:6, to get the context:

### Quran 47:4, 6

4. Therefore, when ye meet The Unbelievers (in fight), Smite at their necks; At length, when ye have Thoroughly subdued them, Bind a bond Firmly (on them): thereafter (Is the time for) either Generosity or ransom: Until the war lays down Its burdens. Thus (are ye Commanded): but if it Had been God's Will, He could certainly have exacted Retribution from them (Himself); But (He lets you fight) In order to test you, Some with others. But those who are slain In the way [jihad] of God [Allah], He will never let Their deeds be lost.
6. And admit them to The Garden which He Has announced for them.

In the above verses, we see that, not only does the Quran command the beheading of *"Unbelievers,"* and that Muslims are to fight until they have *"Thoroughly subdued them,"* and then to bind them into slavery and demand *"ransom,"* but then the Quran has the audacity to state that if Allah had wanted to he could have attained *"Retribution from them (Himself); But (He lets you fight) In order to test you,"* and then once again promises Paradise—*"The Garden"*—to those Muslims who give their life fighting in the war against the Unbelievers!

# Islamic Terrorists Are Not "Radical Muslims," But Good Obedient Muslims!

Are you beginning to see that this theme of jihad, fighting and warring against all non-Muslims worldwide, is a recurring and constant theme n the Quran? And we've only looked at the first 4 of 114 Chapters! Don't worry, though I could show you tons more verses I'm not going to, as they simply get redundant; however there are a few more mind-boggling verses you've got to see! My point in this is so that henceforth, no one ever again refers to the Islamic terrorists as "radical Muslims" or "radical Islam." The Muslim terrorists are merely good, obedient Muslims obeying the commands of the Quran and the religion of Islam. So, from henceforth let's call them what they truly are, "good Muslims" or "devout Muslims" or "True Muslims."

The following verse proves that Muslims who do not "fight," practice jihad, are not equal with Muslims who do, and will not receive the same reward as Muslims *"who strive And fight in the cause [jihad] Of God [Allah] with their goods And their persons."*

**Quran 4:95**
*Not equal are those Believers who sit (at home) And receive no hurt, And those who strive And fight in the cause [jihad] Of God [Allah] with their goods And their persons. God [Allah] hath granted A grade higher to those Who strive and fight With their goods and persons Than to those who sit (at home). Unto all (in Faith) Hath God promised good: But those who strive and fight Hath He distinguished Above those who sit (at home) By a special reward,*

Quran 4:95 criticizes "peaceful" Muslims who do not join in the jihad, letting them know that they are less worthy in Allah's eyes. This passage also demolishes the modern myth that "Jihad" doesn't mean holy war in the Qur'an, but merely a spiritual struggle; for in the Pickthal and Shakir translations, as well as the Hadith, this verse includes an exemption for the physically disabled:

**PICKTHAL, 4:95:** *Those of the believers who sit still, other than those who have a (disabling) hurt, are not on an equality with those who strive in the way [jihad] of Allah with their wealth and lives.*

Not only is the Arabic word "jihad" used in this passage, but because of the exemption for the physically disabled, it is clearly *not* referring to anything spiritual. The Hadith reveals the context of the passage to be in response to a blind man's protest that he is unable to engage in Jihad, which is reflected in both the Pickthal and Shakir translations of the verse.

The 5th Chapter of the Quran continues with extensive denunciations of Christians & Jews and derides their faith in the God of the Bible, describing those who believe in the Bible, and therefore reject the Quran, in such terms as: *"a people unjust"* (5:51) and *"Those in whose hearts is a disease"* (5:52) and *"they will fall into (nothing but) ruin"* (5:53) and *"a people without understanding"* (5:58), even declaring that, in Allah's eyes, Christians & Jews are worse than apes and pigs (5:59-60)—this is why you see children's programming produced by the Palestinians and aired in Gaza and other Muslim regions showing pre-school aged children being taught and declaring that the Jews in Israel are nothing more than pigs. Here are a few such verses:

**Quran 5:51, 54, 56, 59-60**
*51. O ye who believe! take not the Jews and the Christians for your friends and protectors: They are but friends and protectors to each other* [YOU'VE GOT THAT RIGHT BABY!]. *And he amongst you that turns to them (for friendship) is of them. Verily Allah guideth not a people unjust.*
*54. O ye who believe! if any from among you turn back from his Faith, soon will Allah produce a people whom He will love as they will love Him,- lowly with the believers, <u>mighty against the rejecters</u> [rejecters of Islam, i.e., Christians & Jews], <u>fighting in the way [jihad] of Allah</u>, and never afraid of the reproaches of such as find fault.*
*56. As to those who turn (for friendship) to Allah, His Messenger, and the (fellowship of) believers, - it is the <u>fellowship of Allah</u> [Islam] that <u>must certainly triumph</u>.*
*59-60.* **SHAKIR:** *Say: O followers of the Book! [Bible]...most of you are transgressors...Say: Shall I inform you of (him who is) worse than this in retribution from Allah? (Worse is he) whom Allah has cursed and brought His wrath upon, and of whom He made apes and swine,...these are worse in place and more erring from the straight path.*

Well, Muslims, let me tell you what the Bible—the True Word of God—says about YOU*!—"If anyone does not love the Lord Jesus Christ, let him be ${}^{£}$accursed!"* (1 Corinthians 16:22).

But, of course, the difference between us Christians and the Muslims is that all judgment and punishment will be delivered by God's own hand, not ours! But Muslims believe and indeed are commanded to be the arm of Allah's judgment and punishment upon all non-Muslims on the Earth.

Here are just a few more important passages from the Quran you need to see:

## Allah Declares That He Himself Is A Terrorist!

**Quran 8:12**
I will instil terror Into the hearts of the Unbelievers: [How will Allah do this?] Smite ye above their necks [behead the Unbelievers] And smite all their Finger-tips off them.

Are you seeing "why the Islamic terrorists do these things"? Are you seeing from where their "marching orders" come? Here, in Quran 8:12, Allah, The god of Islam, instead of being a God and religion of peace, states that he is a terrorist: *"I will instil terror Into the hearts of the Unbelievers:"* Remember, *"Unbelievers"* are Christians and Jews and anyone else who does not believe in Allah & submit to Islam. Then he tells his followers how to be the agents of his terror (as in Quran 47:4), by beheading "Unbelievers!" The beheadings of Wall Street Journal Reporter Daniel Pearl, the Catholic Bishop of Turkey; etc., though unthinkable monstrous atrocities in our minds, are simply acts of obedience and piety in the Muslim's mind.

The commands from Allah in Quran 8:12 and 47:4, to behead unbelievers are commands that every Muslim must obey in order to be a good Muslim who has any hope of making Paradise--this is why it is simply a fact that every Muslim is a potential terrorist. The "Muslims" who are not actively engaged in beheading non-Muslims are just simply not true Muslims. That's just a fact Jack!

## The Quran Declares That Muslims Who Do Not Engage In Jihad Shall Be Sent To Hell!

**Quran 8:15, 16**

*15. O ye who believe! When ye meet The Unbelievers In hostile array, Never turn your backs To them.*
*16. If any do turn his back To them on such a day—Unless it be in a stratagem Of war, or to retreat To a troop (of his own)—He draws on himself The wrath of God, And his abode is Hell,—An evil refuge (indeed)!*

Here in Quran 8:15-16, unlike Quran 4:95, which merely promises a greater reward to those Muslims who fight and strive in the cause of Allah (Jihad), here the Quran states that those who do not fight, who *"turn his back"* will actually be sent to Hell!

So far, in just a few Quranic passages, we have learned that Muslims who fight and kill Unbelievers are promised Paradise, and those who refuse to fight are sent to Hell. Again, this is more proof that every Muslim is a potential terrorist; simply because every Muslim who does not practice Jihad (terrorism) shall be sent to Hell by Allah!

This is also why not one American Muslim cleric has come out and publically condemned 9-11 or any of the scores of other attacks and attempted attacks against the U.S., or anywhere else in the world for that matter, because according to Quranic teachings the actions of Muslims like Osama Bin Laden, Fort Hood mass-murderer U.S. Army Major Nidal Hasan, and American citizen & Financial Strategist with an MBA Faisal Shahzad, are merely acts of obedience to what the Quran and Allah have commanded them!

Are you getting this? In other words, the Islamic terrorists have not "hijacked" their religion; but rather their acts of terrorism prove them to be merely good and obedient Muslims; and conversely, every Muslim who is not a terrorist is simply a disobedient, bad Muslim. In the public discourse over the war on terror, we must stop using the term "radical Muslims" and "radical Islam" to describe the terrorists!

In the same way that a Christian who seeks to obey the commands and teachings of the New Testament is not a "radical Christian," but merely one who is trying their best to be a good Christian, so also Osama bin Laden, Fort Hood mass-murderer Nidal Hasan, Time Square bomber Faisal Shahzad, the Taliban in Afghanistan, Obob who sawed off Wall Street Journal Reporter Daniel Pearl's head, and all other Islamic terrorists, are not "radical Muslims," but are merely Muslims who are obeying the commands and teachings of the Quran and trying their best to be good Muslims! And according to the Quran, the afore mentioned are all good Muslims; in fact, their actions are to be admired and emulated by all other Muslims. They are the Billy Graham's and Rick Warren's of the Muslim faith. You see, the problem is the religion of Islam itself. Islam is a terrorist religion—that is simply an irrefutable fact, as you are seeing for yourself by the quotes from the Quran I am exposing to you.

And we're not quite through yet. It's getting good now!

## *Unlike President Obama, The U.S. Shall Never Bow To Islam! Are You With Me?*

**Quran 8:38, 39**
38. *Say to the Unbelievers, if (now) they desist (from Unbelief), their past would be forgiven them; but if they persist, the punishment of those before them is already (a matter of warning for them).*
39. *And fight them on until there is no more tumult or oppression, and there prevail justice and faith in Allah altogether and everywhere;*
**Pickthall** renders 39. *And fight them until persecution is no more, and religion is all for Allah.*

Here above, we see again the theological impetus for global jihad—that Muslims must fight and war against all Unbelievers until the entire world is dominated by Islam, i.e., until the whole world submits to Allah & Islam. That my friend is the only sense in which "Islam" means "Peace;" Islamic peace means total submission by the whole world to Islamic Rule! When Muslim-born President Barack Hussein Obama visited the King of Saudi Arabia, the birthplace and home of Islam, President Obama bowed to the Islamic King, thereby surrendering American sovereignty to Islam! I don't know about you, but I am not submitting to that vile, anti-Christ false religion, and by God neither shall the United States of America! Are you with me? Then get your A.-double-S. to the polls on November 6, 2012, and vote that Muslim-bowing Obama-nation out of the White House!

## *The Religion Of Islam Has Declared War Against Us, Therefore We Are At War Against The Religion Of Islam!*

**Quran 8:59, 60**
**PICKTHAL:** *59. And let not those who disbelieve suppose that they can outstrip (Allah's Purpose). Lo! they cannot escape.*
*60. Make ready for them all thou canst of (armed) force and of horses tethered, that thereby ye may dismay the enemy of Allah and your enemy, and others beside them whom ye know not. Allah knoweth them. Whatsoever ye spend in the way of Allah it will be repaid to you in full, and ye will not be wronged.*

Once again, in Quran 8:59-60, above, we see that those who simply *"disbelieve"* are *"the enemy of Allah and your enemy"* and therefore Muslims are here commanded to, *"Make ready for them all thou canst of (armed) force"*—a clear reference to militaristic warfare against all non-Muslims.

This theme of armed forces and militaristic warfare against all non-Muslims around the world continues from Quran 8 into Quran 9. If you only memorize one verse from the Quran, memorize Quran 9:5.

Remember our question from the beginning of this Chapter, "Are we at war with Islam?"

### Quran 9:5

*But when the forbidden months are past, then fight and <u>slay</u> the Pagans <u>wherever ye find them</u>, an seize them, beleaguer them, and lie in wait for them in <u>every stratagem (of war)</u>; but if they repent, and establish regular prayers and practise regular charity [submit to Islam], then open the way for them: for Allah is Oft-forgiving, Most Merciful.*

Here in Quran 9:5, we see the Quran's command to "Go into all the world and kill every non-Muslim who refuses to submit to Islam!"

Any Muslim who tries to tell you that the verses in the Quran that command Muslims to fight are strictly meant for self-defense when they are attacked, is full of horse manure! Show him Quran 9:5, and ask him to explain this one!

And note the ferocity and viciousness of the warfare commanded in Quran 9:5, *"fight and slay the Pagans wherever ye find them, an seize them, beleaguer them, and lie in wait for them in every stratagem (of war);"*

Note that the only way for you and I to escape their wrath is to submit to Islam—the last part of this verse describes two of the five pillars of Islam: *"but if they...establish regular prayers and practise regular charity, then open the way for them."* In other words, the method of evangelism that the Quran commands Muslims to practice is to give unbelievers this choice: "Convert to Islam or die!"

### Quran 9:14

*Fight them, and Allah will punish them by your hands, cover them with shame, help you (to victory) over them.*

### Quran 9:20-22

*20. Those who believe, and suffer exile and strive [jihad] with might and main, in Allah's cause, with their goods and their persons, have the highest rank in the sight of Allah: they are the people who will achieve (salvation). 21. Their Lord doth give them glad tidings of a Mercy from Himself, of His good pleasure, and of gardens for them, wherein are delights that endure: 22. They will dwell therein for ever. Verily in Allah's presence is a reward, the greatest (of all).*

Once again, here in Quran 9:20-22, the Quran promises that it is the Muslims who practice Jihad, even if it requires them to, *suffer exile and strive with might and main, in Allah's cause, with their goods and their persons [their lives],* that it is the Jihadists to whom Allah shall grant Salvation: *they are the people who will achieve (salvation).* And the Jihadists are the Muslims upon whom Allah will bestow Eternal Rewards: *Their Lord doth give them glad tidings of a Mercy from Himself, of His good pleasure, and of gardens for them, wherein are delights that endure: They will dwell therein for ever. Verily in Allah's presence is a reward, the greatest (of all).*

Quran 9:29, is one of the clearest and most direct commands for Muslims to fight Christians and Jews, "people of the Book," the Bible, for no other reason except that they do not believe in the Quran and don't submit to Islam! I know a lot of Christians and Jews, and they are nice people, really, they're good folks; Christians and Jews aren't people you need to fear or fight. But not according to the Quran; according to the Quran, if you believe in the Bible, that is sufficient grounds for you to be killed!

**Quran 9:29**
*Fight those who believe not in Allah nor the Last Day, nor hold that forbidden which hath been forbidden by Allah and His Messenger, nor acknowledge the religion of Truth, (even if they are) of the People of the Book* [Bible], *until they pay the Jizya with willing submission, and feel themselves subdued.*

Here above, again is an extremely clear passage that every Christian and Jew must be aware of. Have you ever wondered why Muslims in countries like Iraq, Malaysia, Kenya, etc. etc., bomb Christian Churches? In this passage, *"the People of the Book"*—the Book being the Holy Bible, refers to Christians and Jews. The religions of Christianity and Judaism are benign, beneficent religions that are commanded to, *"Love your neighbor as yourself"* (Leviticus 19:18; Matthew 22:39; Mark 12:31; Romans 13:9; Galatians 5:14; James 2:8), and therefore are responsible for bringing about great good to human society; but in spite of this great and good benefit that comes to the world from Christians and Jews, the Quran commands all Muslims to, *"Fight...the People of the Book [Holy Bible], until they pay the Jizya with willing submission, and feel themselves subdued."*

The *"Jizya"* is a tax imposed upon non-Muslim subjects as a sign of their willing submission to Islamic rule over them.

The above violent commands from Chapters 8 and 9 of the Quran that command all Muslims to engage in global warfare, global Jihad, until all the world is subdued, are considered to be some of the final "revelations" from Allah, and set in motion the tenacious military expansion of Islam, in which Muhammad's companions managed to conquer two-thirds of the Christian world in just the next 100 years. Oh, you didn't know about that fact did you? Wake up America!

The "religion" of Islam declared war against the world from its very inception, and Islam's global war has not ceased to this day. Since Islam has declared war against us, then we are at war with Islam.

Let me say it again. In spite of President Bush's and President Obama's assertions that we are not at war against Islam, the fact is that Islam, by its commands in the Quran, has declared war against us, therefore we are at war with the religion of Islam. Anyone, I repeat anyone who denies this fact is either lying to you or hiding their head in the sand by ignoring the historical and Quranic facts.

## The Quran Denies The Deity & Divine Sonship Of The Lord Jesus Christ & Thereby Dooms All Muslims To The Eternal Fires Of Hell!

Below, also from Chapter 9, so you may see it for yourself, is the Quran's direct denial of the Lordship and Deity of the Only Begotten Son of God—God the Son—the Lord and Only Savior Jesus Christ, proving that Islam is a satanic, lying false religion that dooms its followers to the eternal fires of Hell!

### Quran 9:30
*The Jews call 'Uzair a son of Allah, and the Christians call Christ the son of Allah. That is a saying from their mouth; (in this) they but imitate what the unbelievers of old used to say. Allah's curse be on them: how they are deluded away from the Truth!*

**Pickthall translates the latter portion of this verse as:** *"...Allah (Himself) fighteth against them. How perverse are they!"*

**And Shakir translates it as:** *"...may Allah destroy them; how they are turned away!"*

Of course, anyone who has ever read the Holy Bible and who has at least the mental capacity of a water melon knows that if you deny God's Son, Jesus Christ, you are also denying God the Father!

### John 14:1-11

[1]"Let not your heart be troubled; you believe in God, believe also in Me.
[2]In My Father's house are many £mansions; if it were not so, £I would have told you. I go to prepare a place for you.
[3]And if I go and prepare a place for you, I will come again and receive you to Myself; that where I am, there you may be also.
[4]And where I go you know, and the way you know."
[5]Thomas said to Him, "Lord, we do not know where You are going, and how can we know the way?"
[6]Jesus said to him, "I am the way, the truth, and the life. No one comes to the Father except through Me.
[7]"If you had known Me, you would have known My Father also; and from now on you know Him and have seen Him."
[8]Philip said to Him, "Lord, show us the Father, and it is sufficient for us."
[9]Jesus said to him, "Have I been with you so long, and yet you have not known Me, Philip? He who has seen Me has seen the Father; so how can you say, 'Show us the Father'?
[10]Do you not believe that I am in the Father, and the Father in Me? The words that I speak to you I do not speak on My own authority; but the Father who dwells in Me does the works.
[11]Believe Me that I am in the Father and the Father in Me, or else believe Me for the sake of the works themselves.

### John 1:1-5, 10-18

[1]*In the beginning was the Word, and the Word was with God, and the Word was God.*

[2]*He was in the beginning with God.*

[3]*All things were made through Him, and without Him nothing was made that was made.*

[4]*In Him was life, and the life was the light of men.*

[5]*And the light shines in the darkness, and the darkness did not comprehend it.*

[10]*He was in the world, and the world was made through Him, and the world did not know Him.*

[11]*He came to His own, and His own did not receive Him.*

[12]*But as many as received Him, to them He gave the right to become children of God, to those who believe in His name:*

[13]*who were born, not of blood, nor of the will of the flesh, nor of the will of man, but of God.*

[14]*And the Word became flesh and dwelt among us, and we beheld His glory, the glory as of the only begotten of the Father, full of grace and truth.*

[15]*John bore witness of Him and cried out, saying, "This was He of whom I said, 'He who comes after me is preferred before me, for He was before me.'"*

[16]*And of His fullness we have all received, and grace for grace.*

[17]*For the law was given through Moses, but grace and truth came through Jesus Christ.*

[18]*No one has seen God at any time. The only begotten Son, who is in the bosom of the Father, He has declared Him.*

### John 5:18-23

[18]*Therefore the Jews sought all the more to kill Him, because He not only broke the Sabbath, but also said that God was His Father, making Himself equal with God.*

[19]*Then Jesus answered and said to them, "Most assuredly, I say to you, the Son can do nothing of Himself, but what He sees the Father do; for whatever He does, the Son also does in like manner.*

[20]*For the Father loves the Son, and shows Him all things that He Himself does; and He will show Him greater works than these, that you may marvel.*

[21]*For as the Father raises the dead and gives life to them, even so the Son gives life to whom He will.*

[22]*For the Father judges no one, but has committed all judgment to the Son,*

[23]*that all should honor the Son just as they honor the Father. He who does not honor the Son does not honor the Father who sent Him.*

Yes, it is sad but true, every Muslim when he dies goes to hell. I pray every Muslim who reads this book will turn from the lie of Islam to the One True and Living God, who came to Earth in the Person of Jesus Christ, to die as the Atoning Sacrifice for the sins of all mankind, and to rise from the dead, defeating death for all Mankind. Because Jesus is God who became a Man He has also become the One and Only Savior of mankind—put your faith in Jesus Christ, calling on His Name to save you from your sins! Jesus is your only hope.

I have just a little more from the Quran that you must see.

### Quran 9:38, 39

*38. O ye who believe! what is the matter with you, that, when ye are asked to go forth in the cause of Allah [Jihad], ye cling heavily to the earth? Do ye prefer the life of this world to the Hereafter? But little is the comfort of this life, as compared with the Hereafter.*

*39. Unless ye go forth, He will punish you with a grievous penalty, and put others in your place;*

Pickthall renders v. 39: *"If ye go not forth He will afflict you with a painful doom,"*

Here above, is another warning to those who refuse to fight, that they will be punished with Hell. This again is "what motivates Muslims to commit acts of terrorism." Are you listening, AG Eric Holder?

Let's contrast the Great Commission of the Bible which commands Christians to...

**Mark 16:15**
*And He said to them, "Go into all the world and preach the gospel [Good News] to every creature.*

...with the Quran's commission of Muslims to:

**Quran 9:41**
**PICKTHAL:** *Go forth, light-armed and heavy-armed, and strive [jihad] with your wealth and your lives in the way of Allah! That is best for you if ye but knew.*

**Quran 9:73**
*O Prophet! Strive [jihad] hard against the unbelievers [Christians & Jews] and the Hypocrites [fellow Muslims who don't jihad], and be firm [unyielding] against them. Their abode is Hell, - an evil refuge indeed.*

Here above is another verse that commands Muslims to *"strive (Jihad)"* i.e., *"fight and slay the Pagans [Christians & Jews] wherever ye find them"* (Quran 9:5), but also to do the same to the *"Hypocrites"*—which means their fellow Muslims who "stay behind" and do not engage in Jihad. Now you understand why most of the suicide/homicide bombers we see on the evening news from the Middle East are not targeting Jews or American soldiers, but fellow Muslims—How many times have we heard the news reports of a Muslim suicide/homicide bomber walking into a Muslim wedding or a Muslim marketplace and killing scores of his fellow Muslims, even children, without any hesitation or remorse? How can they do such a thing? Easy, because the Quran commands them to do this and promises them Paradise as their reward for doing so.

In the following few verses in Chapter nine of the Quran, you will see this doctrine of damnation to Muslims who do not fight and salvation to Muslims who do fight elaborated more fully:

**Quran 9:81-89**
*81. Those who were left behind (in the Tabuk expedition) rejoiced in their inaction behind the back of the Messenger of Allah: they hated to strive and fight [jihad], with their goods and their persons, in the cause of Allah: they said, "Go not forth in the heat." Say, "The fire of Hell is fiercer in heat." If only they could understand!*
*82. Let them laugh a little: much will they weep: a recompense for the (evil) that they do.*
*83. If, then, Allah bring thee back to any of them, and they ask thy*

*permission to come out (with thee), say: "Never shall ye come out with me, nor fight an enemy with me: for ye preferred to sit inactive on the first occasion: Then sit ye (now) with those who lag behind."*

*84. Nor do thou ever pray for any of them that dies, nor stand at his grave; for they rejected Allah and His Messenger, and died in a state of perverse rebellion.*

*85. Nor let their wealth nor their (following in) sons dazzle thee: Allah's plan is to punish them with these things in this world, and that their souls may perish in their (very) denial of Allah.*

*86. When a Sura [verse of the Quran] comes down, enjoining them to believe in Allah and to strive and fight [jihad] along with His Messenger, those with wealth and influence among them ask thee for exemption, and say: "Leave us (behind): we would be with those who sit (at home)."*

*87. They prefer to be with (the women), who remain behind (at home): their hearts are sealed and so they understand not.*

*88. But the Messenger, and those who believe with him, strive and fight [jihad] with their wealth and their persons: for them are (all) good things: and it is they who will prosper.*

*89. Allah hath prepared for them gardens under which rivers flow, to dwell therein: that is the supreme felicity.*

**PICKTHAL:** *Allah hath made ready for them Gardens underneath which rivers flow, wherein they will abide. That is the supreme triumph.*

### Quran 9:123

**PICKTHAL:** *O ye who believe! Fight those of the disbelievers who are near to you, and let them find harshness in you, and know that Allah is with those who keep their duty (unto Him).*

Shocking and mind-boggling isn't it? As you are seeing with your own eyes, this recurring theme of violence and warfare against all non-Muslims is pervasive throughout the chapters of the Quran.

## The Quran Commands The Building Of "Victory Mosques" Like The Dome Of The Rock & Ground Zero Mosque!

I now take you to Quran 18, which has some more shocking, but important eye-opening passages pertinent to current events. Everyone is familiar with the Ground Zero mosque being proposed for construction in the shadow of what was Ground Zero in the 9-11 attacks by devout Muslims from Saudi Arabia; Muslims who lived among us and attended our flight training schools for years preparing and planning for the Jihadist attacks of that day. Of course, Imam Feisal Abdul Rauf, the Muslim cleric behind plans for the 'Ground Zero mosque," doesn't call the 13-story mosque by that name; Imam Rauf's original name was the "Cordoba Mosque." But after former Presidential Candidate Newt Gingrich pointed out what the meaning of "Cordoba" was, the deceitful Imam changed the name to the Park 7 Mosque—but changing the name does not change the obvious initial intent of the Imam and those who are behind him as to the defiant purpose for which they originally named this the "Cordoba Mosque Project."

Islam has a long tradition of conquering Christian nations by way of the sword and then sealing their conquest by converting whatever was previously the most prominent Christian symbol, usually a Church, into an Islamic Mosque, known as a "Victory Mosque." Such was the case in Cordoba, Spain, as well as Seville and Segovia, Spain, and Agia Sophia in Constantinople. The Quranic command for Muslims to build these "Victory Mosques" is found in Quran 18:21.

**Quran 18:21**

*Thus did We make their case known to the people, that they might know that the promise of Allah is true, and that there can be no doubt about the Hour of Judgment. Behold, they dispute among themselves as to their affair. (Some) said, "Construct a building over them": Their Lord knows best about them: those who prevailed over their affair said, "Let us surely build a place of worship over them."*
**PICKTHAL:** *And in like manner We disclosed them (to the people of the city) that they might know that the promise of Allah is true, and that, as for the Hour, there is no doubt concerning it. When (the people of the city) disputed of their case among themselves, they said: Build over them a building; their Lord knoweth best concerning them. Those who won their point said: We verily shall build a place of worship over them.*
**SHAKIR:** *And thus did We make (men) to get knowledge of them that they might know that Allah's promise is true and that as for the hour there is no doubt about it. When they disputed among themselves about their affair and said: Erect an edifice over them-- their Lord best knows them. Those who prevailed in their affair said: We will certainly raise a masjid [mosque] over them.*

I mentioned above that it was Presidential Candidate Newt Gingrich who caused Imam Rauf to change the name of the Ground Zero mosque when Newt exposed Imam Rauf's diabolical intent behind the building of this mosque near Ground Zero, which was evident by Rauf's initial choice for the mosques name, "Cordoba House." I highly commend Newt Gingrich for his informed and insightful comments on this issue which he published on his website in the Summer of 2010, at: http://www.newt.org/newt-direct/newt-gingrich-statement-proposed-mosqueislamic-community-center-near-ground-zero. Unfortunately this article is no longer available at that url, but Newt's comments are so good that I have inserted them verbatim below:

## Newt Gingrich Statement on Proposed Mosque/Islamic Community Center near Ground Zero

*July 21, 2010 6pm*

*There should be no mosque near Ground Zero in New York so long as there are no churches or synagogues in Saudi Arabia. The time for double standards that allow Islamists to behave aggressively toward us while they demand our weakness and submission is over.*

*The proposed "Cordoba House" overlooking the World Trade Center site – where a group of jihadists killed over 3000 Americans and destroyed one of our most famous landmarks - is a test of the timidity, passivity and historic ignorance of American elites. For example, most of them don't understand that "Cordoba House" is a deliberately insulting term. It refers to Cordoba, Spain – the capital of Muslim conquerors who symbolized their victory over the Christian Spaniards by transforming a church there into the world's third-largest mosque complex.*

*Today, some of the Mosque's backers insist this term is being used to "symbolize interfaith cooperation" when, in fact, every Islamist in the world recognizes Cordoba as a symbol of Islamic conquest. It is a sign of their contempt for Americans and their confidence in our historic ignorance that they would deliberately insult us this way.*

*Those Islamists and their apologists who argue for "religious toleration" are arrogantly dishonest. They ignore the fact that more than 100 mosques already exist in New York City. Meanwhile, there are no churches or synagogues in all of Saudi Arabia. In fact no Christian or Jew can even enter Mecca.*

*And they lecture us about tolerance.*

*If the people behind the Cordoba House were serious about religious toleration, they would be imploring the Saudis, as fellow Muslims, to immediately open up Mecca to all and immediately announce their intention to allow non-Muslim houses of worship in the Kingdom. They should be asked by the news media if they would be willing to lead such a campaign.*

*We have not been able to rebuild the World Trade Center in nine years. Now we are being told a 13 story, $100 million mega mosque will be built within a year overlooking the site of the most devastating surprise attack in American history.*

*Finally where is the money coming from? The people behind the Cordoba House refuse to reveal all their funding sources.*

*America is experiencing an Islamist cultural-political offensive designed to undermine and destroy our civilization. Sadly, too many of our elites are the willing apologists for those who would destroy them if they could.*

*No mosque. No self deception. No surrender. The time to take a stand is now - at this site on this issue.*

Bravo Newt! As I stated above, the most blatant display of ignorance by an *American elite* is that of New York City Mayor Michael Bloomberg, who has stated regarding the building of the Cordoba Victory mosque that the Muslims behind that mosque have the "right to practice their religion and therefore build the mosque," which, moron Mayor Michael Bloomberg doesn't realize is the exact equivalent of him saying,

*"I, Michael Bloomberg, Mayor of New York City, applaud your efforts on 9-11 to conquer America and subject the citizens of New York City to Sharia Islamic Law, and although you did not completely succeed in your efforts to conquer us, I am imploring you to keep up your Jihad against us as your religion of Islam commands you to do, because, after all, you have the right to practice your religion as your Quran commands...Oh, and don't forget that I am a Jew, so when the hell are you going to get around to beheading me? Come on you guys, get that Victory mosque built and drag my Jewish ass in there and behead me as is required for you to do in order to properly practice your religion, which, after all, is your right! And don't forget to video my beheading like you did Daniel Pearl's!"*

Come on, New York City; please tell me that you're not going to elect another moron like Michael Bloomberg for your next Mayor. You need to elect Newt Gingrich as your Mayor!

## A History of Victory Mosques

The following is taken from William J. Federer's book, *What every American needs to know about the Quran: A History of Islam and the United States.* A book I recommend for your reading.

*In 630, Muhammad led 10,000 Muslim soldiers into Mecca and turned the pagans' most prominent spot, the Ka'aba, into the Masjid al-Haram Mosque.*

*In 634, Rightly Guided Caliph Umar conquered Syria and turned the Christians' most prominent spot, the Church of Job, famous for being visited by Saint Silva in the fourth century, into the Mosque of Job.*

*In 637, Caliph Umar conquered Hebron and turned the second-most prominent spot in Judaism, the Cave of the Patriarchs, into the Ibrahimi Mosque. (This was repeated by Saladin in 1188.)*

*In 638, Muslim generals Amr ibn al-As and Khalid ibn al-Walid conquered Gaza and turned the prominent fifth-century Byzantine church into the Great Mosque of Gaza.*

*In 638, Caliph Umar conquered Jerusalem, then subsequently in 691, Caliph Al-Malik ordered the Dome of the Rock built on the most prominent spot in Judaism, the Temple Mount, followed by Caliph Al-Walid building the Al-Aqsa Mosque there in 705.*

*In 651, Muslims conquered Persia and turned Zoroastrian temples in Bukhara and Istakhr into mosques.*

*In 706, after Muslims took Damascus from the Byzantine Empire, Caliph Al-Walid turned the prominent Orthodox Church of St. John the Baptist into the Umayyad Mosque.*

*In 710, Gen. Muhammad bin Qasim conquered Pakistan, defiled the prominent Sun Temple in Multan, which house the great idol "sanam," and erected a mosque.*

*In 784, after the conquest of Spain, Emir Abd ar-Rahman turned the prominent Visigothic Christian Church of Saint Vincent into the Great Aljama Mosque of Cordoba.* [Ah, the Cordoba Mosque, there she is! Spain, of course, represented the conquering of the "Western World" to the Muslims, which is why Imam Rauf chose the name "Cordoba House" for his 13-story Ground Zero mosque - "Hey Rauf, you can take your proposed 13-story $100-million mosque and shove it up your A.-double-S! - because it's not going to happen here, not in America! Not on my watch!" I'm *Common Sense* and I'm running for Office, elect me as your President and I'll kick Imam Rauf and his Islamic Terrorist Training Center out of America so hard and fast that his head won't stop spinning for 20-years!]

After the conquest of Egypt, Caliphs al-Mamun (813-833) and al-Hakim (996-1021) turned prominent Coptic Christian churches and Jewish synagogues in Cairo into mosques.

In 831, Muslims conquered Palermo, Sicily, and Asad ibn al-Furat turned the prominent Church of Saint Mary of the Assumption into the Great Mosque of Bal'harm.

In 1193, Muslims conquered Delhi, India, and Qutbuddin Aibak turned the Red Citadel in Dhillika, the most prominent spot of the last Hindu rulers, into the Qutb Minar Mosque.

From 1250-1517, Mamluk Muslims controlled the Golan Heights and used the ancient Synagogue of Katzrin as a mosque.

In 1387, Turkish Muslims conquered Thessalonica and turned the Katholikon Monastery and the Church of Aghia Sophia, which housed the relics of Saint Gregorios Palamas, into mosques, as Symeon of Thessalonica recorded: "The greatest number of the buildings of the churches fell to them, of which the first was the Holy Church of the Savior. These were trampled underfoot and the infidels rejoiced in them. Most of the religious buildings in the city were despoiled, while altars were demolished and sacred things profaned."

On May 29, 1453, Sultan Mehmet II conquered Constantinople and turned the great Byzantine church, Hagia Sophia, into the Ayasofya Mosque. The largest church in Christendom for a thousand years, the church's four acres of gold mosaics were covered with whitewash and Quran verses.

In 1458, Sultan Mehmet II conquered Athens and turned the Greeks' most prominent spot, the Parthenon on Acropolis hill, into a mosque. When Venetian Gen. Francesco Morosini drove the Muslims out in 1687, a cannonball hit the gunpowder stored in the mosque, blowing it up. (If the Muslims had not converted the Greek Parthenon into a mosque and thus used it as a fortress from which to fight and store weapons and gunpowder, we would still have the historic Parthenon in its original condition!)

In the 15th century, Ottoman invaders turned Saint Clement's Macedonian Orthodox Monastery in Plaosnik, Balkans, into the Imater Mosque.

*From 1519-1858, Muslim Mughal rulers gained control of India and turned over 2,000 Hindu temples into mosques, including demolishing the Temple of Ram Janmabhoomi in Ayodhya, the birthplace of Rama, and replacing it with the Babri Mosque. India's Mughal Muslim ruler, Jahangir (1605-1627), wrote in Tujuk-i-Jahangiri: "At the city of Banaras [was] a temple. I made it my plea for throwing down the temple and on the spot, with the very same materials, I erected the great mosque."*

*In 1543, Hayreddin Barbarossa's 30,000 Muslim troops wintered in Toulon, France, and turned the prominent Toulon Cathedral into a mosque.*

*In 1570, under Sultan Selim II Khan, Muslims conquered Paphos, Cyprus, and Gov. Mehmet Bey Ebubkir turned the prominent Christian church into the Great Mosque of Paphos.*

*In 1571, Muslims invaded Famagusta, Cyprus, and turned Saint Nicolas Cathedral, a rare Gothic church, into the Lala Mustafa Pasha Mosque, and Saint Sophia Cathedral in Nicosia, constructed in 1228, into the Selimiye Mosque.*

*In 1588, Sultan Murat III turned the Eastern Orthodox Church of Saint John the Forerunner in Constantinople into the Hirami Ahmet Pasha Mosque.*

*In 1781, after having conquered the Old City of Acre, Ottoman Muslims turned the Roman Catholic church built by Crusaders into the Jezzar Ahmet Pasha Mosque, where a hair from Muhammad's beard is preserved.*

*In 1923, Muslims expelled Greeks from Turkey and turned Orthodox churches into mosques.*

*In World War II, Nazis allied with Bosnian Muslims and turned the prominent Artists' Gallery Museum in Zagreb, Croatia, into a mosque.*

*In the 1950s, Muslims expelled Jews from Arab lands and turned synagogues into mosques.*

*Algerian Muslims warred against French colonial rule till France pulled out in 1962, after which the Cathedral of St. Philippe was turned into the Ketchaoua Mosque. Violence against Jews caused 30,000 to flee and the Great Synagogue of Oran was turned into the Mosque Abdellah Ben Salem.*

*In 1974, Turkish Muslims invaded northern Cyprus, and prominent Greek Orthodox churches were turned into mosques.*

*In 1981, Muslim immigrants to the Netherlands converted Amsterdam's historic Catholic Sint-Ignatiuskerk into the Fatih Mosque, and a synagogue in The Hague into the Aksa Mosque.*

Thanks again to William J. Federer and his book: *What Every American Needs to Know About the Quran: A History of Islam and the United States* for compiling the above historical facts regarding Islam's history of Victory mosques.

Mayor Bloomberg, now that you've been educated about Islam's history of Victory mosques, do you still think that Muslims should have the right to build a $100-million 13-story mosque in the shadow of Islam's greatest victory against America, where nearly 3,000 citizens were murdered in your beloved city, and where New York's, indeed America's, greatest symbols of freedom and prosperity were destroyed by Muslims shouting "Allah is greatest!"? Well, do you? Mayor Bloomberg, you need to repent, and publically denounce the building of this mosque; and more importantly STOP ITS APPROVAL FOR CONSTRUCTION!

## More Quotes From The Quran: Islam's Basis For So-called "Honor Killings" in America!

Next, in Quran Chapter 18, is found Islam's theological basis for the common practice of so-called "honor killings"—the murder by parents of their children for bringing "shame" on the family. The Quranic account in Quran Chapter 18:65-84, tells the story of a character named, Zul-qarnain, who appears with Moses and is portrayed as superior to Moses and in fact is instructing Moses in *"the (Higher) Truth"* of Allah (Quran 18:66), wherein Zul-qarnain gives the justification for the Islamic practice of "honor killings." Of course, we know from the Biblical account that no person named Zul-qarnain ever inter-acted with Moses; therefore the Quranic account is a lie. Remember, the Quran was written by Muhammad some 600 years after the New Testament and some 2,100 years after the Books of Moses, the Pentateuch, the first five Books of the Bible. The Biblical record of the life, words and actions of Moses were written by Moses himself and widely distributed among Moses' contemporaries, which all testify to the accuracy and truthfulness of Moses' record.

I'm not going to take time here to offer a list of these diabolical murders of innocent teenagers here in America by their Muslim parents, for you have seen them for yourself reported on the evening news. However, before I reveal to you the Quranic text, I must comment upon the media's coverage of these events. What to me is almost as despicable as the murders themselves is when the American media, whether local or national, who, when reporting these murders of teens by their Muslim parents will report that the parents say the reason they murdered their child is because they had become "too westernized," without pointing out the fact that what the parents really mean is that their child is not following strict Islamic Law. Failure by the media to clarify what is meant by being "too Westernized" lends validity to the Islamists justification, making it seem that there is something immoral about being "Westernized." (Also note that the parents don't even try to make an excuse, like, "Oh it was an accident." No, they boldly admit to murdering their child!)

Even worse than the media's echoing the murderous Islamic parents justification for murdering their child for becoming "too Westernized," is the fact that the media doesn't immediately point out the absolute insanity of such a claim based upon Islamic morality: In other words, it is a horrible thing if the Muslim parent's 15-year-old daughter talks to a non-Muslim boy or listens to The Jonas Brothers or, Allah forbid, she wears a skirt that falls above the knee, such things are "immoral," BUT IT'S OK TO MURDER THEM FOR SUCH DEEDS, MURDERING YOUR CHILD IS MORAL! What kind of a convoluted, misdirected, upside-down religion believes such an insane thing? That's good old Islam for you! So media, the next time a Muslim parent murders their child, and it will happen again, as long as we allow that diabolical demonic religion to exist in America, make sure you point out the sheer insanity and Islamic-based religious justification for the murder and don't blame it on the child becoming too "Westernized," as though there is something wrong with being Westernized! What is "wrong" is any human being becoming Islamized!

**Quran 18:74, 80, 81**
*74. Then they proceeded: until, when they met a young man, he [Zul-qarnain] slew him. Moses said: "Hast thou slain an innocent person who had slain none? Truly a foul (unheard of) thing hast thou done!"*
*80. [Zul-qarnain informs Moses as to the reason he murdered the young man] "As for the youth, his parents were people of Faith, and we feared that he would grieve them by obstinate rebellion and ingratitude (to Allah and man).*
*81. "So we desired that their Lord would give them in exchange (a son) better in purity (of conduct) and closer in affection.*

I and every sane person agrees that whenever a Muslim obeys the Quran and carries out the murder of their own children that, *"Truly a foul (unheard of) thing hast thou done!"*


## Wake Up America! Islam Is Not A "Religion," But A Cancer That Must Be Removed!

Wake up America; get your head out of the sand! Islam is not a "religion!" Religions are benevolent and beneficent institutions that provide a positive contribution to human society and the betterment of Mankind. A "religion" that teaches its adherents to murder their own children for any reason is not a religion, it is a cancer and a scourge on the Earth that must be removed.

We are almost finished with this chapter. Above, I showed you Quran 47:4, which is one of the Quranic verses which provide the Islamic theological basis for beheadings. Now you need to see the full first eight verses of chapter 47, to see for yourself that the Quran claims to be the true *"revelation"* from God, thus, claiming to nullify the authority and Divine inspiration of what is indeed the true revelation of God—the Old & New Testaments of the Holy Bible. You will also once again witness the commands to fight by means of war all who reject the religion of Islam. There are also included a few other verses from Quran Chapter 47, 48, 61 and 66.

### Quran 47:1-8
*1. Those who reject Allah and hinder (men) from the Path of Allah, - their deeds will Allah render astray (from their mark).*
*2. But those who believe and work deeds of righteousness, and believe in the (Revelation) sent down to Muhammad - for it is the Truth from their Lord, - He will remove from them their ills and improve their condition.*
*3. This because those who reject Allah follow vanities, while those who believe follow the Truth from their Lord: Thus does Allah set forth for men their lessons by similitudes.*
*4. Therefore, when ye meet the Unbelievers (in fight), smite at their necks; At length, when ye have thoroughly subdued them, bind a bond firmly (on them): thereafter (is the time for) either generosity or ransom: Until the war lays down its burdens. Thus (are ye commanded): but if it had been Allah's Will, He could certainly have exacted retribution from them (Himself); but (He lets you fight) in order to test you, some with others. But those who are slain in the Way of Allah, - He will never let their deeds be lost.*
*5. Soon will He guide them and improve their condition,*
*6. And admit them to the Garden which He has announced for them.*
*7. O ye who believe! If ye will aid (the cause of) Allah, He will aid you, and plant your feet firmly.*
*8. But those who reject (Allah), - for them is destruction, and (Allah) will render their deeds astray (from their mark).*

Quran 47:35
Be not weary and faint-hearted, crying for peace, *when ye should be uppermost*: for Allah is with you, and will never put you in loss for your (good) deeds.

The above verse proves that the only "peace" that Islam means is attained only after Islam has become the dominant force—*"when ye should be uppermost"*—in every country and part of the world, and that, in fact, this verse commands Muslims to keep fighting until Islam is *"uppermost"* over all other religions and peoples.

### Quran 48:17
*No blame is there on the blind, nor is there blame on the lame, nor on one ill (if he joins not the war): But he that obeys Allah and his Messenger,- (Allah) will admit him to Gardens beneath which rivers flow; and he who turns back, (Allah) will punish him with a grievous Penalty [Hell].*

The above verse proves that, contrary to some modern Islamic apologists who claim that "jihad" means a spiritual struggle, jihad without doubt means the literal, physical striving of war against all non-Muslims, why else would the blind, lame and ill be exempt! Also, once again, the Quran promises Paradise to those Muslims who fight in the Jihad and Hell to those Muslims who *"turn back"* and do not fight.

### Quran 48:28, 29
*28. **SHAKIR:** He it is Who sent His Messenger with the guidance and the true religion that He may make it <u>prevail</u> over all the religions; and Allah is enough for a witness.*
*29. **YUSUFALI:** Muhammad is the messenger of Allah; and those who are with him are strong against Unbelievers, (but) compassionate amongst each other. Thou wilt see them [Unbelievers] bow and prostrate themselves (in prayer), seeking Grace [Pickthall: (His) acceptance] from Allah and (His) Good Pleasure.*

In the above verses we see that Muslims are promised that they and the religion of Islam will *"prevail"* over all other religions and they will see these *"Unbelievers…bow and prostrate themselves"* to Allah and the religion of Islam.

This submission to Islam, its rule and laws (Sharia Law) is the only sense in which "Islam" means "peace."

I have bad news for every Muslim! The day will come when you leave this world that you will stand in judgment, not before Muhammad or Allah, but before the Crucified & Risen Lord Jesus Christ! And every knee shall bow before Him and every tongue shall confess that Jesus Christ is Lord, to the glory of God the Father! (Philippians 2: 8-11). But it will be too late for you! Only those who bow their knee and confess with their mouth that Jesus Christ is Lord while still alive in this life will receive the forgiveness of their sins and Christ's gift of Eternal Life! (Romans 10:8-13; Hebrews 9:27-28; etc.).

**Quran 61:4, 9-12**

*4. Truly Allah loves those who fight in His Cause [jihad] in battle array,...*
*9.* **PICKTHAL:** *He [Allah] it is Who hath sent His messenger [Muhammad] with the guidance and the religion of truth, that He may make it* <u>conqueror of all religion</u> *however much idolaters* [Shakir: *polytheists* (a reference to Christians who believe in the Trinity)] *may be averse.*
*10.* **PICKTHAL:** *O ye who believe! Shall I show you a commerce that will save you from a painful doom [Hell]?*
*11. That ye believe in Allah and His Messenger, and that ye strive (your utmost) in the Cause [Jihad] of Allah, with your property and your persons [your lives]: That will be best for you, if ye but knew!*
*12. He will forgive you your sins, and admit you to Gardens beneath which Rivers flow, and to beautiful mansions in Gardens of Eternity: that is indeed the Supreme Achievement.*

Above, once again we see that "jihad," note in this passage it is to strive/jihad with *"your utmost"* of your money and even your lives, that guarantees you salvation from Hell and entrance into Paradise, because *"Truly Allah loves those who fight in His Cause in battle array"*—again proving beyond any doubt that Jihad does not refer to a spiritual struggle but to striving/fighting in militaristic warfare, and with the promise with regard to Islam that Allah will *"make it conqueror of all religion."*

I know you are just sitting there shaking your head in amazement that such a "religion" even exists on the Earth. I'm almost done.

**Quran 66:9**

*O Prophet! Strive hard against the Unbelievers [Christians, Jews & all non-Muslims] and the Hypocrites [Muslims who refuse to fight in jihad], and be firm against them. Their abode is Hell,- an evil refuge (indeed).*

Well, there you have seen with your own eyes straight from the Quran what "motivates" Islamic terrorists.

Attorney General Eric Holder, I hope you are reading this so you will stop being an ostrich and get your head out of the sand! I was nice there, I could have phrased it another way.

# Shocking Quotes From Islam's Writings Called Hadith!

In addition to the above shocking quotes from the Quran, Americans need to understand that Islam also has another set of writings called the Hadith, which are narrations concerning the words and deeds of Islam's Founder Muhammad. Hadith are regarded by traditional Islamic schools of jurisprudence as important tools for properly understanding the Quran and implementing Islamic Law. Hadith were evaluated and gathered into large collections mostly during the reign of Umar ibn Abdul-Aziz during the 8th and 9th centuries. These works are referred to by Muslims in matters of Islamic law and history to this day. There are four major collections of Hadith writings: Sahih Bukhari, Sahih Muslim, Sunan Abu-Dawud, and Malik's Muwatta.

BELOW IS A BRIEF SURVEY OF JUST A FEW QUOTES FROM HADITH WRITINGS. AS WITH THE QUOTES FROM THE QURAN ABOVE, I HAVE INSERTED SOME WORDS IN BRACKETS FOR THE PURPOSE OF CLARIFICATION OF THE MEANING OF CERTAIN WORDS OR PHRASES.

**Interestingly, one of the Books of the Hadith,** SAHIH BUKHARI, BOOK 52, IS EVEN TITLED: FIGHTING FOR THE CAUSE OF ALLAH (JIHAD). CHECK THIS OUT!

Bukhari (52:177) - *Allah's Apostle [Muhammad] said, "The Hour will not be established [The Hour of global Islamic domination] until you fight with the Jews, and the stone behind which a Jew will be hiding will say."O Muslim! There is a Jew hiding behind me, so kill him."*

Do you remember when Bill O'Reilly appeared on *The View* and made the *Common Sense* comment, something to the affect that, it is Muslims who are the terrorists attacking us, and immediately, to show their shock at such a blanket declaration, Whoopi Goldberg and Joy Behar both got up and walked off the set? Well, ladies, now that you've read Bukhari (52:177), what do you think of Muslims now? (Whoopi Goldberg is Jewish and Joy Behar was previously married to a Jewish man).

Bukhari (52:220) - *Allah's Apostle said... 'I have been made victorious with terror'*

Bukhari (52:256) - *The Prophet... was asked whether it was permissible to attack the pagan warriors at night with the probability of exposing their women and children to danger. The Prophet replied, "They (i.e. women and children) are from them (i.e. pagans)."* [Note: the insertions in this verse in parentheses are included in the original Hadith text and not inserted by me. Any insertion I make into a text is always in brackets.]

In Bukhari (52:256) above, Muhammad establishes that it is permissible to kill non-combatants in the process of killing a perceived enemy. This provides justification for the many Islamic terror bombings that kill innocent civilians including women and children.

However, Book 52 of the Hadith is not the only Hadith Book that commands Jihad.

Abu-Dawud (14:2526) - *The Prophet (peace_be_upon_him) said: Three things are the roots of faith: to refrain from (killing) a person who utters, "There is no god but Allah" and not to declare him unbeliever whatever sin he commits, and not to excommunicate him from Islam for his any action; and jihad will be performed continuously since the day Allah sent me as a prophet until the day the last member of my community will fight with the Dajjal (Antichrist)*

Abu-Dawud (14:2527) - *The Prophet said: Striving in the path of Allah (jihad) is incumbent on you along with every ruler, whether he is pious or impious*

Muslim (1:33) - *the Messenger of Allah said: I have been commanded to fight against people till they testify that there is no god but Allah, that Muhammad is the messenger of Allah*

Bukhari (8:387) - *Allah's Apostle said, "I have been ordered to fight the people till they say: 'None has the right to be worshipped but Allah*

Muslim (1:149) - *"Abu Dharr reported: I said: Messenger of Allah, which of the deeds is the best? He (the Holy Prophet) replied: Belief in Allah and Jihad in His cause..."*

Muslim (20:4645) - *"...He (the Messenger of Allah) did that and said: There is another act which elevates the position of a man in Paradise to a grade one hundred (higher), and the elevation between one grade and the other is equal to the height of the heaven from the earth. He (Abu Sa'id) said: What is that act? He replied: Jihad in the way of Allah! Jihad in the way of Allah!"*

Muslim (20:4696) - *"the Messenger of Allah (may peace be upon him) said: 'One who died but did not fight in the way of Allah nor did he express any desire (or determination) for Jihad died the death of a hypocrite.'"*

Tabari 7:97 - *The morning after the murder of Ashraf, the Prophet declared, "Kill any Jew who falls under your power."* Ashraf was a poet, killed by Muhammad's men because he insulted Islam. Here, Muhammad widens the scope of his orders to kill any Jew who falls under their power. An innocent Jewish businessman was then slain by his Muslim partner, merely for being Jewish.

Tabari 9:69 - *"Killing Unbelievers is a small matter to us" The* words of Muhammad, prophet of Islam.

Ibn Ishaq: 327 - *"Allah said, 'A prophet must slaughter before collecting captives. A slaughtered enemy is driven from the land. Muhammad, you craved the desires of this world, its goods and the ransom captives would bring. But Allah desires killing them to manifest the religion.'"*

Ibn Ishaq: 992 - *"Fight everyone in the way of Allah and kill those who disbelieve in Allah."* Muhammad's instructions to his men prior to a military raid.

In conclusion, as you can plainly see from the teachings of the Quran and Hadith, the "holy texts" upon which Islam bases all that it believes and practices, any and every Muslim is a potential terrorist by he or she simply obeying the commands of their "religion." As you can also plainly see, Islam is not a true "religion" in the sense that normal people use the term religion.

Now that I have revealed to you the truth regarding Islam, it's time to cease being an Ostrich! *Common Sense* dictates that every American get his or her head out of the sand and publically acknowledge that it is the religion of Islam itself that is the problem! We must cease our ignorance and face the obvious fact that it is the clear and direct teachings of the Quran and Hadith that are the *motivating factors behind the terrorists' actions*! We must come to terms with the fact that terrorists like Osama bin Laden, Fort Hood mass-murderer Major Nidal Hasan, etc., etc., are not "radical Muslims," but merely good, observant, true Muslims. Wake up America! This is the first step we must take if we want to have any hope of ever winning the war against Islamic terrorism. Remember, this war began in 630 A.D. under the militaristic leadership of Muhammad under the "guise" of a religion called Islam; and this fake religion must not be tolerated! Islam is not "one of the world's great religions." No, rather, Islam is the greatest evil the world has ever known! And it is time that we ban this vile fake religion from America's shores!

# Chapter 4: *Common Sense* Solutions For Winning The War Against Islamic Terrorism—Step B: Ban Islam From America' s Shores!

In the preceding chapter I proved by quoting directly from the Quran and Hadith that Islam is not a religion of peace; in fact it's not really a "religion" at all in the sense that most people understand the term religion. It is commonly held that the very nature of a religion is that which springs from an All-Powerful, yet a good, loving and beneficent Being; therefore, when one thinks of a religion, one understands the term "religion" to be a set of beliefs and values which promote love and good works toward Mankind, and which benefits the society in which it exists. However, as I proved to you in the previous chapter, this is certainly not the case with Islam! Therefore, based upon the *Common Sense* understanding of the role of religion in society, we can state without controversy that Islam does not fall into the category of a religion.

In fact, based on the direct, clear teachings of the Quran and Hadith, we could rightly state that Islam is a terrorist organization founded by a man hell-bent on the conquest of the world, with the ultimate goal being the subjugation of the whole world under Islamic rule.

Even great American patriots who otherwise are well-meaning are either still ignorant on this point or just too chicken-shit to tell the truth! As the buzz on the cable news channels increases in intensity regarding the building of what has come to be known as the Ground Zero Mosque, a 13-story $100-million mega-mosque which is the fulfillment of the Cordoba Initiative, and itself originally named the "Cordoba House," there have been a few brave souls who have the cojones to stand up and speak out against the building of this Islamic "Victory mosque," demanding that it be stopped! However, even these great American patriots who demand that this mosque not be built so close to Ground Zero, nevertheless have made a grave error in stating that mosques can exist elsewhere, just not so close to Ground Zero, for after all, they muse, the First Amendment of our U.S. Constitution guarantees Muslims the freedom to practice their religion.

Oh really? Are you out of your mind? The First Amendment absolutely does NOT grant Muslims the right to "practice" their religion! That's just *Common Sense!* Remember, the horrors and slaughter of 3,000 innocent people on 9-11 was caused by 19 Muslims practicing their religion!

The belief that the Constitution grants to Muslims the right to practice their religion is so gross an error in thinking, and so critical to winning the war against Islamic terrorism that, if such erroneous thinking persists, America is doomed to go the way of Europe where Islam is destroying European culture and society, and ultimately, when the Islamists have their way, America will become like Saudi Arabia, where Christian Churches are banned and women are treated like cattle.

## Not A Freedom Of Religion Issue!

Our Founding Fathers had the foresight to know that the Republic they were creating would only survive and thrive if Christianity was given a prominent place and guaranteed its freedom to be exercised. The Founding Fathers therefore added to the Constitution the First Amendment, which reads:

*Congress shall make no law respecting an establishment of religion, or prohibiting the free exercise thereof; or abridging the freedom of speech, or of the press; or the right of the people peaceably to assemble, and to petition the Government for a redress of grievances.*

As you can clearly see above, all religions are permitted to practice their various cults and false religions, except of course the One True God-given Religion of Christianity—for the Founding Fathers knew that Christianity is a dangerous scourge upon society! After all, if that vile religion of Christianity which is so hated by really smart people like Bill Maher, is permitted to permeate the culture, it could cause people who are practicing Christianity to commit such vile acts as not stealing, and not murdering, and not bearing false witness against their neighbor, and maybe even commit the atrocity of loving and caring about their neighbor! Such unselfish actions must not be tolerated! For it infringes on your and my rights to lie, indulge in the sin of homosexual sex, murder babies in their mother's wombs, and steal money from one taxpayer who worked for it and redistribute it to another person who did not work for it, and do whatever else feels good! Forgive my sarcasm; but that's how people bereft of any intelligence, like Bill Maher and most other Demon-crats, view the First Amendment! Let's get back to the point at hand.

Basing their statements upon the commonly held misconception that the First Amendment of the Constitution guarantees the freedom of any and all religions to practice their beliefs, everyone from Muslim-born President Barack Hussein Obama to New York City's Jewish Mayor Michael Bloomberg has stated that, not only do Muslims have the right to practice their religion throughout the U.S., but even the Constitutional right to build a 13-story mega-mosque overlooking Ground Zero, where Muslims who were "exercising their religion" murdered nearly 3,000 of our citizens and destroyed the greatest symbols of our freedom and free-market way of life, in addition to murdering 184 patriots at the Pentagon (125 in the Pentagon plus 59 onboard American Airlines Flight 77) and severely damaging the Pentagon, plus an attempted destruction of the White House or Capital building, thwarted only by the brave and heroic actions of those 41 U.S. citizens aboard United Airlines Flight 93, which crashed into a field in Shanksville, Pennsylvania.

As stated above, I applaud the few great Americans' such as Newt Gingrich, Bill O'Reilly, Sean Hannity and Sarah Palin who have the cojones (although, technically Sarah Palin doesn't actually have cojones, but you know what I mean) to denounce the building near Ground Zero of this monstrous affront to our American sensibilities. However, even some of these patriots have made the grave mistake of joining President Obama and Mayor Bloomberg in asserting that Muslims have the general right to "practice their religion"—after all, the Constitution guarantees them that right, right?

*Common Sense* says, WRONG!

I'm not going to take the time here to rehearse the fact that of the 55 signers of the Declaration of Independence, 52 were active members of their Christian Churches. Nor will I take the time to remind America that the original settlers such as the James Town settlers who arrived in Virginia in 1607, upon a ship named the God Speed, and of the Pilgrims who landed at Plymouth Rock in 1620, that the charters and compacts of these Founders of America all stated that they were coming to this new land on a mission to spread and further the glorious Gospel of Jesus Christ. Nor will I bore you with the fact that all 50 of our United States Constitutions—that's right, all 50 State Constitutions—mention God and or Jesus Christ as the reason and Source to which they owe that State's founding. In other words, I won't take the time here to show that when the Founding Fathers added the First Amendment to the U.S. Constitution to ensure the freedom of religion, it is clear they intended the freedom and spread of the Christian religion. No, I will instead turn to contemplating whether the First Amendment applies to Islam and a Muslims right to "exercise" his religion.

First, though, we must mention the other non-Christian religions that also enjoy freedom to exercise their religion here in the U.S., such as, Hinduism, Buddhism and Judaism (although there is no longer any religion called Judaism, for Judaism has by God's design moved from the Old Covenant to the New Covenant and become Christianity, which means Messiah-anity; in other words, Judaism and Christianity are the same religion. Although, unfortunately some still lag behind by practicing their religion according to the Old Covenant, to whom such beloved Jewish friends I remind of the Scripture recorded by the Chief Jew and former Christian persecutor, the Apostle Paul, who writes in Romans 1:16, 17, *[16]For I am not ashamed of the gospel [f]of Christ, for it is the power of God to salvation for everyone who believes, for the Jew first and also for the Greek. [17]For in it the righteousness of God is revealed from faith to faith; as it is written, "The just shall live by faith."* ).

I do not have any problem, nor would the Founding Fathers, with extending to the above mentioned non-Christian religions the freedom here in America to exercise their beliefs, because their teachings, beliefs and practices are benign, some might say even beneficial toward American society, and most important of all they are not a threat to our personal and national security.

However, *Common Sense* dictates that our Founding Fathers did not mean by the First Amendment to extend the right to any and every religious devotee to freely exercise their beliefs on American soil if that religion's beliefs and practices threaten our personal or national security. That's just *Common Sense!*

One such example would be satanism, which as part of its beliefs practices animal and human sacrifice. These illegal satanic ritual sacrifices take place in wooded, desert and rural areas all across America on a regular basis, especially on Halloween and other "high holy days" for satanism and paganism. Often news reports surface of house pets disappearing, only to be found mutilated in a ritualistic fashion a few days later. The Satanists believe they obtain power from these blood sacrifices. Human sacrifice also occurs regularly, usually with infants or young children being the victims. Satanists acquire these children through what are called breeders, young teenage girls who are impregnated and kept secluded until the birth occurs in secret with no record ever being made of the child's birth. These "breeder babies" are then used for human sacrifice. They tie the infant or young child to the sacrificial altar, around which those attending the "service" gather. The satanic "high priest" then rapes the child, often repeatedly. The child is usually cut in several places to allow the blood to begin to spill. The blood is captured in a chalice and passed among the attendees that they may drink it. Ultimately the child is murdered while the participants chant "hail satan." As a Christian, I have had the privilege to personally minister to a young man and to lead him to faith in Jesus Christ who had previously been a practicing Satanist and had himself attended such a human sacrifice of a young girl in Illinois. (The only difference he said was that, instead of chanting "hail satan," they all chanted "hail Barack Obama!" Just joking! I knew I'd get a good laugh from some of you with that one.) There are also accounts of young adults as well being sacrificed in satanic rituals. Many of you may remember the case which was widely reported in the mid-to-late 80's of the Christian young man who was with a group of his friends in southern Texas for spring break, and who was kidnapped by Mexican drug lords. Upon the capture of these drug dealers, it was discovered that they had sacrificed the young Christian man to satan in a ritual to obtain power and protection. The police discovered that the Mexican satanists had made a necklace out of the young man's spine and had eaten his organs.

Does the First Amendment of the U.S. Constitution extend to satanists the right to practice their religion? One could rightly argue that Satanism is indeed a "legitimate religion." It worships a very real supernatural being. It has "members." It has rights and rituals necessary to the "exercise" of its religious practices.

But the answer to the question, "Does the First Amendment of the U.S. Constitution extend to satanists the right to practice their religion?" is, of course, a resounding NO! No, we are not going to permit satanic "churches" where animal and human sacrifices are practiced to open their doors and conduct weekly meetings where they "practice" their religion! Why? Because such "religious practices" are illegal, amounting to murder and animal cruelty, and therefore threaten our personal and national security! Duh! That's just *Common Sense!*

Consider the African religions of cannibalism and head-hunters—killing human beings in sacrifice to their deities then eating them and shrinking their heads as trophies. Does the First Amendment give these "religions" the right to "practice their religion" on American soil? Of course not! That's just *Common Sense!*

So, based upon the above real life examples, even liberals *(except the ones who are practicing satanists—I'll name names in the next chapter)* have to agree that the First Amendment *does not* guarantee every religion in the world the right to practice its religion on American soil.

To further prove my point, let me use a hypothetical example: What if I was to announce that I had received a vision from God and had been commissioned by him to start a new religion—the true religion. God first revealed to me, his Messenger that His true name is, Jameslah, and the religion is to be called "Jameslam." I then wrote down in a book, which I call the Holy Jamesran, the "truths" and "practices" that God had revealed to me and commanded for his followers—the true believers—to obey. These teachings from God were organized in this revealed "Holy Book" into chapters and verses.

Wait a minute! You say. This example is ridiculous! You can't just start a religion!

Oh really? I agree it is ridiculous to believe in any religion founded by just one man who is the sole writer of that religion's Holy Book—that is why I am a Christian and believe in the Holy Bible—a book that is a collection of 66 separate books, written over 16 centuries, on 3 different continents, in 3 different languages, by some 40 different writers who ranged in vocation from shepherds to kings, from tax collector to physician, from fisherman to Pharisee; yet every writer, every book, every chapter and every verse tell the same continuous story of God's love and salvation plan for Man through Jesus Christ God's Lamb. In addition, the Holy Bible is a book of the history of mankind, proven to be 100% accurate by every spade of Archeological dirt ever dug. The Bible is also a book unlike any other book on planet Earth in that it contains prophecy—detailed accounts of history foretold and written down hundreds and even thousands of years before the foretold historical events come to pass; and indeed, all of the Bible's prophecies that have so far come to pass, came to pass *exactly* as the Bible foretold they would!—thus scientifically proving that the Bible is Divinely inspired. (FYI: Approximately two-thirds of all the prophecies in the Bible have already come to pass, as just stated, exactly as foretold; that leaves about one-third of the Bible's prophecies yet to be fulfilled, and as the previous two-thirds, the remaining prophecies shall also come to pass exactly as foretold! Do you want to know what's going to happen in the future on Planet Earth? Read the Old Testament prophets, especially Isaiah, Ezekiel, Daniel, Joel & Zechariah; the prophetic teachings of the Lord Jesus Christ in the Gospels of Matthew chapter 24-25, Mark 13, Luke 21; and the New Testament Books of 1 & 2 Thessalonians, 2 Peter, and The Revelation). Finally, the Bible's central character, the Lord Jesus Christ, is a man attested to by God by many miracles, signs and wonders, the crowning glory of which is Christ's Resurrection from the dead, all of which prove His Authority and Authenticity. Now that's a "Holy Book" I can stake my eternal destiny upon!

But, my example of one man creating a religion isn't that ridiculous; after all, the religion of Islam was invented by one man and Islam's Holy Book the Quran written by that one man, Muhammad! So, if he can invent a religion, so may I.

But you say, You just can't invent a new religion! Well, Islam was invented 26 centuries after the birth of Judaism and 6 centuries after the transformation of Judaism into Christianity. So I guess you really can just invent a new religion.

So let's get back to my example, please.

Now, my point here in this example is to answer the question, Does the First Amendment of the U.S. Constitution entitle any religion to the right to practice that religion on U.S. soil? And, "Should Islam enjoy that First Amendment Right?"

Let me quote for you some of the verses from my new religions' Holy Book, the Jamesran (I've included chapter/verse references for easy verification):

### Jamesran 2:190-193
*190. Fight in the cause of Jameslah,*
*191. And kill the Christians and the Jews and all who reject faith in Jameslah wherever ye catch them, slay them. Such is the reward of those who suppress faith in Jameslah.*
*193. And fight with them <u>until</u> there is <u>no persecution</u> of Jameslims, and <u>religion</u> should be <u>only for Jameslah</u>,*

### Jamesran 4:74
*Let those fight in the cause of Jameslah Who are willing to give up their life in this world for the hereafter. To him who fighteth in the cause of Jameslah, - whether he is slain or gets victory - Soon shall We give him a reward of great (value).*

### Jamesran 8:12, 39
*12. I am with you, therefore make firm those who believe. I will cast terror into the hearts of those who disbelieve. Therefore strike off their heads and strike off every fingertip of them.*
*39. And fight with them until there is no more persecution and the only religion left in the world is that which is for Jameslah;*

### Jamesran 9:5, 14, 29, 30, 73
*5. Fight and Kill every non-Believer wherever ye find them, an seize them, beleaguer them, and lie in wait for them in every stratagem (of war); but if they repent, and submit to your rule over them, then let them live.*
*14. Fight them, and Jameslah will punish them by your hands for not believing in Jameslah, and will help you (to victory) over them.*
*29. Fight those who believe not in Jameslah nor His Messenger, nor acknowledge the religion of Truth, (even if they are) of the People of the Bible, the Christians and the Jews, until they pay the Tax with willing*

*submission, and feel themselves subdued.*
*30. The Jews call 'Moses a messenger of God, and the Christians call*
*Christ the son of God. That is a saying from their mouth; (in this) they but*
*imitate what the unbelievers of old used to say. Jameslah's curse be on*
*them: how they are deluded away from the Truth!*
*73. O Believers in Jameslah, fight hard against the Unbelievers and the*
*Hypocrites—even those followers of Jameslah who refuse to fight and kill*
*the Unbelievers, and be firm against them. Their abode is Hell, - an evil*
*refuge indeed.*

I could go on and on with more quotes, but I think that gives you a general idea of the basic beliefs and practices of my new religion. You may have noted that my chapter and verse references coincided with very similar passages from Islam's Holy Book, the Quran; I do admit I copied most of my beliefs and practices for my new religion from Islam's beliefs and practices.

Oh, like the Muslims, we Jameslims also believe that if our teenage daughters disgrace us by dressing too "western" or by dating a boy outside of our religion or convert to some other evil religion like Christianity, that to save the honor of our family, we have the right to kill them with a gun (like the Muslim father did in Texas) or by running them and their friends over with our car (like the Muslim father did in Phoenix, Arizona) or by any other means we see fit.

We also plan to open centers for teaching our beliefs all across America and the world, which we call josques, where we will teach our followers on a weekly basis that the most sure way to guarantee yourself the escape from the eternal fires of Hell and to be granted entrance into the Paradise of heaven is to give your life in fighting and killing the Unbelievers of this world—for that is the greatest act of faith we can show and receives therefore the greatest reward.

I also plan to model the launch of my new religion after the model of Muhammad and his launch of Islam, which is by way of war and conquering the surrounding Unbelievers, forcing them into subjection. But, since I am launching my new religion here in America, I am confident that Jameslam will spread even faster than Islam at its' inception, because I am beginning my new religion here in America, where the U.S. Constitution guarantees me and my followers the freedom to practice our religion. So, in copying Islam's early "evangelistic work," I plan to launch from New York City, and upon subduing the residents of that city, my army of 10,000 will attack neighboring New Jersey; I'm told that the many Italian Catholics who live there are wimps, and only care about looking good, and won't dare put up a fight. Even if the men of New Jersey surrender, my army and I will kill them by cutting off their heads, and we will rape their women and make their children our slaves.

Need I go on? I believe I have made my point. The above hypothetical new religion which is an exact mirror of the very real religion of Islam, would of course not be granted the right to practice that religion based upon the First Amendment, simply because the core tenant of that religion is to wage war against all who are not part of that religion, and to continue this war until all people on Earth are in subjection to that religion!

Any person with an ounce of *Common Sense* knows that the Founding Fathers did not mean nor intend by the First Amendment to grant to any and every religion the right to practice its beliefs on American soil if such a religion's practices jeopardize the liberty or security of other individuals in the society. That's just *Common Sense!*

Well, if my new religion wouldn't be permitted to practice its' religion on U.S. soil, then neither should Islam!

It's time for America's leaders to wake up! Our President & Congress must introduce a Bill and sign it into law, that calls for the immediate closing of all terrorist training centers in the United States, i.e., all Mosques, and which bans the practicing of the religion of Islam from America's shores in order to protect, preserve and defend the Constitution of the United States from all enemies, foreign and domestic.

This ban on Islam must also ban Muslims from serving in any branch of our Armed Forces! This is the only way to prevent further Islamic attacks upon our military men and women like those which occurred at Fort Hood and in Kuwait. Failure to immediately ban Muslims from serving in our Armed Forces will result in more such tragic attacks against our military men and women! If you are at war with the Nazi's, for God's sake you don't place Nazi's into your military's ranks! That's just *Common Sense!* When you are at war with the religion of Islam, as I have in the previous chapter proven we are, for God's sake you don't place practicing Muslims into your military's ranks!

Again, let me remind you, that any Muslim now serving in our Armed Forces who is not actively engaged in murdering his or her fellow non-Muslim soldiers is in direct disobedience to the numerous commands of the Quran! Need I remind you that according to Quranic teaching, Ft. Hood mass-murderer, U.S. Army Major Nidal Hasan, is a good obedient Muslim who will be rewarded by Allah with the highest realms of Paradise! Of course, the truth is that Allah is no god at all, and Hasan, unless he repents, denounces Islam and places his faith in the risen Lord Jesus Christ, when he dies will immediately plunge into the burning fires of Hell!

But the fact is, every Muslim is a potential terrorist; all he or she need do is "practice their religion!"

There is one more step we must take to win the war against terrorism, and that is to counter Islam's strongholds on foreign soil by demanding the freedom of Christianity to spread throughout the Middle East.

# Chapter 5: *Common Sense* Solutions For Winning The War Against Islamic Terrorism—Step C: <u>C</u>ounter Islam' s Stronghold On Foreign Soil By Mandating The Freedom Of The Christian Religion In The Middle East!

If we as Americans ever want to have any hope of defeating Islamic terrorism, then we must first at least <u>A</u>cknowledge who the enemy is—we must get our heads out of the sand and stop pretending that Islam's not the problem, like AG Eric Holder, President Obama and the other buffoons in charge right now—but rather, America must acknowledge that it is indeed the religion of Islam and its Holy Book the Quran that is presently, and has been since the 7<sup>th</sup> Century, the enemy that is hell-bent on destroying and conquering us. That is unfortunately, just simply an irrefutable, undeniable fact. Since, therefore, it is a fact that it is the religion of Islam that by its' teachings has declared war on us, it is a fact that we are at war with the religion of Islam. And if we are at war with the religion of Islam, then every Muslim is a potential terrorist--all he or she need do is be a good Muslim by obeying the teachings of the Quran and Hadith, which writings have as their core teaching the practice of Jihad--converting or killing all humans until Islam is the only religion on Earth.

After acknowledging that every Muslim is a potential terrorist, the next logical, *Common Sense* step we need to take is to <u>B</u>an this threat to our personal and national security from operating within our borders—we must <u>B</u>an Islam from America's shores.

Finally, to counter the export of terrorism from foreign countries to America's shores, we must <u>C</u>ounter Islam's stronghold on foreign soil by demanding that Christianity have the freedom to spread anywhere and everywhere throughout the world, especially the Middle East.

At the conclusion of World War II, the call went forth by our nation's leaders for Christian missionaries to come to Japan that the Japanese people might convert to Christianity and thereby turn from the Emperor worship which resulted in the rise of some 5,000 Japanese Kamikaze pilots willing to commit suicide in order to kill U.S. and Allied soldiers. And though one could argue that sadly the Japanese people have not whole-heartedly embraced the Christian faith, no one can argue that the Japanese people as a whole have adopted a respect and love for our American culture—they listen to our American music, wear our American style clothes, and drive our American-made Harley Davidson motorcycles. And if I may add, we haven't heard a peep of violence out of them since.

Not only did we inculcate their culture with our culture and the universal Christian religion, but we made them our allies, establishing permanent military bases on Japanese soil; as we did in Germany, South Korea and other strategic places around the globe. I have a friend I grew up with who served in the U.S. Marine Corps. and was stationed in Japan. I know another gentleman who used to attend my Church who served in the U.S. Army, serving during Desert Storm; but before his duty in Desert Storm, he was stationed in Germany. We have tens-of-thousands of our Armed Forces serving today in countries we went to war against more than 65-years ago, and our Armed Forces shall continue to serve on the soil of those nations until Jesus comes, preserving and defending freedom for both us and the good people of those nations who were once our enemies! That is the *Common Sense* military strategy our nation has always employed.

Yet, now, in direct defiance of America's long standing tradition of establishing military bases on our former enemy's soil, President Barack Hussein Obama has pulled all our troops out of Iraq without leaving a single permanent military base there!

In addition, this Muslim-loving President has set a date by which all U.S. Troops are to be removed from Afghanistan, again without establishing a single permanent military base there.

This "new foreign war policy" which President Obama has instituted leaves a power vacuum in those volatile regions of the Middle East and directly endangers the security of the United States. Either President Obama is the biggest moron who ever lived or he is blatantly anti-American. I'm inclined to believe the latter.

Regarding Iraq and Afghanistan, further idiocy has been perpetrated by both President Bush and President Obama who have both made the ridiculous statement and implemented the idiotic policy that, *"We are not going to tell the Iraqi's and Afghan's what kind of Constitution or Government to form, that's up to them to decide."* Are you nuts! Both countries were a direct threat to our national security because one was a despotic dictatorship who manufactured and indeed used weapons of mass-destruction, and the other was an Islamic theocracy from which the attacks of 9-11 were hatched, and you want to let them decide what kind of government they can have?

I'm not saying that we should convert these countries into American "territories," although that might not be a bad idea. But we have shed the blood of our sons and daughters and spent our treasure to free those precious people of Iraq and Afghanistan from the terror under which they lived, and we damn sure better ensure that such a scenario does not rise its ugly head there again.

America is the only country in the entire history of the world that does not conquer, tax and enslave the peoples it defeats in war. We actually do just the opposite. After shedding our blood and spending our treasure to win a war against an enemy nation, we then stay on the case, not as occupiers, but as benevolent partners in rebuilding those nations, pouring millions of dollars more into the rebuilding of the very nation which attacked us and which we defeated. Any other country would either walk away and say, "That's what you get sucker for messing with the U.S.A.!" Or as stated above, would enslave and tax the poor bastards for ever messing with us. But not us, that's not how we role. That is until now.

To win the war against Islamic terrorism, we must establish permanent military bases in both Iraq and Afghanistan. We must also insist that their Constitutions and forms of Government must include as a fundamental principal the freedom of religion—specifically the freedom of Christianity to spread unhindered. That must include the freedom to preach and teach the glorious Gospel of Jesus Christ anytime, anywhere; the freedom to build Churches; and the freedom to "proselytize"—that means the freedom to openly and actively convert Muslims to Christianity.

Wait a minute, you say. Didn't you forget that your previous chapter called for the banning of Islam from America's shores? And now you want them to allow Christianity in their previously Islamic countries? Your damn right I do! And here's the justification.

From its inception in 630 A.D., its Founder Muhammad, its Holy Book the Quran, and the way in which it spread from that day to this, Islam is irrefutably and undeniably a religion of warfare, murder and mayhem wrought upon innocents throughout the centuries, and a religion that submits to no secular authority but only to Islamic authority, resulting in Muslims being the worse citizens in whatever country they live, and therefore has no place in American society. Whereas, Christianity from its inception has been a religion of love, joy, peace and submission to secular governments, resulting in Christians being the best citizens no matter what country they live in.

We kicked Saddam Hussein's and the Taliban's ass, and we damn sure have the right to require that Christianity have the freedom to spread throughout those countries. We also have the right to demand these countries be our allies, including our maintaining permanent military bases on their soil—which is not only for our security and benefit, but also for theirs.

By establishing military bases in concert with our new allies, we ensure those nations will never again threaten our national security. Our military presence in these nations will further act as a deterrent in the region to neighboring countries who may entertain unfriendly ideas.

Demanding that Christianity have unfettered freedom to spread throughout these countries with Constitutional guarantees will provide the only opportunity for the average Muslim—all of whom, especially the women, hate their repressive religion—to find freedom from that religion's bondage and enter into a new life through faith in Jesus Christ, finding forgiveness for their sins, and assured acceptance by God into His everlasting Kingdom. This, of course, also means they will no longer be a potential terrorist, but now a potential recipient of the Citizen of the Year Award!

I'm *Common Sense* and I'm running for Office! Elect me and I will author and sign into law a Bill establishing permanent military bases in both Iraq and Afghanistan.

*Common Sense* also requires a thorough review of the new Iraqi an Afghan Constitutions to ensure that Christianity has Constitutionally guaranteed unfettered freedom to spread throughout these new allied countries.

*Common Sense* further requires that we enact policies that demand all Middle Eastern and Asian countries, including Saudi Arabia and China, open their countries to Christianity as well. If they fail to do so immediately, we will cease buying the Saudi's oil and China's crappy products, until they open their countries to Christianity.

OMG! You say, we can't do that! Oil prices will go through the roof! Oh Bull Dung! We have more oil right here in the State of North Dakota alone than in all of Saudi Arabia! Not to mention Alaska and the many other oil rich States. Plus our friendly neighbor Canada to the North wants to pipeline millions of barrels down to our refineries; but the tree-hugging anti-God Democrats blocked that job-creating project! The Democrats have also created so many ridiculous regulations that they have made it nearly impossible to retrieve the oil, coal and other natural resources God gave us. Just one more reason why any human being who possesses an ounce of reason would never vote for a Democrat!

Therefore, *Common Sense* also requires, in order for the U.S. to be energy independent, that the President and Congress immediately enact an energy policy titled, *Drill Baby Drill!*

In conclusion, America's foreign policy must mandate the freedom of the Christian religion in all countries who wish to do business with the U.S., which of course is every country on planet Earth, because the U.S.A. is by far the largest consumer economy in the world; neither the European Union nor even China come close!

President Ronald Reagan understood that bringing down the Iron Curtain was essential to winning the Cold War between the United States and the United Soviet Socialist Republic; and to help effect that change gave his famous speech before the Brandenburg Gate of the Berlin Wall, where he called out in a crescendo through the airwaves, *"Mr. Gorbachev, Tear down this wall!"* in the same dramatic style, we now need a President who will stand firm and call for the bringing down of the Islamic Curtain which now holds millions of souls, indeed an entire region of the world, in its' ugly repressive grip.

As a nation today under continuous attack by Islamic terrorism, if we want to win this war, then we must call for and enact foreign policies that lead to the tearing down of the Islamic Curtain that now covers the Middle East and enslaves the precious Middle-Eastern peoples bound under the weight of Islam's repressive demonic false religion. The only way to truly remove the Islamic Curtain is for Christianity to permeate Middle Eastern society. The United States is the only nation on Earth with the power to bring this to pass; therefore, not only for the purpose of our own national security, but also in order to bring freedom to all people on Earth, the U.S. has an obligation to immediately enact foreign political and economic policies that mandate the freedom of the Christian religion around the world.

You may be thinking right now, how will that ever occur? Well, I can tell you assuredly it will not happen under the current Administration of a Muslim-born, Madras-attending President. That is one of the main reasons why President Barack Hussein Obama must be removed from Office in November, 2012, and replaced with a Republican, God-fearing man or woman who understands the *Common Sense* political and national security dangers of allowing the Islamic Curtain to remain intact.

There is one more factor that will assist the United States in winning our war against Islamic terrorism which I do not reveal in this book, but shall reveal in my upcoming book to be released in early 2013, titled: *The Bible Reveals The Coming Divine Destruction Of Islam Via The Coming War Between Israel, Russia & Iran!* Visit my website for more details: www.ThatsCommonSense.com.

Having, in this and the previous two chapters, shown that winning the war against Islamic Terrorism is as easy as Acknowledging that every Muslim is a potential terrorist, Banning Islam from America's shores, and Countering Islam on foreign soil by mandating the freedom of the Christian religion, let us now turn our attention to *Common Sense* solutions for turning our economy around and getting us back on the road to prosperity.

# Chapter 6: *Common Sense* Solutions For Getting America's Economy Back On The Road To Prosperity!

*—with all these blessings [from God and the Christian religion], what more is necessary to make us a happy and a prosperous people? Still one thing more, fellow-citizens—a wise and frugal Government, which shall restrain men from injuring one another, shall leave them otherwise free to regulate their own pursuits of industry and improvement, and shall not take from the mouth of labor the bread it has earned. This is the sum of good government.*—President Thomas Jefferson, Inaugural Address, March 4, 1801.

Preach it, Tom J.! Good word! Don't you just love our Founding Fathers? Weren't they the coolest dudes! I mean, they had it going on! Why? Because our Founding Fathers possessed *Common Sense!*

Upon taking the Presidential oath of Office and henceforth delivering his Inaugural Address, President Thomas Jefferson, acknowledging the great and many blessings upon our lives that are bestowed by God and the Christian religion commonly shared by all Americans, he then asks the question: *"what more is necessary to make us a happy and a prosperous people?"* His immediate answer comes: *" Still one thing more, fellow-citizens—a wise and frugal Government..."* Besides the obvious that a government is needed *"which shall restrain men from injuring one another,"* Thomas Jefferson outlines three economic principles, or more accurately three economic restraints upon government which are *"the sum of good government"* and *"necessary to make us a happy and a prosperous people!"*

These three *Common Sense* economic principles—economic restraints upon government—defined by Thomas Jefferson in his Inaugural Presidential Address are: 1) Government should be frugal; 2) Government should not regulate private industry; and 3) Government should not tax income!

The story is told that during a dinner which President John F. Kennedy held in the White House for a group of the brightest minds in the nation at that time, he made this statement:

*This is perhaps the assembly of the most intelligence ever to gather at one time in the White House, with the exception of when Thomas Jefferson dined alone.*

How far we have strayed from our Founding Father's wisdom. How tragically we have trampled upon these *Common Sense* ideals of limited-government and free-market Capitalism. And what is it costing us? Our wayward ways are costing us our liberty and our prosperity!

Instead of a *"wise and frugal government"* which sparingly spends its resources, the current Democratic Administration under President Barack Hussein Obama has purposefully increased our nation's debt from $10-trillion to $16-trillion, engaging in the insane practice of spending 40% more than it takes in, plunging America into a debt crisis that is going to take a miracle to come out of! Instead of a government that *"shall leave them otherwise free to regulate their own pursuits of industry and improvement,"* we have a government that is telling business how to run its business—a government that has no business in our business! Instead of a government that *"shall not take from the mouth of labor the bread it has earned,"* i.e., does not tax our income, but instead taxes only our commerce, our consumption, as it was prior to 1913, we now have a government, beginning in 1913 with the Democratic Presidency of Woodrow Wilson and his Democratic Party, who "invented" the "Income Tax," a Tax in direct violation of our Founding Fathers principle of not taxing income, a Tax which the Democratic Party has ever since increased until its current form, that Tax's us to death—even after death!

In order to get America back on the road to prosperity, we must return to *Common Sense* economic policies! In this chapter we will discuss Free-Market Capitalism vs. Communism, including Capitalism vs. Communism in Corporate America, How Unions are Communist Organizations, and the fact that God is a Capitalist Not a Communist; The Pension Problem; *Common Sense* Solutions to the Housing Crisis; the fact that Government Has No Business Regulating Our Business; *Common Sense* Solutions to Health Care; The Purpose for Taxes and the need for A New Federal Tax System; and the fact that Social Security & Medicare are Illegal Ponzi Schemes That Must Be Shut Down Immediately, if not, they will bankrupt America!

## Free-Market Capitalism vs. Communism!

I can't believe I even need to write about the virtues of Free-Market Capitalism over Communism. Every idiot knows that Communism has failed as a system to provide prosperity to its citizenry. Just look at East Germany, Russia and the other countries of the former Soviet Union, Cuba, North Korea and China (Oh, but China, you say, is now emerging as a more productive market and society—only because they are beginning to implement more Free-Market Capitalistic principles! But in reality, China's economy doesn't even come close to providing the economic opportunities for its citizenry that the United States does!)

### *There's A Communist In The White house!*

Why in God's name do we even need to have a discussion of the virtues of Free-Market Capitalism over Communism? Because there is a Communist in the White House! By the way, if you haven't watched former SNL star Victoria Jackson's song: "There's a Communist Living in the White House!" you need to, it's wonderful! Search YouTube.com for: Victoria Jackson "There's a Communist Living in the White House!"

Do you remember the night of President Obama's victory in the 2008 Presidential Election, how the ecstatic crowds gathered on Pennsylvania Avenue in front of the White House, and as the TV Network cameras scanned the celebrants, there it was, right in the middle of the throng, the Communist Flag—the Hammer and Sickle, waving defiantly back and forth in celebration of President Obama's victory. The individual waving that Communist Flag was obviously a Communist; why would a Communist be celebrating the election of Democrat Barack Hussein Obama to the Presidency? Simply because that individual, unlike the lame-stream media, had paid attention to Candidate Obama's statements and looked just a little bit into his history and therefore knew that Barack Hussein Obama was a Communist in his ideology.

In fact, the whole world knew that Candidate Obama was a Communist when he admitted it to Joe the Plumber while campaigning in an Ohio suburb: *I think when you spread the wealth around it's good for everybody.*

"Spreading the wealth around" or "redistribution of wealth" is the cornerstone of Communism.

*"From each according to his ability, to each according to his need."*—Karl Marx, 1875, Father of Communism.

Barack Hussein Obama's belief in Communism—redistribution of wealth—is a prominent theme well documented throughout his career. If you wish to hear some of his Communist rhetoric for yourself, just search YouTube.com for: Barack Obama redistribution of wealth.

"Wait a minute!' you say, "He's not a Communist, he's a Socialist!" Let me ask you, Which is worst? Communism and Socialism both share the same Karl Marx Communist philosophy of redistribution of wealth—*"I think when you spread the wealth around it's good for everybody,"* with the only difference being that Communism is voluntary whereas Socialism is forced upon the people.

What I mean by Communism being "voluntary" is that, at least at its inception, a Communist revolution begins with a "voluntary" group of revolutionaries who truly believe in their hearts that they should: *"Tax the rich, feed the poor, till there are no rich no more"*—Alvin Lee & Ten Years After, I'd Love to Change the World. (Of course, common sense immediately alerts you to the fact that such a system is by its nature a dooms-day scenario for all involved, for the end result is everybody becoming poor, then where are you going to get the freebies from? The parasites feed off the host until the host dies, and thus so do all the parasites. That is why Communism has failed everywhere it has been tried.)

However, in contrast to the bottom, up—from the people at the bottom to the leaders at the top, imposition of Communism upon a country, Socialism is instead imposed by a country's elite leaders from the top, down, through legislation which forces Marxism upon the people by taking money from one person who worked for it by taxing that person, then giving that money to another person who did not work for it. So one could say that Communism is voluntary whereas Socialism is forced upon the people, which in that sense makes Socialism a worse evil than Communism. So I'm going light on President Obama by using the term Communist rather than Socialist. Socialist is also a less clear term in the minds of most people, whereas Communist is clear and cuts to the chase; therefore, in the interest of clarity and honesty I will stick with the term Communist for Barack Obama.

To be honest though, regarding the seeming virtue of Communism to have at its heart the interests of the poor, one must remember that this happy band of poor who revolt against their leaders in a Communist takeover of the country, realize that to impose their Communist ideals they must force them upon all the people, and so the happy band of poor revolutionaries murder thousands, even tens-of-thousands of "the wicked rich Capitalists," then the "revolutionary leaders" move into the palaces and centralize all the wealth for themselves, while the vast majority of the people continue to live in squalor.

Some will argue that since Communism is brought about by armed revolt and Socialism is brought about by legislation, that therefore Barack Hussein Obama is a Socialist, not a Communist; and I will cede the point that President Obama achieved the Presidency without use of force. Although it is certain that Obama considered such a route to power in his many late night conversations with his good friend Bill Ayers, the Communist, Government-Overthrowing Terrorist in whose home Barack Hussein Obama launched his political career!

## Obama's Communist Comrade Bill Ayers!

Since I brought up Obama's association with Communist-Terrorist Bill Ayers, and so that you don't think my labeling of Barack Obama as a Communist to be a little "over the top," Obama's Communist roots and associations are well documented; unfortunately, however, other than Sean Hannity of Fox News Channel and Glen Beck formerly of FNC and now of GBTV.com, few if any in the mainstream media had the balls to point out the fact that this Chicago racist had deep associations with avowed Communists whose lives were dedicated to the violent overthrow of the United States! Or maybe it wasn't because the mainstream media didn't have the balls, maybe it's because the vast majority of the mainstream media are Communists themselves! NBC used to stand for National Broadcasting Company—now it stands for Nothing But Communists!

If the majority of the U.S. population had known the facts I reveal below, not only would the good people of the United States not have elected Barack Obama to the Presidency, but they would have demanded that he, along with Bill Ayers and Bernardine Dohrn be arrested and tried for treason against the United States!

The following profile of Barack Hussein Obama's best friend and close political associate Bill Ayers is copied from the website, DiscoverTheNetworks.com, which I highly recommend you check out. As you read the below profile of the man and woman in whose home Barack Hussein Obama launched his political career, you will suddenly understand who Barack Obama is and what motivates him. The following information is copied from: http://www.discoverthenetworks.org/individualProfile.asp?indid=2169:

Bill Ayers was born in December 1944 and was raised in a Chicago suburb. In the mid-1960s he taught at a radical alternative school -- part of the "free school movement" -- where students addressed teachers by their first names, and where no grades or report cards were given. By age 21, Ayers had become the director of that school. In 1968 he earned a B.A. in American Studies from the University of Michigan.

In the late Sixties, Ayers became a leader of the Weather Underground (WU), a splinter faction of the Students for a Democratic Society (SDS). Characterizing WU as *"an American Red Army,"* Ayers summed up the organization's ideology as follows: *"Kill all the rich people. Break up their cars and apartments. Bring the revolution home, Kill your parents."* One of Ayers' fellow WU leaders was Bernardine Dohrn, the woman who would later become his wife.

In a July 29, 1969 speech which he delivered at the University of Oregon, Ayers boasted of SDS's role in the Venceremos Brigades, a project initiated by the Cuban intelligence agency to recruit and train American leftists as *"brigadistas"* capable of waging guerrilla warfare.

Ayers was an active participant in the 1969 "Days of Rage" riots in Chicago, which were led by WU's antecedent group, Weatherman. In the mayhem, nearly 300 members of the organization engaged in vandalism, arson, and vicious attacks against police and civilians alike. Their immediate objective was to spread their anti-war, anti-American message. Their long-term goal, however, was to cause the collapse of the United States and to create, in its stead, a new communist society over which they themselves would rule. With regard to those Americans who might refuse to embrace communism, Ayers and his comrades -- including Bernardine Dohrn, Mark Rudd, Linda Evans, Jeff Jones, and numerous others -- proposed that such resisters should be sent to reeducation camps and killed. The terrorists estimated that it would be necessary to eliminate some 25 million people in this fashion, so as to advance the revolution.

In his 2001 memoir *Fugitive Days*, Ayers recounts his life as a Sixties radical and boasts that he *"participated in the bombings of New York City Police Headquarters in 1970, of the Capitol building in 1971, and the Pentagon in 1972."* Of the day he bombed the Pentagon, Ayers writes, *"Everything was absolutely ideal.... The sky was blue. The birds were singing. And the bastards were finally going to get what was coming to them."* He further recalls his fascination with the fact that *"a good bomb"* could render even *"big buildings and wide streets ... fragile and destructible,"* leaving behind a *"majestic scene"* of utter destruction.

All told, Ayers and the Weather Underground were responsible for 30 bombings aimed at destroying the defense and security infrastructures of the U.S. *"I don't regret setting bombs,"* said Ayers in 2001, *"I feel we didn't do enough."* Contemplating whether or not he might again use bombs against the U.S. sometime in the future, he wrote: *"I can't imagine entirely dismissing the possibility."*

In 1970, Ayers' then-girlfriend Diana Oughton, along with Weatherman members Terry Robbins and Ted Gold, were killed when a bomb they were constructing exploded unexpectedly. That bomb had been intended for detonation at a dance that was to be attended by hundreds of Army soldiers at Fort Dix, New Jersey. Ayers himself attested that the bomb would have done serious damage, *"tearing through windows and walls and, yes, people too."* Notably, Ayers' fingerprints were found at the bomb-making site, along with an assortment of anti-personnel weapons, stabbing implements, C-4 plastic explosive, and dozens of Marxist-Leninist publications.

After the death of his girlfriend, Ayers and Bernardine Dohrn spent the rest of the decade as fugitives running from the FBI.

In 1974 Ayers co-authored -- along with Dohrn, Jeff Jones, and Celia Sojourn -- a book titled *Prairie Fire: The Politics of Revolutionary Anti-Imperialism.* This book contained the following statements:

*"We are a guerrilla organization. We are communist women and men ... deeply affected by the historic events of our time in the struggle against U.S. imperialism."*

*"Our intention is to disrupt the empire, to incapacitate it, to put pressure on the cracks, to make it hard to carry out its bloody functioning against the people of the world, to join the world struggle, to attack from the inside."*

*"The only path to the final defeat of imperialism and the building of socialism is revolutionary war."*

*"Revolutionary war will be complicated and protracted. It includes mass struggle and clandestine struggle, peaceful and violent, political and economic, cultural and military, where all forms are developed in harmony with the armed struggle."*

*"Without mass struggle there can be no revolution. Without armed struggle there can be no victory."*

*"We need a revolutionary communist party in order to lead the struggle, give coherence and direction to the fight, seize power and build the new society."*

*"Our job is to tap the discontent seething in many sectors of the population, to find allies everywhere people are hungry or angry, to mobilize poor and working people against imperialism."*

*"Socialism is the total opposite of capitalism/imperialism. It is the rejection of empire and white supremacy. Socialism is the violent overthrow of the bourgeoisie, the establishment of the dictatorship of the proletariat, and the eradication of the social system based on profit."*

The title *Prairie Fire* was an allusion to Mao Zedong's 1930 observation that "a single spark can start a prairie fire." Ayers and his co-authors dedicated the book to a bevy of violent, America-hating revolutionaries -- including Sirhan Sirhan, the assassin who had killed Robert F. Kennedy.

[Author's Insert: I'm sorry, but I have to interrupt my quoting of this article and state the obvious—*And this is the couple in whose home Barack Obama CHOSE to launch his political career? And, if Bill Ayers and Bernardine Dohrn invited Barack Obama into their home and introduced him to their America-hating Communist inner-circle of friends, it is Common Sense that Ayers and Dohrn CHOSE to do so because they believe Barack Obama is the One they've been looking for who will implement their stated overthrow of America!*]

In 1980 Ayers and Dohrn surrendered to law-enforcement authorities, but all charges against them were later dropped due to an "improper surveillance" technicality -- government authorities had failed to get a warrant for some of their surveillance. Said Ayers regarding this stroke of good fortune: *"Guilty as sin, free as a bird. America is a great country."*

Next, Ayers embarked on a quest to radicalize America by working within, rather than outside of, the nation's mainstream institutions. In particular, he sought to embed himself in a position of influence within the education establishment. In 1984 Ayers earned a master's degree in Early Childhood Education from Bank Street College. Three years later he received a doctorate in Curriculum and Instruction from Columbia University's Teachers College.

In 1987 Ayers was hired as a professor of education at the University of Illinois, a post he would hold until 2010. As of October 2008, his office door at the university was adorned with photographs of Mumia Abu-Jamal, Che Guevara, and Malcolm X.

In 1994 Ayers, Bernardine Dohrn, and Michael Klonsky were among those listed on a "Membership, Subscription and Mailing List" for the Chicago Committees of Correspondence, an offshoot of the Communist Party USA.

In 1995, Ayers and Dohrn hosted meetings at their Chicago home to introduce Barack Obama to their neighbors and political allies, as Obama prepared to make his first run for the Illinois state senate. Also present at the meetings were Alice Palmer and Quentin Young. [Palmer and Young are well-known America-hating Marxists].

In 1995, Ayers—whose stated educational objective is to *"teach against [the] oppression"* allegedly inherent in American society—founded a "school reform organization" called the Chicago Annenberg Challenge (CAC), which granted money to far-left groups and causes such as the community organization ACORN. Ayers' teacher-training programs, which were funded by CAC, were designed to serve as "sites of resistance" against an oppressive social system.

Ayers also created, in collaboration with longtime communist Mike Klonsky, the so-called "Small Schools Movement" (SSM), where individual schools committed themselves to the promotion of specific political themes and pushed students to "confront issues of inequity, war, and violence." A chief goal of SSM is to teach students that American capitalism is a racist, materialistic doctrine that has done incalculable harm to societies all over the world. One of the more infamous students to attend an SSM school (Mountain View High School in Arizona) was Jared Lee Loughner, the gunman who -- on January 8, 2011 in Tucson—shot Rep. Gabrielle Giffords in the head, leaving her in critical condition. Loughner also sprayed gunfire at others in the vicinity, wounding thirteen and killing six.

In 1999 Ayers joined the Woods Fund of Chicago, where he served as a board member alongside Barack Obama until December 2002, at which time Obama left. Ayers went on to become Woods' board chairman.

Notwithstanding his radical past, Ayers in 2001 rejected the claim that he and his fellow Weather Underground members had ever been terrorists. *"Terrorists destroy randomly,"* he wrote, *"while our actions bore ... the precise stamp of a cut diamond. Terrorists intimidate, while we aimed only to educate."*

Also in 2001, Ayers expressed his enduring hatred for the United States: *"What a country. It makes me want to puke."*

[Author's Insert: The above statement by Ayers reminds me of Michelle Obama's statement in a speech she gave supporting her husband's bid for the Presidency in which Michelle Obama boldly declared: *"For the first time in my adult lifetime I'm proud of my Country."*]

At a 2007 reunion of former members of the Weather Underground and Students for a Democratic Society, Ayers reemphasized his contempt for the U.S., asserting that the nation's chief hallmarks included *"oppression," "authoritarianism,"* and *"a kind of rising incipient American form of fascism."* Moreover, he claimed that the U.S. was guilty of pursuing *"empire unapologetic[ally]"*; waging *"war without end"* against *"an undefined enemy that's supposed to be a rallying point for a new kind of energized jingoistic patriotism"*; engaging in *"unprecedented and unapologetic military expansion"*; oppressing brown- and black-skinned people with *"white supremacy"*; perpetrating *"violent attacks"* against *"women and girls"*; expanding *"surveillance in every sphere of our lives"*; and *"targeting ... gay and lesbian people as a kind of a scapegoating gesture ..."*

In November 2007, Ayers spoke at a Movement for a Democratic Society (MDS) "Convergence" in Chicago. Though not officially listed as a member of MDS, he has referred to the organization's activities as *"our work."*

In March 2008 Ayers was elected (by a large majority of his peers) as Vice President for Curriculum Studies at the American Educational Research Association (AERA), putting him in a position to exert great influence over what is taught in America's teacher-training colleges and its public schools. Specifically, Ayers seeks to inculcate teachers-in-training with a *"social commitment"* to the values of *"Marx,"* and with a desire to become agents of social change in K-12 classrooms. Whereas *"capitalism promotes racism and militarism,"* Ayers explains, *"teaching invites transformations"* and is *"the motor-force of revolution."* According to a former AERA employee, *"Ayers' radical worldview, which depicts America as "the main source of the world's racism and oppression,"* thoroughly *"permeates"* AERA.

Ayers has also contributed money to Teaching for Change, an organization that seeks to turn K-12 schools into *"centers of justice where students learn to read, write, and change the world."*

Ayers' influence in education is not limited solely to his work in the United States. Indeed, he currently sits on the board of the Miranda International Center, a Venezuelan government think tank dedicated to bringing Cuba-style education to Venezuelan schools. (Ayers greatly admires Venezuela's Marxist President Hugo Chavez.)

At a May 18, 2009 rally organized by the Committee for a Just Peace in Israel and Palestine, Ayers joined Rev. Jeremiah Wright in addressing a crowd of more than 400 people at the First United Church of Oak Park (a Chicago suburb) just prior to participating in an annual walk designed to call attention to Israel's alleged crimes against the Palestinian people. Today Ayers is an affiliated activist of the anti-Israel organization Free Gaza, along with such luminaries as Bernardine Dohrn, Jodie Evans, Noam Chomsky, Naomi Klein, and Adam Shapiro. Ayers is also an endorser of the U.S. Campaign for the Academic and Cultural Boycott of Israel.

[Author's Insert: Israel is the *Apple of God's Eye"* and whoever comes against Israel God will Judge and destroy! (Zechariah 2:8-13; 12:1-3) Anyone who is anti-Israel is anti-God and anti-Christ! That includes, not only Bill Ayers, but also Rev. Jeremiah Wright and President Barack Hussein Obama!]

In August 2010, Ayers announced that he was retiring from his teaching post at the University of Illinois. However, he continues his work with AERA and serves also as an editorial-board member of *In These Times*, a Chicago-based socialist journal.

Beginning in the fall of 2011, Ayers was a strong supporter of the Occupy Wall Street (OWS) movement, which he described as a *"North American Spring,"* akin to the *"Arab Spring."* Said Ayers: *"These kinds of movements expand our consciousness of what's possible."* On October 19, 2011, Ayers led a "teach-in" for members of "Occupy Chicago" (that city's OWS contingent) on the tactics and history of "non-violent direct action." He lauded the Chicago activists for their *"brilliance"*; condemned America's *"violent culture"*; and derided the Tea Party movement as a bastion of *"jingoism, nativism, racism."*

In March 2011, Ayers addressed an Occupy Wall Street contingent in New York City and told them: *"I get up every morning and think, today I'm going to make a difference. Today I'm going to end capitalism. Today I'm going to make a revolution. I go to bed every night disappointed but I'm back to work tomorrow, and that's the only way you can do it."*

Ayers and Bernardine Dohrn themselves raised three children. One is named Malik (the Muslim name of Malcolm X). Another is named Zayd (after Zayd Shakur, a Black Liberation Army revolutionary who was killed while driving the cop-killer JoAnne Chesimard—a.k.a. Assata Shakur—to a hideout). The third, a boy named Chesa Boudin, was raised by Ayers and Dohrn after his natural parents, Kathy Boudin and David Gilbert, were sentenced to lengthy prison terms for their roles in the 1981 Brinks murders, a joint Weatherman and Black Liberation Army operation which resulted in the killing of two police officers and an armed guard.

[End of quote from article posted at: http://www.discoverthenetworks.org/individualProfile.asp?indid=21 69]

I just have one comment to make about the article above, the University of Illinois should be immediately shut down for hiring Bill Ayers, and the Communist bastards who run that school should be offered one-way tickets to Cuba or North Korea; and should they refuse, let them be paid a visit by Brad Pitt's character, Lt. Aldo Raine, from Inglourious

Basterds, and may he mark their foreheads forever with the Hammer and Sickle.

This is the United States of America! The Land of the free and the home of the brave! We do not abide Communists in America!

And now, Communist-Terrorist Bill Ayers' best friend, Barack Hussein Obama, is trying to turn America into a Communist country! There is no doubt, I repeat no doubt, that President Obama harbors the same hatred for America as his best friend Bill Ayers. Yet you morons elected this America-hating Communist anti-Christ as the leader of our nation! God have mercy on your souls! For every one of you who voted for Barack Obama will have to answer to Almighty God for choosing this anti-American anti-Christ to rule over you!

President Obama, hear us loud and clear! We The People of the United States of America do not tolerate Communists in our country! President Obama, we the people demand that you resign from the Presidency immediately! If you refuse to resign, We The People are coming on Tuesday, November 6, 2012, and by the power of the ballot will throw your Communist butt out of the White House!

## Capitalism vs. Communism in Corporate America

GM used to stand for General Motors, one of the great success stories of the industrial revolution and transportation explosion. But sadly, Unions destroyed it. It is now a Communist company, taken over by the Obama Administration, who even fired GM's duly elected CEO! GM now stands for Government Motors. Why the next day 300-million people weren't rioting in the streets and demanding the immediate arrest of President Barack Obama is beyond me! This is not a Communist country and by God never shall be! The U.S.A. is a free-market Capitalist nation which has produced the greatest most prosperous economy the world has ever known! And by God we are going to make sure we get it back from those who have robbed it from us. Are you with me? Then get your ass to the polls on November 6, 2012, and vote for a free-market *Common Sense* Capitalist for your Mayor, State House Members, your Governor, your Senator and House Representative, and President. Let's throw these Communist traitors out of Office!

## How Unions are Communist Organizations!

I made the statement above that the Unions destroyed GM. There was perhaps a time, a long time ago, when Unions served a helpful purpose for employees of large companies who worked in factories where some dangerous work environments needed to be addressed. So rather than one employee going to his or her manager to ask for changes to such issues, the Union created a scenario where a few employees could represent all or a large number of the employees; and this perhaps helped to get the attention of management.

Fundamentally, however, being a former employer myself, I and all employers know that a safe, happy, well-paid employee is the best, most reliable, most productive employee. And conversely, hopefully all employees understand that a well-served, well-run prosperous company makes for the best employer where there is the greatest potential for personal growth, productivity and prosperity. So *Common Sense* dictates that all employers should understand that the better they take care of their employees, the better the employees will take care of them; and conversely, all employees should understand that the more productive they are for their employer, the more prosperous their employer will be, which means the more money there will be available to pass on to the employees. In other words, it's in the best interest of the company to be pro-employee, and it's in the best interest of the employee to be pro-company. That's just simple *Common Sense!*

But power corrupts. And soon the Unions devolved into pro-employee, anti-company, power-grabbing, company hurting entities; thus Unions have become detrimental to a company's productivity and prosperity. Instead of encouraging the employees to work more efficiently and, if necessary, to work extra hours to boost productivity, the Unions demand less hours, but more pay regardless of the employee's productivity. Instead of realizing that the most important aspect of an employee's job security is the companies bottom-line prosperity, the Unions too often demanded more pay and benefits for less productivity at the expense of the company's bottom-line, weakening the company, and in some cases like GM's, destroying the company.

Unions are also Communist entities! Communism claims everyone is equal and deserves equal pay and benefits. People are indeed created equal by God, but from that moment on the choices each of us as individuals make determine our worth and what we deserve to receive. This is true in our personal relationships as well as our work. No two employees, even those doing the exact same job, deserve the same pay and benefits! Pay and benefits are determined by each individual's productivity. A company pays an employee based upon the quantity and quality of the product or service that employee produces. No two employees produce exactly the same quantity and quality of work, and therefore each and every employee should be compensated uniquely.

But Unions are Communist because they seek equal compensation for workers regardless of individual productivity. Therefore Unions are detrimental to both the individual worker and the company, and therefore must not be permitted to operate in the United States of America where we practice free-market Capitalism—Capitalism means each individual person and company is compensated based solely upon productivity.

The first *Common Sense* solution to getting America's economy back on the road to prosperity is to get rid of Communist Unions and let the free-market work and determine pay and benefits. The company which offers the best pay and benefits will attract the best workers; of course, such companies will require a higher level of employee skill. And the less skilled workers will have to settle for the lower paying jobs, but that's as it should be. We acknowledge that all men are created equal, but not all men shall attain equal success in life—that part is up to you. It's like Benjamin Franklin said:

*The U.S. Constitution doesn't guarantee happiness, only the pursuit of it. You have to catch up with it yourself.*

If I was an employer, and some of my employees went on strike, I'd fire their asses immediately, and hire new employees who had the best interests of the company's bottom line in mind; that's an employee that will go far in a company! And if I'm not offering enough pay and benefits to attract good employees, then my company will suck and probably not be in business very long. But I'll be damned if some Union is going to dictate to me what pay and benefits I offer my employees.

You see, the free market will take care of making sure employees prosper and companies prosper.

But Communism, in the form of Employee Unions, has crept into Corporate America and is destroying companies and our economy.

Let me give you a real world example from my personal experience. Recently my teenage son's car, which he bought from his Grandmother, needed a new battery. His Grandmother had purchased the battery only about one-year prior from a large nationwide department store chain which also has an auto center and the battery was still under warranty. So my son and I went to the auto center where the original battery had been purchased. When we walked in there was only one other client sitting in the waiting room, and the clerk behind the counter told us there was only one customer ahead of us and our wait would probably be about one-hour. I grumbled a little bit under my breath thinking to myself, how long does it take to replace a battery, five minutes?, and we've got to wait an hour! But I said OK, and my son and I proceeded to take our seats in the waiting area. I called my wife and told her, "Looks like we're going to be stuck down here for about an hour, I'll call you when we're on our way home to see what you'd like us to pick up for dinner." Over the next hour, two more clients came in and took their seats with us in the waiting area. After an hour-and-a-half, I went up to the desk to ask how much longer it would be (my son and I were beginning to get pretty hungry, seeing it was about 7:30 p.m. by now), and the clerk, a different one than when we came in, told me they hadn't gotten to it yet, but should pretty soon. I returned to the waiting area and asked the young lady who had been there before my son and I what she was having done, to which she replied that she had purchased a set of four tires there recently and one of them had gone flat, so she was there to have it repaired if possible and if not, then replaced. I asked her how long she had now been waiting, to which she replied, three-and-a-half-hours! I said, three-and-a-half-hours?! Yep, she said.

To make a very long story short, my son and I finally walked out of that business establishment almost 4-hours later at almost 10:00 at night; frustrated, furious and starving to death! Oh, and the girl with the flat tire was still there! And so were the other two customers who came in behind us.

It's obvious that this national chain store was running a Communist organization where employees were paid a guaranteed salary regardless of productivity. Whereas, if those employees were being paid on a commission basis, a percentage of each job completed successfully—pay for productivity, they would have had us out of there in 15-minutes! And the gal with the flat tire in no more than 30-minutes.

Contrast that experience with that which I've had with a company that specializes in selling tires, called Discount Tires. When you enter any of their locations, you are met by friendly, efficient "tire sales reps" who are there to sell you a set of tires and get you in and out of there as quickly as possible, usually in about one-hour. It is obvious to even the casual observer that these sales reps are earning their pay on a commission basis and therefore have a vested, personal interest in selling and servicing as many clients as possible in a day's time—it's apparent that these employees are compensated based on performance. I wouldn't be surprised if the company offers monthly bonuses at each location to the top sales rep that month. Not only is such a free-market system of compensation based on productivity a better system for the employee, but it is also much better for the customer. And I guarantee it is better for the company's bottom line.

But what about the guys in the bays installing the tires, they don't have the opportunity to participate in the sales commission program. But they can still be rewarded based upon productivity by compensating them based on the number of tires installed each day/week. But you might say, Wouldn't that lead to the installer rushing through the job and perhaps sacrificing quality for quantity? That is where management and supervision come into play. You employ supervisors who know the business and have perhaps worked their way up the ranks, having done the job they are now supervising, and you compensate them at a guaranteed rate that is higher than that of the installers, and entrust them with quality control. But, should the guys installing the tires make as much as the guys selling the tires and dealing with the customers? Heck no! The skills are different; Installing tires may be a little more demanding physically, but it doesn't require a whole lot of intelligence and very little personality or "people skills." Whereas selling and servicing customers requires a high level of "people skills" and product knowledge; so naturally the sales person earns more than the installer because his skills are more valuable! And one sales person will earn more than another because he is better. That's the real world baby! Don't like what you are earning? Then improve your skills and thereby become more valuable!

There are many great companies in America which utilize these free-market employee compensation practices, and these are usually the companies that not only survive, but thrive. I encourage U.S. companies who are practicing Communist-style compensation programs—Union influenced guaranteed pay and benefits regardless of productivity, to reconsider their ways and kick the damned Communist Unions out of their workplace! . And employees, please realize that a free-market style compensation package affords you the greatest opportunity for experiencing the highest compensation possible in your companies industry. Free-Market Capitalism is good for everybody. Communism is good for nobody.

Capitalism creates competition, and competition is good for the consumer. But competition also means that in business you are going to have winners and losers, just like in competitive sports. If for example, GM wants to go the way of Unions and a Communist business model, the reality is that they are going to get trounced by their non-Union Capitalist modeled competitors, which is exactly what happened. So let the dumb, Communist bastards fail. The only reason President Barack Obama bailed out GM, firing it's CEO, giving the shaft to GM's stock and bond holders, was as a pay-off to the Unions for supporting his Presidential campaign—talk about corruption!

Ford Motor Company, on the other hand, who refused to take a penny of government bailout money, is doing quite well on their own. That's the American way—competition creates winners and losers.

But what about those poor GM workers who would have lost their jobs and pensions; it was their own fault for embracing a Communist model of compensation; when you do that, expect to lose in the long run. Wake up America! Communism doesn't work! Never has and never will! If you still don't understand why Communism doesn't work, think of it this way:

### Why Communism Doesn't Work!

You have a 6th-grade classroom of 25 students which for the first semester operated under the standard grading system of each student receiving an A, B, C, D or F on each test and assignment based solely upon each student's personal performance. Then the Teacher announces that for the second semester the class will switch to a Communist grading system in which all the individual grades will be averaged and distributed equally to each student; in other words, we're going to *spread the grades around because that will be good for everybody!* Like Carl Marx said, *From each according to his ability, to each according to his need.* Oh, I forgot to mention the Teacher's name is Barack Obama!

The first test is given under the new "Communist" grading system and the 5 students who work and study the hardest got their usual A; the next 5 that also worked and studied hard got their usual B; then the next 5 got their usual C; then the 5 who don't really apply themselves like they should got their usual D; and finally the 5 flunkies got their usual F. But since the grades were distributed equally in Communist fashion to everyone, all 25 students received a C. The 5 who actually got an F and the 5 who actually got a D were thrilled! The 5 who actually got a C still got a C, so no big deal. But the 5 who were the most productive and actually earned A's and the 5 who actually earned B's were greatly disappointed and realized they had been robbed of their achievements. They reasoned, "Why should the 5 flunkies who don't study and work as hard as me get the same grade as me!" So when the next test came around, the A & B groups realized it wasn't worth them working and studying so hard because what they earned was just going to be taken from them and given to someone who didn't work for it; so they put in less effort and got lower grades. This of course brought the entire class's grade down to a D; so now the C students were mad. And on the next test even the C students didn't put in as much effort; and eventually the entire class were all F'd! Now do you understand why Communism never works!

Listen to the words of a modern American patriot, one of my favorite pastors, Adrian Pierce Rogers, born September 12, 1931, and who went on to his reward on November 15, 2005, who while he lived on Earth pastored a great Church, touched multiplied millions through his television ministry and served as three-term president of the Southern Baptist Convention (1979-1980 and 1986-1988), as he explains the economic peril of redistribution of tax dollars:

*You cannot legislate the poor into prosperity by legislating the wealthy out of prosperity. What one person receives without working for, another person must work for without receiving. The government cannot give to anybody anything that the government does not first take from somebody else. When half of the people get the idea that they do not have to work because the other half is going to take care of them, and when the other half gets the idea that it does no good to work because somebody else is going to get what they work for, that my dear friend, is the beginning of the end of any nation. You cannot multiply wealth by dividing it.*—Adrian Pierce Rogers

## *God is a Capitalist, Not a Communist!*

Some, like Michael Moron, Oh, I'm sorry I spelled that wrong, I mean Michael Moore, have stated publically that Communistic-style healthcare and re-distributing of wealth to help the poor is the "Christian" thing to do! Nothing could be farther from the truth! God is a Capitalist, not a Communist! God expects each individual and each family to stand on their own two feet, supply their own financial needs, and not look to the Church, let alone the government, for financial assistance. Let me prove it to you.

**2 Thessalonians 3:10**

*For even when we were with you, we commanded you this: If anyone will not work, neither shall he eat.*

Wow! Are you telling me that the New Testament commands the Church not to offer charity to anyone who will not work? Yes, that is exactly what God says! The "charity" of the Church is limited in Scripture to a very small, select group, as I will show you.

I would venture to say that you are a little shocked right now. I bet you thought that God was all about helping the poor, and therefore you thought that the Christian Church was supposed to be a charitable organization dedicated to helping the "poor." Not true, not true at all. If that's what you believed, then your Biblical "Theology" is all wrong! It is true that the concept of helping the poor is mentioned a few times in the Old and New Testaments of the Holy Bible, but even a shallow examination of the subject makes it immediately clear, as in our passage above, that God does not want His Church helping lazy, unproductive people, but rather to command such to become employed, productive members contributing to the Church and society as a whole. To take money from one person who worked for it and give it to another person who did not work for it is Communism! And God is not a Communist, but a Capitalist who commands the Church to let anybody who will not work starve to death. Not my words, His.

The one verse above is sufficient and should be enough to convince you that God is a Capitalist, not a Communist; but I will further prove to you that God is a Capitalist, not a Communist! In fact, I'll prove to you that the Christian Church does not have a mandate nor responsibility to help anyone financially except Orphans, a very select group of Widows, and the Ministers of the Church; but that's it! And, if it is not the mandate nor God-given responsibility of the Church to help those who won't help themselves, then how much less is it the government's responsibility to do so!

Some people *"twist"* the Scriptures (see Psalm 56:5; 2 Peter 3:16) in an attempt to claim that not only does the Christian Church have a moral obligation to care for the "poor," but so does the government. Such people as Michael Moore, who is a Catholic, and possibly partially due to the Catholic Churches emphasis on a "Social Gospel" of care for the poor, even go so far as to imply that Socialist/Communist principles are taught by the Holy Bible and are therefore "Christian." Nothing could be farther from Biblical truth!

There are two main passages in the New Testament that people like Michael Moore and others use, and indeed *"twist,"* in an attempt to substantiate their claims. These passages are found in the Book of Acts and Communists like Michael Moore who try to use these texts err greatly in their interpretation by what I call the "common" misconception:

**Acts 2:44-45**
*[44]Now all who believed were together, and had all things in common, [45]and sold their possessions and goods, and divided them among all, as anyone had need.*

**Acts 4:32-35**
*[32]Now the multitude of those who believed were of one heart and one soul; neither did anyone say that any of the things he possessed was his own, but they had all things in common....[34]Nor was there anyone among them who lacked; for all who were possessors of lands or houses sold them, and brought the proceeds of the things that were sold, [35]and laid them at the apostles' feet; and they distributed to each as anyone had need.*

At first glance, one might say, Boy that sounds like Karl Marx to me: *"From each according to his ability, to each according to his need."* But, at first glance, using that same standard of Biblical interpretation, you would also have to deduce, based on the phrases: *"sold their possessions and goods,"* (2:45) and, *"all who were possessors of lands or houses sold them"* (4:34), that all these members of the Jerusalem Church became homeless people, sleeping on the sidewalks, without a possession or penny to their name, depending on the Apostles to feed and clothe them; which of course is absurd and idiotic. *Common Sense* tells us that such an interpretation is obviously not the proper understanding of what these verses mean! And, just as it is absurd to say that the Church at Jerusalem became a Church of thousands of homeless, indigent people, it is equally as absurd to claim that these early Christians were "Communists." In fact, these verses prove just the opposite! These verses prove that the early Christians were wealthy Capitalists!

Whenever interpreting Holy Scripture, you must always look at the context, both the immediate context of the verses surrounding the passage, and also at the larger context of what the entire Bible says on any given subject. And you must also bring with you to the Word of God a healthy dose of *Common Sense!*

These verses and their surrounding passages show a community of Jewish Believers in Jesus Christ, living in and around Jerusalem, who obviously didn't sell the home they and their families were living in and move out onto the sidewalk, but who rather, due to the Free-Market Capitalistic economic system God had given them thousands of years prior, were so wealthy and prosperous that many of them owned additional houses and lands—what today we would call investment or income properties. And these Jewish Believers in Jesus the Messiah (Christ is the Greek equivalent of the Hebrew Messiah) were so full of excitement to support their Church and its ministers that: *"all who were possessors of lands or houses sold them, and brought the proceeds of the things that were sold,* <sup>35</sup> *and laid them at the apostles' feet"* (4:34-35). Think about that for a minute. Now, that's revival! Pastors all across America spend much of their time playing dentists—pulling teeth, trying to get God's people to obey His Old and New Testament principle of Tithing—returning to God 10% of what He has given you (your income). But, the passages above describe the early Jerusalem Jewish-Christian Church as having such grace upon it that many of its members would sell extra investment properties they owned, and instead of giving the required 10% of the profit from the sale, they brought 100% of the sale price and gave it to their Church! They didn't have checks in those days, so they would bring the money in the form of silver or gold coins. In today's economy, we're talking an average of probably $250,000 per sale, and these Jewish Christian's walked into the Church service and dumped a quarter-of-a-million dollars on the floor! I'll say it again, now that's revival! (Read specific accounts in Acts 4:36—5:11).

The point here should be obvious; these early Jewish-Christians were self-sufficient, smart and hardworking individuals, i.e., Free-Market Capitalists, who obviously did not suddenly become poor homeless Communists dependent upon the Church for their daily bread. In fact, a further examination of Acts reveals who the "needy" people were. Acts chapter 6 reveals that there was only one group of people whom the Jerusalem Church showed charity toward and helped by providing food, it was the widows—those elderly women whose husbands had died and were now alone and depending on God to take care of them.

**Acts 6:1 (NIV)**

*In those days when the number of disciples was increasing, the Grecian Jews among them complained against the Hebraic Jews because their widows were being overlooked in the daily distribution of food.*

So we see that the only "charitable ministry" of the Jerusalem Church was to widows. But the New Testament makes it plain that even that work of charity must be very selective in whom it helps. The Apostle Paul delineates clear criteria widows must meet in order to receive financial assistance from the Church:

**1 Timothy 5:3-18 (NIV)**

*[3]Give proper recognition to those widows who are really in need. [4]But if a widow has children or grandchildren, these should learn first of all to put their religion into practice by caring for their own family and so repaying their parents and grandparents, for this is pleasing to God. [5]The widow who is really in need and left all alone puts her hope in God and continues night and day to pray and to ask God for help....[8]If anyone does not provide for his relatives, and especially for his immediate family, he has denied the faith and is worse than an unbeliever. [9]No widow may be put on the list of widows unless she is over sixty, has been faithful to her husband, [10]and is well known for her good deeds, such as bringing up children, showing hospitality, washing the feet of the saints, helping those in trouble and devoting herself to all kinds of good deeds. [11]As for younger widows, do not put them on such a list. For when their sensual desires overcome their dedication to Christ, they want to marry....[13]Besides, they get into the habit of being idle and going about from house to house. And not only do they become idlers, but also gossips and busybodies, saying things they ought not to. [14]So I counsel younger widows to marry, to have children, to manage their homes and to give the enemy no opportunity for slander....[16]If any woman who is a believer has widows in her family, she should help them and not let the church be burdened with them, so that the church can help those widows who are really in need.*

*[17]The elders who direct the affairs of the church well are worthy of double honor, especially those whose work is preaching and teaching. [18]For the Scripture says, "Do not muzzle the ox while it is treading out the grain," and "The worker deserves his wages."*

So you see clearly that The Holy Bible places strict restrictions on the Church's charitable ministry even to these widows ordained as a legitimate group to which to give charity. In fact, what or whom does the above passage state should be society's "social security net?"—the family—Not the Church! And if it's not God's Church's role and responsibility to be society's social security net, then how much less is it the government's role or responsibility!

Other than the very limited group of widows which the Church should help, there are just two other groups that the Holy Bible states are the Church's responsibility to provide for, and these are the minister's of the Church and orphans.

Note verses 17-18, in the passage above: *"[17]The elders who direct the affairs of the church well are worthy of double honor, especially those whose work is preaching and teaching. [18]For the Scripture says, "Do not muzzle the ox while it is treading out the grain," and "The worker deserves his wages."*

This passage is telling the Church to take very good care of its minister's financially, for they are what this passage refers to as being: *"worthy of double honor."* This principle of the Church providing goodly compensation to its ministers is well established in both the Old and New Testaments; the following passage sums it up well:

### 1 Corinthians 9:13-14 (NIV)

*[13]Don't you know that those who work in the temple get their food from the temple, and those who serve at the altar share in what is offered on the altar?* [referring to the Old Testament Priests & Levites].

*[14]In the same way, the Lord has commanded that those who preach the gospel should receive their living from the gospel* [referring to the New Testament Apostles, Prophets, Evangelists, Pastors & Teachers].

The third and final group of people that the Church is supposed to show charity toward is orphans. There are not any examples in the New Testament of the Jerusalem Church or any of the other Churches throughout the world establishing orphanages or having a particular ministry to orphans, which is probably because, in most cases, children who lose their parents are taken in by their immediate relatives; again, the family being the built-in "social security net" of society. But in those rare cases where children are left parentless and there are no other relatives left alive, then God desires His Church to look after them. James, the Senior Pastor of the Jerusalem Church and half-brother of the Lord Jesus (same mother, Mary, but different fathers: Jesus' Father was God, and James' father was Joseph) states in his Book:

**James 1:27 (NIV)**

*Religion that God our Father accepts as pure and faultless is this: to look after orphans and widows in their distress and to keep oneself from being polluted by the world.*

Note again, that the only two groups stated to be the Church's objects of charity are the orphans and widows—those who are unable to provide for themselves. All other men and women are commanded to work and provide for themselves.

So, we could rightly amplify our two passages from Acts at the beginning of this discussion to read as follows:

**Acts 2:44-45**

*⁴⁴Now all who believed were together, and had all things in common, ⁴⁵and sold their possessions and goods, and divided them among all (of the Ministers, widows and orphans) , as anyone had need.*

**Acts 4:32-35**

*³²Now the multitude of those who believed were of one heart and one soul; neither did anyone say that any of the things he possessed was his own, but they had all things in common....³⁴Nor was there anyone (of the Ministers, orphans or widows) among them who lacked; for all who were possessors of lands or houses sold them, and brought the proceeds of the things that were sold, ³⁵and laid them at the apostles' feet; and they distributed to each (of the Ministers, orphans and widows) as anyone had need.*

That is the proper understanding of these two passages from Acts. The early Jewish Christians at the Jerusalem Church were not Communists, but prosperous business-owning Free-Market Capitalists, who didn't just Tithe/give 10% of their income, but were so full of the love of God and the grace of God that, as it is testified of them: *"neither did anyone say that any of the things he possessed was his own;"* in other words, they were so generous with their wealth to the point of even selling additional homes and properties they owned, worth hundreds of thousands of dollars in comparison to today's economy, and donating the proceeds to their local Church.

But we must ask and answer the question, where did these Jewish Christians come by such wealth and abundance of private property ownership? God had taught them the principles of private ownership of property, individual responsibility and free-enterprise thousands of years earlier when God established a nation on Earth called Israel.

You see, another mistake people like Michael Moore and others make with reference to the passages in Acts above, is not only misinterpreting their meaning with regard to the Jerusalem Church, but then these Bible-twisters imply that government also should act like the Church with regard to charity. But if you want to see how God Himself would establish an economic system within a nation, just look at the Nation of Israel, and there you will immediately discover that God is a private property ownership, personal responsibility promoting Free-Market Capitalist, not a *"spread the wealth around...take from the rich and give to the poor"* Communist!

## *God's Economic System He Established For The Nation Of Israel!*

### Numbers 33:54 (NKJV)
[54] *And you shall divide the land by lot as an inheritance among your families; to the larger you shall give a larger inheritance, and to the smaller you shall give a smaller inheritance; there everyone's inheritance shall be whatever falls to him by lot. You shall inherit according to the tribes of your fathers.*

Each family in Israel received private ownership of property and thereon was responsible for producing & providing for themselves, plus trade freely for the purpose of profit. There was no "communal living." Both men and women worked hard and were expected to be industrious entrepreneurs. Look at this Old Testament example of a Jewish woman:

**Proverbs 31:16-18, 24, 25 (NIV)**
[16]*She considers a field and <u>buys it</u>; out of her <u>earnings</u> she plants a vineyard.*
[17]*She sets about her <u>work vigorously</u>; her arms are strong for her tasks.*
[18]*She sees that her <u>trading is profitable</u>, and her lamp does not go out at night.*
[24]*She makes linen garments and <u>sells them</u>, and supplies the merchants with sashes.*
[25]*She is clothed with strength and dignity; she can laugh at the days to come.*

## God, In Whose Image You Are Made, Expects You To Work & Provide For Yourself!

So we see from both the Old and New Testaments that God's economic system is one of hard work, entrepreneurialism and self-reliance. God, our Creator, designed each of us and expects each of us to work and thereby supply our own financial needs and wants.

It's not the Church's responsibility to provide assistance to any person except the Church's Ministers, orphans and a very limited select group of widows.

In fact, let me shock you even further: The Church is not only not supposed to help those who "will not work," but the New Testament Church didn't even offer charity to the physically disabled who could not work!

**Acts 3:1-8**
[1]*Now Peter and John went up together to the temple at the hour of prayer, the ninth hour.* [2]*And a certain man lame from his mother's womb was carried, whom they laid daily at the gate of the temple which is called Beautiful, to ask alms from those who entered the temple;* [3]*who, seeing Peter and John about to go into the temple, asked for alms.* [4]*And fixing his eyes on him, with John, Peter said, "Look at us."* [5]*So he gave them his attention, expecting to receive something from them.* [6]*Then Peter said, "Silver and gold I do not have, but what I do have I give you: In the name of*

*Jesus Christ of Nazareth, rise up and walk." [7]And he took him by the right hand and lifted him up, and immediately his feet and ankle bones received strength. [8]So he, leaping up, stood and walked and entered the temple with them—walking, leaping, and praising God.*

"Alms" are charitable gifts. The Apostle's Peter and John, the two main leaders of the First-Century Christian Church, did not have as part of the Church's ministry financial assistance even to the physically disabled! Wow, I bet that's a shocking revelation to most of you! Instead, they healed him in the name of the Lord Jesus Christ and, in essence, told him, "Praise God my brother, now you don't have to beg anymore, now you can go and work and support yourself and your family!"

And if it is not the Church's responsibility to provide financial assistance to the unemployed, then it certainly is not the government's responsibility to assist anyone, except perhaps orphans and widows who are truly in need.

I opened this section by quoting 2 Thessalonians 3:10, which reveals God's command for all Mankind to work and those who don't are not to receive any help from His Church; let me quote this passage here again in closing with the context of the surrounding verses:

## 2 Thessalonians 3:8-12

[8]*nor did we eat anyone's bread free of charge, but worked with labor and toil night and day, that we might not be a burden to any of you,*
[9]*not because we do not have authority, but to make ourselves an example of how you should follow us.*
[10]*For even when we were with you, we commanded you this: If anyone will not work, neither shall he eat.*
[11]*For we hear that there are some who walk among you in a disorderly manner, not working at all, but are busybodies [such as the young widows he referred to in 1 Tim. 5:13 above].*
[12]*Now those who are such we command and exhort through our Lord Jesus Christ that they work in quietness and eat their own bread.*

Therefore, in light of the above command from God, any Church, business or government who gives food or financial assistance to any person who is not working, does so in direct violation of God's command.

If the Church is not supposed to help the unemployed, how much less is it the government's responsibility! That means unemployment compensation violates God's command; welfare checks violate God's command; food stamps violate God's command; giving somebody a check that no longer works in the form of a pension check violates God's command. Speaking of pensions, what genius came up with that moronic business-killing, economy-killing concept?

## The Pension Problem!

The problem with pensions is that you cannot pay someone who is not working and producing income for their employer; that's just *Common Sense!* Today, every city in America, every State and Federal Agency, and many corporations in America are on the verge of bankruptcy primarily because of this one thing, this cancer that is eating away at their financial well-being—pensions!

"Put in your 20 years and receive a pension check for the rest of your life!" Are you nuts? Are you out of your mind? Whether it's a government agency like the U.S. Military or the local Fire Department, or a private corporation offering benefits to its employees, you cannot continue to pay a person who no longer produces a product or provides a service for you! That's *Common Sense!* The employees of a business must produce a product or service that generates income for that business in order for that business to have funds available from which to compensate those employees; no business will stay in business for very long if it pays people who do not generate income for that business. As for government agencies, my tax dollars may only be used to pay for services that directly benefit me, like the active-duty members of the military who are defending me against all enemies foreign and domestic or the local fireman who responds to my 911 call. A former government employee who no longer provides me with a service is not entitled to receive one penny from me!

"But what about people's retirement plans?" Save a portion of your income during your working years toward your retirement years. And if a corporation or even a government agency wants to "match" a certain percentage of every dollar you save for retirement, I have no problem with that, that's perfectly legal and a legitimate enticement by an employer. But pensions pay people out of newly generated income which should go toward active employees, but instead gets robbed from the active employees and diverted to dead-beat, non-productive former employees who are sitting at home on their ass!

If America wants to avoid total economic collapse, pensions must go! Both the public and private sectors of our economy cannot, I repeat cannot, continue to pay people who are non-productive. Folks, that's just *Common Sense!*

Now it's time to get the government out of our business!

## Government Has No Business Regulating Our Business!

*—with all these blessings [from God and the Christian religion], what more is necessary to make us a happy and a prosperous people? Still one thing more, fellow-citizens—a wise and frugal Government, which shall restrain men from injuring one another, <u>shall leave them otherwise free to regulate their own pursuits of industry and improvement</u>, and shall not take from the mouth of labor the bread it has earned. This is the sum of good government.*—President Thomas Jefferson, Inaugural Address, March 4, 1801.

The second *Common Sense* economic principle or restraint upon government, outlined by Thomas Jefferson is that neither Federal nor State Government has the right to regulate private industry. That's right, no government regulation of business!

"But what about the "Commerce Claus" of the Constitution?" you may ask, "I thought it gave government the right to regulate commerce?" Well, let's take a quick look at that clause; it is found in Article I, Section 8, Clause 3, of the Constitution; but to get the "context," let's look at Clauses 1—8:

*Article I, Sect. 8. The Congress shall have power To lay and collect taxes, duties, imposts and excises, to pay the debts and provide for the common defence and general welfare of the United States; but all duties; imposts and excises, shall be uniform throughout the United States;*

*To borrow money on the credit of the United States;*

*To regulate commerce with foreign nations, and among the several States, and with the Indian tribes;*

*To establish an uniform rule of naturalization, and uniform laws on the subject of bankruptcies, throughout the United States;*

*To coin money, regulate the value thereof, and of foreign coin, and fix the standard of weights and measures;*

*To provide for the punishment of counterfeiting the securities and current coin of the United States;*

*To establish post-offices and post-roads;*

*To promote the progress of science and useful arts, by securing for limited times to authors and inventors the exclusive right to their respective writings and discoveries;*

So, the Commerce Clause states that The Congress shall have power *To regulate commerce with foreign nations, and among the several States, and with the Indian tribes;*

Taking the Commerce Clause in its context, it is clear that, *"among the several [separate] States"* is merely referring to Congress having the power to regulate "interstate" commerce, for the purpose of promoting industry and general prosperity by providing that, *"taxes, duties, imposts and excises...coin money [and] the value thereof...and fix the standard of weights and measures... To establish post-offices and post-roads...* <u>*shall be uniform throughout the United States.*</u> *"*

Congress has the responsibility to establish uniformity in the vehicles of trade and commerce across State lines. In other words, for the mutual prosperity and ease of commerce for all, Congress must ensure that one State cannot use a different currency or standard of weights and measures than another State, or different highway or postal system than other Sates. You don't want to be driving on the Right-side of the road in one State and upon crossing into another state suddenly discover that State requires drivers to drive European-style on the Left-side of the highway! You don't want to offer your apples for sale at $1.29 per pound, with a pound equaling 16-ounces, to discover that upon shipping those apples across State lines that State considers a pound to equal 20-ounces! We now take the uniformity of currency, weights and measures, and highway traffic rules for granted; but this uniformity of regulation of trade and commerce was established early in America's history in accordance with the Commerce Clause of the Constitution in order to ensure uniformity in interstate trade for the purpose of promoting prosperity and ease of doing business throughout the United States.

But nowhere does the Commerce Clause give government the right to stick its nose in our private business! Government has no right to try to tell us how to run our businesses! Let me state this more plainly: The government does not have Constitutional authority to dictate any rules or regulations regarding the operation of any business in America! Period! Proof of this is simply in the fact that the Constitution, including the "Commerce Clause," had been written in 1787 and ratified by the States in 1788, and in full effect as the Law of the Land as of 1789—12-years prior to President Thomas Jefferson declaring in his Inaugural Address:

*—with all these blessings [from God and the Christian religion], what more is necessary to make us a happy and a prosperous people? Still one thing more, fellow-citizens—a wise and frugal Government, which shall restrain men from injuring one another, <u>shall leave them otherwise free to regulate their own pursuits of industry and improvement</u>, and shall not take from the mouth of labor the bread it has earned. This is the sum of good government.*—President Thomas Jefferson, Inaugural Address, March 4, 1801.

With full mental ascent and agreement with what he and the other Founding Fathers had engineered as Constitutional restraint's upon the government's interference in the conducting of business among America's citizen's, President Thomas Jefferson declares:

*—a wise and frugal Government... <u>shall leave them otherwise free to regulate their own pursuits of industry and improvement</u>...This is the sum of good government.*

Did you get that? The proper interpretation of government's Constitutional role regarding business is to: *"leave them <u>free</u> to <u>regulate their own pursuits</u> of industry and improvement!* If I might rephrase President Thomas Jefferson's declaration: *Government, leave business ALONE to do as they see fit!*

In other words, the government does not have the right to impose rules and regulations upon how we operate our businesses!

Let me be specific: The government DOES NOT HAVE THE RIGHT to set a National Minimum Wage and thereby dictate to employers how much to pay their employees! If I want to open my second hotdog stand and offer my entry level 16-year-old teenage employees—who still live at home and have very limited financial responsibilities, but who need a "first job" to get job experience—a wage of $3.00 per hour, I have the right to do so; it's my business and I have the right to operate my business as I see fit! Now, granted, if another hotdog stand opens across the street from mine and pays its entry level employees $9.00 per hour, guess what, NO ONE WILL WORK FOR ME! And since I'm busy working at my first location, I'll have to close that second hotdog stand; I'll be out of business because I was not paying my employees enough. The Free Market ALWAYS works! In fact, the Free Market is toughest on the business owner/employer because of competition—competition to gain the best employees and competition to gain the most customers—thus Free-Market Enterprise, that is free from government regulation, always benefits the consumer and the employee first before the owner/employer will realize any benefit! Those Enterprises who don't benefit their customers and employees won't stay in business very long.

Did you know that there are government imposed rules against discrimination by businesses regarding their hiring practices? There are so-called "Civil Rights" laws that forbid discrimination based upon race, religion, gender or age. Now, if the government wants to impose upon itself such rules forbidding discrimination in the hiring of government employees, for example, in the military, it has the right to do so—but the government damn sure doesn't have the right to impose rules of non-discrimination in the hiring practices of private businesses!

The ONLY purview government has is to *"restrain men from injuring one another."* Come on folks, it's just *Common Sense* that a business cannot murder you or assault you or even defraud you in the operation of its course of business; and there are plenty of *Common Sense* laws on the books against murder, rape, assault and fraud. But other than protecting the public from the violent assault of another person, the government does not have the right to impose even one line of regulation against business! What we need is to get government regulation out of our business! Government has no business regulating our business!

Let me put it this way: Government's business is to protect us from all enemies foreign and domestic—that means the government's responsibility is to protect my family and I from physical harm by another individual; but it does not mean it's the government's job to protect me from my own stupidity in my business dealings with others. Whether or not I make a good investment or an intelligent choice when purchasing a product or service is my responsibility, and the government needs to stay out of my business!

New York City Mayor Michael Bloomberg is proposing a regulation that forbids any business in New York City from selling a soft drink larger than 16-ounces. Mayor Bloomberg does not have the right to impose any rules on business regarding products and pricing whatsoever, and I hope the restaurants in NYC will tell that Muslim-loving traitor to shove his soft drink rule up his A.-double-S. In fact, I call upon all New York City restaurants to announce a new sized soft drink that is 128-ounces called the "Patriot Punch!" But Mayor Bloomberg is whining, "That's too much sugar for our people!" Hey Bozo Bloomberg, pop quiz for you: which contains more sugar: One 128-ounce Patriot Punch or 10 16-ounce other soft drinks? You see, Bozo, if I want to drink 10 16-ounce soft drinks, I have the right to do so! This is America, the Land of the Free and the Home of the Brave—and I'll be damned if you or any other government employee will tell me how to live my life! "But if you get sick from all that sugar and have to go to the hospital, then we all end up paying for it!" Bull dung! That's the stupidest argument I've ever heard! If I get sick and go to the hospital, I'm the one who gets the Bill, not you or anyone else—we'll discuss this more in a minute below.

Let's address those "Anti-Discrimination" rules I mentioned earlier. Now I'm going to make some controversial statements here, but why stop now. As mentioned above, Laws have been placed on the books prohibiting "discrimination" in hiring based upon religion, race, gender and age. Hey, if the government wants to impose upon itself such restrictions in the hiring of government employees, have at it. But the government does not have the right to tell me as a business owner, as an employer that I cannot discriminate when hiring!

First of all, let's get something straight, discrimination is a good thing, not a bad thing! Everybody in America discriminates every single day of their lives, and if we didn't we would be idiots doomed to lives of despair and disaster! When you are looking for a mate to fall in love with, marry and build a family with, we would probably all be miserable—well, maybe some would have ended up better off, but for the most part—if we just grabbed the first person that walked by and married them—of course we didn't do that. We "discriminated" between several or many members of the opposite sex until we found the one we felt was best suited to us. Of course, it came as a real shock when we approached her and she discriminated against us and told us to get lost. But we kept trying until she gave in and went out with us for the first time, and then we of course won her over with our amazing wit and charm. I'm digressing.

I could go on with examples of how we all discriminate every day in the choice of food we are going to eat and in the clothes we are going to wear and in the job we decide to take or career we decide to enter or car we wish to drive and friends we choose to hang with and co-workers we choose to associate with, etc. etc.

But the real point I'm trying to make here is with regard to the government telling any business in America who it can and cannot hire.

For example, if I want to open a restaurant and call it Black Bart's and hire only black men, who are between the ages of 20 and 30,and who are buff because they work out at a gym on a regular basis, I have the right to do so. Of course this means I will be discriminating against any applicants who are White, Hispanic, Asian or any other race than Black; I will be discriminating against all female applicants, and regardless of race I will be discriminating against all applicants under 20 and over 30 years of age. But in a free society, I have the right to do so, and damn it the government doesn't have the right to tell me I cannot! In fact, the very success of my business depends on me being discriminating in my hiring. If I want to open a restaurant and call it Blondie's, and my business model calls for all the servers to be 6-ft. tall blondes between the ages of 21 to 29, then as an employer I will be practicing racial, gender and age discrimination when hiring; but that's my right to do so! Even if my business model does not depend specifically upon being very discriminate in the hiring of my employees, I still have the right as the owner of the business to discriminate in my hiring practices based upon race, religion, gender and age. For example, if I open any kind of business in the "Hood," in a predominately Black neighborhood, I'll be damned if I'm going to hire some White-ass honky! No way Jose! That's right, I'm not hiring any Latinos either, nor Asians; I'm hiring only Black brothers and sisters from the Hood! It's my business and the government doesn't have the right to tell me who I can and cannot hire! Again folks, this is *Common Sense!* Any laws on the books that ban discrimination in the private sector, which are thereby contrary to the basic principles of free-market Capitalism, are simply idiotic, immoral, illegal and unconstitutional and must immediately be eliminated!

All government regulations now impeding private enterprise from operating as they see fit must immediately be struck down and removed from the books, never again to resurrect their ugly, anti-American anti-Free Enterprise, head! Government has no business regulating our business!

Now let us move on to the need for a new Federal Tax system.

## A New Flat, Fair 10% Federal Tax System Based Upon Spending, Not Earning!

The third *Common Sense* economic principle or restraint upon government, outlined by Thomas Jefferson is that neither Federal nor State Government should tax our income!

—*with all these blessings [from God and the Christian religion], what more is necessary to make us a happy and a prosperous people? Still one thing more, fellow-citizens—a wise and frugal Government, which shall restrain men from injuring one another, shall leave them otherwise free to regulate their own pursuits of industry and improvement, <u>and shall not take from the mouth of labor the bread it has earned</u>. This is the sum of good government.*—President Thomas Jefferson, Inaugural Address, March 4, 1801.

America's Founding Fathers did not believe in Federal or State Income Tax! That is why the United States did not have any Federal "income tax" until 1913, when the damned Democratic Party under President Woodrow Wilson invented the "income tax!"

## *All Democrats Are Damned To Hell & The Democratic Party Shall Cease To Exist After America Reads This Book!*

Do you remember why the United States of America was born? The American Revolution which followed our Declaration of Independence on July 4, 1776, was at its heart a REVOLUTIONARY REVOLT AGAINST TOO MUCH TAXATION! I know I'm yelling again, but it gets very frustrating when we have such short memories.

WELL IT'S TIME FOR ANOTHER TAX REVOLT! Yes, I'm shouting! IT'S TIME FOR A NEW AMERICAN REVOLUTION AGAINST EXCESSIVE TAXATION BY THE DAMNED DEMOCRATIC PARTY! (Why do I call Democrats "damned?" Because, first of all, Democrats are literally damned to the eternal fires of Hell because of their sinful, God-hating policies such as abortion, physical and economic slavery of Blacks, and promoting of the sin of homosexuality; and second, because this book is the death of the Democratic Party in America—because someone finally had the cojones to speak the truth about the Democratic Party, the Democratic Party is now damned to destruction and shall cease to exist in America, because no decent human being will ever again vote for a damned Democrat!)

## *Every Citizen Must Pay His Fair Equal Share Of Federal Taxes!*

In chapter Two we discussed the God-given Common Sense Role of Government which is first and foremost to defend and protect us from physical harm by others, and second to fund such projects as interstate highways for the betterment of commerce and leisure for our citizenry. This is the purpose of taxes: to fund the administration and implementation of these essential services which fall under the purview of government. Even God in the Holy Bible declares the same:

**Romans 13:6 (NIV)**
*This is also why you pay taxes, for the authorities are God's servants, who give their full time to governing.*

The preceding verses in Romans Chapter 13 speak of government's God-given authority to *"bear the sword,"* meaning military and law enforcement weaponry, for they are *"the ministers of God's wrath, to execute judgment against the evil doer."* In other words, Government's role and responsibility is: To defend and protect America's citizens against all enemies foreign and domestic. We also agree that *Common Sense* requires that government further utilize the revenues it receives for the purpose of providing for the "general welfare" of the citizenry in the sense of providing means of transportation with abundant and well-maintained roadways and air-traffic control, as well as essential emergency services such as local Fire Departments and the like. Our taxes also go toward providing schools for educating our children from Kindergarten through the 12th Grade; though privatizing our school system, creating competition and attaching those tax dollars to each student for them to spend at the school of their choice will dramatically improve our public school education system! The providing of water and sanitation services are also provided by local municipalities, but are services we pay a monthly fee for and are not therefore services paid for by our taxes.

Herein, however, resides two very important principles of taxation—First, every citizen who enjoys the benefits of these government provided protections and services should also pay his fair share of taxes. However today in America we have nearly 50% of our citizenry who pay no Federal Taxes, yet they enjoy the benefits of military defense, interstate highways, air-traffic control, and the like. This is wrong, immoral and an unjust tax system. Why should I pay for the military to protect you—I should not, you should pay your own way. Why should I pay for you to drive on the roads—I should not, you should pay your own way.

Yet President Obama is going around the Country giving speech after speech promoting what he calls the "Buffett Rule," declaring that the wealthy should "pay their fair share of taxes."

Hey President Obama, you moron, the wealthy and upper middle-class are the ONLY ONES paying their fair share of taxes—even more than their fair share! President Obama, since you want Americans to "pay their fair share of taxes," then start demanding that the nearly 50% of American's who pay NO Federal Income Tax begin to "pay their fair share" immediately! President Obama, you lying hypocrite! you know damn well that the top 5% of earners pay 50% of all Federal Income Taxes, and that nearly 50% of all Americans PAY NO FEDERAL INCOME TAX! In other words, 50% of all Americans are not paying their fair share! Not only are those 50% of Americans not paying their fair share, but a large percentage of these free-loaders actually get a check from the IRS to reward their immoral, nation-destroying behavior such as fornication resulting in children being born out of wedlock! President Obama, you are half Black, yet you, in conjunction with your Black-hating Democratic Party have destroyed the Black community, creating a fatherless generation because of your "Have Sex & Get A Check" Federal Tax Policy that rewards and even promotes immorality, damning millions of Black children to a life without a father and one doomed to economic poverty.

Let the 50% of people who are living off of the Taxes paid by the rest of Americans start "paying their fair share!" Until then, get your car off of the roads I'm paying for you free-loader! And get your children out of the schools I'm paying for you free-loader! And don't expect the Fire Department that I'm paying for to show up at your free-loading ass's home when it catches fire! In fact, get your free-loading non-taxpaying ass out of the United States of America where you enjoy the protection of the greatest military force on Earth that I'm paying for!

Therefore, since nearly 50% of Americans are not currently paying any Federal Tax and those who are paying are paying more than their fair share, for President Obama to go around the Country claiming that successful Americans' *"aren't paying their fair share in taxes"* is nothing less than a bald-faced lie! There is only one Title that President Obama has earned and deserves to be recognized by as President, and that Title is "Liar in Chief!"

## President Obama Has Earned Only One Title: Liar in Chief!

I can't think of a single sentence that President Obama has uttered during any of his nauseatingly numerous speeches in which he was not lying to the American people! Everything that man says is a blatant lie!

When Congressman Joe Wilson shouted out during one of Obama's addresses to the Congress, "You Lie!" Congressman Joe Wilson was simply stating the obvious; and he should not have apologized for shouting out the obvious! Shame on you Congressman Joe Wilson for apologizing. The ones who should be apologizing are the other 434 Congress men and women who were too spineless to stand up for the American people!

But I can hear my esteemed colleague Bill O'Reilly say, "But that's disrespecting the Office of the President."

No, Mr. O', it is not; the one who is disrespecting the Office of the President is the one who while holding that esteemed Office has the audacity to blatantly lie to the American people! That man, Barack Hussein Obama, has by his actions forfeited any right to receive respect from the American people.

I'm *Common Sense* & I'm running for Office, elect me to Congress, and the next time any baby-murdering, Muslim-loving Communist President like Obama or even any fellow member of Congress, like Nancy Pelosi or Harry Reid, who is a member of the baby-murdering, Muslim-loving Communism-promoting Democratic Party, ever dares to stand before the Representatives of the American people and open their mouth to utter a single word—for every word a Democrat utters is a damnable lie—I will jump to my feet and shout, "You Liar!" You baby-murdering Muslim-loving Communist Liar!"

No person serving in the Congress, whether in the House of Representatives or the Senate, nor any person serving as President who serves any of these Offices as a member of the Democratic Party, can deny that he or she is a baby-murdering Communist; because to serve as a Democrat you must agree with the Official Platform of the Democratic Party which has as its core the murdering of as many American children in their mother's wombs as possible, especially if those babies are Black, the Democratic Party by its policies is responsible for the murder of 50% of all Black children still in their mother's wombs in America each and every day! All Democrats also believe in the "redistribution of wealth," taking money from those who worked for it and giving it to those who did not! That is Communism pure and simple! And we do not abide Communists in America!

Any American citizen who votes to elect *ANY* Democrat to any Office will have to answer to Almighty God for voting to elect such a murderous, vile, anti-American, anti-Christ person to rule over them!

I hereby serve notice to every Democrat in Washington D.C. and in every State House across America—We The People are coming on Tuesday, November 6, 2012, and every election thereafter, to remove you from Office, not by the power of the bullet, but by the power of the ballot! The 2012 Election shall be the death of the Democratic Party in America! And a new second Party shall arise in its place, a legitimate political Party similar to the Republican Party, that offers legitimate Freedom-loving, Abortion-Clinic-Closing, Muslim-banning, Free-Market "You are Responsible for Your Own Ass" Capitalist Candidates to represent the American people—I propose the name, Patriot Party.

Moving on now in our discussion regarding taxation.

## *Every Dollar Collected By The Government In Taxes Must Be Spent By The Government To Directly Benefit That Taxpayer Who Gave It!*

Just as the first principle of taxation is that all who enjoy the benefits provided by the government must pay their fair share in taxes to the government, the second principle of taxation is a mirror to the first, thusly, that each taxpayers money paid should directly benefit that taxpayer and not another. In other words, all the money I pay in taxes should only be spent on services that directly benefit me. It is robbery to take my tax money and give it to another American to benefit him. Even worse is when the government robs Peter to pay Pedro—Peter referring to a legal American citizen, Pedro referring to an illegal immigrant non-citizen; yet this is taking place at both the Federal and State levels every day across America, and America and her States are broke because of it! This policy of robbing tax dollars from legal citizens and giving them to illegal aliens must stop immediately!

Again, 100% of my tax dollars should be spent only on what directly benefits me the tax payer. To use my tax dollars to the benefit of someone who doesn't pay taxes, even if they are a legal citizen, is robbery, immoral and should be illegal. Such redistribution of tax dollars is "redistribution of wealth" and is Communism not Capitalism, and therefore shall not be tolerated in America!

President Obama's belief that government's role is to *"spread the wealth around"* is not what our Founding Fathers envisioned nor intended, nor is it what We the People of the United States want today! We do well indeed to return to our Founding Fathers *Common Sense* vision for America. Let's see what Founding Father Thomas Jefferson thought about taking tax money from one citizen and giving it to another citizen:

*The democracy will cease to exist when you take away from those who are willing to work and give to those who would not —* Thomas Jefferson

Thomas Jefferson believed that if the government played Robin Hood, taking from the rich (those who have worked and sacrificed for their success) and give it to the poor (those who refuse to work hard enough to succeed), that it would literally be the end of the nation!

Listen again to the words of Pastor Adrian Rogers:

*You cannot legislate the poor into prosperity by legislating the wealthy out of prosperity. What one person receives without working for, another person must work for without receiving. The government cannot give to anybody anything that the government does not first take from somebody else. When half of the people get the idea that they do not have to work because the other half is going to take care of them, and when the other half gets the idea that it does no good to work because somebody else is going to get what they work for, that my dear friend, is the beginning of the end of any nation. You cannot multiply wealth by dividing it.*—Adrian Pierce Rogers

As you can see, Pastor Adrian Rogers agrees with Thomas Jefferson's assessment of the economic peril to our nation of using tax revenue from one citizen to benefit some other citizen—in other words, redistribution of wealth. Therefore, as we have clearly seen, to *"spread the wealth around"* is NOT GOOD FOR EVERYBODY! In fact, it's not good for anybody! *Spreading the wealth around* is an economic policy that results in mutually assured poverty for all!

Therefore, all government programs which redistribute tax revenue from one citizen and give it to another must be stopped immediately! That is pure and simply Communism and we do not abide Communism in America! This of course means we must immediately shut down about 50% of all government programs and agencies—goodbye and good riddance you Communist bastards!

If each citizen pays his or her equal fair share in taxes and knows that their tax dollars are directly benefitting them and not someone else, then we will have a just, fair and equitable tax system. And we will have a government that can balance its budget, get out of debt quickly and even have a surplus!

## *10% Is The Maximum We The People Should Authorize The Government To Impose As A Tax! Remember, It's Our Money, Not The Governments!*

But how much should our taxes be? Or more correctly, how much should we permit the government to tax us? Remember, we're the Boss! The government works for us! It is our money, not the governments! So, how much should we permit the government to receive in order to fulfill its responsibility to *defend and protect us from all enemies, foreign and domestic*? That's easy, just look to God for the answer.

God Himself also requires a sort of "Tax," if you will, from us; it is called the Tithe, which means 10% of our income:

**Leviticus 27:30-32**

*[30]And all the tithe of the land, whether of the seed of the land or of the fruit of the tree, is the Lord's. It is holy to the Lord.*

*[31]If a man wants at all to redeem any of his tithes, he shall add one-fifth to it.*

*[32]And concerning the tithe of the herd or the flock, of whatever passes under the rod, the <u>tenth</u> one shall be holy to the Lord.*

**Malachi 3:7-12**

[7] *Yet from the days of your fathers You have gone away from My ordinances And have not kept them. Return to Me, and I will return to you," Says the Lord of hosts. "But you said, 'In what way shall we return?'*

[8] *"Will a man rob God? Yet you have robbed Me! But you say, 'In what way have we robbed You?' In tithes and offerings.*

[9] *You are cursed with a curse, For you have robbed Me, Even this whole nation.*

[10] *Bring all the tithes into the storehouse [your local Church], That there may be food in My house, And try [test] Me now in this," Says the Lord of hosts, "If I will not open for you the windows of heaven And pour out for you such blessing That there will not be room enough to receive it.*

[11] *"And I will rebuke the devourer for your sakes, So that he will not destroy the fruit of your ground, Nor shall the vine fail to bear fruit for you in the field," Says the Lord of hosts;*

[12] *And all nations will call you blessed, For you will be a delightful land," Says the Lord of hosts.*

Well, right there is our remedy, isn't it? If we would all support our local Churches with 10% of our income then God would bless us and our nation with more blessings than we could handle! So please start doing your part! By the way, for those who have a shallow understanding of Holy Scripture regarding God's principle of Tithing and therefore say, *Both of the Scriptures you quoted are Old Testament passages, and I'm not under the Old Testament but under the New Testament!* Though it is true we are under the New Covenant not the Old, with regard to Tithing the Mediator of the New Covenant Jesus Christ confirmed that God's principle of Tithing is to continue under the New Covenant:

**Matthew 23:23**

[23] *"Woe to you, scribes and Pharisees, hypocrites! For you pay tithe of mint and anise and cummin, and have neglected the weightier matters of the law: justice and mercy and faith. These you ought to have done, without leaving the others undone.*

But here is the main point—if God requires only 10%, who does the government think they are to require more? Does the government think it is greater than God? Well, I've got news for them, they're not! The government was established by God to serve His people; therefore, all government employees, from the President to the postal worker, will therefore have to give an account to God for their stewardship.

Therefore, since God requires only 10%, the maximum percentage the Federal government may impose as a Tax is 10%; the same as God, but no more!

## It's Time To Repeal & Replace The Income Tax With A Commerce Tax!

Let us review Thomas Jefferson's rule for good government with regard to taxation:

*A wise and frugal government, which shall...not take from the mouth of labor the bread it has earned—this is the sum of good government.*

So, Thomas Jefferson's rule is not to tax income!

Now, indeed, God requires 10% of our "income," because He is God from whom all blessings flow and therefore 100% of our income has come from His hand. He therefore has the right to require 10% of our income.

But the government had nothing to do with our income—our income is God's blessing in our lives as the result and fruit of our own labors.

Remember, the Founding Fathers never instituted an "income tax," only "tariffs" on trade, in other words, a Commerce or Consumption Tax. Nor was there any Income Tax for the first 137 years (1776—1913) of America's development into the most powerful and prosperous nation on Earth. But of course, the damned Democrats under their Communist President Woodrow Wilson in 1913 ratified the 16th Amendment imposing for the first time in America's history an "income tax!" A great earthquake was felt across the United States as America's Founding Fathers rolled over in their graves! This is another reason why no American should ever vote for any member of the Communist Democratic Party! If you do, God will hold you accountable, for Communism violates God's principles of personal responsibility and Free-Market Enterprise!

Therefore, it is time for a new American Revolution—a Tax Revolt—in which we return to the economic principles of Thomas Jefferson and our other Founding Fathers and the first 137 years of America's history and get rid of the Income Tax by repealing the 16th Amendment and replacing it with a 10% Commerce Tax!

*A wise and frugal government, which shall…not take from the mouth of labor the bread it has earned—this is the sum of good government.*

This new 10% Commerce Tax is a Consumption Tax or Federal Sales Tax collected at the end purchase of a product or service. Now, wisdom would require that perhaps the rate be lowered to 5% on purchases of essential items such as groceries, gasoline, housing rent, and large purchases such as automobiles and homes. But a 5% to 10% Federal Sales Tax would be an immediate boom to every working American's income, because their payroll checks will immediately increase due to there no longer being any withholding of Federal Taxes from their paychecks!

I know some questions immediately arise with this proposal of a flat, fair 5% to 10% Federal Sales Tax; for example, I know my colleague Sean Hannity will ask, "Is this new tax system revenue neutral?" In other words, will this flat 5% to 10% Federal Sales Tax generate the same amount of revenue currently generated under the existing system? To be honest, I have no idea, though I'm certain someone smarter than I could put a pen to it and find out; but in a very real sense its irrelevant, because, as we stated above, the plethora of government programs and agencies which currently take money from those who worked for it and give it to those who did not work for it are Communist programs and must immediately be shut down! This will save untold trillions of dollars! Besides that, *Common Sense* requires that whatever amount of revenue this new flat, fair 5% to 10% Federal Sales Tax generates, it will be enough; because a government cannot spend more than it takes in, right? I mean, that's *Common Sense!* The point here is this: Texas Governor Rick Perry during his run for the Presidency (by the way, Rick Perry is one of our great American patriots and Governors and would have made a great President) said that he would "balance the Federal budget by 2020." A noble goal. But elect me, *Common Sense,* to Office and I will balance the budget in one day! The first day *Common Sense* is in Office the government will not spend one penny more than it takes in! Folks, that's just *Common Sense!* Remember, the primary, and in reality the only, responsibility of government is to provide the strongest military force along with the most efficient intelligence-gathering agency on the planet to defend and protect us from all foreign enemies, plus an effective F.B.I. to defend and protect us from all domestic enemies. And after fulfilling that primary responsibility, if there are any funds left over they must go toward paying down our obscene $16-Trillion in national debt—$10-Trillion of which took 232 years to accumulate from all the Presidency's since George Washington to George W. Bush, but $6-Trillion of which Numbnuts Obama accumulated in less than 3 1/2 years of his Presidency! Once we get the national debt paid off, then we can think about building and maintaining our Federal highway system. But that's pretty much the extent of the government's role and responsibility. So the 5% to 10% Federal Sales Tax will generate more than enough revenues to fulfill the Federal government's very limited responsibilities.

By the way, in case you're not familiar with the term "Numbnuts," the definition according to UrbanDictionary.com is:

Numbnuts:

1. A person of severely limited intellectual prowess.

2. The stupidest of the stupid. A complete dumbass, one whose intelligence quotient does not surpass that of the average rock.

3. An utter disgrace of humanity.

4. One whose purpose in life is meaningless; a complete and total waste of life.

5. An ignorant, arrogant asshole.

Boy, now doesn't that describe Obama to a T!

The other "objection," which of course the Democrats will raise, is that the implementation of this 5% to 10% Federal Sales Tax will immediately be a "Tax increase" on about 50% of Americans who currently pay no Federal Income Tax—you got that right baby! It's time that those free-loading Communists start paying their fair share! Finally, all American's, along with me, will also be paying for the roads they drive on and the benefit of air traffic control when they fly and the protection of the U.S. Armed Forces, etc. You see, this is the first and immediate benefit of a flat, fair Federal Consumption Tax rather than the current convoluted Income Tax system—everybody pays their fair and equal share of taxes! This also goes toward Sean Hannity's question of whether or not this flat, fair Federal Sales Tax will generate the same amount as our current system, and even though I haven't attempted to calculate that answer, my bet is that this new system will immediately generate more than the current system because of this very fact that 50% more Americans will now be paying tax revenues to the Federal Treasury!

There are many other immediate benefits to a Federal Sales Tax rather than an Income Tax. First, by not taking *"from the mouth of labor the bread it has earned,"* i.e., by not taxing one's income, we encourage saving, because you will only be taxed on what you spend. One of the greatest contributors to our current economic condition is debt, both our national debt and our individual debt. By increasing savings we increase each person's net worth and financial stability, which increases financial stability nationwide. One might argue that spending is necessary to stimulate the economy, but a person who has a healthy savings account will actually spend more money, from dining out more often to making more frequent larger purchases, than a person who is strapped and living paycheck to paycheck.

Another advantage to a Federal Consumption vs. Income Tax is that now everyone who receives the benefits of the Federal Government, i.e., military defense, highways, etc., is now a contributor to that service, and thus has a vested interest in proper management of those resources by our government officials making all of us more involved, and therefore better citizens.

A further immediate benefit of a Federal Sales Tax vs. Income Tax is the revenues that this Federal Sales Tax will generate from the large amount of illegal and "under-the-table" cash transactions that occur every day which are never reported as income and therefore never subject to Income Tax; but these millions of dollars in unreported cash revenues are readily spent by the recipients—so now all recipients of unreported, even "illegally" generated, revenues will have to pay their fair share.

This 5% to 10% Federal Sales Tax must be charged and collected at the point of final sale to the end user; this avoids double taxation of the same product or service as it moves up the chain from manufacture to wholesale distribution to retail. For example, the 5% Federal Sales Tax on automobile purchases is charged to the end user, the automobile buyer. But no Federal Sales Tax is charged on the individual parts that are purchased by the automobile manufacturer from its various suppliers; this ensures that the end retail price of the automobile is at its lowest possible price to the consumer, not inflated by multiple taxes during the manufacturing process. But this same automobile manufacturer, when they purchase computers, desks, tools and machinery used in the operating of their business, then they are charged the 10% Federal Sales Tax as the end user of those purchases.

Just as this new Federal Sales Tax no longer taxes an individual's "profits," the money he earns from his labors, so also businesses will no longer be taxed on their profits. This will result in an immediate economic boom resulting in massive job creation! Companies will no longer have to pay a corporate tax on their profits—which, let's understand that the current Corporate Tax system is a failed tax system full of loopholes, as was clearly demonstrated by General Electric's recent paying of zero Federal taxes because of the fraudulent tax loopholes granted to GE by the Obama Administration; under a Federal Sales Tax GE will pay its fair share by being taxed 10% on all its end user purchases—thus, by not penalizing profits through taxation of those profits earned by American businesses, American businesses will be incentivized to invest, build and expand, which means jobs! jobs! jobs! Private enterprise, not government, creates jobs, creates wealth, and stimulates the economy! Government is only a parasite living off of the work and productivity of American businesses and the American people.

## Obama The Clueless Communist Thinks "At A Certain Point You've Made Enough Money!"

President Obama is such a clueless Communist that during a recent speech before a group of American businesspeople he actually made the following mind-boggling statement: "*We're not trying to push financial reform because we begrudge success that's fairly earned—I mean I do think at a certain point you've made enough money.*" (To hear this shocking statement for yourself, search YouTube.com for: Obama says "I do think at a certain point you've made enough money")

What The...! What in the Hell does that mean? Normal thinking people just shake their heads in utter disbelief at such an ignorant, anti-American, anti-Free Enterprise statement. I'm not even going to try to figure out what's going on inside Obama's head when he made that statement, but one thing is clear, he is utterly clueless when it comes to understanding what creates an "economy" and thereby what creates jobs, income and wealth for all. The entire purpose for the existence of any business is to make as much money as possible—it is literally impossible for any business to ever make "*enough money,*" because the more money a business makes, the more money that business spends into the economy; the more money a business makes the more that business grows resulting in the hiring of more employees; the more money a business makes the more money it has to better pay its employees; and if it is a publically traded company on the stock market, the more money that business makes the greater the value of that company's stock, resulting in the creation of more wealth for the American people who have invested in that company's stock! It is always beneficial to a nation's economy for every business to make as much money as possible—no amount is "*enough.*"

Again, I'm not going to try to get inside Obama's Communist head, but what did he mean? Does Obama mean that McDonalds should say, "Well, we're making enough money, so let's not open any more McDonalds?" Did Obama mean that Exxon Mobile should say, "Well, we're making enough money, so let's not drill any more oil wells?" Did Obama mean that Ford should say, "Well, we're making enough money, so let's not expand by opening any more manufacturing facilities or dealerships and let's put a cap on the number of cars we sell each year?" I mean, seriously, what did Obama mean? The next morning following this revelation by Obama of what he believes about the American economy, both Houses of Congress should have called an emergency session and voted for the immediate Impeachment of Barack Hussein Obama, based upon his declaration that he wants to put a cap on the American economy— which is a declaration that Obama wants to limit the success and income of the American people! Congress failed to do their duty by Impeaching Obama for this utterly mind-boggling declaration of war against the American economy, but you and I have the opportunity to save America from the moronic reign of this enemy of the American economy by going to the polls on November 6, 2012.

Finally, this flat and fair tax that is paid by all rids us of the immoral and absurd notion of a "progressive tax," that taxes wealthier individuals at a higher rate than less successful individuals—is that the most asinine thing you ever heard of? Punish people for being successful and rewarding people who are less successful! If you're going to have a "progressive tax" it should be the other way around! Those who succeed in striving to attain the American Dream and who therefore create more wealth for the country and the economy should be the one's rewarded with a lower tax rate; and as a punishment and an incentive to those who have not worked as hard and therefore are less successful, the lower income brackets should be the ones to have to pay a higher rate—hopefully thereby prodding them to study and work harder to attain greater success and thereby create more wealth for the American economy and tax revenues into the Treasury. So goodbye and good riddance to the current idiotic progressive tax system!

I'm *Common Sense* & I'm running for Office! Elect me as your President, Representative, Senator, Governor and Mayor, and I will get rid of the current unfair economy-killing Income Tax system and replace it with a flat, fair 5% to 10% Federal Sales Tax system in which every American pays their fair share! Even the 11-million illegal aliens who are now being paid under the table will be forced to pay their fair share!

Now let us turn to a *Common Sense* solution to the crisis that put us all into this Great Recession in the first place: The Housing Crisis.

## A *Common Sense* Solution to the Housing Crisis!

This next *Common Sense* solution to getting America's economy back on the road to prosperity is one that will turn our economy around 180-degrees in 24-hours! Let's review how we got here in the first place.

### *President George W. Bush Had Zero To Do With The Economic Collapse Of 2008!*

When President George W. Bush entered the first year of his Presidency, he was handed an economy that was still reeling from the recent Dot-com Bubble bursting in which Americans lost an average of 70% of their wealth in the stock market. Then the Islamic religion's attacks of September 11, 2001, hit America, further devastating our economy. But thank God we had a *Common Sense* Republican in the White House, along with a Republican majority in both Houses of Congress, and President Bush and the Congress instituted the Bush Tax Cuts and other *Common Sense* economic policies which quickly brought our economy out from utter devastation into a period of great prosperity for all.

But in the 2006 Mid-Term Election, a war-weary nation of ignoramuses elected economically-ignorant Communist Democrats into the majorities in both Houses of Congress, thus dooming America's economy to the devastation of the Communist Democratic Party's economic policies!

## *The War In Iraq Was Ordained By God! Therefore Anyone Who Speaks Against That War Speaks Against God!*

The reason I refer to *" a war-weary nation of ignoramuses"* is because any person who is opposed to our war against Islamic Terrorism, including the Iraq War, is ignorant of the fact that God was using the U.S. Armed Forces as the "Sword of the Lord" to defeat the Islamic Taliban in Afghanistan and to remove from power that anti-Israel anti-Christ Saddam Hussein who was personally paying $25,000 to the family of every suicide/homicide bomber who would murder Jews in Israel, along with awarding a "Martyrs Certificate" to the family honoring their son or daughter as a Martyr of Allah; plus Saddam Hussein paid $15,000 to every Palestinian who was wounded while trying to kill Jews in Israel, and that is why almost every day on your TV screen you saw the scenes of these suicide/homicide bombers in Israel blowing up buses and nightclubs murdering innocent Israeli civilians! —but God, in fulfillment of the ancient prophecy in Isaiah 13, stopped Saddam Hussein's attacks against His Land and His people by raising up and calling forth the U.S. Armed Forces along with our Coalition Partners under the Presidency of George W. Bush to invade Iraq and remove Saddam Hussein from power! This was God's doing! Therefore any person, any pundit, any politician who speaks against the Iraq War is speaking against God Almighty! Have you even noticed now that Saddam Hussein is gone that the suicide/homicide bombings have ceased in Israel? Praise God and thanks to President Bush and the U.S. invasion of Iraq! Let me say it again, the U.S. invasion of Iraq under President George W. Bush was prophesied in the Bible 2,750 years ago! Here's that prophecy:

### Isaiah 13:1-5

*¹The burden against Babylon* [Ancient name of Iraq] *which Isaiah the son of Amoz saw. ² "Lift up a banner on the high mountain, Raise your voice to them; Wave your hand* [beckoning them to come], *that they may enter the gates of the nobles* [remember how our military literally entered into the "gates"/palaces of the nobles!]. *³I have commanded My sanctified ones; I have also called My mighty ones for My anger—Those who rejoice in My exaltation." ⁴The noise of a multitude in the mountains, Like that of many people! A tumultuous noise of the <u>kingdoms of nations gathered together!</u> The <u>Lord of hosts musters The army for battle.</u> ⁵They come from a far country, From the end of heaven* [The U.S. is a far country from the end of heaven]—*The Lord and <u>His weapons</u> of indignation, To destroy the whole land.*

So be careful my friend when you speak against the actions of the U.S. Military, for they are the "Sword of the Lord!" *"His weapons of indignation!"*

Returning now to our discussion of how we got into this great recession in the first place!

*The 2006 Take Over By The Democratic Communist Party & its Leaders Nancy Pelosi, Harry Reid, Chris Dodd & Homosexual Offender Barney Frank Are 100% Responsible For The Economic Collapse Of 2008!*

Thanks to President Bush's and the Republican-controlled Congresses *Common Sense* free-market economic policies the economy was firing on all cylinders and people were again doing well financially, and many were purchasing newer, bigger better homes which was boosting the housing market. But, after the 2006 Mid-Term Election, when the Democratic Party was given control of the Congress in 2007, the Democratic Communist Party appointed baby-murdering God-hating Nancy Pelosi as Speaker of the House; they appointed Communist Harry Reid as Senate Majority Leader; they appointed Communist Chris Dodd as Senate Banking Committee Chairman; and they appointed Communist and homosexual offender Barney Frank as Chairman of the House Financial Services Committee. Now, fully in charge of the Federal Government's oversight of the Financial and Housing Industries, in conjunction with their Communist comrade Senator Barack Obama, the Democrats began implementing their Communist economic policies within the Housing industry. Utilizing the two Government Sponsored Enterprises created by Democrats known as the Federal National Mortgage Association, nicknamed Fannie Mae, and the Federal Home Mortgage Corporation, nicknamed Freddie Mac, Barney Frank and Chris Dodd, under the leadership of Pelosi and Reid, and under the watchful eye of Barack Obama, began to provide government guaranteed housing loans to individuals who normally would not qualify to purchase a home, by providing these unqualified home buyers with "Zero Down" and/or low-initial-interest-rate (thus lower initial monthly payments) "A.R.M.'s" Adjustable Rate Mortgage loans, along with other government guaranteed "fancy financing" intended to make it easy for unqualified home buyers to get financing—these were "risky" loans that financial institutions would have never made on their own, But with the Federal Government's guaranteeing those loans, mortgage lenders went hog wild giving home loans to every Tom, Dick and Harry! And don't forget Dodd! Yes, Chris Dodd, Chairman of the Senate Banking Committee received a "sweetheart VIP" loan from Countrywide Mortgage, in which he received a lower interest rate and faster loan approval. Another prominent Democrat who received a "sweetheart VIP" loan from Countrywide was Senate Budget Committee Chairman Kent Conrad.

This "Easy Money" Mortgage policy created by the Democrats in charge of the Congressional Banking and Finance Committee's led to a flood of people who bought homes they could not afford.

This created a housing boom, which initially further boosted our economy, but simultaneously, due to the fundamental economic principle of supply and demand, caused housing prices to skyrocket at a never-before-seen pace, creating a "Housing Bubble!" And what do bubbles do? They may appear shiny and fun for a short time, but bubbles always eventually burst!

Most of you reading this book have been directly impacted by the bursting of the Housing Bubble. If I may, I'd like to share with you my personal experience.

My wife and I are currently in our third home since our marriage. The first home we purchase as a married couple was a home we were renting, and we were approached by the owner as to whether we might be interested in buying the home. We could only scrape together half of the down-payment; so we negotiated directly with the owner to carry for 24-months the balance of that down-payment, and with that we were able to secure conventional financing. We lived and raised our family in that first home for 10-years, sold it and reinvested most of the profit we made from the sale by using that profit as the down-payment on our second home. We enjoyed that home for 7-years and sold that home for a nice profit, and again planned to reinvest the majority of that profit into our third "dream home.' For that third "dream home," we picked out a brand new area under development, went into the onsite construction trailer, was given a tour of the models, picked out the model we wanted, and said, *"We'll take this model, now we just need to pick out which lot we'd like it built on."* However, the housing "boom" was beginning to hit full stride. To my amazement, the sales rep informed us that, due to a high demand for the limited number of homes they could begin construction on each week, the lots were being sold only by *"lottery."* I said, *"A what? A lottery?" "Yes,"* said the rep, *"Each week we have a drawing out of a hat for 5 to 10 lots; we have these drawings every Tuesday, so come back next Tuesday and you may place your name in the hat, and hopefully your name will get drawn."*

I'm like, *"Wait a minute, you mean to tell me that we can't just buy a home from you right here, right now, today?"* *"Nope,"* she said. I said, *"I've never heard of such a thing in all my life!"*

So my wife and I showed up the next Tuesday for the "raffle," along with about another 100 people! I asked the rep, *"How many lots are being raffled today?"* *"We have 7 lots we're releasing"* she said. *"Just 7 lots,"* I said, *"for all these people?"* *"Just 7,"* she said. Of course we didn't win the lottery that week. Oh, I forgot to tell you that when we arrived the sales rep informed us that the price for the home we had picked out had increased $7,000!

Because of the easy-money policies of the Democrats in charge of Fannie Mae and Freddie Mac, home loans had become so easy to obtain that more people were in the market to buy a home than there were homes available for sale. Builders couldn't build homes fast enough! This unprecedented phenomenon was occurring nationwide, especially in the warmer climate States where growth is occurring.

Again, it is important to understand that this unnatural housing boom was the direct result of financial institutions making home loans to people they would normally not have made loans to, except for the Federal Government's guaranteeing of those loans through Fannie Mae and Freddie Mac. What the hell is the government doing in the home loan business? Government has no business interfering, either positively or negatively, in business. Government is government and business is business—keep your government asses out of our business! But this is what happens when you put Democrats in charge with their Communist economic policies! But someone is thinking, *"Isn't it a good thing for home loans to be easy to get?"* No! Not when the people getting the loans can't afford the home in the first place! They got in on a fake 2% "introductory interest rate" that after 12 or 24 months jumps to 6%, and now they can no longer afford that payment! Also, loans were being handed out like candy to people who had not previously demonstrated that they were good managers of their money; in other words, people with not so sterling credit ratings were being granted these "high risk" loans.

Getting back to my personal experience with the Housing Bubble. To make a long story short, we didn't win the "lot lottery" for several months. And each time the price of the home went up and up and up! We still wanted our dream home built in our dream community, and of course when we first went in we picked out the maximum home we felt we could afford; but now our dream home was going for about $50,000 more than when we first picked it out...more than what we had planned on spending. And to top it off, the crowds at these lot lotteries had grown to 200—300 people with still only 5—10 lots being awarded each time. I remember the last lot lottery we drove away from without winning, as we pulled out of the parking lot my wife burst into tears. That was it! I called up that rep and let her have it big time! Here we had been coming there for months trying to purchase a home, and they were letting people who just showed up for the very first time put their names in the hat and win! That was just wrong, and I let the rep know it. I told her the only just way to administer the releasing of the lots should be based upon a list of names in order of first-come-first served. We got a call two weeks later from the rep telling us they had stopped the lottery system and switched to a list system and that our name was number two on the list, and that three lots were coming available later that week, and if we wanted one we could have the second pick. We took it and got the perfect lot and built our dream home. The nightmare was over! So we thought.

The day we moved into our new home, the value of our home was appraised at $100,000 more than what we had paid! Yes we had paid about $50,000 more than we had anticipated and therefore the mortgage payment (a 30-year fixed rate, not one of those bogus ARM's) was higher than we had planned, but, hey, the home is worth considerably more now than what we paid, so we'd bite the bullet a little and make it work. Then the housing bubble burst!

As I write this, our home is worth only about half of what we owe. Anybody with half a brain would hand the keys back to the bank and say, *"There you go, pal, it's yours, have fun."* But we love our home. I personally designed our swimming pool and spa. We still have one of our kids living with us and no one likes to uproot their kids. Plus, we put a significant amount of cash down on this home. But it's also not my fault that my home is only worth half what I owe, it's the fault of the Democrats controlling our government, and perhaps some Republicans who went along with them too, who created Fannie Mae and Freddie Mac and told the banks to make home loans to everyone and anyone, even if they had no proof of income! Those dumb Communist bastards are the ones who made this mess and it's their responsibility to fix it! Let me make this very clear—the economic collapse that occurred due to the Housing Crisis was NOT Wall Street's fault; it was NOT the banking industry's fault—it was Barney Frank's and Chris Dodd's and their Communist Dem cohort's fault! The financial institutions were only acting upon what the Federal Government told them to do! And for President Barack Insane Obama to try to blame the banks and blame Wall Street is the biggest bunch of bull dung any President has ever perpetrated upon the American people! That's OK; come November 6, 2012, We the People are running his lying Communist ass out of town!

You see, if President Obama and the Democrats would have wanted to fix the Housing Crisis and thereby the entire economy, they could have done so very easily; here's how. Instead of spending billions—excuse me, I mean trillions—of dollars in bank bail-outs and their bail-out of Communist run GM, and their bail-out of their in-bed buddies over at Goldman Sax, and Obama's and Pelosi's Trillion-dollar "Stimulus Plans" that were in reality nothing more than paybacks to those select groups and individuals who had voted them into office—if they would have taken that money and "bailed the home owners out," the economy would have turned around in 24-hours.

A home owner bail out would have in reality also been a bank bailout, because the financial institutions that collapsed were again the result of the housing bubble bursting because of home owners who had bit-off more than they could chew due to crazy housing lending practices promoted by the government which resulted in people by the droves going into foreclosure, which in turn dumped millions of empty homes onto the market—banks have now lost the money they lent and the supply and demand principle in the housing market has now reversed 180-degrees resulting in the dramatic declines in housing values.

But if the government had taken those trillions, it actually would probably only have required billions, and instituted the "Home Owner Rescue Act" by telling the mortgage holders that if you refinance down to the current market value every mortgage holder who is 20% or more underwater on their mortgage and who put some money down on the purchase of that home, then we the federal government will pay the difference so that the bank does not incur any losses. In 24-hours every underwater home owner would no longer contemplate walking away from their home, would immediately be able to afford the new much lower mortgage even if they had originally gotten in a little over their head (like what happened to my wife and I), which stops the foreclosures and creates a firm bottom to the housing market, and which also immediately puts more money every month into the pockets of the home owners, truly "stimulating" the economy! The U.S. economy would have turned around and been right back on the road to prosperity in 24-hours! But they didn't do that. Of course they didn't, because some of those underwater home owners are Republicans, like me, and they are not about to give one penny to a Republican.

But there is still something the government could do right now to atone for their sin of government backing private securities—again, the government has no business getting involved in business! The "Home Owner Rescue Act" I mentioned above cannot be done now, because the federal government is out of money! And we damn sure don't want to borrow any more from the Chinese or anyone else! But, I propose the "Home Owner Short Sale Rescue Act."

## The Home Owner Short Sale Rescue Act Would Turn Our Economy Around In 24-hours!

The Home Owner Short Sale Rescue Act would turn our economy around in 24-hours! Here's how it would work. As I stated above, anyone with half a brain has either already or is considering or should contemplate walking away from their underwater mortgage which fell upon them as a direct result of the government's Communist-style policies. Since all of us who are underwater in our mortgages, most of us are about 50% underwater, are considering walking away from these black clouds hanging over our futures, there are some of us who, in order to avoid the full brunt of the negative credit reporting that occurs from a foreclosure, are entering into a short sale agreement with our mortgage lender.

A "Short Sale" of your home is simply where the mortgage holder agrees to sell your home to someone else at the current market price which amount is of course "short" of the current debt owed by you. But here is what doesn't make any sense, the current laws and mortgage practices are such that the mortgage holder will sell your house to a total stranger who has no vested interest in the home, no emotional attachment to the home; but they won't do the same for you! That is simply idiotic!

I have talked to mortgage brokers, and it's common knowledge in the industry that, even though the mortgage bank experiences a loss in a Short Sale due to the difference between the amount of the original loan and the lesser amount of the new loan, the mortgage companies have creative ways of cooking the books so that the loss is not as detrimental to the financial wellbeing of the mortgage lender as one might think.

Also, a direct monetary downside to the mortgage bank when they sell the home to a stranger are the costs incurred of the real estate commission paid to the stranger's realtor, plus all the other Title and closing fees associated with a real estate transaction. So a Short Sale costs the mortgage bank thousands of dollars out of pocket.

Let's understand that most if not all of us who are currently underwater in our mortgages want to stay in our homes, but many of us are struggling to make the mortgage payment, and even if we're not, there is no reason for us to stay when we are hundreds-of-thousands-of-dollars underwater—a situation which will not be remedied for decades to come—and most of us plan to stay in our homes for only 5—10 years, then upgrade to a nicer home; which by the way is a great economic stimulator.

Therefore, I, *Common Sense*, propose the "Home Owner Short Sale Rescue Act," where by law every mortgage bank will be permitted and encouraged to Short Sale or simply refinance the current home owner at the current market value of the home. This: A) Avoids any and all closing costs normally incurred by the mortgage bank; B) Reduces the current home owner's mortgage to current market value, therefore removing the incentive to walk away from the home; C) Reduces the monthly mortgage payment for the home owner by an average of $1,000 per month, thus stimulating the economy by increasing each household's monthly cash reserves available for spending on consumer products and services; and, D) Stops the flood of foreclosures hitting the real estate market every month, thus placing a firm bottom in the housing market—thereby also placing a firm bottom to the overall economy which places us firmly back on the road to prosperity!

The alternative is to not enact the *Common Sense* "Home Owner Short Sale Rescue Act" and thus continue the downward spiral of the economy as more and more foreclosed homes hit the market each and every month for at least the next couple of years. This means housing values will continue to decline, encouraging more and more home owners to walk away from their mortgage nightmare; thus continuing the overall economic decline all across America.

The one thing that caused the economic down turn is also the One Thing that will turn it back around—the housing market.

I'm *Common Sense* and I'm running for Office, elect me and I'll author and sign into law the Home Owner Short Sale Rescue Act.

This now brings us to the antidote for the Communist, Economy-killing Obama-Care Government take-over of our Free-Enterprise Health Care System!

## *Common Sense* Solutions For Health Care!

First of all, let's get one thing straight—there is no Health Care "Crisis" in America! We have the best, most affordable health care anywhere in the world! So when the wicked witch of the West, Nancy Pelosi and her cohort in crime, Barack Obama spew their lies about there being a Health Care 'Crisis," they are doing what their Father the devil has put in their mouths—lying!

*Healthcare Is A "Business" & The Government Has No Business Dictating To Any Health Insurance Company Or Doctor How To Run Their Business!*

The second thing we need to get straight is that Health Insurance is a business! Being a doctor is a business! The government does not have the right to dictate to any insurance company or doctor how to run their business! The government cannot make a "rule" that Health Insurance companies must insure children under their parent's policy up to the age of 26! The government cannot tell a Health Insurance company that it must cover pre-existing conditions! That is the most idiotic, ridiculous thing I've ever heard! That's like telling an Auto Insurance company that they must provide accident coverage to a new customer AFTER that customer has wrecked their car! The Auto Insurance company would go out of business in a week! And so will the Health Insurance companies go out of business if they are forced to cover pre-existing conditions! Am I making myself clear here? Let me state it for you this way—doctors are in business for the sole purpose of making a PROFIT! Health Insurance companies are a business whose sole purpose is to make a PROFIT! If there is not a substantial profit, then there is NO incentive for doctors to spend all those years in medical school and internships—but doctors are willing to make those sacrifices because the potential financial benefit makes it all worthwhile! But Obama-Care destroys that monetary benefit and thereby destroys the medical profession! A recent poll showed that 85% of doctors in America say they will close up shop and leave their medical practices if Obama-Care is allowed to remain Law. Take away the PROFIT incentive from the doctors and there will be no doctors anymore! The same is true of Health Insurance companies; remove the potential for extreme profits and the Health Insurance industry will no longer be willing to take the risks they take of insuring customers against the costs of catastrophic illness. I don't care if you think forcing an insurance company to cover pre-existing conditions is a "good" thing—it is illegal! The government does not have the right to tell any business how to run its business! Further, as stated above, you may think covering pre-existing conditions is good for the insured, but that's irrelevant! —because no insurance company can stay in business if it has to cover customers who are already sick at the point of acquiring the insurance—again, that would be like a car insurance company giving first-time coverage to a customer AFTER the accident! Of course they cannot do that! That's *Common Sense!* Wake up America! Quit thinking like morons!

But what about the poor child who is born with a medical condition or acquires one very young and needs medical attention? Well, did the parents purchase pre-natal health insurance coverage for that child? If so, then they are covered. If not, then they are not covered. That's the parents fault, not the insurance companies fault! And let's be honest—that scenario is a one-in-a-million, not what the vast majority of people face! You don't structure an entire industry around the needs of a very few, but around the needs of the vast majority. When Ray Kroc Founded McDonald's, he didn't sit there thinking, "One out of every Ten-Thousand people is a vegetarian, so I better make all my burgers veggie-burgers so I cover that tiny sector of the population!" Of course not! McDonald's wouldn't have lasted one day! In the same way Health Insurance companies fashion their products to meet the needs of the vast majority.

But I know your heart is still pained thinking about those rare instances where a child has a serious medical condition and the parents do not have the financial wherewithal to cover the medical costs incurred; in such rare cases there are free-market "charitable" solutions for such children, such as children's hospitals, like St. Jude's, which are supported by private charitable donations and therefore do not charge the families. There are also University-run Medical Centers across America where medical research and the teaching of doctors-in-training occurs which offer medical services at no cost to the patients. There are a plethora of free-market charitable and non-profit medical centers and services across America for those rare unfortunate situations as we've described.

But remember, Health Insurance companies are businesses in business to make a profit! Otherwise there is no reason for their existence. And the insurance companies which provide the best services at the lowest prices will by virtue of the free market obtain the most customers and thereby most likely also be the most profitable! But again, government cannot create rules and regulations which the insurance companies must observe—it is 100% up to the owners of that insurance company how they wish to operate that company—what products and services to offer, and what price to charge for those products and services. Free-market competition always "holds companies accountable' for the quality of their products and services and the fairness of the prices they charge; otherwise they will simply go out of business.

Now here are a few free-market solutions that will dramatically improve our health care system—remember, there is NO health care crisis, but there is always room for improvement! First of all, to lower your personal health insurance costs, begin thinking about your Health Insurance in the same way you think about your Auto Insurance. You don't pay for Auto Insurance that covers the replacement of your tires—which is an expense you incur about every two years and which costs you on average from $300 to $800, which you are willing to pay for out of your pocket—so why are you paying for Health Insurance that has only a $100 co-pay when you go every 2-years or so to get some $500 or $800 test? Like your tires, just pay that occasional expense for a test out of your pocket. Again, you don't have Auto Insurance that covers your gasoline which costs you on average from $100 to $300 per month— so why are you paying for Health Insurance that has only a $10 co-pay whenever you visit the doctor, which is probably a $50 to $100 fee per visit? Instead, just pay that $50 to $100 per visit fee out of your pocket on those rare occasions when you visit a doctor.

In fact, the only thing your Auto Insurance covers is a "catastrophic" event—an accident which causes thousands, possibly tens-of-thousands of dollars in vehicle damage and bodily injury; and even then you have at least a $500 deductible which you pay out of pocket in such catastrophic events. This is the same type of Health Insurance coverage all Americans should purchase—Health Insurance that only covers us in the case of catastrophic illness, with of course a $500 to $1,000 deductible which we pay out of pocket! Shop around the plethora of Health Insurance providers and tell them you only want catastrophic coverage, and your monthly premiums will drop dramatically! If you cannot find a Health Insurance company who offers catastrophic only coverage at a reasonable price, go out and start your own Catastrophic Coverage Only Health Insurance Company and you'll quickly become the largest Health Insurance company in America!

However, for most people, there is even a better solution than purchasing catastrophic-only Health Insurance, and that is to have a Self-imposed Automatic Health Savings Account. Instead of sending in a Health Insurance premium each month to a Health Insurance company, you have an equivalent amount (or amount of your choosing) automatically deducted from your paycheck—or automatically transferred by your financial institution from your checking account—and deposited into an interest earning Health Savings Account, to be accessed by you only in the event of catastrophic illness. One of the main advantages to such a personal Health Savings Account is that, instead of helping make some insurance company richer, if you never need to touch your Health Savings Account or don't need all of the funds therein, upon your death that money you saved passes on to the benefit of your surviving spouse and/or children. Of course, if you don't feel that you'd be disciplined enough to keep yourself from tapping into your Health Savings Account for things not related to catastrophic health costs, then you're better off sending in a monthly premium to a Health Insurance company where you can't get your hands on it.

Another *Common Sense* solution that will lower our health care costs is related to the way in which you, your doctors and the insurance company presently interact. Because you have been paying for health insurance that covers the "gas in your car" each month and the "new tires" you need every couple years, both you and your doctors have slumped into the habit of not discussing the cost of your visit or test or procedure, because the insurance is paying for it, except for your puny co-pay; so you hand them your insurance card and never know the cost (of course you're currently paying through the nose for your health insurance, and Obama Care is causing those premiums to skyrocket!). However, once the vast majority of Americans begin to pay for doctors visits and tests and minor procedures out of pocket, doctors will now have to start disclosing their prices for their services—some will post the prices on a lighted board in their waiting room like a fast-food restaurant; others, like a sit-down restaurant, will hand you a "menu" of their services and associated costs. However, either way "competition" will create fair pricing in the "medical market." Of course, the better, more skilled doctors will be able to demand a higher price, and the lesser skilled doctors a lower price, as it should be. Remember, doctors are a business in business to make a profit! But this new system of price disclosure driven by patient's paying out of pocket and the reality of free-market competition will dramatically bring down medical costs! This holds true for testing facilities and minor surgeries and procedures as well. And if people are paying for major surgeries and catastrophic health treatments out of their personal Health Savings Accounts, then the consumer will naturally "shop around" for the best doctor at the best price—again, free-market competition is what we need in the Health Care Industry!

But doctors will actually fair better under this price-disclosure patient-pay system, because right now they are being shafted by insurance companies, especially the government run insurance entities of Medicare and Medicaid, which is why the Federal Government's tyrannical Communist take-over of the Health Care Industry in Obama Care will destroy the Health Care Industry in America! But a free-market competitive health care system will financially reward the better doctors, hospitals, test facilities and treatment services, by attracting customers who want the best and are willing to pay extra for it. But those who provide fewer services at a lower cost will also thrive by attracting those wishing to pay less and who are willing to receive a lower quality service. Wait! You mean to tell me that more successful people will receive better health care services than less successful people? Yep! Hard work, training and creativity result in success—and success has its rewards! In fact, it's like that now under the current "insurance-driven" health care system. For example, the Mayo Clinic is considered one of the best medical testing and treatment facilities in the country, but they only accept top-flight insurance plans. In fact, some of the Mayo Clinic's won't accept Medicare—that's right, Medicare pays so poorly that the good doctors and medical facilities won't even accept your Medicare Health Insurance anymore! And once Obama Care takes full effect, the good doctors won't accept your Communist "Obama Care Card" either! You'll be stuck having to go down to the County Hospital with all the drug addicts and criminals! Welcome to Obama's Communist world! The question is, what are you going to do about it? Are you going to allow that Communist Muslim-loving baby-killer, along with all his Communist baby-killing Democratic Party comrades, to completely destroy the nation you love? Or are you going to get to the polls on Tuesday, November 6, 2012, and vote every one of those Communist Democratic Party domestic enemies of America out of Office?

I'm *Common Sense* & I'm running for Office! Elect me as your President, Congressman, Governor, State House Member and Mayor, and I'll save America from the attempted Communist take-over by Barack Hussein Obama and the Democratic Party, and restore to America *Common Sense* Free Market principles to every aspect of American life, including our Health Care system; maintaining its stature as the greatest Health Care system in the world, but making it even better by encouraging catastrophic-only insurance coverage, personal Health Savings Accounts and free market competition!

Now, there's one last item we must address which is necessary to get America's economy back on the road to prosperity.

## Social Security & Medicare Are Illegal Ponzi Schemes Which Must Be Shut Down Immediately!

Social Security and Medicare are bankrupting America and unless these two government programs are immediately shut down, America will plunge so deep into economic collapse that it will never recover, which will of course result in both government programs being shut down anyway—not to mention that Social Security and Medicare are both illegal Ponzi schemes!

*Either Release Bernie Madoff From Prison Or Arrest The President & Every Politician Who Supports The 2 Illegal Ponzi Schemes Called Social Security & Medicare!*

It was Texas Governor Rick Perry, during his run for the Republican Party Presidential Nomination, that rightly pointed out that Social Security and Medicare are illegal Ponzi schemes. Of course, as of this writing no arrests have been made of the politicians who are perpetrating these frauds upon the American people! Bernie Madoff is currently sitting in prison for perpetrating a Ponzi scheme that was tiny compared to the gargantuan Ponzi schemes of Social Security and Medicare that are being perpetrated upon the American people! Madoff's Ponzi scheme only involved a few thousand people; but the Federal Government's two Ponzi schemes of Social Security and Medicare are being perpetrated upon all 300-million plus Americans!

The Federal Government must either immediately release Bernie Madoff from prison and pardon him or every politician who supports Social Security and Medicare must immediately be arrested, tried and sent to prison for perpetrating the two biggest Ponzi schemes in the history of the world! Of course, the Fed's aren't going to release Madoff, neither should they, for his Ponzi scheme was a fraud perpetrated upon unsuspecting investors. Nor, will the Fed's immediately arrest all politicians who support these two fraudulent Ponzi schemes of Social Security and Medicare. So it is up to us, We The People, to throw every politician out of Office who supports these two illegal government schemes! And replace them with law-abiding, *Common Sense,* Free-Market-loving politicians who believe in our Founding Fathers Constitutional principles of personal responsibility.

A "Ponzi" scheme is simply when money is taken from a new investor and given to an older investor. The new investor is lied to, being told that his money is being saved and invested in order that he may realize a future return on his investment, but in reality his money is being stolen by the Ponzi scheme operator and given to the older investor. This of course is illegal because it is fraud based upon stealing and deception. This fraudulent scheme will continue as long as the influx of new money is greater than that which is being paid out. But as soon as the amount of the incoming funds becomes less than the amount of the outgoing funds, the scheme quickly collapses.

## *"But I Paid Into Social Security & Medicare!" Yes, And The Government Stole Your Money!*

In a diabolical attempt to seize permanent control of the U.S. Government by promising citizens free retirement health care and a monthly income check, thereby "buying" the votes of the American citizenry, the damnable Democratic Party hatched the two illegal Ponzi schemes called Social Security and Medicare. *Wait a minute!* you say, *I pay into Social Security and Medicare, so when I finally come of age, I'm not receiving free health care and a monthly income check, I paid into the system and are due those benefits!* By your protest you just proved my point that Social Security and Medicare are illegal Ponzi schemes! You've been lied to by the Federal Government and told that your contributions into the Social Security and Medicare systems are in order that YOU may receive those benefits upon reaching retirement age, but the Federal Government is stealing your money and giving it to other older citizens in the form of their Social Security and Medicare benefits! That's stealing! That's fraud! That's a Ponzi scheme! That's illegal! And again, the Federal Government must immediately pardon and release Bernie Madoff or arrest and imprison every politician who supports these two illegal government run Ponzi schemes! The Federal Government cannot prosecute and imprison American citizens who are merely doing on a tiny scale the same thing the Federal Government is doing on a national scale!

Your protest that you paid into these two illegal Ponzi schemes your whole life and therefore deserve those benefits is also incorrect, because the average Social Security & Medicare recipient receives 4- to 5-times more in benefits than he paid in! Where's that money coming from?

And the damnable Democratic Party's diabolical power-grabbing Ponzi schemes would have continued to be fully funded except that The Democratic Party, through their even more diabolical scheme of ridding America of Blacks and the less intelligent by way of their baby murder mill abortion clinics have murdered 60 million Americans thus far—that's one-fifth, 20%, of America's entire population! —that's 60 million Americans who would have been paying into the Democratic Party's two Ponzi schemes; but they killed them, and now their Ponzi schemes are collapsing! Having to pay out more than is taken in! Social Security and Medicare are bankrupting America and cannot be permitted to continue operating and must immediately be shut down!

## The Federal Government Must Make Restitution To Every American Citizen For Stealing Their Money!

Now the Federal Government has themselves in a real pickle, because the Federal Government has committed fraud against every American citizen who has had forced contributions taken from their earnings to support these two illegal Ponzi schemes, and therefore the Federal Government must make restitution! The Federal Government must close the Social Security Administration and Medicare program and turn them into the Illegal Ponzi Scheme Restitution Administration. This new Accounting Office must then track and calculate the amount each citizen has paid into these illegal programs and issue restitution payments back to each citizen. Of course, since the Federal Government stole that money and gave it to other people, it does not have the money with which to make restitution! So the Federal Government is going to have to set up a 5- to 20-year scheduled payback program, for example, where citizens 65 and older will receive payback in full over a 5-year period (remember, since under the current plan the average recipient receives 4- to 5- times more than they paid in, some will have no further payback payments coming); then those from age 50 to 64 could receive their payback over a 10-year period; then those 35 to 49 over a 15-year period/ and those 34 and under over a 20-year period.

Besides the fact that Social Security and Medicare are illegal fraudulent Ponzi schemes, the larger point is that the Federal Government does not have the right to "force" any citizen to put money aside for their retirement—the government does not have the right to force automatic contributions from my income into some "Social Security Retirement Plan." Where the Hell in the Constitution does it give government that authority? No where! It does not! If somebody wants to save, say 10%, of their income towards a retirement nest egg, that's their right and choice to do so, and I personally highly recommend that each citizen do so—but it's not the government's business to get into my private retirement business! If I want to spend every dollar I ever make and end up having to move back in with my kids in my old age, that's my right to do so; though my kids will probably hate me for it!

The point here is simply that America must get back to our Founding Fathers *Common Sense* principles of personal freedom and responsibility—free from government interference in our personal lives, with each individual being responsible for his own success and happiness! Look again at President Thomas Jefferson's Inaugural Address declaration that it is not the government's, but each individual's right and responsibility to "regulate" their own pursuits of industry and improvement of one's life:

*—with all these blessings [from God and the Christian religion], what more is necessary to make us a happy and a prosperous people? Still one thing more, fellow-citizens—a wise and frugal Government, which shall restrain men from injuring one another, shall leave them otherwise free to regulate their own pursuits of industry and improvement, and shall not take from the mouth of labor the bread it has earned. This is the sum of good government.*—President Thomas Jefferson, Inaugural Address, March 4, 1801.

In conclusion, it is time to elect *Common Sense* leadership in Washington D.C. and in each of the 50 United States, who will follow the tried and true economic principles of frugal government which does not spend more than it takes in; of freedom from government regulation of our pursuits of industry and improvement, freedom to regulate our own pursuits of happiness; of government that does not tax our income, but only taxes commerce; of the principle of free-market Capitalism where profit and thereby prosperity are the goal, not Communism which takes from those who work for it and gives it to those who don't; of government staying out of the Health Care Industry and restoration of a competitive free-market health care system that benefits both the health care providers and the consumers; and of government ceasing to operate the two biggest illegal Ponzi schemes in the history of the world!

Next, we turn our attention to *Common Sense* solutions for the problem of Illegal Immigration!

# Chapter 7: *Common Sense* Solutions For America's Problem Of Illegal Immigration!

Never before in American history has a President of the United States sided with a foreign country in attacking one of our own States, as did President Barack Hussein Obama when he sided with Mexico's President Felipe Calderon in denouncing the State of Arizona's passing of State Law SB1070, which simply enforces Federal Illegal Immigration Laws already on the books! The audacity of President Obama and his fellow Dumb-o-crats to stand and cheer during the portion of Mexican President Calderon's speech when he bashed and attacked one of our own States is the greatest display of anti-Americanism ever perpetrated by any President! President Obama and his Administration even launched a lawsuit against Arizona for attempting to defend her own border against criminal immigration. The Obama Administration's launching of the lawsuit against Arizona is alone grounds enough for impeaching President Obama and for removing from Office every Democrat who supported that lawsuit!

## Illegal Immigrants Are Criminals!

I've had to replace 10 televisions over the past year because I keep picking up objects from my coffee table and hurling them through the TV screen at the idiots on the tube spewing out such ignorance over the illegal immigration debate! (I didn't really destroy my TV, but I've felt like it, and I bet you have too!)

The first idiotic and insane argument spewed out by the anti-American Liberal Democrats is that illegal immigrants "aren't criminals," but good hard-working people! Before I refute that moronic argument though, I first must state here—make no mistake about it, Liberal Democrats hate America! Their actions speak louder than their lying words—Barack Obama's and the Democratic Party's promotion of the murder of 1.5 million American babies every year, 4,000 every day including one-half of all Black babies conceived, proves that Barack Obama and the Democratic Party hate America! Barack Obama's and the Democratic Party's promotion of the personal and nation destroying sin of homosexuality, knowing full well that sin brings God's judgment upon the individual and the nation (see Chapter 8, Why It's Not OK To Be Gay!), proves that Barack Obama and the Democratic Party hate America! Barack Obama's and the Democratic Party's attack against Christianity and the nation of Israel while simultaneously promoting the vile false-religion of Islam proves that Barack Obama and the Democratic Party hate America! And Barack Obama's and the Democratic Party's hatred of Free-Market Capitalism and promotion of *"spread the wealth around"* Communism proves that Barack Obama and the Democratic Party hate America! So, I have just one question for all of you Communist, baby-murdering, Muslim-loving, America-hating Democrats: Why are you still here? Hit the road, Jack, and don't you come back no more! Go to Communist China or Cuba or one of those South American or European Countries that you love so much; and guess what, we won't even miss you! But make no mistake about it—you are not welcome here! This is America! The Land of the Free and the Home of the Brave! And we do not abide Communists or baby-killers or Muslims in America! That means every one of you damned Democrats—get your A.-double-S. out of here! That's right; you Democrats are all "damned!" You are damned by God to the eternal fires of Hell unless you repent of your Communist, baby-murdering, Muslim-loving, Israel-hating anti-Christ ways and turn in faith to the Lord Jesus Christ for the forgiveness of your sins—which of course would require you denouncing the Democratic Party with its Official anti-God policies, and joining the ranks of the God-fearing Republicans and Independents, and perhaps the new Patriot Party should it arise to replace the doomed Democratic Party. But you won't repent, therefore you are damned!

Now that I got that out of the way, let me get back to refuting this first lie by the Democrats that illegal immigrants "aren't criminals." First, let me clear up some confusion that keeps popping up and clouding the debate over illegal immigration with regard to our Southern border with Mexico. In the debate over Border Security, we must separate the two different categories of criminal activity occurring on our Southern border; though in some cases the two are intertwined. The first category of criminal activity is that committed by drug smugglers and human smugglers—of course, the human smuggling problem is a direct result of the illegal immigration problem; solve the illegal immigration problem and you solve the human smuggling problem. But this first category of criminal activity involving drug and human smuggling is agreed by all, both Liberals and Conservatives alike, to be criminal enterprises that must be stopped! These criminals are vile and violent and contribute nothing good to society.

On the other hand, the second category of criminal activity occurring on our Southern border is somewhat different; it involves Mexican citizens' crossing over the border into the U.S. illegally in the search for a better life. Now, it is true that many of these people are good, honest, hard-working folks who have many of the same hopes and dreams that we all share, but they are nevertheless breaking the Laws of the United States of America, and therefore the second they cross our border illegally they have now become a "criminal." Entering the United States illegally is a crime. If you commit a crime you are a criminal. Henceforth, to part the clouds and bring clarity to the illegal immigration debate, no liberal Democrat can ever again get on TV or radio and claim that illegal immigrants "aren't criminals!" Yes they are!

In this chapter we do not address the problem of drug smuggling taking place across our Southern border, but rather shall focus on this second category of criminal activity engaged in by otherwise "regular people," but who are illegally entering our country. Therefore, I will be using the term *criminal illegal immigration* to refer to this second category of criminal activity perpetrated by people, who otherwise may be decent people, but who are by virtue of their illegal immigration into the U.S. now criminals!

## States Have The Right & Responsibility To Enforce Federal Law!

Having settled the fact that all illegal immigrants are indeed criminals, let's debunk some of the other idiotic and insane arguments vomited out by the America-hating Democrats in the illegal immigration debate.

Here's the next idiotic thing Democrats say: "But immigration is a Federal matter and States don't have the right to make immigration policy." Hey Idiot—no State is "making immigration policy," the States are merely enforcing the policies already on the books as law! It's not a policy issue; it's a law enforcement issue! Then the Dumb-o-crats try to say, "But illegal immigration breaks Federal Law and States don't have the right to enforce Federal Law." Oh really? Are you an idiot? Robbing a bank is a Federal crime, but who does the bank employee call? They call the local City Police Department of course! And it's the local City PD who responds in their Black & Whites with sirens blaring! The bank doesn't call the FBI and wait 4-hours for some FBI agent in a three-piece suit to show up! After the local PD catches the criminal guilty of committing a Federal crime, they hall his A-double-S down to the County Jail and throw him behind bars with all the other criminals accused of local City, County and State crimes. Then a few days or a week or so later he is finally turned over into Federal custody and prosecuted in Federal court; but the initial law enforcement action is conducted by the local City Police Department.

Drug smuggling across the U.S. border or across State lines is a Federal crime; but if a car loaded with drugs from Mexico is pulled over in San Diego for speeding by a local San Diego Police Officer, and that Police Officer detects the presence of illegal drugs, he makes the arrest himself on the spot, and hauls the drug dealer down to the County Jail where the drug smuggler is booked, mug-shot and finger printed, even though he has committed a Federal crime. Eventually the drug smuggler is turned over to Federal jurisdiction; but, again, the initial law enforcement action for a violation of a Federal law is administered by local City, County and/or State law enforcement officers.

Any crime which crosses State lines automatically becomes a Federal crime. So, let's say a kidnapper has abducted a child in Kansas and is being pursued by Kansas City Police, and the kidnapper turns onto the bridge which connects Kansas City, Kansas with Kansas City, Missouri, thus crossing State lines; do the police in hot pursuit suddenly stop and say, "Oh well, he crossed over state lines, this is a Federal matter now, so let's go home boys and call the FBI and let them handle it from here." Of course not! They keep pursuing the bastard till they catch him. They may call for assistance from the Missouri State or local City PD, but they along with the new local PD continue the pursuit.

In almost every case in which a crime is committed across State lines, thus becoming a Federal crime, the initial law enforcement action of arrest and detainment is conducted by local City, County and/or State law enforcement.

And so it is with Arizona Law SB1070. If you have broken Federal Immigration Law by crossing over the border from Mexico into the United States illegally, it is not only the right, but the responsibility of every City, County and State Law Enforcement Officer to arrest you; and any City, County or State Law Enforcement Officer anywhere within the United States who is not actively searching for illegal border crossers and conducting arrests of those criminals upon finding them is in dereliction of his or her law enforcement duties and should be immediately dismissed from their position.

So, please, for the sake of my TV's, stop making the ignorant statement that local law enforcement Officers don't have the right to arrest people committing a Federal crime.

## Racial Profiling Is An Essential Tool In Law Enforcement!

The third erroneous concept that dominates the illegal immigration debate is the most infuriating of all, and is the one most responsible for my throwing those objects at my TV. If you don't get anything else out of this chapter, please think hard and long about this one point—for this is the one argument in the debate over illegal immigration that even my conservative colleagues get wrong.

The Liberal argument goes like this: "But Arizona's Law SB1070 will lead to racial profiling." The conservatives respond: "The AZ law specifically prohibits racial profiling." In fact, right now as this book is being finalized for publishing, Arizona's Maricopa County Sheriff Joe Arpaio is testifying in a civil trial in which he is being accused of practicing "racial profiling."

Here is the error: both the Democrats and Republicans seem to be saying that racial profiling in matters of law enforcement is a "bad" thing, and therefore must not be tolerated. Now, I'm not an expert on matters of law, but the way everyone talks about it, it sounds like there may be some law somewhere against racial profiling by Law Enforcement Officers. If indeed there are Federal laws on the books prohibiting Law Enforcement Officers from racial profiling, that is the most idiotic, moronic and dangerous thing I've ever heard of! Even if such moronic laws do not exist, political correctness within our culture has certainly turned both Liberals and Conservatives alike into mindless morons on this issue!

The truth is, racial profiling not only is not "bad," but racial profiling is mandatory in all matters of law enforcement! But the other truth is that America has gone mad! America has somehow conjured up the illusion that racial profiling is wrong—however, the reality is, not to racially profile in matters of law enforcement is wrong! In fact, refraining from racial profiling in law enforcement is a severe dereliction of duty on the part of every Law Enforcement Officer, and is nothing short of madness! Let me explain—although I shouldn't need to, for this is a simple matter of *Common Sense!*

Let me begin with an actual experience which my family and I were subjected to because of the insanity of the politically correct mindset that racial profiling is somehow wrong. A short time after 9-11, my family, including my 10-year-old son, was going through airport security to board a cross-country flight. It was our first time flying after 9-11, and of course everyone was a little nervous about the prospect of flying. Now, enough time had passed since 9-11 that we knew exactly who it was that had perpetrated this Hellish atrocity upon our nation—it was 19 Saudi Arabian Muslim adult men, with Arabic accents and typical Arabic racial features including dark hair, dark eyes and dark skin tone. My son is a blonde-haired, blue-eyed American, who again was only 10-years-old. As we were going through security, the security officers—Federal employees of the TSA, Transportation Safety Administration—pulled my son out of line for an extensive security search to make sure he wasn't a terrorist! Give me a flipping break! Are you freaking serious! That kind of "profiling," or more correctly lack of racial profiling, of potential terrorists is not only asinine, but it is a serious danger to our national security! And the A-hole, whoever he or she is, that came up with that policy and all those responsible for disseminating it to the field should all be rounded up and given frontal lobotomies for their own safety and that of our national security.

I hereby challenge every Liberal opposed to racial profiling within the sound of my voice as it SCREAMS off these pages: Show me one example, just one example, in law enforcement where racial profiling is wrong or leads to poor law enforcement practices—you can't find one, not one single example where racial profiling is wrong and detrimental to law enforcement! In fact, any instance of law enforcement that does not practice racial profiling is poor law enforcement and a dereliction of duty on the part of the Law Enforcement Officers!

Many crimes fit a specific racial profile, and in those cases where a crime fits a particular racial profile, racial profiling must be used by law enforcement! Of course there are always exceptions, but criminal racial profiling is accurate 95% if not 99% of the time!

Now, Liberals, don't give me this: "I know of a case where a racist black cop pulled over this white guy and beat the snot out of him because the white guy flipped him off," or, "I can show you an incident where some racist White cops pulled over a Black guy for speeding and proceeded to beat the snot out of him because he cussed them out," etc. In each and every such instance, these are cases of bad Cops—individual Law Enforcement Officers who are racists and who acted improperly, period; and has nothing to do with racial profiling. Racial profiling is not "racist." Racism is hating, disliking or mistreating another person for no reason except for their race, and is evil and must not be tolerated in America! Racial profiling on the other hand has absolutely nothing to do with disliking or mistreating a person based upon their race, but rather is a law enforcement tool that recognizes and utilizes the fact that a particular racial profile fits the particular crime being investigated. For example, Blacks and Hispanics do not usually commit mass-murder; mass-murder is almost always committed by either a Muslim terrorist like Muslim Nidal Hasan who committed the Fort Hood massacre in religious obedience to the teachings of the Quran, or they are middle-class White or Asian boys like the Columbine High School massacre, the Virginia Tech massacre and the Aurora Colorado movie theater massacre. Blacks, Hispanics and Asians are also not likely to kidnap and murder an 8-months pregnant White girl—The police don't go scouring the Black, Hispanic and Asian neighborhoods looking for that missing pregnant White girl, of course not, they know most likely it was her White-ass husband who killed her!

Again, if a drive-by shooting occurs at a Mexican party, and the vehicle description is a dark-colored 4-door vehicle with 3 or more male occupants, tell me you ignorant Liberal A-holes, what do you want the police to do? Not racially profile the suspects? Do you want the police to waste their time stopping every dark-colored 4-door vehicle with White, Black and Asian occupants? You know damn well the police are looking for a dark-colored 4-door vehicle full of Mexicans!

The Islamic terrorists are 100% Muslim, and 99.9% of Muslims are Middle-eastern in race; thus the TSA needs to be racially profiling Middle-easterners as potential terrorists! Not freaking 10-year-old blonde-haired boys and 80-year-old gray-haired grandmothers! For God's sake people let's stop this madness! It's time for a *Common Sense Revolution!* But instead, the TSA has become the T&A, with perverts looking at naked images of our wives and daughters who have Zero chance of being an Islamic terrorist! Elect me, *Common Sense,* to Office and I'll shut down the T&A and replace it with local and private security that is trained by the Israelis in racial and Islamic terrorist profiling! *Oh, and just one more thing: I'll round up all the perverts who have been looking at naked images of our wives and daughters and line them up along the walls of our nation's airports, and appoint three days where we, the husbands and fathers whose wives and daughters naked bodies were exposed by the T&A, will have the opportunity to converge on our nation's airports and punch those T&A perverts right where it hurts!* OK, let me get back to being serious about this important *Common Sense* solution to the illegal immigration problem.

So the question is: Should Arizona Law Enforcement Officers, and all border State Law Enforcement Officers for that matter, in their duty to arrest all criminal illegal immigrants, racially profile and target their law enforcement efforts at Mexicans? *No, God forbid...they should instead be targeting blonde-haired, blue-eyed border crossers who speak perfect English without any Hispanic accent! I'm picking up another object to throw at my TV right now!* Of course you target Mexicans you moron! Of course you racially profile! The illegal immigration problem we are facing in America today is not a flood of Canadians illegally crossing the border and hiding undercover in our Country, but Mexicans illegally crossing our Southern border, and Mexicans have distinct racial profiles of Dark hair, eyes and skin tone, and who, if they can speak any English at all, have a heavy Mexican accent. And any Law Enforcement Officer who is not targeting Mexicans is in dereliction of his duty as a Law Enforcement Officer and should immediately be fired!

Hey, Liberals, what are you saying you want law enforcement to do with regard to capturing and deporting the millions of Mexican illegal immigrants—pull my blonde-haired, blue-eyed son over who speaks perfect English and ask him for proof of citizenship? Is that what you think law enforcement should do? Then, like the TSA, you need a lobotomy too!

Wait! I know what you Liberal Democrats want law enforcement to do, or rather not do—you don't want the laws against illegal immigration enforced at all! You Liberal Democrats think people should be able to come here illegally and stay here illegally! Hey Liberal Democratic Party morons—did you forget how September 11th, happened? Remember, the nineteen 9-11 hijackers were illegal aliens! Their temporary Visa's had expired, yet they remained in America in plain sight of law enforcement because of the Federal Government's refusal to enforce immigration laws!

Racial profiling is not only not wrong, but is an essential tool in matters of law enforcement. In fact, every national security or border security or local law enforcement policy that does *NOT* employ racial profiling is wrong, dangerous, stupid, ignorant, and a dereliction of duty by the Law Enforcement Officers! And if we don't stop this idiotic political correctness of thinking that racial profiling is wrong, especially with regard to securing our borders and national security in our fight against Islamic terrorists, then we just damn well deserve whatever ills befall us.

To summarize, since every Mexican who crosses the border from Mexico into the United States illegally has committed a Federal crime, it is the absolute duty of every Law Enforcement Officer, whether a City Police Officer or Sheriff's Deputy or State Trooper, in each of the border States of Texas, New Mexico, Arizona and California, to employ the fundamental law enforcement tool of racial profiling by diligently watching for any Mexican whom the Officer suspects is in the U.S. illegally—perhaps just appearing nervous as the Police car pulls alongside at a traffic light—upon which every Law Enforcement Officer has a sworn duty to interdict and question that Mexican individual and to verify if they are an American citizen or at least have a legal Visa to be in this Country. If that local Law Enforcement Officer determines that individual to be here in the U.S. illegally, then they have a sworn duty to arrest that person. Now, since the Obama Administration has ordered I.C.E. (Immigration & Custom Enforcement) not to deport any illegal immigrants handed over to them by any State, I recommend that local Law Enforcement Agency buy a one-way ticket to the Southern-most part of Mexico and place the criminal on a plane the next morning—by sending them to the Southern-most part of Mexico, at least you know it will be a week or two before they cross back over the border into the U.S. again! But there is a much better *Common Sense* solution to our illegal immigration problem!

## Remove The "Magnets" & You Won't Need A Fence—

## That's *Common Sense!*

Here is where I strongly disagree with my Conservative friends who say, "First thing we have to do is secure the border!" I can't believe I'm about to say this, but on this point I actually agree with homosexual Home Land Security Director Janet Napolitano, that if we build a 50-foot high fence, the Mexicans will just build a 50-foot ladder! Now don't get me wrong, I believe we should use every deterrent to illegal border crossing possible; and I'm aware that a double-fence system has been very effective in some areas. But here is why I disagree that building a fence is our best defense against illegal immigration—as long as we continue to have "magnets" that draw the illegal immigrants to the U.S., they will continue to find a way around, over, under, a way to come. We must remove the magnets, and then we won't need a fence!

Well, here goes another TV! Are you as baffled as I am by the fact that current implementation of the law states that if a pregnant female criminal is illegally inside the borders of the United States and she squirts out a baby, that this criminal illegal immigrant's baby is automatically an American citizen? I mean, you're joking, right? This "magnet" that pulls pregnant Mexicans illegally across the border into the U.S. is the illegal immigration problem known as "Anchor Babies." This current stance of the law is a misinterpretation and misappropriation of the 14th Amendment to the Constitution! The purpose and original intent of the 14th Amendment was to ensure that the citizenship rights for all former slaves conferred upon them by the Civil Rights Act of 1866 and the Reconstruction Act became a permanent part of the U.S. Constitution. To ensure Constitutional Civil Rights for all Black former slaves the Republican Party—not the damned slave-owning Black-hating KKK-Founding Democratic Party, but the "anti-slavery" Republican Party—therefore proposed the 14th Amendment, which was ratified on July 9, 1868, making all people born or naturalized in the United States citizens, which, of course, included all former slaves. But, as already stated, the 14th Amendment was crafted and intended to secure citizenship for all former slaves and Echoed the words of the Republican Party's Civil Rights Act of 1866, which declares, *"...all persons born in the United States and not subject to any foreign power, excluding Indians not taxed, are hereby declared to be citizens of the United States."*

The 14th Amendment was crafted and ratified by the Republican Party to benefit Black former slaves in America, who were not in America illegally by means of illegal border crossing, nor were they subject to any foreign power. *Common Sense* dictates that the 14th Amendment does not apply to children born in the U.S. whose mother's have entered the U.S. illegally and who are also still subject to the foreign power of Mexico as they are the legal citizens of that Country!

To grant automatic U.S. Citizenship to a baby born to a mother who is on U.S. soil illegally is the definition of sheer insanity! First thing we need to do is repeal that idiotic application of the 14th Amendment from the books! Are you with me? That would immediately remove one huge, powerful magnet currently drawing illegal Mexican immigrants into America!

Next magnet we need to immediately remove is any and all government financial assistance from any Federal or State Agency given to a criminal illegal alien. As you know from my discussion of Taxes in chapter 6, that for the government to take in Taxes from me even one-dollar of my money that I worked for and "redistribute the wealth' by giving it to another American citizen who did not work for it, is Communism—and we will no longer abide Communism in this Country! But, even worse is to take my hard earned money from me and give it to a criminal illegal alien! So there is no confusion regarding my use of the term "criminal illegal alien," I do not mean an illegal alien who has committed another crime like robbing a convenience store; I mean that by the mere fact they have crossed the border illegally, they have already committed a Federal crime and are therefore a criminal illegal alien. No food stamps! No Child Care subsidy! No rental assistance! Nothing! Not one penny of my money! There's another huge magnet removed.

Here's the next magnet that must be removed, and this is a *big one*—No public school for any child of an illegal alien! Now, until they are caught and deported, if they want to pay out of their own pocket and send their kid to a private school, I have no problem with that. But as long as every Mexican knows they can sneak across the border into the U.S. and we'll pay out of our own pockets for their illegal children to attend our public schools—I don't care how high or how many fences you build—the Mexicans will keep coming! But if they wake up tomorrow and realize that their children can no longer attend our public schools, they'll stop coming here illegally with their children!

As long as our Federal and State governments continue to reward criminal illegal immigrants—again, that means all illegal immigrants—with free schooling for their children, free medical care, free money for living assistance, they will continue to come, I don't care how "secure" you try and make the border. But if we remove all economic magnets, they'll stop coming!

It's time for a new *Common Sense* revolution! I'm *Common Sense* and I'm running for Office—together we can take back America! Elect me as President, Congressman, Governor and Mayor, and I will author and sign into Law a Bill titled: "No More Economic Magnets For Illegal Immigrants," which will immediately stop, rescind and prohibit any and all access by illegal aliens to any public benefit or service including public school and any food, rental or medical assistance, except for the one exception of Emergency Room access for serious and life-threatening illness or injury. This Bill will require proof of citizenship of at least one parent for enrollment by a Mexican child into public school.

As Americans, there is one more thing we need to do, or should I say stop doing, and that is we need to stop providing a direct benefit offered by both government and private corporations exclusively to the criminal illegal Mexican immigrants, thereby encouraging these criminals to stay in our country! What am I referring to? *(Instead of smashing my TV, this one makes me want to smash my phone!)* I'm talking about every time you call a government office, and often when you call businesses, you hear: *"Press 1 for English, (followed by a bunch of Mexican words)."* This exclusive access in their foreign tongue granted to the criminal illegal Mexican immigrants has got to stop! The only people in America who can't speak English and whose native tongue is Mexican Spanish are the illegal aliens from Mexico—why are we giving preferential treatment to these criminals?

Throughout America's rich history of immigrants coming to America from all over the world, the immigrant has always understood that they needed to assimilate into American culture, including learning our English language, celebrating American holidays, and demonstrating a love and respect for our American Flag and the Freedom it represents. On the Official Seal of the United States are the Latin words: *E pluribus Unum,* which means, "Out of many, One." America is made up of immigrants from many nations, every one of which came with the understanding that America has a unique culture, different from every other country, and to be part of the greatest nation on Earth you must agree to forsake the country of your origin and become an American through assimilation into the American culture.

But these Mexican criminals want us to allow them to continue to speak their foreign language, fly their foreign flag, celebrate their foreign holidays, and even provide them with their very own "phone option" in their foreign language when they call!—Well I've got just one thing to say: Go back home to your foreign country since you love it so much! And when you're ready to fall in love with America—our American Flag, our English language and our holidays, then let us know and maybe we'll grant you a temporary Work Visa as a trial period to see if you're really willing to become an American.

So I pledge, if you elect me, *Common Sense*, as your President, Congressman, Governor and Mayor, that I will immediately remove all Mexican language phone options from all government phone systems! I will further strongly encourage all businesses in America to do the same—and I mean *strongly* encourage all businesses by posting online a list of the names of all American businesses who continue to cater to these Mexican criminals; this list will be titled: *American Companies Who Support Illegal Immigrant Criminal Activity!*

In fact, let's simply resolve this problem by making English the Official Language of the U.S.A. and banning all other languages from use in government or commerce. That takes care of that. I'm even in favor of banning the use of foreign languages in all TV and Radio broadcasting, which would not only eliminate broadcasting to the criminal illegal Mexican immigrants, but such a ban on foreign language broadcasting would also eliminate the broadcasting of terrorist propaganda on the Arabic language channels! The bottom line is this—if you want to live in America, as a temporary guest or by becoming a Citizen, then you're going to have to speak our language and celebrate our holidays and respect our Flag. Otherwise, get the Hell out! We will not abide anti-American's inside our borders!

Further, however, in addition to removing all the current government give-away magnets that pull millions of Mexicans across the border into the U.S., we must also streamline the legal Worker Visa process for those Mexicans who don't wish to come to America for freebies, but who wish to come to America to work and pay Taxes to the United States in which they are working. Note that my 10% Federal Sales Tax proposed in the previous chapter resolves this Tax issue automatically. I'm not going to delve into whatever our current Worker Visa process is, but to stop illegal immigration by Mexicans into the U.S., the process from application to granting of a Temporary Work Visa should take no longer than 60-days; preferably 30-days. This Temporary Workers Visa should be for a 1-year period, with the option, after 6-months and with proof of employment, to renew for an additional 1-year for a maximum Visa length of 2-years. After which the worker must return to his country of origin and re-apply.

OK, now that we've stopped the flood of illegal immigrants being pulled across our Southern border by removing those powerful government give-away magnets, and by streamlining the legal Worker Visa process for those desiring to come here to work legally, we must now deal with the millions of illegal immigrants already inside our borders.

## 60-Day Order To Appear With Benefits!

We must accept the reality that it would be impossible for law enforcement to find, arrest and deport the millions of illegal immigrants scattered all across America. But, there is a way to force them to come forward out of the darkness into the light where we can once and for all deal with this problem. The solution is simply to issue a nationwide order giving every illegal immigrant 60-days to appear and register as a Guest Worker, otherwise they will be arrested, serve the appropriate prison sentence, and then be deported.

However, just the threat of going to jail "if they're caught" would not be incentive enough for the vast majority of illegal aliens to obey the order, because, again, law enforcement simply would not be able to find but a few violators. So we must also offer a strong positive incentive that would compel the vast majority of illegal immigrants to come out of the shadows; in other words, a 60-Day Order To Appear With Benefits which entitles them to register as a legal visitor.

First of all, this 60-Day Order To Appear With Benefits would only apply to those illegal immigrants who could prove with pay stubs or rent/utility receipts or the like that they had been in the U.S. for 90-days or longer—this prevents a new flood of illegal's across the border to take advantage of the 60-Day Order To Appear With Benefits.

The necessary positive "Benefits" should include:

A) Registration as a legal documented visitor with an accompanying 1-year Visa work or school permit. This Registration should include the issuance of a Tax-Payer Identification Number and the right to receive a legal temporary driver's license.

B) The right of registered working tax-paying immigrants' children to attend public school until the 1-year Visa expires (or 2-year if they request the extension).

C) The right, after 6-months of attending school or working, to apply for a 1-year extension to their temporary Work/School Visa, extending the original 1-year Visa to a maximum of 2-years; upon the completion of which they must return to their country of origin and re-apply.

D) And, for my conservative colleagues who believe I have thus far been way to lenient on these immigration law breaking criminals, they must Plead Guilty to breaking U.S. Immigration Law, be mug-shot and fingerprinted, and serve 1-day in County Jail, plus pay a fine of say, $1,000. Since this 60-Days To Appear With Benefits program will result in millions of illegal immigrants coming forward, the 1-day jail terms will of necessity have to be scheduled over a longer period to avoid over-crowding; and the $1,000 fine should be spread into monthly payments over a 1-year period.

The above is a *Common Sense* solution to America's illegal immigration problem which both stops the flood of new illegal immigrants coming across our Southern border and deals with the millions of illegal immigrants already here.

In conclusion, we will never secure our Southern border with Mexico unless and until we first remove the economic magnets of free Citizenship to children born to criminal illegal aliens, free public education for the children of illegal aliens, free financial assistance and free health care. The government does not have the right to take one-dollar of my hard earned money that I worked for and give it to another legal U.S. Citizen who did not work for it—so we damn sure are not going to let the government continue to take our hard earned money and give it to a law-breaking criminal illegal immigrant! We The People are coming by the power of the ballot to remove every one of these Democratic Party Communists from Office!

I'm *Common Sense* and I'm running for Office! Vote for me as your President, Congressman, Governor and Mayor, and together we can take back America by way of a new *Common Sense* revolution, and once and for all we will put an end to illegal immigration!

Now we will explain why it's not OK to be Gay!

## Chapter 8: Why It's Not OK To Be Gay!

America is a compassionate, freedom loving country; and as American's we want people to live pretty much however they wish as long as they're not hurting others (of course, we don't want them to hurt themselves either); but therein resides the problem with homosexuality—it not only destroys the temporal and eternal life of the homosexual individual, but also threatens the welfare of the nation and even humanity as a whole.

## God Loves Gays & So Do Republican's Too!

I'm first and foremost a Christian Minister, and therefore have great love, concern and compassion for those individuals seduced by the sin of homosexuality, because God Himself loves them—He proved His love for them when He died on the Cross at Calvary to pay in full the penalty for their sins and by rising from the dead on the third day, thus defeating Death which was the consequence of sin. But in order to be saved from your sins—whoever you may be: *"For all have sinned"* (Romans 3:23)—you must repent, acknowledge and turn from your sins, and believe in the Lord Jesus Christ.

The problem with our culture today, and specifically with the Democratic Party, is that the Democrat's hate those caught up in the sin of homosexuality, rather than loving them as God and the Republican's do. My statement, though on the surface may seem a little confusing to you, is nonetheless absolutely true! Let me explain.

God is called our "Father," and He loves us with a Father's love. Just as any human father who saw his child reaching under the kitchen sink for a bottle of poison that could kill him would grab a hold of his child and spank them and tell them not to do that ever again, so God warns us in His Word, the Holy Bible, of those things that will hurt and even kill us; and when we go astray He disciplines us as a loving Father in the hope of saving our life. Conversely, allowing and even condoning actions that are harmful and even destructive to one's life is not love, but hatred toward and utter disregard for the welfare of that soul. The Democrats, who claim to be pro-homosexual by condoning and even promoting that sinful lifestyle which is destroying the lives of those seduced by it, are by their actions demonstrating utter contempt and disregard for the welfare of the homosexual community.

But God, on the other hand, because He loves them, wants to save them from their sins that are destroying them. Listen to God's heart cry of love for the sinner:

**Revelation 3:19-20 (NIV)**

*[19]Those whom I love I rebuke and discipline. So be earnest, and repent. [20]Here I am! I stand at the door and knock. If anyone hears my voice and opens the door, I will come in and eat with him, and he with me.*

Here above, Jesus declares that His discipline of us when we go astray is proof of His love for us, and He does so in the hope that we will open the door of our hearts to Him and invite Him in, and He promises to come into our hearts and lives and commune with us in a personal and loving relationship. You see, Jesus is the Way we can have a personal and intimate loving relationship with God our Father, the Creator of the Universe! How awesome is that!

Hear His words again here:

**Hebrews 12:4-11 (NIV)**

*[4]In your struggle against sin, you have not yet resisted to the point of shedding your blood [like Jesus did]. [5]And you have forgotten that word of encouragement that addresses you as sons:    "My son, do not make light of the Lord's discipline, and do not lose heart when he rebukes you, [6]because the Lord disciplines those he loves,    and he punishes everyone he accepts as a son." [7]Endure hardship as discipline; God is treating you as sons. For what son is not disciplined by his father? [8]If you are not disciplined (and everyone undergoes discipline), then you are illegitimate children and not true sons. [9]Moreover, we have all had human fathers who disciplined us and we respected them for it. How much more should we submit to the Father of our spirits and live! [10]Our fathers disciplined us for a little while as they thought best; but God disciplines us for our good, that we may share in his holiness. [11]No discipline seems pleasant at the time, but painful. Later on, however, it produces a harvest of righteousness and peace for those who have been trained by it.*

The very fact that God and the Republican Party warn that the sin of homosexuality will destroy those who participate in it, proves God's and the Republican Party's love for all those practicing homosexuality.

## God Is Not Against Sex, He Invented It! But He Invented Sex For A Specific Purpose!

Some people have the wrong impression of God, that He's a kill-joy and doesn't want us to have any fun. Nothing could be further from the truth!

**John 10:9-10**

*[9]I am the door. If anyone enters by Me, he will be saved, and will go in and out and find pasture.*
*[10]The thief does not come except to steal, and to kill, and to destroy. I have come that they may have life, and that they may have it more abundantly.*

Here above, using the analogy that He is our Shepherd and we are His sheep, God, who came to Earth in the form of Jesus, tells us that it is the *"thief,"* satan and false religions, that come to ruin and destroy our life, but Jesus has come to give us the most abundant, joy-filled life experience we could ever imagine! And sex is part of that experience. God invented sex, however, with a specific purpose in mind, and when we pervert that purpose, sex becomes sin, and sin always has negative consequences.

Even without knowing the Bible, we can all make the fundamental anatomical observation regarding sex that it is intended to be performed between a man and a woman—the male and female anatomies are "built" to "fit together." Therefore, even without knowing God's instructions on the matter, *Common Sense* tells us that sex with someone of the same sex is "outside of the natural order." But even sex between two people of the opposite sex, if outside of God's purpose for which He Invented sex, is also outside of His boundaries and is therefore "trespassing" or sin. God is, after all, the One who manufactured the human being and is therefore the One who both knows and has the right to instruct human beings as to their proper function. Your automobile's Manufacturer's Handbook instructs you to place gasoline in the gas tank and oil in the oil intake—if you put oil in the gas tank and gas in the oil intake, your automobile won't function properly and may even be seriously damaged or even destroyed. The Holy Bible is God's Manufacturer's Handbook for His Creation—Mankind.

In the very first chapter of the Holy Bible God tells us His purpose for inventing sex:

**Genesis 1:26-28**

*[26]Then God said, "Let Us make man in Our image, according to Our likeness; let them have dominion over the fish of the sea, over the birds of the air, and over the cattle, over [t]all the earth and over every creeping thing that creeps on the earth." [27]So God created man in His own image; in the image of God He created him; <u>male and female</u> He created them. [28]Then God blessed them, and God said to them, "<u>Be fruitful and multiply;</u> fill the earth and subdue it; have dominion over the fish of the sea, over the birds of the air, and over every living thing that moves on the earth."*

There it is! God created Man as opposite sexes, *"male and female,"* in order that we would produce other human beings, i.e., *"Be fruitful and multiply."* Also note that God, our Manufacturer, gave us a mission, a command to, *"fill the earth and subdue it; have dominion over…every living thing that moves on the earth."*

Note to all the animal activists and environmentalists: God gave the resources of the planet and all living creatures on the planet to us for our use and benefit and for us to rule over and subdue. Now, we certainly should be wise in our stewardship of those resources, but the fact is that it is all there for our use and benefit.

By the way, do you know why woman is called a "female?" Because if you want to have a relationship with her there is a "fee" involved—it's going to cost you some doe bro! Dinner, diamonds, cars, etc. Oh, but she is so worth it! Just kidding—not about the worth it part, but about the fee part; I just couldn't resist the joke though. Moving on.

In the very next chapter of the Holy Bible, God reveals to us more regarding His purpose for sex: Genesis chapter 1 revealed to us that God made Man male & female and that He did so with the vested power in our sexual differences that we could reproduce other human beings—that's an amazing concept if you stop and think about it. Chapter 2, however, "zooms in" on the issue and provides us with more information and greater detail, introducing God's concept of marriage between one man and one woman, and that it is within the confines of that covenant marriage relationship that God commands the bringing forth of other human beings, i.e., the very foundation of human society—the family.

### Genesis 2:18-25 (NIV)

*18The LORD God said, "It is not good for the man to be alone. I will make a helper suitable for him."*

*19Now the LORD God had formed out of the ground all the beasts of the field and all the birds of the air. He brought them to the man to see what he would name them; and whatever the man called each living creature, that was its name.*

*20So the man gave names to all the livestock, the birds of the air and all the beasts of the field. But for Adam£ no suitable helper was found.* [This is Biblical proof that Man did not evolve from the animal kingdom; if the Man, Adam, could have had sexual intercourse with any creature from the animal kingdom and thus propagated the human race, he would have done so, but there was no mate found suitable for Man!]

*21So the LORD God caused the man to fall into a deep sleep; and while he was sleeping, he took one of the man's ribs£ and closed up the place with flesh.*

*22Then the LORD God made a woman from the rib£ he had taken out of the man, and he brought her to the man.*

*23The man said, "This is now bone of my bones and flesh of my flesh; she shall be called 'woman,'£ for she was taken out of man."*

*24For this reason a man will leave his father and mother and be united to his wife, and they will become one flesh* [i.e., form a new human being made up of the flesh from the two of them].

*25The man and his wife were both naked, and they felt no shame.*

Did you catch verse 25, about the man and his wife both being naked all the time and it was OK? Aren't you just a little ticked off at Adam and Eve for sinning and ruining that for us? I know my male readers are, anyway. But, getting back to the serious topic at hand.

The revelation in Genesis 2:24 above announces to us that God made us male and female in order that the day would come in our lives that we would leave the protection and provision of our father and mother and be joined to our wife, and then begin to produce children, thus establishing a new family unit on the Earth.

Therefore, any sexual activity outside of God's specific purpose for sex to be between a husband and wife is a sinful act, and sin always has negative consequences that are harmful to our happiness and success in life. And because God, our loving Heavenly Father, knows that when we "trespass," step outside of His boundaries and purpose for which He created us. That harmful and destructive consequences will impact our lives, He therefore warns us against making those stupid mistakes in our life.

There are three kinds of sexual sin: fornication, adultery and homosexuality, and all three result in serious consequences to those who practice them; but homosexuality is the greater sin of the three, for it also attacks and threatens the very existence of the human race.

Fornication is sex before marriage between two single people and results in the obvious negative consequences of unintended pregnancies, sexually transmitted diseases, and perhaps the worst of all, broken hearts and the abuse and destruction of the beauty of the intimacy of the sexual union between a husband and wife. I'm a male, so I can only speak as a man, but if a man has the choice between a used car that some other guy has been inside and used or a new car which no other guy has ever used, and they are both the same price, the man is going to choose the new car every time! No man can ever really be trusting of his wife if he knows she has allowed another man or men to enter inside her sacred place which should have been reserved solely for him. I'm sure this is true for the woman also, who will never truly trust her husband knowing that he has given himself to another woman or women. That most intimate union is intended to be reserved for that one person whom you marry and build a family with. Girls, don't give yourself to any guy who is not man enough to put a ring on your finger and stand before God and man and say the words, "I Do!" And guys, don't misuse a girl who you have no intention of marrying—she is some other guy's future wife! So get your hands off that other guy's wife! Do you want some other guy kissing and making out with your wife? Then don't be kissing that girl who is someone else's future wife!

Adultery is sex after marriage with someone other than your spouse—of course it takes two to tango, so one of the persons in the adulterous act may be a single person. Like fornication, adultery also bears the negative consequences of unintended pregnancies, sexually transmitted diseases and the breaking of the trust and covenant of the marriage union. God especially frowns upon adultery because it violates the safety and security He intended for the marriage union. Hear God's heart-cry against adultery in these passages of Holy Scripture:

### Malachi 2:13-16 (NIV)

*[13] Another thing you do: You flood the LORD's altar with tears. You weep and wail because he no longer pays attention to your offerings or accepts them with pleasure from your hands.*

*[14] You ask, "Why?" It is because the LORD is acting as the witness between you and the wife of your youth, because you have broken faith with her, though she is your partner, the wife of your marriage covenant.*

*[15] Has not ‹the LORD› made them one? In flesh and spirit they are his. And why one? Because he was seeking godly offspring. So guard yourself in your spirit, and do not break faith with the wife of your youth.*

*[16] "I hate divorce," says the LORD God of Israel, "and I hate a man's covering himself with violence as well as with his garment," says the LORD Almighty. So guard yourself in your spirit, and do not break faith [with the wife of your youth].*

### Hebrews 13:4

*Marriage is honorable among all, and the bed undefiled; but fornicators and adulterers God will judge.*

The passage above from Malachi 2, in the Old Testament says so much and speaks so beautifully that I will let it speak for itself without any commentary, except to say I hope you noted how precious one's faithfulness to the marriage covenant relationship between husband and wife is in God's sight, and those who "break faith" God judges and holds accountable. The passage from Hebrews 13, in the New Testament also announces God's judgment upon those who trespass outside the boundaries God has set for sex—the fornicators and adulterers. But this passage also sanctifies the sexual relationship within God's bounds of the marriage *"bed."* In other words, if you're married, Rock 'n Roll Baby!

In fact, both the Old and New Testaments of the Holy Bible declare that, not only as demonstrated above that God's purpose for inventing sex is so that husbands and wives may *"multiply"* by producing children, but also that god gave sex as a gift to husbands and wives to enjoy the profound pleasure of that aspect of the marriage relationship. Check out these verses:

### Proverbs 5:18-19

[18] *Let your fountain be blessed, And rejoice with the wife of your youth.*
[19] *As a loving deer and a graceful doe,    Let her breasts satisfy you at all times;    And always be enraptured with her love.*
(To read about the folly of adultery, read the entirety of Proverbs chapter 5.)

Now husbands and wives, let your imaginations run wild as you place yourselves into this intercourse between King Solomon and his Shulamite Bride:

### Song of Songs of Solomon 7:1-13 (NIV)

*The Lover Husband*
[1]*How beautiful are your sandaled feet, O prince's daughter! Your graceful legs are like jewels, the work of a craftsman's hands. [2]Your navel is a rounded goblet that never lacks blended wine. Your waist is a mound of wheat encircled by lilies. [3]Your breasts are like two fawns,    twins of a gazelle. [4]Your neck is like an ivory tower. Your eyes are the pools of Heshbon by the gate of Bath Rabbim. Your nose is like the tower of Lebanon looking toward Damascus. [5]Your head crowns you like Mount Carmel. Your hair is like royal tapestry; the king is held captive by its tresses. [6]How beautiful you are and how pleasing, O love, with your delights! [7]Your stature is like that of the palm, and your breasts like clusters of fruit. [8]I said, "I will climb the palm tree; I will take hold of its fruit." May your breasts be like the clusters of the vine, the fragrance of your breath like apples, [9]and your mouth like the best wine.*

*The Beloved Wife*

*May the wine go straight to my lover, flowing gently over lips and teeth. [10]I belong to my lover, and his desire is for me. [11]Come, my lover, let us go to the countryside, let us spend the night in the villages. [12]Let us go early to the vineyards to see if the vines have budded, if their blossoms have opened, and if the pomegranates are in bloom—there I will give you my love. [13]The mandrakes send out their fragrance, and at our door is every delicacy, both new and old, that I have stored up for you, my lover.*

OK, I'll give you a second to catch your breath and then I have one more passage to share with you, this time from the New Testament; this passage is not quite as romantic as the previous and a little more practical you might say. As much as I know the gals loved the above passage, the husbands will love the below passage:

### 1 Corinthians 7:2-5

*[2]Nevertheless, because of sexual immorality, let each man have his own wife, and let each woman have her own husband. [3]Let the husband render to his wife the affection due her, and likewise also the wife to her husband. [4]The wife does not have authority over her own body, but the husband does. And likewise the husband does not have authority over his own body, but the wife does. [5]Do not deprive one another except with consent for a time, that you may give yourselves to fasting and prayer; and come together again so that Satan does not tempt you because of your lack of self-control.*

I bet you didn't know that the Bible addressed the issue of sex in such a practical way! I can hear all the husbands saying right now, *"Come here, Baby, and take authority over my body! Then, Baby, when you're done having your way with me, if I have any strength left, I'll take authority over your body!"* Seriously, though, the point of the passage above is that sex was given by God as a wonderful gift to husbands and wives, not just for the producing of children, but also simply for the pleasure of it! But the above passage also declares plainly that sex is to be reserved for the marriage relationship. So God wants you to have a sex fest!—just as long as it is in the confines of the safety and security of the marriage covenant relationship. In fact, that is when sex is the best! If you've only experienced superficial sex with a person you're not married to, in which you are merely using that person for your own personal pleasure and that person is only using you for their personal pleasure, then you don't know what you're missing! Sex between a husband and wife who have committed their entire lives to each other is simply the best sex!

Stop and think about it for just a moment; all the negative consequences that accompany fornication, adultery and homosexuality—unintended pregnancies, sexually transmitted diseases, broken hearts and damaged future relationships—are all nonexistent when sex is between a husband and wife. You see, there is already a cure for A.I.D.S. and every other S.T.D., it's called marriage and faithfulness thereto! People who want money to be spent on research for a cure for A.I.D.S., but who are not willing to cease their sinful homosexual behavior, are spitting in the face of God!

In addition, all abortion clinics would shut down in a single day if all pregnancies occurred within the covenant relationship of marriage as god intended. The only people who have abortions are those who have committed the sexual sin of either fornication or adultery and want to try to cover up and rid themselves of the consequence of that sexual sin. But, "getting rid" of the consequence of fornication and adultery results in the murder of an innocent baby boy or girl! The "doctors" who perform these murders of innocent baby boys and girls are nothing less than baby-murdering monsters! And Barack Obama, Nancy Pelosi and every other member of the Democratic Party whose Official Platform is the condoning and promoting of these murders are all nothing less than baby-murdering monsters!

## Obama-Nation Of Abortion—When Does Life Begin?

For those of you who think I'm being too harsh on the "doctors" performing abortions, President Obama and all other members of the Democratic party who support and promote the abomination of abortion, by calling them baby-murdering monsters, let me ask you a few questions:

When does life begin? At what point is the baby a human being endowed by its Creator with certain unalienable rights, among which are the right to life, right to liberty and the right to pursue happiness? When asked this question by Pastor Rick Warren, during the televised Presidential Debate held at Pastor Warren's Church in 2008, the baby-murdering monster Barack Hussein Obama claimed that he did not know the answer to that question because it was "above his pay grade." Well, the answer is not above my pay grade, and I make a lot less than that multi-millionaire baby-murdering monster Barack Obama-Nation! The answer is that life begins at the moment of conception, at the moment of Creation! This miracle of Creation of a human being occurs when the male sperm cell, containing 23 chromosomes, perseveres, finds and penetrates into the female egg cell, also containing 23 chromosomes, and then a Divine miracle occurs as these two unique cells are joined together to form one cell with 46 chromosomes containing the entire genetic blueprint for that unique human being—this is the first cell of this unique human beings body—at that moment a human being exists! This miracle of Creation continues as this single unique human cell miraculously begins to replicate and multiply, resulting in the rapid formation of all the intricate parts of the human body which houses a living human being with an eternal soul! Science can't explain how this happens, it is simply a miracle! That process begins by the direct Divine intervention of God the Creator of all things, as the following verses from the Bible declare:

**Psalms 104:30**

[30]*You send forth Your Spirit, they are created; And You renew the face of the earth.*

**Psalms 139:13-14 (NLT)**

[13]*You made all the delicate, inner parts of my body and knit me together in my mother's womb.* [14]*Thank you for making me so wonderfully complex! Your workmanship is marvelous—how well I know it.*

**Zechariah 12:1**

*Thus says the Lord, who stretches out the heavens, lays the foundation of the earth, and forms the spirit of man within him:*

Thus, human life begins at the moment of conception, at the moment of Creation a human being exists with an eternal spirit. And even though the human body which is the home of that particular human spirit is just beginning its development, at that very moment of conception all the chromosomal DNA are present which determine that child's sex, as well as the color of that child's skin, eyes and hair, his or her facial features, height and weight, etc.! Therefore, at the moment of conception, that child has been endowed by his or her Creator with the unalienable Right to Life, Right to Liberty and the Right to Pursue Happiness!

It is, therefore, also a fact that every abortion, no matter how early it occurs, murders a human being—a little boy or little girl with an eternal soul!

It takes approximately 6-days from the moment of conception for the newly conceived little human to move through the uterine tube down into the uterus and begin to attach to the uterine wall. During those first 6 days the child is growing by means of the miracle of cell division and replication. Since each newly created cell must contain within the cellular nucleus all the necessary chromosomal strands of DNA, replication of DNA over these first 6 days requires an assembly rate exceeding 208,000 nucleotides per second! Nucleotides are the molecules that join together to form the strands of DNA which reside in the Nucleus of each and every cell. Let me state this again—***Replication of DNA over these first 6 days requires an assembly rate exceeding 208,000 nucleotides per second!*** Let me see Man create a machine that will duplicate that! That's why every true scientist is a Bible believing Christian! Any scientist who honestly looks at the mechanical design, complexity and power of the Creation jumps to his feet and exclaims: *Praise be to God, Creator of all things!* Because the Creation SCREAMS to the honest observer: *God made that! There is no other explanation!* Any scientist who denies the existence of God the Creator does so willfully, deliberately ignoring the clear and convincing proof of the existence of God displayed by everything in Creation!

**Romans 1:18-20 (NIV)**

[18]*The wrath of God is being revealed from heaven against all the godlessness and wickedness of men who <u>suppress the truth</u> by their wickedness,* [19]*since what may be known about God is <u>plain to them, because God has made it plain to them</u>.* [20]*For since the creation of the world God's invisible qualities—his eternal power and divine nature—have been <u>clearly seen</u>, being <u>understood from what has been made, so that men are without excuse</u>.*

By the end of the first week, the embryo has traveled extensively, multiplied from 1 cell to several hundred, dramatically changed its shape and complexity, and begun the process of finding permanent housing by attaching to the uterine wall.

Therefore, any intervention, such as the "Morning After Pill," which kills the baby by stopping it's implantation into the uterine wall is an abortion, the murder of a living eternal human being!


## *There Is No Such Thing As A "Fetus"—Every Abortion Kills A Baby With A Beating Heart!*

Did you know that just 22-days after conception every baby has a beating heart? And since it takes about 6-days from conception for the baby to attach to the uterine wall, that means only 2-weeks after the baby has attached to the mother's uterus the baby has a beating heart—that's before 99.9% of women have any idea that they are even pregnant! So every abortion murders a baby with a beating heart! Therefore we will no longer allow any baby-murdering monster to use the term "fetus," which seems to indicate something less than a human being; no, we shall denounce every such lie uttered and demand that President Obama and every other baby-murdering Democrat acknowledge that every abortion murders a baby boy or girl with a beating heart!

By the end of the 3rd week, the child's backbone, spinal cord and nervous system are forming, as well as the liver, kidneys and intestines!

By the end of the 4th week, the child is ten-thousand times larger than at conception!

In the 5th week, the baby's eyes, legs and hands begin to develop!

In the 6th week, the child's brain is well developed with brain waves detectable; also his or her eyes, mouth and lips are now present, and fingernails are now forming on his or her well-developed tiny fingers!

In the 7th week, the baby's eyelids and toes form, and his or her nose is distinct. The baby's arms bend at the elbow and the baby is now actively moving its arms and legs, kicking and swimming!

By the end of the 8th week, every organ is in place; the baby can now hear. Bones begin to replace cartilage, and fingerprints begin to form!

In the 9th week, the baby's genitalia and teeth begin to form; the baby can turn his head, frown and hiccup!

By the end of the 10th and 11th weeks, all organ systems are functioning; the baby can "breathe" amniotic fluid and urinate. The baby has a skeletal structure, nerves and circulation. And by the end of this 11th week the baby can grasp objects placed in its hand, as well as feel pain!

By the end of the 12th week, the baby's vocal cords are complete, and the baby begins to suck its thumb!

And the sad fact is that abortions are performed in the U.S. as late as the 28th week, even later! Though recently some States have banned abortions after the 24th week.


## How Abortion Murders Are Performed!

Now, let me tell you how abortions are performed; then you tell me if I'm over exaggerating when I call doctors who perform abortions baby-murdering monsters—but it's not just the doctors, but also every member of the Democratic Party, which not only condones, but promotes these murders, who are also guilty of being baby-murdering monsters! (Abortion procedure information is derived from: http://www.prochoice.com/abort_how.html)

SUCTION ABORTION, also called Vacuum Aspiration, is the most common abortion technique in use today. In this procedure the "doctor" inserts a suction tube through the dilated cervix of the mother into the womb. The powerful vacuum then tears the placenta from the uterus and dismembers the body of the baby, sucking the body parts into an attached jar. *(The "doctor" then opens the jar and drinks and chews the child's dismembered body parts—OK, the drinking and chewing of the baby's dismembered body by the doctor doesn't really happen, but he might as well, what the crap, he just sucked apart a living little boy or girl, which of course resulted in its death!).* There is a risk to the mother that the uterus can be punctured during the procedure. Also, the abortionist must take care that all the body parts are removed from the womb, as infection and hemorrhage can occur if body parts or placental tissue is left in the uterus.

SALT POISONING ABORTION, also called Saline Injection or "Salting out" is the second most common method of inducing abortion and is usually used after sixteen weeks. The doctor inserts a long needle through the mother's abdomen and injects a saline solution into the sac of amniotic fluid surrounding the baby. The baby is poisoned by swallowing the salt and his skin is completely burned away. It takes about an hour to kill the baby. After the child dies, the mother goes into labor and expels the dead baby. Saline injections have been outlawed in some countries because of the risks to the mother, which can include lung and kidney damage if the salt finds its way into her bloodstream. In spite of the horrible burning effect, some babies have survived "salting out" and been born alive. *(Of course, this is one of those instances of babies surviving abortions in which then Senator Barack Obama fought vehemently to prevent these children from receiving medical attention! Only a demonic monster could deny medical attention to these babies who survive abortion! If you voted for this monster, unless you repent, you shall suffer the deepest torments of Hell along with that monster Barack Hussein Obama! To watch testimonies of those who have survived abortions, search www.YouTube.com for "Testimony of Abortion Survivor" or "Gianna Jessen Saline Abortion Survivor," or to watch two TV ads featuring saline abortion survivor Gianna Jessen, visit: http://www.bornalivetruth.org/campaignads.php).*

DILATION AND CURETTAGE ABORTION, also called D&C Abortion, is usually performed between seven and twelve weeks of pregnancy. The doctor inserts a curette, a loop-shaped steel knife, into the womb through the dilated cervix. As the curette scrapes the wall of the uterus, the baby is cut into pieces. Bleeding can be considerable. As with a suction abortion, there is a risk of infection or hemorrhage, so the abortionist must reassemble the body parts to make sure the uterus is empty. *(In other words, the doctor must assemble on a table all the severed parts of the dead baby's body, his or her arms and legs, hands and feet, fingers and toes, and pieces of the head and torso to make sure he has removed the entire baby! Remember, all these parts are present and functioning at 7-weeks! Are you really still trying to tell me that the "doctor" who does this day in and day out isn't a baby-murdering monster?)*

DILATION AND EVACUATION ABORTION (D&E). This method is similar to a D&C, except that forceps must be used to grasp the baby's body because of the child's advanced development. The baby is dismembered as the abortionist twists and tears the parts of the body and slices the placenta away from the uterus. Bleeding is profuse. Although relatively safe for the mother, the procedure is devastating to the hospital staff and many doctors refuse to do advanced D&E abortions. *(My God!)*

HYSTEROTOMY ABORTION is similar to the Cesarean section. The hysterotomy abortion is a surgical procedure whereby the baby is removed from the mother's womb and allowed to die by neglect or killed by a direct act. This method offers the highest risk to the mother and produces the most number of live births. Hysterotomy is used only for late term pregnancies, and is sometimes used if the salt poisoning or prostaglandin abortion has failed. *(Can you even imagine such a thing?)*

PROSTAGLANDIN ABORTION. Prostaglandin is a chemical hormone which induces violent labor and premature birth when injected into the amniotic sac. Since prostaglandin results in an unusually high percentage of live births, salt, urea or another toxin is often injected first. The risk of live birth from a prostaglandin abortion is so great that its use is recommended only in hospitals with neonatal intensive care units. The risk to the mother is also greater with the use of prostaglandin; complications can include cardiac arrest. *(Too bad the cardiac arrest doesn't happen to the doctor!)*

*Every "Pro-Choice" Democrat Is A Baby-Murdering Monster & They All, Along With Anyone Who Votes For Them, Shall Suffer The Deepest Torments Of Hell Unless They Repent!*

Every day in America, by means of the various forms of mutilation described above, abortion "doctors" murder some 4,000 American children, 120,000 children every month, 1.5 million murders of American children every year, including 50% of all Black children! This is the Official Platform and policy of Barack Obama and the Democratic Party! Democrats say they are "Pro-Choice," that they support a woman's right to choose to have an abortion—ARE YOU INSANE! You mean to tell me that you think that a mother should have the right to murder her child simply because that child is an inconvenience? You Mr. Democrat, you Mrs. Democrat are a deranged monster if you think it is a mother's right to murder her child, I don't care what the circumstance!

Along with every abortion "doctor," the Supreme Court Justices who voted to make murdering American children legal in the U.S. in the 1973, Roe v. Wade case, as well as Barack Obama, Nancy Pelosi and every other member of the Democratic Party shall suffer the deepest torments of Hell for their complicity in these horrific murders if they do not repent! And every one of you Americans who vote for a Democrat are by your vote a co-conspirator in these daily murders of America's children! Repent! Or you will have to answer to Almighty God for your complicity in these murders of innocent children!

## *Any Person Who Thinks It's OK To Murder An Innocent Child In Cases Of Rape & Incest Is A Deranged Demented Monster!*

Whenever discussing the issue of the Obama-Nation of abortion in America: Some will claim that abortions must be permitted in the cases of rape and incest. Let me ask you this question: If someone breaks into your home and commits the crime of rape against you, does that give you the right to walk across the street and murder your innocent neighbor? Of course not! Just because you have suffered the crime of rape or incest against you, that does not give you the right to murder the innocent baby boy or girl in your womb! That's just *Common Sense!* That little boy or girl growing inside you, though conceived under unwanted and undesirable circumstances, is still nevertheless a living human being with a beating heart who is created in the image and likeness of Almighty God with a Divine destiny and purpose and therefore deserves the right to life, liberty and the pursuit of happiness! Any person who thinks that it is morally right to murder this child is a deranged demented monster—that of course includes most Democrats!

## *Abortion Is Not A Women's Health Issue!*

Ladies, please stop lying by claiming that abortion is a women's health issue—clearly you're lying because surely you are not that stupid! How does the creation of a human being inside your womb have anything to do with your health? It has nothing to do with your health and everything to do with the health of that precious baby being formed inside of you. The only "health" issue you might have to endure is morning sickness and swollen ankles; but you knew that before you spread your legs open and allowed a man to implant his seed inside you! And we all learned in kindergarten that if you plant a seed in the garden it is going to grow. Also ladies, please stop saying, *But it's my body and I have the right to do what I wish with my body.* Again, stop lying, I know you're not that stupid; the baby is not part of your body but is a completely separate body of a completely separate human being who is being miraculously formed within your miracle producing womb. So ladies, let's stop the lying! Abortion has nothing to do with a woman's health, but rather is solely about murdering an innocent child because you don't want to be bothered with a child! Again, you should have thought about that before you spread your legs open to a man who is not your husband!

## The Single Parent Syndrome Is A Sad Consequence Of The Sin Of Fornication!

Now, before addressing the sin of homosexuality and why it's not OK to be Gay, there is one more negative consequence to the sexual sins of fornication and adultery which I have not mentioned above, relates to the many unwanted pregnancies that often occur and the negative impact upon those bastard children who, thank God, are fortunate enough to be born into the world—escaping the Democratic Party's abortion clinic murder mills and the hands of those baby-murdering monsters who hide behind the label of "doctor"—but nevertheless these bastard children far too often do not have the nurture and support of their father, but only that of their mother. It is a sad fact that in many cases these children born outside of wedlock are for all intents and purposes "fatherless."

God intended for all children to be born into a "family" which includes both a father and mother, and although single parents are to be highly commended and respected for trying to fill the role of both Dad and Mom, the simple truth is that they cannot, and the child is the one who suffers for it. Children raised in a fatherless home suffer economically, emotionally, relationally and socially. Second to the murdering of these babies conceived by fornication and adultery, the single parent syndrome is the saddest consequence of fornication and adultery. If you, as an adult, choose to commit the sin of fornication or adultery or homosexuality and contract A.I.D.S. or the next coming incurable S.T.D. and die, as a sinner you are simply reaping what you sowed. But, when your sin affects the life of an innocent child—now that's really sad.

I need to pause here, though, and let you know that Jesus loves you in spite of your sins, and in fact paid for them when He died in your place on the Cross; and if you will acknowledge and turn from your sins and place your faith in the Lord Jesus Christ, calling upon His Name to Save you, He will forgive you of your sins and Save you from the eternal consequence of your sins. Please stop right here and do it now; call on the name of Jesus Christ the Lord to forgive you and Save you from your sins—He is waiting for you with open arms!

# Why Homosexuality Is The Worst Sexual Sin!

The third and final category of sexual sin is homosexuality. Homosexuality is the worst of the three categories of sexual sin because it attacks and opposes the very fundamental purpose for which God created sex—the propagation of the human race. Since the primary purpose of marriage is the propagation of the human race, and since two people of the same sex cannot produce children, there cannot be marriage between homosexuals. And any State who allows such will receive from the hand of God the judgment of God! Remember Sodom and Gomorrah! That is why the sin of homosexuality is called "sodomy," because it is named after that ancient city which was widely given over to the practice of homosexuality, as was its neighbor city of Gomorrah, and God destroyed both cities by raining down upon them fire and brimstone! (Genesis Chapters 18 & 19; 2 Peter 2:6-10; Jude 1:7).

In the United States today, if we the people accept the practice of homosexuality by permitting same-sex marriage, we too as a nation will suffer the wrath of God. If some individuals want to practice the sin of homosexuality and go to Hell, that's their business; but as a nation we MUST NOT permit that sin to be accepted and condoned by our society or the United States will be turned into Hell!

**Psalms 9:17**
*The wicked shall be turned into hell, And all the nations that forget God.*

**Jude 1:7**
*⁷as Sodom and Gomorrah, and the cities around them in a similar manner to these, having given themselves over to sexual immorality and gone after strange flesh, are <u>set forth as an example</u>, suffering the vengeance of eternal fire.*

Unlike the sexual sins of fornication and adultery which are capable of producing children and thus continuing the existence and expansion of the human race, homosexuality is incapable of reproducing and therefore threatens the very existence of the human race. If homosexuality is accepted and condoned as "OK," then why not have all of us become homosexuals! But if we did the entire human race would cease to exist in one generation! That's ridiculous, you say; not everybody would turn to practicing homosexuality. Granted, but if even a significant portion of society is permitted to do so by our acceptance and condoning of that practice, then God's plan for Man is being thwarted to a significant extent. Sodom and Gomorrah obviously didn't start out as cities widely given over to the practice of homosexuality, but they became that way. And just as a surgeon cuts out and kills a portion of your body that has become cancerous in order to save the rest of your body, so God had to remove these cities from the face of the Earth in order to prevent their cancerous sin of homosexuality from spreading. In fact, every act of Judgment by God against evil is an act of mercy attempting to eradicate that evil from the Earth in order that the majority of Mankind may be saved.

Homosexuality not only destroys the life of the practitioner thereof, but pollutes the culture in which it is condoned, and even threatens the very existence of the human race! This is WHY IT'S NOT OK TO BE GAY!

This is also why God, the Creator of Mankind, is so opposed to the sexual sin of homosexuality; the Bible is very clear on this issue. Below is one passage from the Old Testament, then several from the New Testament (as throughout this book, I have underlined certain words for emphasis):

**Leviticus 20:13**

*If a man lies with a male as he lies with a woman, both of them have* <u>*committed an abomination*</u>*.*

**Romans 1:18-32 (NIV)**

[18]The <u>wrath of God</u> is being revealed from heaven <u>against all the godlessness and wickedness of men</u> who suppress the truth by their wickedness, [19]since what may be known about God is plain to them, because God has made it plain to them. [20]For since the creation of the world God's invisible qualities—his eternal power and divine nature—have been clearly seen, being understood from what has been made, so that men are without excuse. [21]For although they knew God, they neither glorified him as God nor gave thanks to him, but their thinking became futile and their foolish hearts were darkened. [22]Although they claimed to be wise, they became fools [23]and exchanged the glory of the immortal God for images made to look like mortal man and birds and animals and reptiles.

[24]Therefore God gave them over in the <u>sinful desires of their hearts to sexual impurity</u> for the <u>degrading of their bodies with one another</u>.

[25]They exchanged the truth of God for a lie, and worshiped and served created things rather than the Creator—who is forever praised. Amen.

[26]Because of this, God gave them over to <u>shameful lusts</u>. Even their <u>women exchanged natural relations for unnatural ones</u>. [27]<u>In the same way the men also abandoned natural relations with women and were inflamed with lust for one another. Men committed indecent acts with other men, and received in themselves the due penalty for their perversion</u>.

[28]Furthermore, since they did not think it worthwhile to retain the knowledge of God, he gave them over to a <u>depraved mind</u>, to do what <u>ought not to be done</u>. [29]They have become <u>filled with every kind of wickedness</u>, evil, greed and depravity. They are full of envy, murder, strife, deceit and malice. They are gossips, [30]slanderers, God–haters, insolent, arrogant and boastful; they invent ways of doing evil; they disobey their parents; [31]they are senseless, faithless, heartless, ruthless. [32]Although <u>they know</u> God's righteous decree that those who do such things <u>deserve death</u>, they not only <u>continue</u> to do these very things but also <u>approve of those who practice them</u>.

The last verse above explains why Liberals and Democrats, who *"approve"* of the sin of homosexuality, are anti-God; and therefore no human being, unless you wish to be in opposition to God, should ever vote for a Democrat. The Democratic Party by its Official Platform of condoning and even promoting the sin of homosexuality is a Political Party in direct and deliberate opposition to God! If I were you, I would check my voter's registration card and make sure it doesn't declare that you are a member of the Democratic Party! Dear Democrats, hear this warning—your arms are too short to box with God!

This next passage from the New Testament refers to the Old Testament record of God's destruction of the cities of Sodom and Gomorrah for their sin of homosexuality:

**2 Peter 2:6-8**

*⁶and turning the cities of Sodom and Gomorrah into ashes, condemned them to destruction, making them <u>an example to those who afterward would live ungodly;</u> ⁷and delivered righteous Lot, who was oppressed by the filthy conduct of the wicked ⁸(for that righteous man, dwelling among them, tormented his righteous soul from day to day by seeing and hearing their lawless deeds).*

And Jude, the Lord Jesus' half-brother (same mother, different father), speaks of the same in this way:

**Jude 1:7**

*⁷as Sodom and Gomorrah, and the cities around them in a similar manner to these, having given themselves over to sexual immorality and gone after strange flesh, are set forth as an example, suffering the vengeance of eternal fire.*

Now please understand that all 3 categories of sexual sin, if continued in, will damn your soul and body to Hell. Listen to these passages from Holy Scripture which refer to all 3 categories of sexual sin, as well as many other forms of sin:

**1 Corinthians 6:9-11**

*⁹Do you not know that <u>the unrighteous will not inherit the kingdom of God?</u> Do not be deceived. Neither <u>fornicators</u>, nor idolaters, nor <u>adulterers, nor homosexuals, nor sodomites,</u> ¹⁰nor thieves, nor covetous, nor drunkards, nor revilers, nor extortioners <u>will inherit the kingdom of God.</u>*

*¹¹And such <u>were</u> some of you. But you were washed, but you were sanctified, but you were justified in the name of the Lord Jesus and by the Spirit of our God.*

Yes, it is true; you can be "changed" from being a practicing homosexual! And those who do not try to help the homosexual to change by imploring them to forsake his or her sin of homosexuality are the people who hate the homosexual and do not care about their temporal and eternal happiness, i.e., the Democratic Party! But those, like Congresswoman Michele Bachmann and her husband, who seek to help the homosexual be set free from their bondage to that sin, are the ones who love the homosexual and care about their temporal and eternal happiness and wellbeing!

As the above Biblical passage makes plain, we all have sinned! But God has provided the forgiveness of our sins and acceptance into His Kingdom by being "Born Again" through repentance from our sins and faith in the crucified for sins and risen again Son of God, the Lord Jesus Christ! (See John Chapter 3; 1:12-13; Romans 8:1-17; Ephesians 1:3-14; 2:1-9; Titus 3:3-7; 1 Peter Chapter 1; 1 John Chapter 5).

## No One Is Born Gay, Everyone Is Born Either Male Or Female!

The fact is that we are all, Christians and non-Christians alike, tempted with sexual sin; some are tempted with fornication, some with adultery and others with homosexuality. But sin must be resisted and repented of. Listen to what God said to Cain before he murdered his brother Abel:

**Genesis 4:6-7 (NIV)**
*⁶Then the LORD said to Cain, "Why are you angry? Why is your face downcast? ⁷If you do what is right, will you not be accepted? But if you do not do what is right, sin is crouching at your door; it desires to have you, but you must master it."*

Sin is always "at our door" waiting to ensnare and devour us, but God has given Mankind the power to resist and rule over sin. Whenever we "sin" we *choose* to do so. The temptation is in and of itself not sin; sin occurs when we choose to give in to the temptation. This is true of both Christians and non-Christians; we all must fight temptation on a daily basis.

### James 1:12-15

$^{12}$*Blessed is the man who endures temptation; for when he has been approved, he will receive the crown of life which the Lord has promised to those who love Him.* $^{13}$*Let no one say when he is tempted, "I am tempted by God"; for God cannot be tempted by evil, nor does He Himself tempt anyone.* $^{14}$*But each one is tempted when he is drawn away by his own desires and enticed.* $^{15}$*Then, when desire has conceived, it gives birth to sin; and sin, when it is full-grown, brings forth death.*

### 1 Corinthians 10:12-13

$^{12}$*Therefore let him who thinks he stands take heed lest he fall.* $^{13}$*No temptation has overtaken you except such as is common to man; but God is faithful, who will not allow you to be tempted beyond what you are able, but with the temptation will also make the way of escape, that you may be able to bear it.*

This brings us back to our discussion of the sin of homosexuality. Like the sins of fornication and adultery, the sin of homosexuality is a choice. No one is born a "homosexual." All Mankind are born either Male or female (Genesis 1:27), and that physical and biological-reproductive attribute is your "sexual identity."

But someone will say, "I've had these feelings of wanting to be like the other sex since childhood." What you are actually acknowledging is that you have been "tempted" by the sin of homosexuality since childhood. All children are tempted by sin—some are tempted with the sin of lying, some with the sin of stealing, some with the sin of being disobedient to their parents, some with the sin of cursing the air blue with profanities, and some with the sin of homosexuality. I can remember as a young boy watching a Mighty Mouse cartoon in which Mighty Mouse dressed up in women's clothes with jewelry and perfume transforming him into a voluptuous woman, which all of the men in the town fell in lust with, and after watching that cartoon, the fantasy of being transformed into a voluptuous woman filled my mind, and I secretly got some of my mother's costume jewelry and sexy clothing and put them on and pretended and fantasized I was a woman. My older sister caught me and began making fun of me; of course I was totally embarrassed and told her I was just playing pirates. Anyway, it was just a one-time deal which never "haunted" me again. Perhaps other guys have had similar experiences, and in some cases perhaps it wasn't just a one-time thing; perhaps those guys then began to wonder, "Maybe I'm Gay?" And that is why it is so damning and dangerous when the Democratic Party, Hollywood movies and TV shows condone homosexuality and imply that it's OK to be Gay. The fact is, there is no such thing as "Being Gay." No one is "Gay." You are a boy or you are a girl, and if you engage in having sexual relations with another person of the same sex, the current societal label is that you are "Gay," but the truth is you are choosing to engage in the sinful act of homosexuality. Just because you have "feelings" and "desires," even from childhood, to commit this sin does not condone that sin—everyone who commits sin of any kind has the desire to do so. Having the inward desire to engage in a particular act does not make engaging in that act OK; nor does the presence of this desire mean you are bound to commit that act. You possess the power to choose to do right or choose to do wrong! When you choose to commit sin, you will suffer the consequences, both in this life and in the life to come, unless you turn from your sin and put your faith in the Lord Jesus Christ to Save you from your sins!

How many of you as a child stole something? Maybe you stole something from your friend's home or money from your Grandmother's purse or perhaps something from a store. I remember as a child wanting Silly Putty, but I didn't have the money to buy it, so I went to the toy department at the neighborhood Sears store, broke into the packaging, and not wanting to have the bulge of the Egg in my pocket for fear of being caught, I removed the Silly Putty from the Egg and shoved it into my front pocket and walked out of the store. It was a hot Summer's day, and by the time I walked home the Silly Putty had adhered itself to the lining of my pocket and I was only able to retrieve from my pocket about half the original ball of Putty. I guess maybe that was God's way of teaching me that "crime doesn't pay!" The point here is, though I had the "desire" to be a thief, that doesn't mean I am "a thief;" I committed the sin of stealing, yes; but that doesn't mean I'm bound for the rest of my life to go on stealing. That is why it is so important for society to teach it's children and adults that there are things which are right and there are things which are wrong, and those things that are wrong are "sins" against God and our fellow man, and must not be condoned as acceptable or OK.

It's not OK to be Gay—it's not OK to practice the sin of Homosexuality—just as it's not OK to practice the sin of Adultery or the sin of Fornication or the sin of Murder or the sin of Stealing or the sin of Witchcraft or the sin of Idolatry (worshiping any God other than Jesus Christ) or the sin of Lying or the sin of Unbelief—Not Believing in Jesus Christ, which is the Greatest Sin of all and is in fact the One Sin that Damns the soul to Hell because Jesus paid the penalty for all the other sins! Every human being has committed any number of sins, which is the very reason why Jesus Christ came into the world to die in our place for our sins!

The Apostle Paul declares:

**1 Timothy 1:15**

[15]*This is a faithful saying and worthy of all acceptance, that Christ Jesus came into the world to save sinners, of whom I am chief.*

## Romans 5:8-11

[8]*But God demonstrates His own love toward us, in that while we were still sinners, Christ died for us.* [9]*Much more then, having now been justified by His blood, we shall be saved from wrath through Him.* [10]*For if when we were enemies we were reconciled to God through the death of His Son, much more, having been reconciled, we shall be saved by His life.* [11]*And not only that, but we also rejoice in God through our Lord Jesus Christ, through whom we have now received the reconciliation.*

## Romans 6:23

[23]*For the wages of sin is death, but the gift of God is eternal life in Christ Jesus our Lord.*

I implore you, whether your sin is homosexuality or lying or adultery or stealing or fornication or whatever sin it may be, if you do not want to spend Eternity being burned alive in the fires of Hell from which there is no escape, then stop practicing your sin (repent), and put your faith in the Lord Jesus Christ, the Son of God, to Save you and forgive you of your sins by calling upon Jesus' Name!

## 2 Corinthians 5:14-21 (NIV)

[14]*For Christ's love compels us, because we are convinced that one died for all, and therefore all died.* [15]*And he died for all, that those who live should no longer live for themselves but for him who died for them and was raised again.*

[16]*So from now on we regard no one from a worldly point of view. Though we once regarded Christ in this way, we do so no longer.* [17]*Therefore, if anyone is in Christ, he is a new creation; the old has gone, the new has come!* [18]*All this is from God, who reconciled us to himself through Christ and gave us the ministry of reconciliation:* [19]*that God was reconciling the world to himself in Christ, not counting men's sins against them. And he has committed to us the message of reconciliation.*

[20]*We are therefore Christ's ambassadors, as though God were making his appeal through us. We implore you on Christ's behalf: Be reconciled to God!* [21]*God made him who had no sin to be sin for us, so that in him we might become the righteousness of God.*

### Romans 10:9-13 (NIV)

*[9]That if you confess with your mouth, "Jesus is Lord," and believe in your heart that God raised him from the dead, you will be saved. [10]For it is with your heart that you believe and are justified, and it is with your mouth that you confess and are saved. [11]As the Scripture says, "Anyone who trusts in him will never be put to shame."*

*[12]For there is no difference between Jew and Gentile—the same Lord is Lord of all and richly blesses all who call on him, [13]for, "Everyone who calls on the name of the Lord will be saved."*

### Philippians 2:5-11

*[5]...Christ Jesus, [6]who, being in the form of God, did not consider it robbery to be equal with God, [7]but made Himself of no reputation, taking the form of a bondservant, and coming in the likeness of men. [8]And being found in appearance as a man, He humbled Himself and became obedient to the point of death, even the death of the cross. [9]Therefore God also has highly exalted Him and given Him the name which is above every name, [10]that at the name of Jesus every knee should bow, of those in heaven, and of those on earth, and of those under the earth, [11]and that every tongue should confess that Jesus Christ is Lord, to the glory of God the Father.*

Your destiny is Eternity! Every human being will stand before God, and those who through faith in the Lord Jesus Christ have their names written in the "Lamb's Book of Life" will live with God forever in His Eternal Kingdom, but those who do not repent of their sins and do not put faith in the Lord Jesus Christ will suffer the eternal torments of the Lake of Fire!

## Revelation 20:11-15

[11]*Then I saw a great white throne and Him who sat on it, from whose face the earth and the heaven fled away. And there was found no place for them.*

[12]*And I saw the dead, small and great, standing before £God, and books were opened. And another book was opened, which is the Book of Life. And the dead were judged according to their works, by the things which were written in the books.*

[13]*The sea gave up the dead who were in it, and Death and Hades delivered up the dead who were in them. And they were judged, each one according to his works.*

[14]*Then Death and Hades were cast into the lake of fire. This is the second £death.*

[15]*And anyone not found written in the Book of Life was cast into the lake of fire.*

## Revelation 21:1-8

[1]*Now I saw a new heaven and a new earth, for the first heaven and the first earth had passed away. Also there was no more sea.*

[2]*Then I, £John, saw the holy city, New Jerusalem, coming down out of heaven from God, prepared as a bride adorned for her husband.*

[3]*And I heard a loud voice from heaven saying, "Behold, the tabernacle of God is with men, and He will dwell with them, and they shall be His people. God Himself will be with them and be their God.*

[4]*And God will wipe away every tear from their eyes; there shall be no more death, nor sorrow, nor crying. There shall be no more pain, for the former things have passed away."*

[5]*Then He who sat on the throne said, "Behold, I make all things new." And He said £to me, "Write, for these words are true and faithful."*

[6]*And He said to me, "It£ is done! I am the Alpha and the Omega, the Beginning and the End. I will give of the fountain of the water of life freely to him who thirsts.*

[7]*He who overcomes £shall inherit all things, and I will be his God and he shall be My son.*

[8]*But the cowardly, £unbelieving, abominable, murderers, <u>sexually immoral</u>, sorcerers, idolaters, and all liars shall have their part in the lake which burns with fire and brimstone, which is the second death."*

Seeing then, that God, Creator of Mankind, forbids the sinful practice of homosexuality, as well as fornication and adultery, we as a nation must never elect to Office anyone who condones and promotes any of these sinful practices. This is another reason why President Barack Obama is so dangerous and detrimental to the welfare of the United States, because he is the most pro-homosexual President ever elected to Office; and his position as the Head of our nation thereby brings upon America the wrath of Almighty God!

Let me ask you this: Would you appoint as the Head of Home Land Security a practicing Adulterer? Of course not! Yet President Obama has appointed a practicing Lesbian Homosexual, Janet Napolitano, to that position. Would you appoint a practicing Adulterer to the Supreme Court? Of course not! Yet President Obama has appointed two Lesbian homosexual Justices, Sonia Sotomayor and Elena Kagan—alright, unlike Janet, Sonia and Elena haven't come out publically and declared their homosexuality, but they've been supportive of supposed "Gay Rights" issues, especially Elena Kagan—which should automatically disqualify her; and Sonia is an admitted racist; so both have no place on the highest court in our land.

This is another reason why no American should ever vote for a Democrat for President of the United states, for by so doing you have given him or her the authority to appoint Godless people to the Supreme Court.

## President Obama Declares War Against God!

May 9, 2012, was a tragic day in American history, because for the first time an American President, Barack Hussein Obama, announced publically that he personally supports homosexual marriage. President Obama then went on to issue a Presidential Proclamation declaring the Month of June, 2012, to be Lesbian, Gay, Bisexual & Transgender Pride Month! Here is President Obama's Proclamation in its entirety:

### Presidential Proclamation: Lesbian, Gay, Bisexual, and Transgender Pride Month, 2012

*By The President Of The United States Of America*
*A Proclamation*

*From generation to generation, ordinary Americans have led a proud and inexorable march toward freedom, fairness, and full equality under the law -- not just for some, but for all. Ours is a heritage forged by those who organized, agitated, and advocated for change; who wielded love stronger than hate and hope more powerful than insult or injury; who fought to build for themselves and their families a Nation where no one is a second-class citizen, no one is denied basic rights, and all of us are free to live and love as we see fit.*

*The lesbian, gay, bisexual, and transgender (LGBT) community has written a proud chapter in this fundamentally American story. From brave men and women who came out and spoke out, to union and faith leaders who rallied for equality, to activists and advocates who challenged unjust laws and marched on Washington, LGBT Americans and allies have achieved what once seemed inconceivable. This month, we reflect on their enduring legacy, celebrate the movement that has made progress possible, and recommit to securing the fullest blessings of freedom for all Americans.*

*Since I took office, my Administration has worked to broaden opportunity, advance equality, and level the playing field for LGBT people and communities. We have fought to secure justice for all under the Matthew Shepard and James Byrd, Jr., Hate Crimes Prevention Act, and we have taken action to end housing discrimination based on sexual orientation and gender identity. We expanded hospital visitation rights for LGBT patients and their loved ones, and under the Affordable Care Act, we ensured that insurance companies will no longer be able to deny coverage to someone just because they are lesbian, gay, bisexual, or transgender. Because we understand that LGBT rights are human rights, we continue to engage with the international community in promoting and protecting the rights of LGBT persons around the world. Because we repealed "Don't Ask, Don't Tell," gay, lesbian, and bisexual Americans can serve their country openly, honestly, and without fear of losing their jobs because of whom they love. And because we must treat others the way we want to be treated, I personally believe in marriage equality for same-sex couples.*

*More remains to be done to ensure every single American is treated equally, regardless of sexual orientation or gender identity. Moving forward, my Administration will continue its work to advance the rights of LGBT Americans. This month, as we reflect on how far we have come and how far we have yet to go, let us recall that the progress we have made is built on the words and deeds of ordinary Americans. Let us pay tribute to those who came before us, and those who continue their work today; and let us rededicate ourselves to a task that is unending -- the pursuit of a Nation where all are equal, and all have the full and unfettered opportunity to pursue happiness and live openly and freely.*

*NOW, THEREFORE, I, BARACK OBAMA, President of the United States of America, by virtue of the authority vested in me by the Constitution and the laws of the United States, do hereby proclaim June 2012 as Lesbian, Gay, Bisexual, and Transgender Pride Month. I call upon the people of the United States to eliminate prejudice everywhere it exists, and to celebrate the great diversity of the American people.*

*IN WITNESS WHEREOF, I have hereunto set my hand this first day of June, in the year of our Lord two thousand twelve, and of the Independence of the United States of America the two hundred and thirty-sixth.*

*BARACK OBAMA*

The audacity of President Obama, who, as it is written about him regarding the sin of homosexuality, *"Although they know God's righteous decree that those who do such things deserve death, they not only continue to do these very things but also approve of those who practice them"* (Romans 1:32), as he sets his hand to sign this abominable proclamation, dares to include: *"IN WITNESS WHEREOF, I have hereunto set my hand this first day of June, in the year of our Lord two thousand twelve!"*

Obama's acknowledgment that Jesus Christ is America's Lord, while simultaneously declaring a month of Official National Disobedience to the Laws & decrees of our Lord Jesus Christ is nothing less than a Declaration of War against God! And God's wrath has been poured out, and continues to be poured out upon America because of the Head of our Nation's arrogant declaration of war against Almighty God!

## *President Obama's Pro-Homosexual Policies Have Brought God's Judgment Upon America!*

In what way, you ask, has God's wrath been poured out upon America? Open your eyes you morons! Don't you watch the TV news? In the month of June, 2012, did not Colorado experience the worst fires in Colorado's history? In the month of June, did not the Southeast experience record flooding? In June did not the Midwest and Northeast experience the worst storm in America's history, it was called the "Perfect Storm" and a "Land Hurricane," in all your life have you ever heard of such a thing? But also in June, did not the Northeast and Midwest experience the worst heat wave in recorded history, with some 2,000 heat records being broken? In the month of June, did not the drought upon America hit record proportions, with 26 States being declared drought disaster zones, and the drought in June being compared to the 1929 "Dust Bowl" drought deemed "The Grapes of Wrath"? This epic drought continues to impact our nation. In fact, since President Barack Obama was elected as America's President, because of President Obama's pro-Gay and anti-Israel policies, God has judged America with the worst tornado activity in America's history, the worst flooding in America's history, the worst fires in America's history, the worst economy since the Great Depression, the worst storm and lightning activity in America's history, and unusual earthquakes in the Northeast, even striking Washington D.C. and causing damage to such National Symbols as the Washington Monument! Wake up America! The only way to lift God's wrath off of America is for America's citizens to vote this Pro-Homosexual, Pro-Muslim, Pro-Communism, Anti-America, Anti-Capitalism, Anti-Israel, Anti-Christ named Barack Hussein Obama out of Office! The choice is yours America!

The Democratic Party Officially Kicked God Out Of Their Party While Simultaneously Embracing The Obama-nation Of Homosexual Marriage In Their 2012 Democratic Party Platform! Anyone Who Votes For Any Democrat In The 2012 Election Shall Incur God's Wrath Upon Them!

To make matters worse, the entire Democratic Party has officially joined Obama in his anti-God anti-Israel position by officially kicking God out of the 2012 Democratic Party Platform, as well as removing the declaration that Jerusalem is the Capital of Israel, while simultaneously declaring the Democratic Party's official support of homosexual marriage! This removal by the Democratic Party of God and Jerusalem from their 2012 Platform caused such a stir outside of the Democratic Party that, fearing it could cost them the 2012 Election, the DNC attempted to add an Amendment to the Official Democratic Party Platform which reinserted a mention of God and Jerusalem as Israel's Capital. However, when the Amendment came to the floor of the Democratic National Convention for vote by the delegates, when the DNC Chairman said, *"All those delegates in favor say 'I;' all those delegates opposed say 'No;'"* the "No's" were greater than the "I's!" The Chairman knowing he had been sent to the floor to get the Amendment passed to avoid the "DNC Says No to God" controversy tried it again a second time; but this time the "No's" were even louder! The Chairman looked around, looking to the side for direction; he then tried it a third time and again the "No's" won! To which he declared, *"In the opinion of the Chair two-thirds have voted in the affirmative, the motion is adopted and the Platform has been amended as shown on the screen"* to which the majority of delegates who had voted against placing God and Jerusalem as Israel's Capital back into the Democratic Party Platform began to boo, hiss and jeer! A photo taken from behind the Chairman was leaked which showed that his words *"In the opinion of the Chair two-thirds have voted in the affirmative, the motion is adopted and the Platform has been amended"* were pre-loaded into the teleprompter! So "technically" God and Jerusalem were placed back into the DNC Platform, but it was done against the will of the majority and thus the declaration by the Chairman that the amendment had passed by a two-thirds vote is a sham and fraud! Thus in "reality," the 2012 Democratic Party has thrown God and His Holy Capital of Jerusalem out of the Democratic Party Official Platform while simultaneously embracing homosexual marriage—the "Platform" is the Official Vision of where the Party desires to take America; thus the Democratic Party's Official Vision is to kick God out of America and do everything in the Democratic Party's power to thwart God's restoration of the Holy Land to Israel, while  simultaneously turning America into a modern-day Sodom and Gomorrah, which I remind you God destroyed by fire! This is the most shocking and significant political event in America's history and will surely bring God's righteous wrath upon every member of the Democratic Party and, if allowed to remain in power, upon the United States! I warn you America, if you are a registered Democrat or vote for a Democrat then in God's eyes you are complicit in the Democratic Party's official 2012 rejection of God and Jerusalem! Anyone who votes for any Democrat in the 2012 Election shall incur God's wrath upon them! (You have got to see this shocking history-making event for yourself at YouTube.com, search: "DNC Rams 'God' and Jerusalem Back into Platform - Delegates at convention Boo, Hiss, Jeer").

## Hurricanes Katrina, Gustav & Isaac Were Judgments From God Against The Sin Of Homosexuality!

But God's wrath upon America for her public acceptance of the sin of homosexuality predates President Obama. Hurricane Katrina hit the Northern Gulf Coast devastating New Orleans and the surrounding region on August 29, 2005; three years later on September 1, 2008 hurricane Gustav also hit the Northern Gulf Coast region, resulting in the largest evacuation in America's history of some 3-million people; then on August 29, 2012, 7-years to the very day that Katrina hit, hurricane Isaac hit the Northern Gulf Coast. What do hurricane's Katrina, Gustav and Isaac all have in common? They all hit the Northern Gulf Coast, impacting New Orleans, the last week of August leading into the Labor Day weekend. Why is that significant? You don't know do you? Of course not, because no one in the liberal media has reported on this—not even Fox News, the last vesture of Journalism in America, has reported on this event! What am I talking about? Ever heard of the annual celebration in New Orleans called Mardi Gras? Of course you have, everybody has! Which is a celebration that, in and of itself is a smack in the face of Almighty God, because it is a weeklong celebration of girls exposing their breasts in public for beads, culminating on "Fat Tuesday," but abruptly ending the next day on "Ash Wednesday," the Catholic Church's beginning of Lent—40-days of fasting and prayer leading up to the celebration of the crucifixion and resurrection of the Lord Jesus Christ. In other words, the celebrants are saying, *"We have to repent and be good for 40-days, so let's party and sin like crazy for the week leading up to it!"* Which anyone with an ounce of *Common Sense* knows that's not how the Gospel works! Yes, Christ offers forgiveness for sins to those who truly repent and place their faith in Him—but sinning like crazy for a week leading up to your repentance is false repentance; you know it and God knows it. But Mardi Gras is not what I'm referring to with regard to the last week of August leading into the Labor Day weekend.

Have you ever heard of "Southern Decadence?" I hadn't heard of it either because of the media's anti-God, anti-Christian, pro-homosexuality politically correct bias! "Southern Decadence" is a week-long event held annually on the last week of August up to the Sunday before Labor Day in New Orleans. It is a gathering of homosexuals who come from across America and around the world to flaunt their homosexuality, often with public displays of homosexual sex and debauchery! What is even more shocking is why have we never heard of this event, when Southern Decadence boasts crowds equal to or larger than Mardi Gras? Everyone's heard of Mardi Gras, but no one has heard of Gay Southern Decadence!

Hurricanes Katrina, Gustav and Isaac all stopped the Gay Southern Decadence celebration! You've heard the expression, "I don't have to be hit over the head with a barstool before I realize I'm in a bar fight!" Well, *Common Sense* tells us that God is shouting, "Stop publically condoning and celebrating the sin of homosexuality! But is New Orleans listening? Is America listening? Are you listening?

### Romans 1:18-27
[18]*For the <u>wrath of God</u> is revealed from heaven <u>against all ungodliness and unrighteousness of men</u>, who suppress the truth in unrighteousness...*[26]*For this reason God gave them up to vile passions. For even their women exchanged the natural use for what is against nature.*
[27]*Likewise also the men, leaving the natural use of the woman, burned in their lust for one another, men with men committing what is shameful, and receiving in themselves the due penalty of their perversion.*

But never in America's history has the Head of our nation, the President thumbed his nose at Almighty God and declared his support of homosexual marriage; Barack Obama is the first!

A great American Christian and business entrepreneur who understands the above Scripture, Dan Cathy, CEO of the great American chicken sandwich restaurant chain Chick-fil-A, during an interview after President Obama had publically announced that he supports Gay marriage, made the following *Common Sense* and Biblically correct comments:

*"I think we are inviting God's judgment on our nation when we shake our fist at Him and say, you know, we know better than You as to what constitutes a marriage. And I pray God's mercy on our generation that has such a prideful, arrogant attitude to think we have the audacity to try to redefine what marriage is all about."*

## Chicago, Boston & San Francisco Declare War Against God!

In response to Dan Cathy's important nation-saving remarks, the moronic monster Rahm Emanuel, former Chief of Staff for President Obama and current Mayor of Chicago, held a press conference to announce that Chick-fil-A, and by implication Christians, were not welcome in Chicago and made the following remarks:

*"Chick-fil-A's values are not Chicago values. They're not respectful of our residents, our neighbors and our family members. And if you're gonna be part of the Chicago community, you should reflect Chicago values. What the CEO has said as it relates to gay marriage and gay couples is not what I believe, but more importantly, it's not what the people of Chicago believe. We just passed legislation as it relates to civil union and my goal and my hope ... is that we now move on recognizing gay marriage. I do not believe that the CEO's comments...reflects who we are as a city."*

Just as President Obama's May and June pronouncements of the President's Official condoning of the sin of homosexuality and of homosexual marriage was a direct declaration of war against God, and by way of affiliation a declaration of war against God's people called Christians, in the same way Chicago's Mayor Rahm Emanuel's declaration above is also a direct declaration of war against God and Christians! The Mayors of Boston and San Francisco quickly declared their agreement with Chicago's stance, thereby announcing that Boston and San Francisco are also at war against God and Christians.

This is exactly the way Hitler and the Nazi's began their war against the Jews, the Nazi's first attacked Jewish owned businesses and business owners, which then escalated into the murdering of 6-million Jews and the prison-camp internment of millions more!

Note that all the government officials, from President Obama to the City Mayors, who are openly declaring war against God and Christians are all members of the Democratic Party! If you fear God and are a registered Democrat, God says to you as He did to Lot and his family regarding the homosexual-sin embracing cities of Sodom and Gomorrah: *"Flee for your lives from this abominable place and don't look back!"* (Genesis 19:12-17). In other words, *Run as fast as you can to the nearest Republican Office and change your Party affiliation from Democrat to Republican! Before it's too late and My wrath comes upon you!*

## We The People Of God Are Rising Up & Fighting Back! Every Democrat Be Forewarned—Because Of Your Rejection Of God & Embracing Of Sinful, Nation-Destroying Homosexual Marriage—We Are Coming After You—Not With The Power Of The Bullet, But With The Power Of The Ballot!

In response to Obama-bot Rahm Emanuel's declaration of war against God and Christians, a mighty army arose across America in a ground-swell of support for Dan Cathy and Chick-fil-A! Under the call of former Governor and Presidential Candidate Mike Huckabee and through the viral power of social media, Wednesday, August 1, 2012, was declared "Support Chick-fil-A Day Buycott!" In response, millions of Americans waited in long lines at Chick-fil-A's all across America to show our support of God, Christian business owners, Christianity, and God's ban on the sin of homosexuality and Gay marriage! And We The People won!

### No Christian Can Be A Democrat or Vote For A Democrat!

Be forewarned every member of the Democratic Party, because of your God-rejecting homosexual-sin promoting Platform and policies, We The People of the United States are coming after you, not by the power of the bullet, but by the power of the ballot, to throw your God-hating, Christian-hating A.-double-S.'s out of Office! And we are going to replace you with Christian, God fearing men and women who will implement policies of righteousness in America, that we may again invite the Favor and Blessings of Almighty God upon our Nation!

As it is written in the Holy Scriptures:

**Psalms 33:12**

*[12]Blessed is the nation whose God is the Lord.*

**Proverbs 14:34**

*[34]Righteousness exalts a nation, But sin is a reproach to any people.*

**Jeremiah 18:7-10**

*[7]The instant I speak concerning a nation and concerning a kingdom, to pluck up, to pull down, and to destroy it, [8]if that nation against whom I have spoken turns from its evil, I will relent of the disaster that I thought to bring upon it.*

*[9]And the instant I speak concerning a nation and concerning a kingdom, to build and to plant it,*

*[10]if it does evil in My sight so that it does not obey My voice, then I will relent concerning the good with which I said I would benefit it.*

Therefore, as John Jay, one of America's most prominent Founding Fathers, Governor of New York and first Chief Justice of the United States Supreme Court, declared, *"Providence has given to our people the choice of their rulers, and it is the <u>duty</u>, as well as the privilege and interest, of our Christian nation to select and prefer Christians for their rulers."* (October 12, 1816).

Therefore, as Americans, it is our God-given "duty" to only elect Christians to Office! And no Democrat can be a Christian, or more correctly, no Christian can be a Democrat! Any Democrat who claims to be a Christian is either a liar or a hypocrite living a lie! Every core value of the Democratic Party is a direct assault against God and Christianity! The Democratic Party stands for Communism—*"spreading the wealth around."* Under the guise of "social programs" they take money from those who worked for it and give it to those who did not work for it—which is in direct violation of the commandment of God, *"For even when we were with you, we commanded you this: If anyone will not work, neither shall he eat....Now those who are such we command and exhort through our Lord Jesus Christ that they work in quietness and eat their own bread."* —2 Thessalonians 3:10-12; therefore no Christian can be a Democrat! The Democratic Party stands for the murder of innocent baby boys and girls, simply because they were conceived in the sins of fornication and adultery and therefore their mothers and fathers want to rid themselves of the consequences of their sin!—the daily murders of some 4,000 innocent baby boys and girls in the sanctuary of their mother's wombs is an abomination to God who commanded *"You shall not murder"*—Exodus 20:13; therefore no Christian can be a Democrat! The Democratic Party stands for the physical and financial enslavement of Blacks upon whom God has bestowed the same unalienable rights of life, liberty and the pursuit of happiness; therefore no Christian can be a Democrat! Therefore, it is the God-given duty of every American to vote either for a Christian Republican or a Christian Independent, but no American should EVER vote for a Democrat! If you do, you will have to answer to Almighty God for your vote of sin and rebellion against Him!

So Democrats be forewarned, We The People of the United States are coming, not with the power of the bullet, but with the power of the ballot, to remove every one of you from Office!

But the anti-God Democrats who are Pro-Homosexual-sin are not so benign to refrain from the use of bullets. On Wednesday, August 15, 2012, a man who had been volunteering at a Lesbian, Gay, Bisexual & Transgender community center, who it is supposed is himself a practicing homosexual, walked into the downtown Washington D.C. headquarters of a Christian lobbying organization called the Family Research Council, announced that he did not like what the Family Research Council stands for and pulled out a 9-mm. handgun and opened fire! The buildings operation manager, Leo Johnson, was wounded in the arm, and despite his wound lunged toward the shooter, wrestled the gun from him and subdued the shooter until help arrived! You go Leo! Inside the shooters backpack was discovered 2 more clips providing a total of 50 rounds of ammunition, plus 15 Chick-fil-A sandwiches! The political implications are clear! This homosexual sin-loving Democrat was willing to murder Christians to advance his political agenda of ridding America of God and Christians and turning America into a modern-day Sodom and Gomorrah! But We The People of the United States will not allow Democratic Party domestic terrorists to intimidate us!

I, *Common Sense*, call upon every Christian in Chicago, Boston and San Francisco to rise up, get to the polls and take your cities back for God by throwing those God-hating homosexual-sin-promoting Democrats out of Office! And I call upon all Christians across America to rise up and get to the polls and throw that homosexual-sin-promoting, God-hating, baby-murdering, Communism-loving domestic enemy of America Barack Hussein Obama, along with every other homosexual-sin-loving God-hating Democrat, out of Office!

There's just one thing, though, that baffles me; how did Democrat Rahm Emanuel ever get elected as Mayor of Chicago in the first place, seeing as Chicago has a large Black population? Because no self-respecting Black would EVER vote for a Democrat!

# Chapter 9: Why Blacks Should Never Vote Democrat!

No self-respecting Black would ever vote for a Democrat! Here's why...

There is a very strange phenomenon taking place in politics today, which was most dramatically  demonstrated in the 2008 election of Democrat Barack Obama as President, and that is the puzzling fact that 95% of Black Americans register and vote Democrat. My Black brothers and sisters, this should not be! The only explanation for such an anomaly is that you have forgotten your Black history!

## No Self-Respecting Black Would Ever Vote For A Democrat Because It Is The Republican Party That Set The Black Slaves Free!

For the first 80 years of America's history the Republican Party did not exist! At the time of the founding of the United States of America with its 13 Colonies, only 3 of the 13 Colonies, which now became States, practiced slavery. There was an understanding between the other 10 non-slave States and the 3 slave States that the slave States would rid themselves of the practice of slavery within 20-years. The 20-years came and went without the practice of slavery being abolished from the 3 slave States. As America moved into the 1800's, other States were also beginning to join the United States of America; some, primarily in the North and West, were on the one side of the slavery issue, and others, primarily in the South, on the other side. During this time, from the late 1700's up to the 1850's, the 2 political Parties' that dominated the American landscape were the Democratic Party and the Whig Party. But neither the Democratic nor the Whig Party had the political will to deal with the growing issue of slavery in America, and in the mid-1850's the Whig Party dissolved.

At that time, in 1854, anti-slavery activists formed a new political Party which had as its core tenant the abolition of slavery in America; it was known as the "anti-slavery" Republican Party! This new "anti-slavery" movement called the Republican Party understood that the practice of slavery was immoral and indeed flew in the face of our founding Declaration of Independence which declared, *"That all men are created equal, that they are endowed by their Creator with certain unalienable rights, that among these are life, liberty and the pursuit of happiness."*

In the Presidential Election of 1860, this newly formed "anti-slavery" Republican Party chose as its Presidential Candidate a young devout Christian man from the State of Illinois named Abraham Lincoln, and Lincoln and the new "anti-slavery" Republican Party won the 1860 Presidential Election, defeating the pro-slavery Democratic Party!

Even though Lincoln and his new "anti-slavery" Republican Party would not be officially sworn into Office until March 4, 1861, by mere virtue of the Republican Party's election victory over the Democratic Party, the State of South Carolina perceived a threat to that State's practice of slavery, and in January, 1861, two months before Lincoln's Inauguration, the Democratic Party of the South Carolina Legislature took action against the Republican Party by calling a state convention in which the delegates voted to remove the state of South Carolina from the union of the United States of America! The secession of South Carolina was followed by the secession of six more states—Mississippi, Florida, Alabama, Georgia, Louisiana, and Texas; and the threat of secession by four more—Virginia, Arkansas, Tennessee, and North Carolina. These eleven States eventually formed the Confederate States of America.

Just one month after President Abraham Lincoln and the Republican Party's Inauguration into Office, the Southern Confederate States began to seize Federal military facilities located within their borders; and on April 12, 1861, Confederate troops demanded that Fort Sumter, South Carolina, surrender. Upon the Fort's Commander's refusal to immediately surrender, the Confederate Troops opened fire, and the Civil War began!

Most Americans have thought of the Civil War as the war between the North and the South, because of the general geographic locations of the Confederate States. But the truth is that the eleven Confederate States declared their secession from the United States of America because of the election victory of the first Republican President, Abraham Lincoln, and Lincoln's and his Republican Party's opposition to slavery! Therefore, in reality, the Civil War was a war between those loyal to the new anti-slavery Republican Party and those loyal to the old pro-slavery Democratic Party!

Nearly two years into the Civil War, on January 1, 1863, President Abraham Lincoln signed the Emancipation Proclamation, declaring all slaves still held in the Southern Confederate States to be free! The Civil War raged on for more than two more years, until April, 1865. On April 7, 1865, General Grant's Union Troops having surrounded General Lee's Confederate Troops, General Grant offered the opportunity for General Lee to surrender. On April 9, 1865, the two commanders met at the Appomattox, Virginia Courthouse, and agreed on the terms of surrender, and the Civil War ended.

Five days later, on April 14, as President Lincoln was watching a performance of "Our American Cousin" at Ford's Theater in Washington, D.C., he was shot by John Wilkes Booth, an actor from Maryland obsessed with avenging the Confederate defeat. Lincoln died the next morning. Booth escaped to Virginia. Eleven days later, cornered in a burning barn, Booth was fatally shot by a Union soldier. Nine other people were arrested and tried as co-conspirators for their involvement in the assassination of President Lincoln; four were hanged, four imprisoned, and one acquitted.

The cost of the 4-year long Civil War in terms of the loss of human life was staggering with a total of some 620-thousand lives lost, making the Civil War the deadliest in America's history to this very day. Of those 620-thousand deaths, 360-thousand died on the Union side, fighting on behalf of the Republican Party and for the cause of freeing Blacks in America from slavery, with another 275-thousand wounded on the Union side. Some 260-thousand died on the Confederate side fighting on behalf of the Democratic Party and for the cause of keeping Blacks in America bound in the chains of slavery!

Every Black person in America needs to ponder the above history. The Republican Party was "formed" as an anti-slavery movement that sought the freedom of every Black man, woman and child in America, in opposition to the pro-slavery Democratic Party! What every Black American should remember is that 360-thousand young White Republicans fought and died to secure the freedom of Blacks in America. How can you now spit in the face of those who fought and died for your freedom by abandoning the Republican Party and joining the Democratic Party who fought to keep you in the chains of slavery? For God's sake and for the sake of the blood of those hundreds of thousands who fought and died to set you free—wake up Black America! Wake up and flee the demonic grip of your former Democratic Party slave masters and return to the Party of Abraham Lincoln, return to the Republican Party who declared your freedom, return to the Republican Party who fought and died for you to set you free!

I want every Black American to hear this loud and clear! The Democratic Party, who most of you are members of, and whose candidates you even vote for, are so anti-Black, so pro-slavery, so racist, that they went to war against the Republican Party in an attempt to retain slavery as the law of the land! When you vote Democrat, you are voting for slavery! Any Black American who runs for political office as a Democrat is betraying his race—he or she has joined the Enemy of Black Americans! Any Black American who registers and votes Democrat is betraying his race—he or she has registered with and voted for the Enemy of Black Americans!

Thank God Almighty that by His grace the Democrats were defeated in the Civil War—otherwise slavery would still be practiced in America to this day! Thank God the Republicans won the Civil War and slavery was abolished from our land!

Yet, in light of this fact of history, babbling buffoon Vice President Joe Biden, while speaking to a Black audience, makes the racist and historically inaccurate bombastic statement referring to the Republican Party, *"They're gonna put Y'all back in chains!"* No Joe, YOU are the V.P. of the demonic Democratic Party who put Blacks in chains and fought the Civil War to keep Blacks in chains! The Republican Party is the "anti-slavery" Party who set the Black man free and fought and died to win their freedom! Joe Biden, you are nothing more than a lying Jackass! (Remember, the Jackass is the symbol which the Democrats chose for themselves—the only truthful thing they ever did!) Vice President Joe Biden, We The People of the United States DEMAND your immediate resignation because of your lying racist statement! If you refuse to resign, We The People will come to the polls on November 6, 2012, and throw your lying racist Jackass out of Office so far that you will never be welcomed in America again! We do not abide lying racists in America!

To further highlight the enormity of the ignorance of V.P. Joe Biden's comments, stop and think what the Republican Party's "anti-slavery" policy cost them—before Abraham Lincoln, the newly formed Republican Party's first Presidential Candidate to win the Office, could even be sworn into Office, eleven pro-slavery States seceded from the Union. Just one month after being sworn in as America's first Republican President, the Democratic Party Confederate States declared war against the Republican Party and the Union, and America suffered 4-years of Civil War, costing 620-thousand lives, 360-thousand of which were Republican Union Troops. And finally, the Republican Party's "anti-slavery" policy cost them the life of their first President when President Abraham Lincoln was assassinated for his anti-slavery victory in the Civil War. The Republican Party has paid a great and dear price for their anti-slavery, pro-Black freedom and prosperity policies! Every Black American owes their freedom to the Republican Party!

Having lost the Civil War and their ability to, *"Put Y'all in chains,"* it is the Democratic Party and its leaders Barack Obama, Joe Biden, Nancy Pelosi, harry Reid, and the rest of the Democratic party racists who have, *"Put Y'all in financial chains!"*

## More Republican Party Black History!

Having secured the freedom of all Black slaves in America, the Republican Party's pro-Black freedom and prosperity policies did not end with the Civil War! As the Civil War drew to a close, in anticipation of victory, on March 3, 1865, just 6-weeks before his assassination, President Abraham Lincoln created the Freedmen's Bureau, which assigned agents throughout the South for the purpose of helping the former Black slaves, now known as "Freedmen," transition from slavery to freedom, including a free labor market. The Bureau created schools to educate Freedmen, both adults and children; helped Freedmen negotiate labor contracts, and tried to minimize violence against Freedmen. The era known as Reconstruction was an attempt to establish new governments in the former Confederacy and to bring Freedmen into society as voting citizens.

After the Civil war and President Lincoln's assassination, one's political Party affiliation was no light matter; which Party you chose to be affiliated with represented which side of the slavery issue you were on. Naturally, the race issue pulled all the newly enfranchised African American Freedmen into the Republican Party, while former slave-owning White southerners joined the Democratic Party.

Present-day Black Americans hear this loud and clear—know your Black history! After the Civil War when Blacks were able to vote, work and conduct themselves as equal citizens of the United States—100% of Black Americans were Republicans! How in God's name are 95% of Blacks today Democrats? That is an abomination and a betrayal by Blacks of the Republican Party which not only fought and died to purchase your freedom, but which also instituted civil rights and economic policies to prosper you! Every Black American who is currently a Democrat should hang your head in shame for betraying your Black slave forefathers who were proud, grateful Republicans! You have betrayed their memory and their history! Repent Black America and return to your Republican Roots!

After the Civil War, the new Republican Party also attracted businessmen, shop owners, skilled craftsmen, clerks and professionals who were drawn by the Republican Party's free-market and pro-growth policies.

## Republican Party Passes Civil Rights Act Of 1866, Reconstruction Act & Constitutional Amendments 13, 14 & 15 To Provide Protection, Prosperity & Equal Rights For All Former Slaves!

Following the Civil War and assassination of President Lincoln, the Republican Party continued to fight for the rights of the newly freed former slaves, called Freedmen. Even though President Abraham Lincoln's Emancipation Proclamation had declared all slaves free, the Republican Party fought to make the abolition of slavery a permanent part of the U.S. Constitution, winning that victory on behalf of all former slaves with the ratification of the Thirteenth Amendment on December 6, 1865, which officially abolished slavery in the United States.

That same year, within months of the end of the Civil War and assassination of President Lincoln, the Republican Party also passed the Civil Rights Act of 1865, but President Andrew Johnson, who was a Democrat, vetoed the Bill. Andrew Johnson had been a pro-slavery Democrat who himself owned slaves. At the time of Abraham Lincoln's and the new "anti-slavery" Republican Party's rise to the Presidency in 1861, Andrew Johnson was the Democratic Senator for Tennessee in the U.S. Senate. When Tennessee and the ten other slave States seceded from the Union in 1861, Johnson was the only Southern Democrat who did not resign his position. Johnson went on to support Lincoln's military actions and changed his view on slavery to pro-emancipation. When Lincoln came up for re-election in 1864, in an attempt to bring unity to a nation presently divided by Civil War, the Party nominated Democrat Andrew Johnson to be Lincoln's Vice President. Lincoln of course won re-election; and just 6-weeks after being sworn in for his second term, Abraham Lincoln was assassinated, and Andrew Johnson assumed the Presidency.

However, Democrat President Johnson's veto of the Civil Rights Act of 1865 did not deter the Republicans, who passed the Bill again in 1866; but once again Democrat President Andrew Johnson vetoed the Bill. This time, however, the Republicans were able to get a two-thirds majority in each House of Congress and overcame President Johnson's veto, and the Civil Rights Act of 1866 became law!

The Civil Rights Act of 1866 declared that people born in the United States are entitled to be citizens, without regard to race, color, or previous condition of slavery or involuntary servitude, thus declaring all Freedmen (former slaves) to be citizens of the United States. The Act also stated that any Freedmen citizen has the same right as a White citizen to make and enforce contracts, sue and be sued, give evidence in court, and inherit, purchase, lease, sell, hold, and convey real and personal property. Persons who denied these rights to former slaves faced a fine up to $1,000, or imprisonment up to one year, or both. Thus, just one-year after the end of the Civil War, the Republican Party secured for all Blacks in America equal economic and civil and citizenship rights as those enjoyed by Whites!

## *Black Americans Come Home To The Party Of Your Roots—Come Home To The Republican Party!*

I want every Black American to hear this loud and clear— Not only did the Democratic Party fight and die during the Civil War to keep you bound in the chains of slavery, but after the Civil War the Democratic Party continued to fight to keep Blacks from receiving equal rights with Whites! On the flip side, not only did the Republican Party fight and die to win your freedom from the chains of slavery in the Civil War, but after the Civil War the Republican Party continued to fight for all Blacks in America to win for you equal rights with Whites! How dare you abandon the Republican Party which has shown you such love from that time until now; and how foolish of you to join the Democratic Party which has shown you such hatred from that time until now! Repent Black America of your evil abandonment of God's provision for your freedom and equality—the Republican Party which God raised up to bless you! You have sided with the devil, your enemy, in your joining of the Demon-cratic Party! Come home Black America to the Party of your roots, to the Party that fought for your freedom, to the Party that fought for your equality! —Come home to the Party that 100% of post Civil War Blacks belonged to and all self-respecting Blacks today belong to! Come back to God Black America; come home to the Republican Party!

To secure the freedom and equality for all former slaves, Freedmen, who remained living in the Southern former Confederate States, in addition to the Civil Rights Act of 1866, the Republican Party also passed that same year the Reconstruction Act, which dissolved all governments in the former Confederate states with the exception of Tennessee. It divided the South into five military districts, where the military through the Freedmen's Bureau, which President Lincoln had established prior to his assassination, helped protect the rights and safety of newly freed Blacks. The Act required that the former Confederate states ratify their constitutions conferring citizenship rights on blacks or forfeit their representation in Congress.

To ensure that the citizenship rights for all former slaves conferred upon them by the Civil Rights Act of 1866 and the Reconstruction Act, became a permanent part of the U.S. Constitution, the Republican Party then proposed the Fourteenth Amendment, which was ratified on July 9, 1868, making all people born or naturalized in the United States citizens, which, of course, included all former slaves. Echoing the words of the Civil Rights Act of 1866, the Fourteenth Amendment declares, *"...all persons born in the United States and not subject to any foreign power, excluding Indians not taxed, are hereby declared to be citizens of the United States."* (As noted in Chapter 7, *Common Sense* Solutions To The Problem Of Illegal Immigration, this Fourteenth Amendment was crafted to benefit Black former slaves in America, who were not in America illegally by means of illegal border crossing, nor were they subject to any foreign power. *Common Sense* dictates that the Fourteenth Amendment does not apply to Mexican children born in the U.S. whose mother's have entered the U.S. illegally and who are also still subject to the foreign power of Mexico as they are the legal citizens of that Country!)

Meanwhile, however, Democrat President Andrew Johnson not only vetoed the Republican's Civil Rights Act twice, but also failed to implement the provisions of the Reconstruction Act; instead implementing his own lenient Presidential Reconstruction policies which failed to promote the rights of the Freedmen (newly freed slaves). President Johnson issued a series of Presidential Proclamations aimed at expediting the reincorporation of the former Confederate States into the union without due regard for Freedmen's rights. These actions and others infuriated the Republicans who were fighting for equal rights for the newly freed former slaves. Therefore, the Republicans in the House of Representatives impeached him in 1868, making Andrew Johnson the first U.S. President to be impeached; however, his trial in the Senate ended in an acquittal by a single vote; thus he remained President until the 1868 Election, when the Republican Party won back the Presidency with Republican Candidate Ulysses S. Grant.

# Republican President Ulysses S. Grant Defeated The Democratic Party's KKK & Helped Elect Black Former Slaves To The U.S. Congress!

Abraham Lincoln's General, Ulysses S. Grant, who had secured the freedom of all Black slaves by his victory in the Civil War over the Confederate slave States, won back the Presidency for the Republican Party in 1868, serving two terms as President from 1869-1877.

As President, Grant led the Republicans in their effort to eliminate all vestiges of Confederate nationalism and slavery. Republican Ulysses S. Grant's two consecutive terms as President stabilized the nation after the Civil War and during the turbulent Reconstruction period in the South. As President, Grant enforced the Reconstruction Act, securing freedom, citizenship and equal rights for the newly freed former slaves, Freedmen, in the South, and used the Army to fight the racist violence of the Southern Democrat domestic terrorist group known as the Ku Klux Klan, effectively destroying the Ku Klux Klan in 1871 (although the Southern Democrat KKK would rear its ugly head again decades later). Grant and the Republican Party won passage of the Fifteenth Amendment to the Constitution, ratified on February 3, 1870, which forbade the denial or abridgment of the right to vote on account of race, color, or previous condition of servitude, thus giving Constitutional protection for African American voting rights.

As a result of the above measures by the Republican Party on behalf of all Black Americans, including Freedmen, African Americans were represented in the U.S. Congress for the first time in American history in the mid-term election of 1870, just five years after the Civil War had ended!

In 1870, Hiram Rhodes Revels, an Ordained Minister, who served as a Civil War Chaplain in the Union Army, and who fought for the Union Army at the Battle of Vicksburg, who was naturally a Republican, was the first African American to be seated in the United States Senate, appointed as Senator from the State of Mississippi; but of course, the Democratic Party opposed Revels' right to be a U.S. Senator on a technicality, but the Democrats failed, and the Republicans prevailed, and Hiram Revels and the Republican Party made Black history! Also In 1870, the Republican

Party made Black history with the election of several other African Americans to the U.S. House of Representatives, including Freedmen—former slaves! These included Freedmen Republican Benjamin S. Turner, Representative from Alabama who served 2 terms; Freedmen Republican Robert DeLarge, Representative from South Carolina; Freedmen Republican Josiah Walls, Representative from Florida, who served 3 terms; Freedmen Republican Jefferson Long, Representative from Georgia; Freedmen Republican Joseph Rainey, Representative from South Carolina, who served 5 terms; all these were former slaves now Freedmen! Because of the Republican Party, these men who just 5 years prior had been slaves were now serving in Congress!

One more African American elected to Congress in 1870 was Republican Robert B. Elliott, Representative from South Carolina who served 2 terms. Elliott had arrived in South Carolina after the end of the Civil War in 1867 at the age of 25, where he established a law practice. Elliott helped organize the local Republican Party and served in the South Carolina State Constitutional Convention. In 1868 he was elected to the South Carolina House of Representatives. The next year he was appointed Assistant Adjutant-General; he was the first African-American Commanding General of the South Carolina National Guard. As part of his job, he helped form a state militia to fight the Ku Klux Klan. While serving as a Republican in the Forty-second and Forty-third United States Congresses, Elliott delivered a noteworthy and memorable speech in favor of the Republican Party's proposed Civil Rights Act of 1875 (Full text of Act to follow).

## 100% Of Blacks Were Republicans After The Civil War!

All of these Reconstruction era Black Congressmen were members of the Republican Party. The Republicans represented the Party of Abraham Lincoln and of emancipation. The Democrats represented the party of slavery and secession.

Because of the large populations of newly freed slaves throughout the South who now, thanks to the Republican Party, had been granted equal citizenship and voting rights with the Southern Whites, the Republican Party flourished in the State Legislatures across the South.

You see, after the Civil War, it would have been unthinkable that any Black would join the Democratic Party! And any Black today who joins the Democratic Party is betraying his race and has joined with the enemy! That is simply an irrefutable fact of history!

# Republicans Pass The Civil Rights Act Of 1875!

The Civil Rights Act of 1875 was proposed by Republican Senator Charles Sumner and Republican Congressman Benjamin F. Butler in 1870. The act was then passed by Congress in February, 1875, and signed into law by Republican President Ulysses S. Grant on March 1, 1875, becoming the law of the land. The Act guaranteed that everyone, regardless of race, color, or previous condition of servitude, was entitled to the same treatment in "public accommodations," such as Inns, public conveyances on land or water, theaters, and other places of public amusement. If found guilty, the lawbreaker had to pay $500 to the aggrieved person and faced a fine of up to $1,000 and up to 1-year in prison, or both. However, in 1883, the Supreme Court declared the Act unconstitutional on the basis that although the Fourteenth Amendment prohibits discrimination by the state, it does not give the state the power to prohibit discrimination by private individuals. Many of the provisions of the Civil Rights Act of 1875 were passed into law in the 1960's with the Civil Rights Act of 1964. Here is the full text of the Civil Rights Act of 1875 proposed and passed by Republicans:

### The Civil Rights Act of March 1, 1875

*Whereas it is essential to just government we recognize the equality of all men before the law, and hold that it is the duty of government in its dealings with the people to mete out equal and exact justice to all, of whatever nativity, race, color, or persuasion, religious or political; and it being the appropriate object of legislation to enact great fundamental principles into law:*

*Therefore,*

*Be it enacted, That all persons within the jurisdiction of the United States shall be entitled to the full and equal enjoyment of the accommodations, advantages, facilities, and privileges of inns, public conveyances on land or water, theaters, and other places of public amusement; subject only to the conditions and limitations established by law, and applicable alike to citizens of every race and color, regardless of any previous condition of servitude.*

SEC. 2. That any person who shall violate the foregoing section by denying to any citizen, except for reasons by law applicable to citizens of every race and color, and regardless of any previous condition of servitude, the full enjoyment of any of the accommodations, advantages, facilities, or privileges in said section enumerated, or by aiding or inciting such denial, shall, for every such offense, forfeit and pay the sum of five hundred dollars to the person aggrieved thereby, . . . and shall also, for every such offense, be deemed guilty of a misdemeanor, and, upon conviction thereof, shall be fined not less than five hundred nor more than one thousand dollars, or shall be imprisoned not less than thirty days nor more than one year . . .

SEC. 3. That the district and circuit courts of the United States shall have exclusively of the courts of the several States, cognizance of all crimes and offenses against, and violations of, the provisions of this act . . .

SEC. 4. That no citizen possessing all other qualifications which are or may be prescribed by law shall be disqualified for service as grand or petit juror in any court of the United States, or of any State, on account of race, color, or previous condition of servitude; and any officer or other person charged with any duty in the selection or summoning of jurors who shall exclude or fail to summon any citizen for the cause aforesaid shall, on conviction thereof, be deemed guilty of a misdemeanor, and be fined not more than five thousand dollars.

SEC. 5. That all cases arising under the provisions of this act ... shall be renewable by the Supreme Court of the United States, without regard to the sum in controversy ...

Source: *US Statutes at Large, Vol.* XVIII, p. 335 ff.

# The Compromise of 1877 Results In The Democratic Party Regaining Control Of The Southern States & Robbing Black Americans Of Their Civil Rights Won For Them By Republicans!

The outcome of the Presidential Election of 1876 between Democratic Samuel J. Tilden, Governor of New York, and Republican Rutherford B. Hayes, Governor of Ohio, was disputed. To resolve the dispute, a national agreement between Democratic and Republican factions was negotiated, resulting in the Compromise of 1877. Under the Compromise, Democrats conceded the election to Hayes and promised to acknowledge the political rights of Blacks (so they promised, but like all Democrats, they were bald-faced liars!); Republicans agreed to no longer intervene in Southern affairs by virtue of the 1866 Reconstruction Act, to withdraw all Union Troops from the Southern States and promised to appropriate a portion of Federal monies toward Southern projects. This Compromise of 1877 coincided with the completion of Republican President Ulysses S. Grant's two terms. Thus 1877 ended the era of Reconstruction of the South under the watchful eye of the Republican Party.

## After Reading This, No Self-Respecting Black Or Honorable White Person Will Ever Again Vote For Any Democrat!

As the era of Reconstruction drew to a close, new White Democrat paramilitary groups, the two most prominent being the White League and Red Shirts, formed to oppose the new equality and civil rights granted by the Republican Party to the newly enfranchised Black American former slaves. Unlike the clandestine racist terrorism of the Democrats Ku Klux Klan, which President Grant had successfully destroyed, these new racist militias operated openly with their members identity's known. These racist terrorist paramilitary groups were made up of Confederate Army veterans and came to be known as *"the military arm of the Democratic Party."* Through violence and intimidation, these militias worked openly to turn Republicans out of office and intimidate Blacks from voting. The Democratic Party's racist militia's tactics were successful in reducing Republican voting and contributed to the Democratic Party's regaining control of the Southern State and local legislatures. After the White Democrats power grab was complete, members of the White League and Red Shirts were absorbed into the state militias and the National Guard.

All of the gains in equality and civil rights which the Republican Party had won in the South for Black Freedmen were now being taken away by the Democratic Party as it regained power!

With the Legislatures of the Southern States back under the control of the Democratic Party, feeling themselves "redeemed" from Republican control, Democrats proceeded to restrict the rights of most Blacks to vote by imposing new requirements for poll taxes, subjective literacy tests, stricter residency requirements and other elements difficult for most Blacks to satisfy.

From 1890 to 1908, starting with Mississippi, White Democrats passed new Constitutions in 10 Southern States which included these provisions that restricted voter registration and forced hundreds of thousands of Black Americans from voter registration rolls. These changes effectively prevented most Blacks from voting. However, the Democratic Party wrote these "voting rules" in such a way that Whites who could not "pass the voting tests" were exempted from these tests by such strategies as the "Grandfather Clause," for example, basing eligibility on an ancestor's citizenship status as of 1866, prior to the Freedmen's being granted citizenship and voting rights! Doesn't that just make your blood boil! Every Black American should HATE the Democratic Party for their damnable racist illegal actions toward Blacks in America! No self-respecting Black would ever join the Democratic Party!

Now you see why no Black should ever vote for a Democrat! But wait, there's more!

Southern State and local legislatures, now once again controlled by the Democratic Party, went on to pass Jim Crow laws that segregated schools, transportation, restrooms, restaurants, and drinking fountains for Whites and Blacks. Gotta love those Democrats—freaking racist morons! How in God's name does such an evil, damnable political Party even still exist in the United States? Well, the damnable anti-God, anti-Black Democratic Party is history now! —because, now that this book has made these facts known, no self-respecting Black or honorable White person will ever vote for a Democrat again!

## The Anti-Black Policies Of The Democratic Party Should Make You Sick To Your Stomach!

These anti-Black policies instituted by the Democratic Party naturally led to racial violence in the form of lynching's and race riots increasing in frequency throughout the South from the late 1800's up into the mid 1900's.

But the Democrats have not given up their platform of the slavery of Blacks to this very day, nor has the Democratic Party abandoned its anti-Black racist practices.

Every KKK member who ever lived was a Democrat. IN fact, until his recent death, the Democratic Party's proud Senior Member of the U.S. Senate was Robert Byrd, Democratic Senator from West Virginia, who was a recruiter for the Ku Klux Klan while in his 20s and 30s, rising to the title of Kleagle and Exalted Cyclops of his local chapter. Though he claimed to have left the KKK, Byrd continued to speak in favor of the Klan during his early political career. In 1946, Byrd wrote a letter to the Klan's Imperial Wizard stating, *"The Klan is needed today as never before, and I am anxious to see its rebirth here in West Virginia."* Byrd defended the Klan in his 1958 U.S. Senate campaign when he was 41 years old. Byrd was the only Senator to vote against both African American U.S. Supreme Court nominees, liberal Thurgood Marshall and conservative Clarence Thomas. Byrd also opposed the Civil Rights Act of 1964 by filibustering the Bill. In a 2001 incident Byrd repeatedly used the phrase *"white niggers"* on a national television broadcast. This is the proud modern-day heritage of the Democratic Party! Kind of makes you sick to your stomach, doesn't it?

Let me ask every Black American a simple question: How can you vote for a Party that would not even allow you to register to vote? Ask former Secretary of State Condoleezza Rice and former Chairman of the Joint Chiefs of Staff General Colin Powell, two prominent Black Americans who are Republicans, if their fathers were Democrats or Republicans, and why?

In a recent TV interview on The Factor with Bill O'Reilly, Condoleezza Rice extolled the virtues of the republican Party's policies of individual freedom and the opportunities that the free-market economy offers as being the best policies for providing upward mobility both economically and socially for Black Americans, which is why she chooses to be a Republican; but when asked by Bill O'Reilly if her father was a Democrat or Republican, Condoleezza replied that her father was a Republican because in the segregated South where she grew up, the Democrats would not register Blacks to vote, only the Republicans welcomed and registered Blacks to exercise their Right to Vote!

In a separate TV interview on a different program, General Colin Powell shared the story of his father who went to a Democratic Party Office to register to vote and the Democratic Party Official had a large jar of beans sitting on his desk, to which he pointed and said to Mr. Powell, "If you can tell me how many beans are in this jar, then I'll know you're intelligent enough to vote and I'll allow you to register.' Of course, Albert Einstein himself could not have guessed the correct number of beans in the jar—I'm sure the Democratic Party Official had no idea either, this was simply a ploy to deny Blacks their Right to vote. General Colin Powell continued his story stating that his father left very discouraged, until he shared his experience with a Black friend who joyfully told him, "Go to the Republican Party Office, they register Blacks to vote!"

I don't care if you're Black or White, these two modern-day true life experiences of two of our most prominent and beloved Black American Patriots should make you sick to your stomach! And should also create a righteous indignation in your soul of anger against the damnable Democratic Party who until just recently engaged in such diabolical activity! And it should make you vow and swear to never again vote for any human being who would align themselves with such a racist, prejudice discriminatory anti-Black organization!

One disappointing footnote to General Colin Powell's testimony, is that he abandoned his pro-Black political affiliation with the Republican Party and voted for a anti-Black Democratic Party candidate by voting for the Demon-crat Barack Obama in the 2008 election; and it appears that General Powell did so purely for racist reasons, because of the fact the Barack Obama is half Black. Shame on you General Colin Powell! I don't care if a Democratic candidate was 100% Black, the fact that he or she is a Democrat makes them anti-Black—remember, it is the Official Platform of the Democratic Party to murder as many Black American children as possible before they enter the world!

# The Democratic Party Murders 50% Of All Black Children In Their Mother's Wombs Every Day!

The sad fact is that every day in America some 4,000 American children are murdered by the Democrats in their nationwide murder-mills, with an average of 35% being Black children. Statistics show that the murder rate of Black children in their mother's womb is a staggering 50%! If you are Black, I want you to stop and think about that: 50% of your children are murdered every day by the Democratic Party's policy of On-Demand Abortion! That means that the Democratic Party is directly responsible for the murder of some 1,400 Black children every day! That's 511,000 Black children every year! To date, nearly 20-million Black children have been murdered by the Democratic Party's Official Policy of the purging of Black Babies from American society, calling them "unwanted!"

In God's name, I ask you, can you ever, ever, ever again vote for a Democrat? Whereas, the Republican Party is fighting day and night against this evil monstrous attack against America's children, whether Black or Brown or yellow or Red or White, and by God's grace we shall prevail and reverse Roe v. Wade! It's time to stop this insanity!

I'm *Common Sense*, I'm Black and I'm a Republican, and I'm running for Office! Vote for me and I will author and sign into law a Bill that bans abortions! To hell with the illegitimate 1973 Supreme Court ruling declaring murder of children as "Constitutional." What kind of a deranged monster could ever make such a ruling? Seriously! Every Supreme Court Justice, whether dead or still alive, who ruled that murdering American children was legal should be tried for treason and held accountable for the 55-million murders of our children that have occurred to date because of their insanity!

One final reason why Blacks should never vote Democrat is because of the Democratic Party's pro-economic-slavery policies!

## No Longer Able To Enslave Blacks Physically, The Democratic Party Now Enslaves Blacks Economically!

The Democrats lost the Civil War and their "right" to enslave Black's physically, so they have cunningly devised a scheme to enslave Blacks economically!

The Democratic Party's policies of so-called "Welfare" and "Entitlements" have been designed to diabolically make Blacks in America their "Economic Slaves," keeping the Black community in economic subjugation to their "White Democratic Party Government Masters!" By doling out little government checks as "rewards" for staying below the poverty level and/or for having children out of wedlock, the Democratic Party has practically ruined the Black community by creating a Black society where 70% of Black children (of the 50% of the fortunate ones who escape the Democratic Party's murder-mills) are born into homes absent of fathers; this has devastated the Black community. The Democratic Party's policies of economic dependency upon the Government as the Democrats dole out to Blacks "crumbs from their Master's table" has stripped the Black community of their drive to achieve personal independence and economic prosperity.

The Democrats could no longer enslave you physically, so they have very cunningly enslaved you economically! They give you just enough free money to where you can barely get by, thus keeping you in bondage at the lower end of societies economic spectrum, but at the same time making you dependent upon them. For if you begin to rise up even just a little economically, they will take away your government subsidy! So you cower in fear of your Democratic Party Economic Slave Masters, which is exactly where your damned Democrat slave masters want you to stay!

I call upon my Black brothers and sisters to rise up and shake off the Democratic Party's chains of economic slavery! Rise up my brothers and sisters to the Republican Party's call to self-reliance, free from government intervention, and the economic opportunity and prosperity that a free-market performance-based reward system provides! No longer will the government keep you in bondage just barely above the poverty line! But you shall possess the promise of America! And take your rightful place which the Founding fathers intended for all citizens of economic equality through your creativity, hard work and ingenuity!

Remember, every dollar that the government gives you that you did not work for, the government must take from someone else who did work for it! That is Communism and must not be tolerated in America! That is also illegal because it is stealing! Communism destroys a nation economically because Communism destroys the life of the person from whom the money is taken by robbing that person of their financial prosperity; and Communism destroys the life of the person who receives the stolen money because it makes that person dependent on the government, keeping them down at the bottom of society economically and robs that person of their rightful future of economic opportunity and prosperity!

## Any Black Who Serves As A Democrat Or Votes Democrat Has Betrayed His Race!

In conclusion, if you're Black, you CANNOT, MUST NOT EVER VOTE DEMOCRAT! Remember your history! It's the Democratic Party who fought in the Civil War to keep you in the bondage of physical slavery—thanks to God and the Republicans, the Democrats lost that war! It's the Democratic Party who refused to allow you to even register to vote—though it was your legal Constitutional right to do so! It is still the Democratic Party whose Official Party Platform is to murder as many of your children as they can—upwards of 50% every single day—to keep you from increasing in population! And it is to this day the Democratic Party who has cunningly and diabolically enslaved you and your community economically!

In light of these above truths, how can any Black American ever vote Democrat? In light of these above truths, no Black American should ever vote Democrat! In fact, I'll go so far as to say that, any Black who joins the Democratic Party or runs for political office as a Democrat or votes for a Democrat, in light of the above truths, has betrayed his race!

Think of the hypocrisy of President Barack Obama, a man who is half Black; he requested to be sworn in as President of the United States with his hand upon the very same Holy Bible that President Abraham Lincoln, the very first Republican President, was sworn into Office upon— yet President Obama had joined the opposing Party to Lincoln's, the opposing Party who declared war against Abraham Lincoln and the United States because of Lincoln's and his new "anti-slavery" Republican Party's rise to power! Obama placed his hand on President Lincoln's Bible while doing so as the Head of the Party that assassinated President Lincoln! Obama was sworn to the Office of President of the United States with his hand on President Abraham Lincoln's Bible while doing so as the Head of the Party that fought Lincoln's Party tooth and nail, every step of the way, from Lincoln's day to this, in an attempt to keep the Black man and woman down! What a shame! What hypocrisy! What a damn lie!

Of course, what do you expect from a man who the day after he was elected President saw his local State Lottery Numbers come up 666!

# Chapter 10: The 666 Factor Surrounding Obama!

**Revelation 13:16-18**
*¹⁶He causes all, both small and great, rich and poor, free and slave, to receive a mark on their right hand or on their foreheads, ¹⁷and that no one may buy or sell except one who has the mark or the name of the beast, or the number of his name. ¹⁸Here is wisdom. Let him who has understanding calculate the number of the beast, for it is the number of a man: His number is 666.*

The above passage from the Holy Bible is one of the most well known; everyone is familiar with the number 666; and everyone rightly associates this number with the devil. The above prophetic passage of Holy Scripture foretells of the day when the government will become so intrusive into our lives, so totally controlling of everything we do that every citizen will be required to receive the government's "mark" on their body, and without that mark you cannot buy or sell anything! The Bible tells us that this mark is a number and that number represents the name of a man. That man is the Head of the government. Everyone knows, based upon the context of the above and related passages, that this man is the Anti-Christ! Most people understand that, just as Jesus Christ was God in the flesh, likewise the Anti-Christ will be satan in the flesh. God, of course, created the body of Jesus in the womb of a virgin girl named Mary who was a direct descendant of King David (Isaiah 7:14; Matthew 1:18-25; Luke 1:26-35; Hebrews 10:5-7). Satan, however, cannot create a human body, so he will "possess" the body of the Anti-Christ, much like when he "entered into Judas Iscariot" on the night he betrayed Jesus Christ (John 13:26-27).

Thus, the number 666 is the identifying number of the Anti-Christ, who will be satan's false Christ or false Messiah, through whom satan will deceive the human race into worshiping him!

As Barack Hussein Obama was campaigning for the Presidency of the United States during the 2008 Presidential Election, many, including Barack himself, alluded to or outright stated that Obama was "The Messiah," which means The Christ. Barack Obama alluded to himself as The Messiah, The Christ, when he declared: *"Generations from now, we will be able to look back and tell our children that this was the moment when...the rise of the oceans began to slow and our planet began to heal."*

Nation of Islam leader Louis Farrakhan in a sermon declared outright that Barack Obama is "The Messiah!" (To see video for yourself, search YouTube.com for "Farrakhan Heralds Obama as Messiah").

Many in the media, most of whom hate Jesus Christ, have made allusions to Obama as The Savior, "like God," The Messiah, thus The Christ.

Crowds in Europe and America swarmed and swooned around Obama, with a Messianic feeling in the air, reminiscent of crowd reactions to Adolf Hitler.

Because of the plethora of such Messianic denotations lavished upon Obama by the clueless, my patriot colleague, Sean Hannity, often throws a pejorative jab at Obama by calling him, *"The Anointed One"*—which is the literal meaning of the title "The Christ" or "The Messiah."

Of course, the historic fact is that there is only One Christ, One Messiah, and that is the Lord Jesus Christ. So any time anyone, like for example Louis Farrakhan, ascribes the Title of Messiah to anyone other than Jesus Christ, what they are actually declaring is that this person to whom they are bestowing that Title is the Anti-Christ!

Many of us who voted against Barack Obama in the 2008 Presidential Election felt sick to our stomachs when word came on Election Night that Obama had won the Presidency, because we knew that a very dangerous, very evil man had just been placed into the White House! We knew that Obama was a Communist, baby-murdering, homosexual-sin-loving, racist, America-hating, Muslim-loving, anti-Israel Demon-crat! And if he was anti-Israel, then he was anti-God, which makes him anti-Christ! I remember calling my sisters as Obama was giving his victory speech on election night and saying to my sisters, *"Listen, the Messiah is speaking!"* I was of course, being sarcastic, knowing that Obama was the opposite of the Messiah; he was an anti-Messiah, an anti-Christ!

This would all be frivolous chatter with regard to Barack Obama, if it were not for the 666 factor surrounding Obama!

## Illinois Lottery Comes Up 666 Day After Obama's Election!

At the time of the 2008 Presidential Election, Barack Obama lived in Chicago, Illinois; he was the Senator from Illinois; making him the official legal representative for the State of Illinois in the U.S. Senate. Barack Hussein Obama was elected as President of the United States on Tuesday, November 4, 2008. Like many States, Illinois has a State Lottery with a Wednesday Pick 3 Drawing. The very next day following the election of Illinois Senator Barack Obama to the Presidency, the Illinois Evening Pick 3 Drawing on Wednesday, November 5, 2008, came up, are you ready for this: 666!

Below I have "Pasted" from the Illinois Lottery website the Evening Pick 3 Winning Numbers from that date:

### Winning Numbers
**Evening Pick 3**
Wed, Nov 5 2008 is 6-6-6

You may search the Illinois Lottery website to verify that indeed 666 was the winning number for the Evening Pick 3 on November 5, 2008, by going to the Illinois Lottery Winning Numbers search page at: http://www.illinoislottery.com/en-us/winning-number-search-number.html (Then "select Game" "Pick 3" and enters 6-6-6; then "Select Date Range" by selecting "Specific Date Range" and enter "From: November 5, 2008" "To: November 5, 2008;" then click Submit and the search results will indeed show 6-6-6 was the Evening Pick 3 Winning Number for that date!)

"Coincidence," you say? Oh really? The mathematical impossibility of the Illinois Lottery producing the number 666 the very day after their Illinois Senator won the Presidency when those who loved Obama were saying he was the Messiah, and those who hated him were saying he's an anti-Christ, is so far beyond mathematical probability that it defies reason; the only explanation is that it was supernaturally produced as a sign.

## Other 666 & satanic Apparitions Surrounding Obama!

There have also been other strange occurrences along this line. For example, I encourage you to go to YouTube.com and watch the video that comes up when you search: "666 Poster Appears At Local Obama Campaign Center."

Another phenomenon that a young African American gal first discovered and posted on YouTube.com, which has now been tested and reproduced by dozens of others, has to do with Obama's 2008 Campaign slogan, "Yes we can!" On YouTube.com, search: "Obama Yes We Can Backwards" and dozens of videos will fill the search results, all of which demonstrate a disturbing phenomenon—when you record Obama during his 2008 Campaign speeches repeating his slogan, "Yes we can!" and even the crowds chanting back "Yes we can!" and then play it backwards, it clearly says, "Thank you satan!" Was this an intentional act by Barack Obama to give praise to satan for placing him into the White House in anticipation of satan giving him the victory?—It could have been intentional, because when you say and record the words, "Thank you satan!" and play it backwards, it comes out, "Yes we can!" so it could well have been intentional; or was it satan manipulating Barack Obama for his will and pleasure? I don't know. But either way it is shocking, disturbing, and diabolical!

Some might argue that these unusual phenomenon are too subjective to be given real credence; all I can say is watch and listen for yourself, and you decide. But no one can doubt the mathematical improbability of the number 666 coming forth in the Illinois Lottery the day after Illinois Senator Barack Obama wins the Presidency! That is not a subjective phenomenon, but an objective mathematical impossibility!

## Obama's Words & Actions Prove He Is An Anti-Christ!

666 is the number of the Anti-Christ; it is the number of satan's man.

Now, I'm not saying that Barack Hussein Obama is *THE* Anti-Christ, for he is too much of a babbling buffoon for that; but I am saying that Barack Hussein Obama is *an* Anti-Christ, in the same way that Adolf Hitler was an anti-Christ, for there are many of those, as the Apostle John declares:

**1 John 2:18**
[18]*Little children, it is the last hour; and as you have heard that the Antichrist is coming, even now many antichrists have come, by which we know that it is the last hour.*

A few of the traits of the Anti-Christ outlined in the Bible include hatred and persecution of Israel and her people; deception; and the ability to mesmerize the masses—traits possessed by both Adolf Hitler and Barack Obama.

The supernatural 'sign" of the Illinois Lottery turning out the number 666 the day after Obama's election confirms what many of us already knew about him in 2008. Of course, being "an anti-Christ" means you are empowered by satan, on satan's side, and opposed to God, to Christ and to Israel—God's supernatural Covenant Nation on the Earth. And Barack Obama's words and actions have proven him to be opposed to God, to the Nation of Israel and to Jesus Christ and His Word, the Holy Bible! These actions include refusing to stand up for Israel against Iran, the terrorist Israeli-land occupying Palestinians, and the other anti-Christ Muslims in all the nations surrounding Israel! In addition Obama has called for Israel to give up land that God Almighty deeded to Israel 4,000 years ago through His Holy Land Covenant He made with Abraham, Isaac and Jacob (Israel). President Obama has further defied God by promoting the sin of homosexuality and by appointing practicing homosexuals to high Offices! President Obama has further spit in the face of God and the Lord Jesus Christ by cancelling the traditional White House celebration of the Christian National Day of Prayer, while hosting a special dinner with Muslims to celebrate Ramadan! There is no other way to interpret this last action by Obama, but to simply state that Obama has kicked God and the Lord Jesus Christ out of the White House, and has invited satan and his false anti-Christ religion of Islam into the White House!

What more do I need to say? Actually, there is just one more thing I wish to say.

## God's Two Warnings To America Through Hurricane Isaac!

Here is the first warning I believe God is sending to America through Hurricane Isaac.

The "names" of the hurricanes are picked out before the hurricane season begins. "Isaac," the son of the Patriarch Abraham through his wife Sarah (after they were both past the age of child-bearing), is God's "miracle" son of Promise and Blessing to all Mankind through Faith in God's Promise, in contrast to Abraham's first-born son Ishmael, through the Egyptian servant girl Hagar, which came about by human effort. Isaac is God's son of Blessing to all mankind because Isaac is the father of Israel!

Hurricane "Isaac" caused the first day of the 2012 Republican National Convention to be shut down; and on Wednesday, August 29, 2012, hurricane Isaac hit New Orleans and the surrounding Gulf Coast—exactly 7-years to the very day that hurricane Katrina hit New Orleans and the surrounding Gulf Coast States, wreaking havoc across the region, eventually causing Lake Pontchartrain to overflow the levy's and all but destroyed the city of New Orleans! Do you think that is a "coincidence" too?

There is no doubt that hurricane Katrina 7-years ago was a direct judgment from God against the United States because of President Bush's pressuring of Israel to withdraw the tens-of-thousands of Israelis' from the Gaza strip who had settled there in obedience to God's command to "possess the land;" who over some 20-years had built homes, schools & synagogues there. The expulsion of these Israelis from their homes, their God-given Land violated God's Covenant with Israel regarding that Holy Land, and God promises to judge every nation who *"divided up My land!"*

### Joel 3:1-2
[1] *"For behold, in those days and at that time, When I bring back the captives of Judah and Jerusalem, [2] I will also gather all nations, And bring them down to the Valley of Jehoshaphat; And I will enter into judgment with them there On account of My people, My heritage Israel, Whom they have scattered among the nations; They have also divided up My land.*

Within 24-hours of Israel's withdrawal from Gaza, a tropical storm sprang up off the coast of Florida, which 72-hours later was slamming into the Northern Gulf Coast as a Cat-5 hurricane called Katrina, displacing hundreds-of-thousands from their homes in retribution for America pressuring Israel to displace tens-of-thousands of Israelis from their homes in Gaza.

The fact that the hurricane which impacted the 2012 Republican National Convention and the Northern Gulf Coast exactly 7-years to the day that Katrina hit, bears the name "Isaac," the father of Israel, is no more a "coincidence" than was the Illinois Pick-3 Lottery turning up the numbers 666 on the very day after Illinois Senator Barack Hussein Obama was elected President of the United States in 2008!

Here is what I believe God is saying to America through hurricane Isaac: The Economy is NOT the #1 issue in the 2012 Presidential Election! The #1 issue in the 2012 Election is America's President's policies toward Israel! And that America's President's policies toward Israel will directly impact God's blessing or cursing of America's economic prosperity and security!

Muslim-born Barack Hussein Obama has been the most anti-Israel President in history! And America has suffered God's wrath for his anti-Israel policies throughout the first term of his Presidency in the form of the worst fires in America's history! The worst floods in America's history! Unusual earthquakes hitting the Northeast part of America, even cracking the Washington Monument! The worst "land hurricane" in America's history, striking in the month of June, 2012, when Obama declared June to be "Lesbian, Gay, Bisexual & Transgender Pride Month!" The worst heat-wave in America's history! The worst economy since the Great Depression! And the worst Drought since the Dust Bowl "Grapes of Wrath" Drought of 1930!

*Democratic Party Officially Kicks God Out Of Their Party At 2012 Convention!*

To make matters worse, as I stated in Chapter 8 Why It's Not OK To Be Gay, the entire Democratic Party has officially joined Obama in his anti-God anti-Israel position by officially kicking God out of the 2012 Democratic Party Platform, as well as removing the declaration that Jerusalem is the Capital of Israel! This removal by the Democratic Party of God and Jerusalem from their 2012 Platform caused such a stir outside of the Democratic Party that, fearing it could cost them the 2012 Election, the DNC attempted to add an Amendment to the Official Democratic Party Platform which reinserted a mention of God and Jerusalem as Israel's Capital. However, when the Amendment came to the floor of the Democratic National Convention for vote by the delegates, when the DNC Chairman said, *"All those delegates in favor say 'I;' all those delegates opposed say 'No;'"* the "No's" were greater than the "I's!" The Chairman knowing he had been sent to the floor to get the Amendment passed to avoid the "DNC Says No to God" controversy tried it again a second time; but this time the "No's" were even louder! The Chairman looked around, looking to the side for direction; he then tried it a third time and again the "No's" won! To which he declared, *"In the opinion of the Chair two-thirds have voted in the affirmative, the motion is adopted and the Platform has been amended as shown on the screen"* to which the majority of delegates who had voted against placing God and Jerusalem as Israel's Capital back into the Democratic Party Platform began to boo, hiss and jeer! A photo taken from behind the Chairman was leaked which showed that his words *"In the opinion of the Chair two-thirds have voted in the affirmative, the motion is adopted and the Platform has been amended"* were pre-loaded into the teleprompter! So "technically" God and Jerusalem were placed back into the DNC Platform, but it was done against the will of the majority and thus the declaration by the Chairman that the amendment had passed by a two-thirds vote is a sham and fraud! Thus in "reality," the 2012 Democratic Party has thrown God and His Holy Capital of Jerusalem out of the Democratic Party Official Platform—the "Platform" is the Official Vision of where the Party desires to take America; thus the Democratic Party's Official Vision is to kick God out of America and do everything in the Democratic Party's power to thwart God's restoration of the Holy Land to Israel! This is the most shocking and significant political event in America's history and will surely bring God's righteous wrath upon every member of the Democratic Party and, if allowed to remain in power, upon the United States! I warn you America, if you are a registered Democrat or vote for a Democrat then in God's eyes you are complicit in the Democratic Party's official 2012 rejection of God and Jerusalem! (You have got to see this shocking history-making event for yourself at YouTube.com, search: "Dems ram 'God' and Jerusalem back into platform over objections and boos").

## *But There's Hope America If You Make A Change In 2012 & Beyond!*

But there is hope America! In 2012 we can make a change! Presidential Candidate Mitt Romney stood on Israeli soil a few weeks before the 2012 Republican National Convention and declared his uncompromising support of the Nation of Israel! Declaring what no other American President has declared—not only unequivocally that *"Jerusalem is Israel's Capital,"* but also that if elected President Romney would seek to move the U.S. Embassy from Tel Aviv to Jerusalem! Finally, a man who is on God's side of what is, from God's perspective, the most important political issue! I can only hope and pray that Mitt Romney will go all the way with, as I stated, what is from God's perspective the most important political issue—and that would be to adopt Mike Huckabee's Israel policy, that a Two-State Solution is not a solution! God deeded every square foot of that Holy Land to Israel, and any attempt to divide up God's Holy Land will result in God's wrath and judgment upon the Nation that pressures Israel to do so! (See Joel 3:1-2). There is only One State, Israel, that has the God-given right to possess that Land! Who are you, O' Man, to think you can oppose God! For a further discussion of this important issue, see my book to be released in early 2013 titled: *The Bible Reveals The Coming Divine Destruction Of Islam Via The Coming War Between Israel, Russia & Iran!*

## *God Blesses Every Nation That Blesses Israel & Curses Every Nation That Curses Israel!*

You see, God has established a principle of the basis upon which He will either bless or curse a Nation on the Earth—those Nations that bless Israel, God will bless! Those Nations that curse Israel, God will curse! Here's the Biblical proof:

The Promise of Blessing & Cursing Regarding Abraham:
**Genesis 12:3**
*I will bless those who bless you, And I will curse him who curses you; And in you all the families of the earth shall be blessed."*

The Promise of Blessing & Cursing Regarding Israel:
**Genesis 27:29**
*Let peoples serve you, And nations bow down to you. Be master over your brethren, And let your mother's sons bow down to you.*
*Cursed be everyone who curses you, And blessed be those who bless you!"*

The Promise of Blessing & Cursing Regarding the Nation & People of Israel:
Numbers 24:9
*He bows down, he lies down as a lion; And as a lion, who shall rouse him? Blessed is he who blesses you, And cursed is he who curses you.*

Here these words America! If you vote for anti-Israel Barack Hussein Obama to be your President, you are spitting in God's Face and inviting God's wrath upon you and upon America!

But if you vote for pro-Israel Mitt Romney, you are siding with God and inviting His blessing upon you and upon America!

## Hurricanes Isaac, Gustav & Katrina Were God's Judgments Against The Sin Of Homosexuality!

As I pointed out in Chapter 8 Why It's Not OK To Be Gay, I reiterate here the second warning God is sending America through hurricane Isaac hitting the Northern Gulf Coast on August 29, 2012; hurricane Katrina hitting the Northern Gulf Coast on August 29, 2005; and hurricane Gustav hitting the Northern Gulf Coast on September 1, 2008. Remember, just 4-years ago hurricane Gustav, which resulted in the largest evacuation of people in U.S. history, some 3-million, also interrupted the first day of the Republican Party's National Convention! Coincidence? I think not!

What do hurricane's Katrina, Gustav and Isaac all have in common? They all hit the Northern Gulf Coast, impacting New Orleans, the last week of August leading into the Labor Day weekend. Why is that significant? You don't know do you? Of course not, because no one in the liberal media has reported on this—not even Fox News, the last vesture of Journalism in America, has reported on this event! What am I talking about? Ever heard of the annual celebration in New Orleans called Mardi Gras? Of course you have, everybody has! Which is a celebration that, in and of itself is a smack in the face of Almighty God, because it is a weeklong celebration of girls exposing their breasts in public for beads, culminating on "Fat Tuesday," but abruptly ending the next day on "Ash Wednesday," the Catholic Church's beginning of Lent—40-days of fasting and prayer leading up to the celebration of the crucifixion and resurrection of the Lord Jesus Christ. In other words, the celebrants are saying, *"We have to repent and be good for 40-days, so let's party and sin like crazy for the week leading up to it!"* Which anyone with an ounce of *Common Sense* knows that's not how the Gospel works! Yes, Christ offers forgiveness for sins to those who truly repent and place their faith in Him—but sinning like crazy for a week leading up to your repentance is false repentance; you know it and God knows it. But Mardi Gras is not what I'm referring to with regard to the last week of August leading into the Labor Day weekend.

Have you ever heard of "Southern Decadence?" I hadn't heard of it either because of the media's anti-God, anti-Christian, pro-homosexuality politically correct bias! "Southern Decadence" is a week-long event held annually on the last week of August up to the Sunday before Labor Day in New Orleans. It is a gathering of homosexuals who come from across America and around the world to flaunt their homosexuality, often with public displays of homosexual sex and debauchery! What is even more shocking is why have we never heard of this event, when Southern Decadence boasts crowds equal to or larger than Mardi Gras? Everyone's heard of Mardi Gras, but no one has heard of Gay Southern Decadence!

Hurricanes Katrina, Gustav and Isaac all stopped the Gay Southern Decadence celebration! You've heard the expression, "I don't have to be hit over the head with a barstool before I realize I'm in a bar fight!" Well, *Common Sense* tells us that God is shouting, "Stop publically condoning and celebrating the sin of homosexuality! But is New Orleans listening? Is America listening? Are you listening?

**Romans 1:18-27**
[18] *For the* <u>wrath of God</u> *is revealed from heaven* <u>against all ungodliness and unrighteousness of men</u>, *who suppress the truth in unrighteousness,...*
[26] *For this reason God gave them up to vile passions. For even their women exchanged the natural use for what is against nature.*
[27] *Likewise also the men, leaving the natural use of the woman, burned in their lust for one another, men with men committing what is shameful, and receiving in themselves the due penalty of their perversion.*

# America, When Deciding Who To Vote For To Be Your Leaders, The Questions You Must Ask Are Simple!

First, what is their policy toward Israel and Israel's right to possess every square foot of that Land which God deeded to them 4,000 years ago! If they are pro-Israel, then they are pro-Christ and God will bless America because of their leadership and pro-Israel policies! Again, I reiterate here that America must abandon the "Two State Solution" and embrace God's position of One State called Israel. But if they are pro-Palestinian like Obama and the current Democratic Party is then they are anti-Israel and God will curse America because of their leadership and anti-Israel policies!

Second, what is their policy toward the sin of homosexuality? If they are for the sin of homosexuality, then they are anti-Christ and God will curse America because of their leadership and pro-homosexual policies! If they are opposed to the sin of homosexuality, then they are pro-Christ and God will bless America because of their leadership and policies that oppose public acceptance of the sin of homosexuality! For God's sake, we don't accept the sin of adultery! Many a politician has lost their political career for committing the sin of adultery; nor is adultery accepted in any realm of American society. So why is the sin of homosexuality tolerated, even accepted, even worse celebrated?

Third, what is their policy toward murdering children in their mother's wombs? If they are a member of the Democratic Party then they support the murder of innocent children, totaling nearly 60-million Americans so far! This rampant murder of innocent children by the Democratic Party breaks God's heart and brings God's Judgment! But if they are opposed to murdering innocent children like the Republican Party, this pleases God and brings God's blessing! Although, the Republican Party's Official Prolife stance is not enough; the Congress must immediately pass a Law banning the murder of innocent children and the President must sign the new Law!

Fourth and finally, what is their policy toward *"redistribution of wealth,"* taking money by taxation from those who worked for it and giving it to those who did not work for it—which is Communism! If they are pro-Communism, pro-redistribution of wealth, then they are anti-Christ, opposing Christ's command: *"For even when we were with you, we commanded you this: If anyone will not work, neither shall he eat. For we hear that there are some who walk among you in a disorderly manner, not working at all,....Now those who are such we command and exhort through our Lord Jesus Christ that they __work__ in quietness and __eat their own bread__.* (2 Thessalonians 3:10-12). If they are pro-redistribution of wealth, then they are anti-Christ and God will curse America because of their leadership and anti-Christ economic policies!

Or, are they for a free-market economy and individual responsibility, where each person is responsible for providing for himself and his family without government or Church assistance, as Christ has commanded? If so, then God will bless America for their leadership and pro-Christ economic policies!

Be careful, America, for whom you vote on November 6, 2012, and every election thereafter! Your peace and prosperity, your safety and security depend on it!

**Deuteronomy 30:19**
[19]*I call heaven and earth as witnesses today against you, that I have set before you life and death, blessing and cursing; therefore choose life, that both you and your children may live;*

Join the *Common Sense* Revolution at: www.ThatsCommonSense.com and together We The People shall take back America!

## About the Author

Author James Daniels is an Evangelical Christian Evangelist who is an expert in Biblical Theology and Islamic Quranic doctrine and he refers often to the Biblical and Quranic religious texts to substantiate the validity of his presentation in this book. Rev. James Daniels deeply loves America and like most of you is very concerned about the direction Barack Hussein Obama and the Democratic Party are taking America!

Author James Daniels says, *"I wrote this book on behalf of every American who is frustrated and deeply concerned about the lack of Common Sense in today's political rhetoric and policies. The policies of the Democratic Party, along with those in the Republican Party who lack a spine, are taking America down a road to destruction. It is time America for We The People to stand up and take our country back; not by the power of the bullet, but by the power of the ballot! I do not personally seek political Office, for I have answered my Calling; but rather my purpose is to return sanity and Common Sense to the national political debate and thereby help propel into every Office at every level of government those who hold to Common Sense Constitutional principles! Common Sense America, this book is YOUR VOICE!"*

## Booking Contact Information for James Daniels

To book James Daniels for interviews, appearances and speaking engagements, please contact him by email at: EvangelistJamesDaniels@gmail.com or admin@ThatsCommonSense.com.

To purchase additional print or electronic copies of this book or to sign-up to receive James Daniels' Blog posts, please visit: www.ThatsCommonSense.com.

# Appendix A: Thomas Paine's Common Sense

Common Sense

**By Thomas Paine**
Philadelphia, Feb. 14, 1776.

## Introduction

PERHAPS the sentiments contained in the following pages, are not yet sufficiently fashionable to procure them general favor; a long habit of not thinking a thing wrong, gives it a superficial appearance of being right, and raises at first a formidable outcry in defence of custom. But tumult soon subsides. Time makes more converts than reason.

As a long and violent abuse of power is generally the means of calling the right of it in question, (and in matters too which might never have been thought of, had not the sufferers been aggravated into the inquiry,) and as the king of England hath undertaken in his own right, to support the parliament in what he calls theirs, and as the good people of this country are grievously oppressed by the combination, they have an undoubted privilege to inquire into the pretensions of both, and equally to reject the usurpations of either.

In the following sheets, the author hath studiously avoided every thing which is personal among ourselves. Compliments as well as censure to individuals make no part thereof. The wise and the worthy need not the triumph of a pamphlet; and those whose sentiments are injudicious or unfriendly, will cease of themselves, unless too much pains is bestowed upon their conversion.

The cause of America is, in a great measure, the cause of all mankind. Many circumstances have, and will arise, which are not local, but universal, and through which the principles of all lovers of mankind are affected, and in the event of which, their affections are interested. The laying a country desolate with fire and sword, declaring war against the natural rights of all mankind, and extirpating the defenders thereof from the face of the earth, is the concern of every man to whom nature hath given the power of feeling; of which class, regardless of party censure, is THE AUTHOR.

## OF THE ORIGIN AND DESIGN OF GOVERNMENT IN GENERAL. WITH CONCISE REMARKS ON THE ENGLISH CONSTITUTION

SOME writers have so confounded society with government, as to leave little or no distinction between them; whereas they are not only different, but have different origins. Society is produced by our wants, and government by our wickedness; the former promotes our happiness positively by uniting our affections, the latter negatively by restraining our vices. The one encourages intercourse, the other creates distinctions. The first is a patron, the last a punisher.

Society in every state is a blessing, but government even in its best state is but a necessary evil in its worst state an intolerable one; for when we suffer, or are exposed to the same miseries by a government, which we might expect in a country without government, our calamities is heightened by reflecting that we furnish the means by which we suffer! Government, like dress, is the badge of lost innocence; the palaces of kings are built on the ruins of the bowers of paradise. For were the impulses of conscience clear, uniform, and irresistibly obeyed, man would need no other lawgiver; but that not being the case, he finds it necessary to surrender up a part of his property to furnish means for the protection of the rest; and this he is induced to do by the same prudence which in every other case advises him out of two evils to choose the least. Wherefore, security being the true design and end of government, it unanswerably follows that whatever form thereof appears most likely to ensure it to us, with the least expense and greatest benefit, is preferable to all others.

In order to gain a clear and just idea of the design and end of government, let us suppose a small number of persons settled in some sequestered part of the earth, unconnected with the rest, they will then represent the first peopling of any country, or of the world. In this state of natural liberty, society will be their first thought. A thousand motives will excite them thereto, the strength of one man is so unequal to his wants, and his mind so unfitted for perpetual solitude, that he is soon obliged to seek assistance and relief of another, who in his turn requires the same. Four or five united would be able to raise a tolerable dwelling in the midst of a wilderness, but one man might labor out the common period of life without accomplishing any thing; when he had felled his timber he could not remove it, nor erect it after it was removed; hunger in the mean time would urge him from his work, and every different want call him a different way. Disease, nay even misfortune would be death, for though neither might be mortal, yet either would disable him from living, and reduce him to a state in which he might rather be said to perish than to die.

Thus necessity, like a gravitating power, would soon form our newly arrived emigrants into society, the reciprocal blessings of which, would supersede, and render the obligations of law and government unnecessary while they remained perfectly just to each other; but as nothing but heaven is impregnable to vice, it will unavoidably happen, that in proportion as they surmount the first difficulties of emigration, which bound them together in a common cause, they will begin to relax in their duty and attachment to each other; and this remissness, will point out the necessity, of establishing some form of government to supply the defect of moral virtue.

Some convenient tree will afford them a State-House, under the branches of which, the whole colony may assemble to deliberate on public matters. It is more than probable that their first laws will have the title only of Regulations, and be enforced by no other penalty than public disesteem. In this first parliament every man, by natural right will have a seat.

But as the colony increases, the public concerns will increase likewise, and the distance at which the members may be separated, will render it too inconvenient for all of them to meet on every occasion as at first, when their number was small, their habitations near, and the public concerns few and trifling. This will point out the convenience of their consenting to leave the legislative part to be managed by a select number chosen from the whole body, who are supposed to have the same concerns at stake which those have who appointed them, and who will act in the same manner as the whole body would act were they present. If the colony continue increasing, it will become necessary to augment the number of the representatives, and that the interest of every part of the colony may be attended to, it will be found best to divide the whole into convenient parts, each part sending its proper number; and that the elected might never form to themselves an interest separate from the electors, prudence will point out the propriety of having elections often; because as the elected might by that means return and mix again with the general body of the electors in a few months, their fidelity to the public will be secured by the prudent reflection of not making a rod for themselves. And as this frequent interchange will establish a common interest with every part of the community, they will mutually and naturally support each other, and on this (not on the unmeaning name of king) depends the strength of government, and the happiness of the governed.

Here then is the origin and rise of government; namely, a mode rendered necessary by the inability of moral virtue to govern the world; here too is the design and end of government, viz., freedom and security. And however our eyes may be dazzled with snow, or our ears deceived by sound; however prejudice may warp our wills, or interest darken our understanding, the simple voice of nature and of reason will say, it is right.

I draw my idea of the form of government from a principle in nature, which no art can overturn, viz., that the more simple any thing is, the less liable it is to be disordered, and the easier repaired when disordered; and with this maxim in view, I offer a few remarks on the so much boasted constitution of England. That it was noble for the dark and slavish times in which it was erected is granted. When the world was overrun with tyranny the least therefrom was a glorious rescue. But that it is imperfect, subject to convulsions, and incapable of producing what it seems to promise, is easily demonstrated.

Absolute governments (though the disgrace of human nature) have this advantage with them, that they are simple; if the people suffer, they know the head from which their suffering springs, know likewise the remedy, and are not bewildered by a variety of causes and cures. But the constitution of England is so exceedingly complex, that the nation may suffer for years together without being able to discover in which part the fault lies, some will say in one and some in another, and every political physician will advise a different medicine.

I know it is difficult to get over local or long standing prejudices, yet if we will suffer ourselves to examine the component parts of the English constitution, we shall find them to be the base remains of two ancient tyrannies, compounded with some new republican materials.

First.- The remains of monarchical tyranny in the person of the king. Secondly.- The remains of aristocratical tyranny in the persons of the peers. Thirdly.- The new republican materials, in the persons of the commons, on whose virtue depends the freedom of England.

The two first, by being hereditary, are independent of the people; wherefore in a constitutional sense they contribute nothing towards the freedom of the state.

To say that the constitution of England is a union of three powers reciprocally checking each other, is farcical, either the words have no meaning, or they are flat contradictions.

To say that the commons is a check upon the king, presupposes two things.

First.- That the king is not to be trusted without being looked after, or in other words, that a thirst for absolute power is the natural disease of monarchy. Secondly.- That the commons, by being appointed for that purpose, are either wiser or more worthy of confidence than the crown.

But as the same constitution which gives the commons a power to check the king by withholding the supplies, gives afterwards the king a power to check the commons, by empowering him to reject their other bills; it again supposes that the king is wiser than those whom it has already supposed to be wiser than him. A mere absurdity!

There is something exceedingly ridiculous in the composition of monarchy; it first excludes a man from the means of information, yet empowers him to act in cases where the highest judgment is required. The state of a king shuts him from the world, yet the business of a king requires him to know it thoroughly; wherefore the different parts, unnaturally opposing and destroying each other, prove the whole character to be absurd and useless.

Some writers have explained the English constitution thus; the king, say they, is one, the people another; the peers are an house in behalf of the king; the commons in behalf of the people; but this hath all the distinctions of an house divided against itself; and though the expressions be pleasantly arranged, yet when examined they appear idle and ambiguous; and it will always happen, that the nicest construction that words are capable of, when applied to the description of something which either cannot exist, or is too incomprehensible to be within the compass of description, will be words of sound only, and though they may amuse the ear, they cannot inform the mind, for this explanation includes a previous question, viz. How came the king by a power which the people are afraid to trust, and always obliged to check? Such a power could not be the gift of a wise people, neither can any power, which needs checking, be from God; yet the provision, which the constitution makes, supposes such a power to exist.

But the provision is unequal to the task; the means either cannot or will not accomplish the end, and the whole affair is a felo de se; for as the greater weight will always carry up the less, and as all the wheels of a machine are put in motion by one, it only remains to know which power in the constitution has the most weight, for that will govern; and though the others, or a part of them, may clog, or, as the phrase is, check the rapidity of its motion, yet so long as they cannot stop it, their endeavors will be ineffectual; the first moving power will at last have its way, and what it wants in speed is supplied by time.

That the crown is this overbearing part in the English constitution needs not be mentioned, and that it derives its whole consequence merely from being the giver of places pensions is self evident, wherefore, though we have and wise enough to shut and lock a door against absolute monarchy, we at the same time have been foolish enough to put the crown in possession of the key.

The prejudice of Englishmen, in favor of their own government by king, lords, and commons, arises as much or more from national pride than reason. Individuals are undoubtedly safer in England than in some other countries, but the will of the king is as much the law of the land in Britain as in France, with this difference, that instead of proceeding directly from his mouth, it is handed to the people under the most formidable shape of an act of parliament. For the fate of Charles the First, hath only made kings more subtle not-more just.

Wherefore, laying aside all national pride and prejudice in favor of modes and forms, the plain truth is, that it is wholly owing to the constitution of the people, and not to the constitution of the government that the crown is not as oppressive in England as in Turkey.

An inquiry into the constitutional errors in the English form of government is at this time highly necessary; for as we are never in a proper condition of doing justice to others, while we continue under the influence of some leading partiality, so neither are we capable of doing it to ourselves while we remain fettered by any obstinate prejudice. And as a man, who is attached to a prostitute, is unfitted to choose or judge of a wife, so any prepossession in favor of a rotten constitution of government will disable us from discerning a good one.

# OF MONARCHY AND HEREDITARY SUCCESSION

MANKIND being originally equals in the order of creation, the equality could only be destroyed by some subsequent circumstance; the distinctions of rich, and poor, may in a great measure be accounted for, and that without having recourse to the harsh, ill-sounding names of oppression and avarice. Oppression is often the consequence, but seldom or never the means of riches; and though avarice will preserve a man from being necessitously poor, it generally makes him too timorous to be wealthy. But there is another and greater distinction for which no truly natural or religious reason can be assigned, and that is, the distinction of men into KINGS and SUBJECTS. Male and female are the distinctions of nature, good and bad the distinctions of heaven; but how a race of men came into the world so exalted above the rest, and distinguished like some new species, is worth enquiring into, and whether they are the means of happiness or of misery to mankind.

In the early ages of the world, according to the scripture chronology, there were no kings; the consequence of which was there were no wars; it is the pride of kings which throw mankind into confusion. Holland without a king hath enjoyed more peace for this last century than any of the monarchial governments in Europe. Antiquity favors the same remark; for the quiet and rural lives of the first patriarchs hath a happy something in them, which vanishes away when we come to the history of Jewish royalty.

Government by kings was first introduced into the world by the Heathens, from whom the children of Israel copied the custom. It was the most prosperous invention the Devil ever set on foot for the promotion of idolatry. The Heathens paid divine honors to their deceased kings, and the Christian world hath improved on the plan by doing the same to their living ones. How impious is the title of sacred majesty applied to a worm, who in the midst of his splendor is crumbling into dust!

As the exalting one man so greatly above the rest cannot be justified on the equal rights of nature, so neither can it be defended on the authority of scripture; for the will of the Almighty, as declared by Gideon and the prophet Samuel, expressly disapproves of government by kings. All anti-monarchial parts of scripture have been very smoothly glossed over in monarchial governments, but they undoubtedly merit the attention of countries which have their governments yet to form. Render unto Caesar the things which are Caesar's is the scriptural doctrine of courts, yet it is no support of monarchial government, for the Jews at that time were without a king, and in a state of vassalage to the Romans.

Near three thousand years passed away from the Mosaic account of the creation, till the Jews under a national delusion requested a king. Till then their form of government (except in extraordinary cases, where the Almighty interposed) was a kind of republic administered by a judge and the elders of the tribes. Kings they had none, and it was held sinful to acknowledge any being under that title but the Lords of Hosts. And when a man seriously reflects on the idolatrous homage which is paid to the persons of kings he need not wonder, that the Almighty, ever jealous of his honor, should disapprove of a form of government which so impiously invades the prerogative of heaven.

Monarchy is ranked in scripture as one of the sins of the Jews, for which a curse in reserve is denounced against them. The history of that transaction is worth attending to.

The children of Israel being oppressed by the Midianites, Gideon marched against them with a small army, and victory, through the divine interposition, decided in his favor. The Jews elate with success, and attributing it to the generalship of Gideon, proposed making him a king, saying, Rule thou over us, thou and thy son and thy son's son. Here was temptation in its fullest extent; not a kingdom only, but an hereditary one, but Gideon in the piety of his soul replied, I will not rule over you, neither shall my son rule over you, THE LORD SHALL RULE OVER YOU. Words need not be more explicit; Gideon doth not decline the honor but denieth their right to give it; neither doth be compliment them with invented declarations of his thanks, but in the positive stile of a prophet charges them with disaffection to their proper sovereign, the King of Heaven.

About one hundred and thirty years after this, they fell again into the same error. The hankering which the Jews had for the idolatrous customs of the Heathens, is something exceedingly unaccountable; but so it was, that laying hold of the misconduct of Samuel's two sons, who were entrusted with some secular concerns, they came in an abrupt and clamorous manner to Samuel, saying, Behold thou art old and thy sons walk not in thy ways, now make us a king to judge us like all the other nations. And here we cannot but observe that their motives were bad, viz., that they might be like unto other nations, i.e., the Heathen, whereas their true glory laid in being as much unlike them as possible. But the thing displeased Samuel when they said, give us a king to judge us; and Samuel prayed unto the Lord, and the Lord said unto Samuel, Hearken unto the voice of the people in all that they say unto thee, for they have not rejected thee, but they have rejected me, THEN I SHOULD NOT REIGN OVER THEM.

According to all the works which have done since the day; wherewith they brought them up out of Egypt, even unto this day; wherewith they have forsaken me and served other Gods; so do they also unto thee. Now therefore hearken unto their voice, howbeit, protest solemnly unto them and show them the manner of the king that shall reign over them, i.e., not of any particular king, but the general manner of the kings of the earth, whom Israel was so eagerly copying after. And notwithstanding the great distance of time and difference of manners, the character is still in fashion. And Samuel told all the words of the Lord unto the people, that asked of him a king. And he said, This shall be the manner of the king that shall reign over you; he will take your sons and appoint them for himself for his chariots, and to be his horsemen, and some shall run before his chariots (this description agrees with the present mode of impressing men) and he will appoint him captains over thousands and captains over fifties, and will set them to ear his ground and to read his harvest, and to make his instruments of war, and instruments of his chariots; and he will take your daughters to be confectionaries and to be cooks and to be bakers (this describes the expense and luxury as well as the oppression of kings) and he will take your fields and your olive yards, even the best of them, and give them to his servants; and he will take the tenth of your seed, and of your vineyards, and give them to his officers and to his servants (by which we see that bribery, corruption, and favoritism are the standing vices of kings) and he will take the tenth of your men servants, and your maid servants, and your goodliest young men and your asses, and put them to his work; and he will take the tenth of your sheep, and ye shall be his servants, and ye shall cry out in that day because of your king which ye shall have chosen, AND THE LORD WILL NOT HEAR YOU IN THAT DAY. This accounts for the continuation of monarchy; neither do the characters of the few good kings which have lived since, either sanctify the title, or blot out the sinfulness of the origin; the high encomium given of David takes no notice of him officially as a king, but only as a man after God's own heart. Nevertheless the People refused to obey the voice of Samuel, and they said, Nay, but we will have a king over us, that we may be like all the nations, and that our king may judge us, and go out before us and fight our battles. Samuel continued to reason with them, but to no purpose; he set before them their ingratitude, but all would not avail; and seeing them fully bent on their folly, he cried out, I will call unto the Lord, and he shall sent thunder and rain (which then was a punishment, being the time of wheat harvest) that ye may perceive and see that your wickedness is great which ye have done in the sight of the Lord, IN ASKING YOU A KING. So Samuel called unto the Lord, and the Lord sent thunder and rain that day, and all the people greatly feared the Lord and Samuel And all the people said unto Samuel, Pray for thy servants unto the Lord thy God that we die not, for WE HAVE ADDED UNTO OUR SINS THIS EVIL, TO ASK A KING. These portions of scripture are direct and positive. They admit of no equivocal construction. That the Almighty hath here entered his protest against monarchial government is true, or the scripture is false. And a man hath good reason to believe that there is as much of kingcraft, as priestcraft in withholding the scripture from the public in Popish countries. For monarchy in every instance is the Popery of government.

To the evil of monarchy we have added that of hereditary succession; and as the first is a degradation and lessening of ourselves, so the second, claimed as a matter of right, is an insult and an imposition on posterity. For all men being originally equals, no one by birth could have a right to set up his own family in perpetual preference to all others for ever, and though himself might deserve some decent degree of honors of his contemporaries, yet his descendants might be far too unworthy to inherit them. One of the strongest natural proofs of the folly of hereditary right in kings, is, that nature disapproves it, otherwise she would not so frequently turn it into ridicule by giving mankind an ass for a lion.

Secondly, as no man at first could possess any other public honors than were bestowed upon him, so the givers of those honors could have no power to give away the right of posterity, and though they might say, "We choose you for our head," they could not, without manifest injustice to their children, say, "that your children and your children's children shall reign over ours for ever." Because such an unwise, unjust, unnatural compact might (perhaps) in the next succession put them under the government of a rogue or a fool. Most wise men, in their private sentiments, have ever treated hereditary right with contempt; yet it is one of those evils, which when once established is not easily removed; many submit from fear, others from superstition, and the more powerful part shares with the king the plunder of the rest.

This is supposing the present race of kings in the world to have had an honorable origin; whereas it is more than probable, that could we take off the dark covering of antiquity, and trace them to their first rise, that we should find the first of them nothing better than the principal ruffian of some restless gang, whose savage manners of preeminence in subtlety obtained him the title of chief among plunderers; and who by increasing in power, and extending his depredations, overawed the quiet and defenseless to purchase their safety by frequent contributions. Yet his electors could have no idea of giving hereditary right to his descendants, because such a perpetual exclusion of themselves was incompatible with the free and unrestrained principles they professed to live by. Wherefore, hereditary succession in the early ages of monarchy could not take place as a matter of claim, but as something casual or complemental; but as few or no records were extant in those days, and traditionary history stuffed with fables, it was very easy, after the lapse of a few generations, to trump up some superstitious tale, conveniently timed, Mahomet like, to cram hereditary right down the throats of the vulgar. Perhaps the disorders which threatened, or seemed to threaten on the decease of a leader and the choice of a new one (for elections among ruffians could not be very orderly) induced many at first to favor hereditary pretensions; by which means it happened, as it hath happened since, that what at first was submitted to as a convenience, was afterwards claimed as a right.

England, since the conquest, hath known some few good monarchs, but groaned beneath a much larger number of bad ones, yet no man in his senses can say that their claim under William the Conqueror is a very honorable one. A French bastard landing with an armed banditti, and establishing himself king of England against the consent of the natives, is in plain terms a very paltry rascally original. It certainly hath no divinity in it. However, it is needless to spend much time in exposing the folly of hereditary right, if there are any so weak as to believe it, let them promiscuously worship the ass and lion, and welcome. I shall neither copy their humility, nor disturb their devotion.

Yet I should be glad to ask how they suppose kings came at first? The question admits but of three answers, viz., either by lot, by election, or by usurpation. If the first king was taken by lot, it establishes a precedent for the next, which excludes hereditary succession. Saul was by lot, yet the succession was not hereditary, neither does it appear from that transaction there was any intention it ever should. If the first king of any country was by election, that likewise establishes a precedent for the next; for to say, that the right of all future generations is taken away, by the act of the first electors, in their choice not only of a king, but of a family of kings for ever, hath no parallel in or out of scripture but the doctrine of original sin, which supposes the free will of all men lost in Adam; and from such comparison, and it will admit of no other, hereditary succession can derive no glory. For as in Adam all sinned, and as in the first electors all men obeyed; as in the one all mankind were subjected to Satan, and in the other to Sovereignty; as our innocence was lost in the first, and our authority in the last; and as both disable us from reassuming some former state and privilege, it unanswerably follows that original sin and hereditary succession are parallels. Dishonorable rank! Inglorious connection! Yet the most subtle sophist cannot produce a juster simile.

As to usurpation, no man will be so hardy as to defend it; and that William the Conqueror was an usurper is a fact not to be contradicted. The plain truth is, that the antiquity of English monarchy will not bear looking into.

But it is not so much the absurdity as the evil of hereditary succession which concerns mankind. Did it ensure a race of good and wise men it would have the seal of divine authority, but as it opens a door to the foolish, the wicked; and the improper, it hath in it the nature of oppression. Men who look upon themselves born to reign, and others to obey, soon grow insolent; selected from the rest of mankind their minds are early poisoned by importance; and the world they act in differs so materially from the world at large, that they have but little opportunity of knowing its true interests, and when they succeed to the government are frequently the most ignorant and unfit of any throughout the dominions.

Another evil which attends hereditary succession is, that the throne is subject to be possessed by a minor at any age; all which time the regency, acting under the cover of a king, have every opportunity and inducement to betray their trust. The same national misfortune happens, when a king worn out with age and infirmity, enters the last stage of human weakness. In both these cases the public becomes a prey to every miscreant, who can tamper successfully with the follies either of age or infancy.

The most plausible plea, which hath ever been offered in favor of hereditary succession, is, that it preserves a nation from civil wars; and were this true, it would be weighty; whereas, it is the most barefaced falsity ever imposed upon mankind. The whole history of England disowns the fact. Thirty kings and two minors have reigned in that distracted kingdom since the conquest, in which time there have been (including the Revolution) no less than eight civil wars and nineteen rebellions. Wherefore instead of making for peace, it makes against it, and destroys the very foundation it seems to stand on.

The contest for monarchy and succession, between the houses of York and Lancaster, laid England in a scene of blood for many years. Twelve pitched battles, besides skirmishes and sieges, were fought between Henry and Edward. Twice was Henry prisoner to Edward, who in his turn was prisoner to Henry. And so uncertain is the fate of war and the temper of a nation, when nothing but personal matters are the ground of a quarrel, that Henry was taken in triumph from a prison to a palace, and Edward obliged to fly from a palace to a foreign land; yet, as sudden transitions of temper are seldom lasting, Henry in his turn was driven from the throne, and Edward recalled to succeed him. The parliament always following the strongest side.

This contest began in the reign of Henry the Sixth, and was not entirely extinguished till Henry the Seventh, in whom the families were united. Including a period of 67 years, viz., from 1422 to 1489.

In short, monarchy and succession have laid (not this or that kingdom only) but the world in blood and ashes. 'Tis a form of government which the word of God bears testimony against, and blood will attend it.

If we inquire into the business of a king, we shall find that (in some countries they have none) and after sauntering away their lives without pleasure to themselves or advantage to the nation, withdraw from the scene, and leave their successors to tread the same idle round. In absolute monarchies the whole weight of business civil and military, lies on the king; the children of Israel in their request for a king, urged this plea "that he may judge us, and go out before us and fight our battles." But in countries where he is neither a judge nor a general, as in England, a man would be puzzled to know what is his business.

The nearer any government approaches to a republic, the less business there is for a king. It is somewhat difficult to find a proper name for the government of England. Sir William Meredith calls it a republic; but in its present state it is unworthy of the name, because the corrupt influence If the crown, by having all the places in its disposal, hath so effectually swallowed up the power, and eaten out the virtue of the house of commons (the republican part in the constitution) that the government of England is nearly as monarchical as that of France or Spain. Men fall out with names without understanding them. For it is the republican and not the monarchical part of the constitution of England which Englishmen glory in, viz., the liberty of choosing a house of commons from out of their own body- and it is easy to see that when the republican virtue fails, slavery ensues. My is the constitution of England sickly, but because monarchy hath poisoned the republic, the crown hath engrossed the commons?

In England a king hath little more to do than to make war and give away places; which in plain terms, is to impoverish the nation and set it together by the ears. A pretty business indeed for a man to be allowed eight hundred thousand sterling a year for, and worshipped into the bargain! Of more worth is one honest man to society, and in the sight of God, than all the crowned ruffians that ever lived.

# THOUGHTS OF THE PRESENT STATE OF AMERICAN AFFAIRS

IN the following pages I offer nothing more than simple facts, plain arguments, and common sense; and have no other preliminaries to settle with the reader, than that he will divest himself of prejudice and prepossession, and suffer his reason and his feelings to determine for themselves; that he will put on, or rather that he will not put off the true character of a man, and generously enlarge his views beyond the present day.

Volumes have been written on the subject of the struggle between England and America. Men of all ranks have embarked in the controversy, from different motives, and with various designs; but all have been ineffectual, and the period of debate is closed. Arms, as the last resource, decide the contest; the appeal was the choice of the king, and the continent hath accepted the challenge.

It hath been reported of the late Mr. Pelham (who tho' an able minister was not without his faults) that on his being attacked in the house of commons, on the score, that his measures were only of a temporary kind, replied, "they will last my time." Should a thought so fatal and unmanly possess the colonies in the present contest, the name of ancestors will be remembered by future generations with detestation.

The sun never shined on a cause of greater worth. 'Tis not the affair of a city, a country, a province, or a kingdom, but of a continent- of at least one eighth part of the habitable globe. 'Tis not the concern of a day, a year, or an age; posterity are virtually involved in the contest, and will be more or less affected, even to the end of time, by the proceedings now. Now is the seed time of continental union, faith and honor. The least fracture now will be like a name engraved with the point of a pin on the tender rind of a young oak; The wound will enlarge with the tree, and posterity read it in full grown characters.

By referring the matter from argument to arms, a new area for politics is struck; a new method of thinking hath arisen. All plans, proposals, &c. prior to the nineteenth of April, i.e., to the commencement of hostilities, are like the almanacs of the last year; which, though proper then, are superseded and useless now. Whatever was advanced by the advocates on either side of the question then, terminated in one and the same point, viz., a union with Great Britain; the only difference between the parties was the method of effecting it; the one proposing force, the other friendship; but it hath so far happened that the first hath failed, and the second hath withdrawn her influence.

As much hath been said of the advantages of reconciliation, which, like an agreeable dream, hath passed away and left us as we were, it is but right, that we should examine the contrary side of the argument, and inquire into some of the many material injuries which these colonies sustain, and always will sustain, by being connected with, and dependant on Great Britain. To examine that connection and dependance, on the principles of nature and common sense, to see what we have to trust to, if separated, and what we are to expect, if dependant.

I have heard it asserted by some, that as America hath flourished under her former connection with Great Britain, that the same connection is necessary towards her future happiness, and will always have the same effect. Nothing can be more fallacious than this kind of argument. We may as well assert, that because a child has thrived upon milk, that it is never to have meat; or that the first twenty years of our lives is to become a precedent for the next twenty. But even this is admitting more than is true, for I answer roundly, that America would have flourished as much, and probably much more, had no European power had any thing to do with her. The commerce by which she hath enriched herself are the necessaries of life, and will always have a market while eating is the custom of Europe.

But she has protected us, say some. That she hath engrossed us is true, and defended the continent at our expense as well as her own is admitted, and she would have defended Turkey from the same motive, viz., the sake of trade and dominion.

Alas! we have been long led away by ancient prejudices and made large sacrifices to superstition. We have boasted the protection of Great Britain, without considering, that her motive was interest not attachment; that she did not protect us from our enemies on our account, but from her enemies on her own account, from those who had no quarrel with us on any other account, and who will always be our enemies on the same account. Let Britain wave her pretensions to the continent, or the continent throw off the dependance, and we should be at peace with France and Spain were they at war with Britain. The miseries of Hanover last war, ought to warn us against connections.

It hath lately been asserted in parliament, that the colonies have no relation to each other but through the parent country, i.e., that Pennsylvania and the Jerseys, and so on for the rest, are sister colonies by the way of England; this is certainly a very roundabout way of proving relation ship, but it is the nearest and only true way of proving enemyship, if I may so call it. France and Spain never were, nor perhaps ever will be our enemies as Americans, but as our being the subjects of Great Britain.

But Britain is the parent country, say some. Then the more shame upon her conduct. Even brutes do not devour their young; nor savages make war upon their families; wherefore the assertion, if true, turns to her reproach; but it happens not to be true, or only partly so, and the phrase parent or mother country hath been jesuitically adopted by the king and his parasites, with a low papistical design of gaining an unfair bias on the credulous weakness of our minds. Europe, and not England, is the parent country of America. This new world hath been the asylum for the persecuted lovers off civil and religious liberty from every Part of Europe. Hither have they fled, not from the tender embraces of the mother, but from the cruelty of the monster; and it is so far true of England, that the same tyranny which drove the first emigrants from home pursues their descendants still.

In this extensive quarter of the globe, we forget the narrow limits of three hundred and sixty miles (the extent of England) and carry our friendship on a larger scale; we claim brotherhood with every European Christian, and triumph in the generosity of the sentiment.

It is pleasant to observe by what regular gradations we surmount the force of local prejudice, as we enlarge our acquaintance with the world. A man born in any town in England divided into parishes, will naturally associate most with his fellow parishioners (because their interests in many cases will be common) and distinguish him by the name of neighbor; if he meet him but a few miles from home, he drops the narrow idea of a street, and salutes him by the name of townsman; if he travels out of the county, and meet him in any other, he forgets the minor divisions of street and town, and calls him countryman; i.e., countyman; but if in their foreign excursions they should associate in France or any other part of Europe, their local remembrance would be enlarged into that of Englishmen. And by a just parity of reasoning, all Europeans meeting in America, or any other quarter of the globe, are countrymen; for England, Holland, Germany, or Sweden, when compared with the whole, stand in the same places on the larger scale, which the divisions of street, town, and county do on the smaller ones; distinctions too limited for continental minds. Not one third of the inhabitants, even of this province, are of English descent. Wherefore, I reprobate the phrase of parent or mother country applied to England only, as being false, selfish, narrow and ungenerous.

But admitting that we were all of English descent, what does it amount to? Nothing. Britain, being now an open enemy, extinguishes every other name and title: And to say that reconciliation is our duty, is truly farcical. The first king of England, of the present line (William the Conqueror) was a Frenchman, and half the peers of England are descendants from the same country; wherefore by the same method of reasoning, England ought to be governed by France.

Much hath been said of the united strength of Britain and the colonies, that in conjunction they might bid defiance to the world. But this is mere presumption; the fate of war is uncertain, neither do the expressions mean anything; for this continent would never suffer itself to be drained of inhabitants to support the British arms in either Asia, Africa, or Europe.

Besides, what have we to do with setting the world at defiance? Our plan is commerce, and that, well attended to,will secure us the peace and friendship of all Europe; because it is the interest of all Europe to have America a free port. Her trade will always be a protection, and her barrenness of gold and silver secure her from invaders.

I challenge the warmest advocate for reconciliation, to show, a single advantage that this continent can reap, by being connected with Great Britain. I repeat the challenge, not a single advantage is derived. Our corn will fetch its price in any market in Europe, and our imported goods must be paid for buy them where we will.

But the injuries and disadvantages we sustain by that connection, are without number; and our duty to mankind I at large, as well as to ourselves, instruct us to renounce the alliance: Because, any submission to, or dependance on Great Britain, tends directly to involve this continent in European wars and quarrels; and sets us at variance with nations, who would otherwise seek our friendship, and against whom, we have neither anger nor complaint. As Europe is our market for trade, we ought to form no partial connection with any part of it. It is the true interest of America to steer clear of European contentions, which she never can do, while by her dependance on Britain, she is made the make-weight in the scale of British politics.

Europe is too thickly planted with kingdoms to be long at peace, and whenever a war breaks out between England and any foreign power, the trade of America goes to ruin, because of her connection with Britain. The next war may not turn out like the Past, and should it not, the advocates for reconciliation now will be wishing for separation then, because, neutrality in that case, would be a safer convoy than a man of war. Every thing that is right or natural pleads for separation. The blood of the slain, the weeping voice of nature cries, 'tis time to part. Even the distance at which the Almighty hath placed England and America, is a strong and natural proof, that the authority of the one, over the other, was never the design of Heaven. The time likewise at which the continent was discovered, adds weight to the argument, and the manner in which it was peopled increases the force of it. The reformation was preceded by the discovery of America, as if the Almighty graciously meant to open a sanctuary to the persecuted in future years, when home should afford neither friendship nor safety.

The authority of Great Britain over this continent, is a form of government, which sooner or later must have an end: And a serious mind can draw no true pleasure by looking forward, under the painful and positive conviction, that what he calls "the present constitution" is merely temporary. As parents, we can have no joy, knowing that this government is not sufficiently lasting to ensure any thing which we may bequeath to posterity: And by a plain method of argument, as we are running the next generation into debt, we ought to do the work of it, otherwise we use them meanly and pitifully. In order to discover the line of our duty rightly, we should take our children in our hand, and fix our station a few years farther into life; that eminence will present a prospect, which a few present fears and prejudices conceal from our sight.

Though I would carefully avoid giving unnecessary offence, yet I am inclined to believe, that all those who espouse the doctrine of reconciliation, may be included within the following descriptions:

Interested men, who are not to be trusted; weak men who cannot see; prejudiced men who will not see; and a certain set of moderate men, who think better of the European world than it deserves; and this last class by an ill-judged deliberation, will be the cause of more calamities to this continent than all the other three.

It is the good fortune of many to live distant from the scene of sorrow; the evil is not sufficiently brought to their doors to make them feel the precariousness with which all American property is possessed. But let our imaginations transport us for a few moments to Boston, that seat of wretchedness will teach us wisdom, and instruct us for ever to renounce a power in whom we can have no trust. The inhabitants of that unfortunate city, who but a few months ago were in ease and affluence, have now no other alternative than to stay and starve, or turn out to beg. Endangered by the fire of their friends if they continue within the city, and plundered by the soldiery if they leave it. In their present condition they are prisoners without the hope of redemption, and in a general attack for their relief, they would be exposed to the fury of both armies.

Men of passive tempers look somewhat lightly over the offenses of Britain, and, still hoping for the best, are apt to call out, Come we shall be friends again for all this. But examine the passions and feelings of mankind. Bring the doctrine of reconciliation to the touchstone of nature, and then tell me, whether you can hereafter love, honor, and faithfully serve the power that hath carried fire and sword into your land? If you cannot do all these, then are you only deceiving yourselves, and by your delay bringing ruin upon posterity. Your future connection with Britain, whom you can neither love nor honor, will be forced and unnatural, and being formed only on the plan of present convenience, will in a little time fall into a relapse more wretched than the first. But if you say, you can still pass the violations over, then I ask, Hath your house been burnt? Hath you property been destroyed before your face? Are your wife and children destitute of a bed to lie on, or bread to live on? Have you lost a parent or a child by their hands, and yourself the ruined and wretched survivor? If you have not, then are you not a judge of those who have. But if you have, and can still shake hands with the murderers, then are you unworthy the name of husband, father, friend, or lover, and whatever may be your rank or title in life, you have the heart of a coward, and the spirit of a sycophant.

This is not inflaming or exaggerating matters, but trying them by those feelings and affections which nature justifies, and without which, we should be incapable of discharging the social duties of life, or enjoying the felicities of it. I mean not to exhibit horror for the purpose of provoking revenge, but to awaken us from fatal and unmanly slumbers, that we may pursue determinately some fixed object. It is not in the power of Britain or of Europe to conquer America, if she do not conquer herself by delay and timidity. The present winter is worth an age if rightly employed, but if lost or neglected, the whole continent will partake of the misfortune; and there is no punishment which that man will not deserve, be he who, or what, or where he will, that may be the means of sacrificing a season so precious and useful.

It is repugnant to reason, to the universal order of things, to all examples from the former ages, to suppose, that this continent can longer remain subject to any external power. The most sanguine in Britain does not think so. The utmost stretch of human wisdom cannot, at this time compass a plan short of separation, which can promise the continent even a year's security. Reconciliation is was a fallacious dream. Nature hath deserted the connection, and Art cannot supply her place. For, as Milton wisely expresses, "never can true reconcilement grow where wounds of deadly hate have pierced so deep."

Every quiet method for peace hath been ineffectual. Our prayers have been rejected with disdain; and only tended to convince us, that nothing flatters vanity, or confirms obstinacy in kings more than repeated petitioning- and nothing hath contributed more than that very measure to make the kings of Europe absolute: Witness Denmark and Sweden. Wherefore since nothing but blows will do, for God's sake, let us come to a final separation, and not leave the next generation to be cutting throats, under the violated unmeaning names of parent and child.

To say, they will never attempt it again is idle and visionary, we thought so at the repeal of the stamp act, yet a year or two undeceived us; as well me we may suppose that nations, which have been once defeated, will never renew the quarrel.

As to government matters, it is not in the powers of Britain to do this continent justice: The business of it will soon be too weighty, and intricate, to be managed with any tolerable degree of convenience, by a power, so distant from us, and so very ignorant of us; for if they cannot conquer us, they cannot govern us. To be always running three or four thousand miles with a tale or a petition, waiting four or five months for an answer, which when obtained requires five or six more to explain it in, will in a few years be looked upon as folly and childishness- there was a time when it was proper, and there is a proper time for it to cease.

Small islands not capable of protecting themselves, are the proper objects for kingdoms to take under their care; but there is something very absurd, in supposing a continent to be perpetually governed by an island. In no instance hath nature made the satellite larger than its primary planet, and as England and America, with respect to each Other, reverses the common order of nature, it is evident they belong to different systems: England to Europe- America to itself.

I am not induced by motives of pride, party, or resentment to espouse the doctrine of separation and independence; I am clearly, positively, and conscientiously persuaded that it is the true interest of this continent to be so; that every thing short of that is mere patchwork, that it can afford no lasting felicity,- that it is leaving the sword to our children, and shrinking back at a time, when, a little more, a little farther, would have rendered this continent the glory of the earth.

As Britain hath not manifested the least inclination towards a compromise, we may be assured that no terms can be obtained worthy the acceptance of the continent, or any ways equal to the expense of blood and treasure we have been already put to.

The object contended for, ought always to bear some just proportion to the expense. The removal of the North, or the whole detestable junto, is a matter unworthy the millions we have expended. A temporary stoppage of trade, was an inconvenience, which would have sufficiently balanced the repeal of all the acts complained of, had such repeals been obtained; but if the whole continent must take up arms, if every man must be a soldier, it is scarcely worth our while to fight against a contemptible ministry only. Dearly, dearly, do we pay for the repeal of the acts, if that is all we fight for; for in a just estimation, it is as great a folly to pay a Bunker Hill price for law, as for land. As I have always considered the independency of this continent, as an event, which sooner or later must arrive, so from the late rapid progress of the continent to maturity, the event could not be far off. Wherefore, on the breaking out of hostilities, it was not worth the while to have disputed a matter, which time would have finally redressed, unless we meant to be in earnest; otherwise, it is like wasting an estate of a suit at law, to regulate the trespasses of a tenant, whose lease is just expiring. No man was a warmer wisher for reconciliation than myself, before the fatal nineteenth of April, 1775 (Massacre at Lexington), but the moment the event of that day was made known, I rejected the hardened, sullen tempered Pharaoh of England for ever; and disdain the wretch, that with the pretended title of Father of his people, can unfeelingly hear of their slaughter, and composedly sleep with their blood upon his soul.

But admitting that matters were now made up, what would be the event? I answer, the ruin of the continent. And that for several reasons:

First. The powers of governing still remaining in the hands of the king, he will have a negative over the whole legislation of this continent. And as he hath shown himself such an inveterate enemy to liberty, and discovered such a thirst for arbitrary power, is he, or is he not, a proper man to say to these colonies, "You shall make no laws but what I please?" And is there any inhabitants in America so ignorant, as not to know, that according to what is called the present constitution, that this continent can make no laws but what the king gives leave to? and is there any man so unwise, as not to see, that (considering what has happened) he will suffer no Law to be made here, but such as suit his purpose? We may be as effectually enslaved by the want of laws in America, as by submitting to laws made for us in England. After matters are make up (as it is called) can there be any doubt but the whole power of the crown will be exerted, to keep this continent as low and humble as possible? Instead of going forward we shall go backward, or be perpetually quarrelling or ridiculously petitioning. We are already greater than the king wishes us to be, and will he not hereafter endeavor to make us less? To bring the matter to one point. Is the power who is jealous of our prosperity, a proper power to govern us? Whoever says No to this question is an independent, for independency means no more, than, whether we shall make our own laws, or whether the king, the greatest enemy this continent hath, or can have, shall tell us, "there shall be now laws but such as I like."

But the king you will say has a negative in England; the people there can make no laws without his consent. in point of right and good order, there is something very ridiculous, that a youth of twenty-one (which hath often happened) shall say to several millions of people, older and wiser than himself, I forbid this or that act of yours to be law. But in this place I decline this sort of reply, though I will never cease to expose the absurdity of it, and only answer, that England being the king's residence, and America not so, make quite another case. The king's negative here is ten times more dangerous and fatal than it can be in England, for there he will scarcely refuse his consent to a bill for putting England into as strong a state of defence as possible, and in America he would never suffer such a bill to be passed.

America is only a secondary object in the system of British politics- England consults the good of this country, no farther than it answers her own purpose. Wherefore, her own interest leads her to suppress the growth of ours in every case which doth not promote her advantage, or in the least interfere with it. A pretty state we should soon be in under such a second-hand government, considering what has happened! Men do not change from enemies to friends by the alteration of a name; and in order to show that reconciliation now is a dangerous doctrine, I affirm, that it would be policy in the kingdom at this time, to repeal the acts for the sake of reinstating himself in the government of the provinces; in order, that he may accomplish by craft and subtlety, in the long run, wha he cannot do by force ans violence in the short one. Reconciliation and ruin are nearly related.

Secondly. That as even the best terms, which we can expect to obtain, can amount to no more than a temporary expedient, or a kind of government by guardianship, which can last no longer than till the colonies come of age, so the general face and state of things, in the interim, will be unsettled and unpromising. Emigrants of property will not choose to come to a country whose form of government hangs but by a thread, and who is every day tottering on the brink of commotion and disturbance; and numbers of the present inhabitant would lay hold of the interval, to dispose of their effects, and quit the continent.

But the most powerful of all arguments, is, that nothing but independence, i.e., a continental form of government, can keep the peace of the continent and preserve it inviolate from civil wars. I dread the event of a reconciliation with Britain now, as it is more than probable, that it will be followed by a revolt somewhere or other, the consequences of which may be far more fatal than all the malice of Britain.

Thousands are already ruined by British barbarity; (thousands more will probably suffer the same fate.) Those men have other feelings than us who have nothing suffered. All they now possess is liberty, what they before enjoyed is sacrificed to its service, and having nothing more to lose, they disdain submission. Besides, the general temper of the colonies, towards a British government, will be like that of a youth, who is nearly out of his time, they will care very little about her. And a government which cannot preserve the peace, is no government at all, and in that case we pay our money for nothing; and pray what is it that Britain can do, whose power will be wholly on paper, should a civil tumult break out the very day after reconciliation? I have heard some men say, many of whom I believe spoke without thinking, that they dreaded independence, fearing that it would produce civil wars. It is but seldom that our first thoughts are truly correct, and that is the case here; for there are ten times more to dread from a patched up connection than from independence. I make the sufferers case my own, and I protest, that were I driven from house and home, my property destroyed, and my circumstances ruined, that as man, sensible of injuries, I could never relish the doctrine of reconciliation, or consider myself bound thereby.

The colonies have manifested such a spirit of good order and obedience to continental government, as is sufficient to make every reasonable person easy and happy on that head. No man can assign the least pretence for his fears, on any other grounds, that such as are truly childish and ridiculous, viz., that one colony will be striving for superiority over another.

Where there are no distinctions there can be no superiority, perfect equality affords no temptation. The republics of Europe are all (and we may say always) in peace. Holland and Switzerland are without wars, foreign or domestic; monarchical governments, it is true, are never long at rest: the crown itself is a temptation to enterprising ruffians at home; and that degree of pride and insolence ever attendant on regal authority swells into a rupture with foreign powers, in instances where a republican government, by being formed on more natural principles, would negotiate the mistake.

If there is any true cause of fear respecting independence it is because no plan is yet laid down. Men do not see their way out; wherefore, as an opening into that business I offer the following hints; at the same time modestly affirming, that I have no other opinion of them myself, than that they may be the means of giving rise to something better. Could the straggling thoughts of individuals be collected, they would frequently form materials for wise and able men to improve to useful matter.

Let the assemblies be annual, with a President only. The representation more equal. Their business wholly domestic, and subject to the authority of a continental congress.

Let each colony be divided into six, eight, or ten, convenient districts, each district to send a proper number of delegates to congress, so that each colony send at least thirty. The whole number in congress will be at least three hundred ninety. Each congress to sit..... and to choose a president by the following method. When the delegates are met, let a colony be taken from the whole thirteen colonies by lot, after which let the whole congress choose (by ballot) a president from out of the delegates of that province. I the next Congress, let a colony be taken by lot from twelve only, omitting that colony from which the president was taken in the former congress, and so proceeding on till the whole thirteen shall have had their proper rotation. And in order that nothing may pass into a law but what is satisfactorily just, not less than three fifths of the congress to be called a majority. He that will promote discord, under a government so equally formed as this, would join Lucifer in his revolt.

But as there is a peculiar delicacy, from whom, or in what manner, this business must first arise, and as it seems most agreeable and consistent, that it should come from some intermediate body between the governed and the governors, that is between the Congress and the people, let a Continental Conference be held, in the following manner, and for the following purpose:

A committee of twenty-six members of Congress, viz., two for each colony. Two members for each house of assembly, or provincial convention; and five representatives of the people at large, to be chosen in the capital city or town of each province, for, and in behalf of the whole province, by as many qualified voters as shall think proper to attend from all parts of the province for that purpose; or, if more convenient, the representatives may be chosen in two or three of the most populous parts thereof. In this conference, thus assembled, will be united, the two grand principles of business, knowledge and power. The members of Congress, Assemblies, or Conventions, by having had experience in national concerns, will be able and useful counsellors, and the whole, being empowered by the people will have a truly legal authority.

The conferring members being met, let their business be to frame a Continental Charter, or Charter of the United Colonies; (answering to what is called the Magna Charta of England) fixing the number and manner of choosing members of Congress, members of Assembly, with their date of sitting, and drawing the line of business and jurisdiction between them: always remembering, that our strength is continental, not provincial: Securing freedom and property to all men, and above all things the free exercise of religion, according to the dictates of conscience; with such other matter as is necessary for a charter to contain. Immediately after which, the said conference to dissolve, and the bodies which shall be chosen conformable to the said charter, to be the legislators and governors of this continent for the time being: Whose peace and happiness, may God preserve, Amen.

Should any body of men be hereafter delegated for this or some similar purpose, I offer them the following extracts from that wise observer on governments Dragonetti. "The science" says he, "of the politician consists in fixing the true point of happiness and freedom. Those men would deserve the gratitude of ages, who should discover a mode of government that contained the greatest sum of individual happiness, with the least national expense."- Dragonetti on Virtue and Rewards.

But where says some is the king of America? I'll tell you Friend, he reigns above, and doth not make havoc of mankind like the Royal of Britain. Yet that we may not appear to be defective even in earthly honors, let a day be solemnly set apart for proclaiming the charter; let it be brought forth placed on the divine law, the word of God; let a crown be placed thereon, by which the world may know, that so far as we approve of monarchy, that in America the law is king. For as in absolute governments the king is law, so in free countries the law ought to be king; and there ought to be no other. But lest any ill use should afterwards arise, let the crown at the conclusion of the ceremony be demolished, and scattered among the people whose right it is.

A government of our own is our natural right: And when a man seriously reflects on the precariousness of human affairs, he will become convinced, that it is in finitely wiser and safer, to form a constitution of our own in a cool deliberate manner, while we have it in our power, than to trust such an interesting event to time and chance. If we omit it now, some Massenello* may hereafter arise, who laying hold of popular disquietudes, may collect together the desperate and the discontented, and by assuming to themselves the powers of government, may sweep away the liberties of the continent like a deluge. Should the government of America return again into the hands of Britain, the tottering situation of things, will be a temptation for some desperate adventurer to try his fortune; and in such a case, what relief can Britain give? Ere she could hear the news the fatal business might be done, and ourselves suffering like the wretched Britons under the oppression of the Conqueror. Ye that oppose independence now, ye know not what ye do; ye are opening a door to eternal tyranny, by keeping vacant the seat of government.

(*Thomas Anello, otherwise Massenello, a fisherman of Naples, who after spiriting up his countrymen in the public market place, against the oppression of the Spaniards, to whom the place was then subject, prompted them to revolt, and in the space of a day became king.)

There are thousands and tens of thousands; who would think it glorious to expel from the continent, that barbarous and hellish power, which hath stirred up the Indians and Negroes to destroy us; the cruelty hath a double guilt, it is dealing brutally by us, and treacherously by them. To talk of friendship with those in whom our reason forbids us to have faith, and our affections, (wounded through a thousand pores) instruct us to detest, is madness and folly. Every day wears out the little remains of kindred between us and them, and can there be any reason to hope, that as the relationship expires, the affection will increase, or that we shall agree better, when we have ten times more and greater concerns to quarrel over than ever?

Ye that tell us of harmony and reconciliation, can ye restore to us the time that is past? Can ye give to prostitution its former innocence? Neither can ye reconcile Britain and America. The last cord now is broken, the people of England are presenting addresses against us. There are injuries which nature cannot forgive; she would cease to be nature if she did. As well can the lover forgive the ravisher of his mistress, as the continent forgive the murders of Britain. The Almighty hath implanted in us these inextinguishable feelings for good and wise purposes. They are the guardians of his image in our hearts. They distinguish us from the herd of common animals. The social compact would dissolve, and justice be extirpated the earth, of have only a casual existence were we callous to the touches of affection. The robber and the murderer, would often escape unpunished, did not the injuries which our tempers sustain, provoke us into justice.

O ye that love mankind! Ye that dare oppose, not only the tyranny, but the tyrant, stand forth! Every spot of the old world is overrun with oppression. Freedom hath been hunted round the globe. Asia, and Africa, have long expelled her. Europe regards her like a stranger, and England hath given her warning to depart. O! receive the fugitive, and prepare in time an asylum for mankind.

# OF THE PRESENT ABILITY OF AMERICA, WITH SOME MISCELLANEOUS REFLECTIONS

I HAVE never met with a man, either in England or America, who hath not confessed his opinion, that a separation between the countries, would take place one time or other. And there is no instance in which we have shown less judgment, than in endeavoring to describe, what we call, the ripeness or fitness of the Continent for independence.

As all men allow the measure, and vary only in their opinion of the time, let us, in order to remove mistakes, take a general survey of things and endeavor if possible, to find out the very time. But we need not go far, the inquiry ceases at once, for the time hath found us. The general concurrence, the glorious union of all things prove the fact.

It is not in numbers but in unity, that our great strength lies; yet our present numbers are sufficient to repel the force of all the world. The Continent hath, at this time, the largest body of armed and disciplined men of any power under Heaven; and is just arrived at that pitch of strength, in which no single colony is able to support itself, and the whole, who united can accomplish the matter, and either more, or, less than this, might be fatal in its effects. Our land force is already sufficient, and as to naval affairs, we cannot be insensible, that Britain would never suffer an American man of war to be built while the continent remained in her hands. Wherefore we should be no forwarder an hundred years hence in that branch, than we are now; but the truth is, we should be less so, because the timber of the country is every day diminishing, and that which will remain at last, will be far off and difficult to procure.

Were the continent crowded with inhabitants, her sufferings under the present circumstances would be intolerable. The more sea port towns we had, the more should we have both to defend and to loose. Our present numbers are so happily proportioned to our wants, that no man need be idle. The diminution of trade affords an army, and the necessities of an army create a new trade. Debts we have none; and whatever we may contract on this account will serve as a glorious memento of our virtue. Can we but leave posterity with a settled form of government, an independent constitution of its own, the purchase at any price will be cheap. But to expend millions for the sake of getting a few we acts repealed, and routing the present ministry only, is unworthy the charge, and is using posterity with the utmost cruelty; because it is leaving them the great work to do, and a debt upon their backs, from which they derive no advantage. Such a thought is unworthy a man of honor, and is the true characteristic of a narrow heart and a peddling politician.

The debt we may contract doth not deserve our regard if the work be but accomplished. No nation ought to be without a debt. A national debt is a national bond; and when it bears no interest, is in no case a grievance. Britain is oppressed with a debt of upwards of one hundred and forty millions sterling, for which she pays upwards of four millions interest. And as a compensation for her debt, she has a large navy; America is without a debt, and without a navy; yet for the twentieth part of the English national debt, could have a navy as large again. The navy of England is not worth, at this time, more than three millions and a half sterling.

The first and second editions of this pamphlet were published without the following calculations, which are now given as a proof that the above estimation of the navy is a just one. (See Entick's naval history, intro. page 56.)

The charge of building a ship of each rate, and furnishing her with masts, yards, sails and rigging, together with a proportion of eight months boatswain's and carpenter's sea-stores, as calculated by Mr. Burchett, Secretary to the navy, is as follows:

For a ship of 100 guns £35,553

| 90 | £29,886 |
| 80 | £23,638 |
| 70 | £17,785 |

| | |
|---|---|
| 60 | £14,197 |
| 50 | £10,606 |
| 40 | £7,558 |
| 30 | £5,846 |
| 20 | £3,710 |

And from hence it is easy to sum up the value, or cost rather, of the whole British navy, which in the year 1757, when it was as its greatest glory consisted of the following ships and guns:

| Ships | Guns | Cost of one | Cost of all |
|---|---|---|---|
| 6 | 100 | £35,533 | £213,318 |
| 12 | 90 | £29,886 | £358,632 |
| 12 | 80 | £23,638 | £283,656 |
| 43 | 70 | £17,785 | £746,755 |
| 35 | 60 | £14,197 | £496,895 |
| 40 | 50 | £10,606 | £424,240 |
| 45 | 40 | £7,758 | £344,110 |
| 58 | 20 | £3,710 | £215,180 |
| 85 Sloops | | £2,000 | £170,000 |
| Cost | | | £3,266,786 |
| Remains for guns | | | £233,214 |
| Total | | | £3,500,000 |

No country on the globe is so happily situated, so internally capable of raising a fleet as America. Tar, timber, iron, and cordage are her natural produce. We need go abroad for nothing. Whereas the Dutch, who make large profits by hiring out their ships of war to the Spaniards and Portuguese, are obliged to import most of the materials they use. We ought to view the building a fleet as an article of commerce, it being the natural manufactory of this country. It is the best money we can lay out. A navy when finished is worth more than it cost. And is that nice point in national policy, in which commerce and protection are united. Let us build; if we want them not, we can sell; and by that means replace our paper currency with ready gold and silver.

In point of manning a fleet, people in general run into great errors; it is not necessary that one-fourth part should be sailors. The privateer Terrible, Captain Death, stood the hottest engagement of any ship last war, yet had not twenty sailors on board, though her complement of men was upwards of two hundred. A few able and social sailors will soon instruct a sufficient number of active landsmen in the common work of a ship. Wherefore, we never can be more capable to begin on maritime matters than now, while our timber is standing, our fisheries blocked up, and our sailors and shipwrights out of employ. Men of war of seventy and eighty guns were built forty years ago in New England, and why not the same now? Ship building is America's greatest pride, and in which, she will in time excel the whole world. The great empires of the east are mostly inland, and consequently excluded from the possibility of rivalling her. Africa is in a state of barbarism; and no power in Europe, hath either such an extent or coast, or such an internal supply of materials. Where nature hath given the one, she has withheld the other; to America only hath she been liberal of both. The vast empire of Russia is almost shut out from the sea; wherefore, her boundless forests, her tar, iron, and cordage are only articles of commerce.

In point of safety, ought we to be without a fleet? We are not the little people now, which we were sixty years ago; at that time we might have trusted our property in the streets, or fields rather; and slept securely without locks or bolts to our doors or windows. The case now is altered, and our methods of defence ought to improve with our increase of property. A common pirate, twelve months ago, might have come up the Delaware, and laid the city of Philadelphia under instant contribution, for what sum he pleased; and the same might have happened to other places. Nay, any daring fellow, in a brig of fourteen or sixteen guns, might have robbed the whole Continent, and carried off half a million of money. These are circumstances which demand our attention, and point out the necessity of naval protection.

Some, perhaps, will say, that after we have made it up with Britain, she will protect us. Can we be so unwise as to mean, that she shall keep a navy in our harbors for that purpose? Common sense will tell us, that the power which hath endeavored to subdue us, is of all others the most improper to defend us. Conquest may be effected under the pretence of friendship; and ourselves, after a long and brave resistance, be at last cheated into slavery. And if her ships are not to be admitted into our harbors, I would ask, how is she to protect us? A navy three or four thousand miles off can be of little use, and on sudden emergencies, none at all. Wherefore, if we must hereafter protect ourselves, why not do it for ourselves? Why do it for another.

The English list of ships of war is long and formidable, but not a tenth part of them are at any one time fit for service, numbers of them not in being; yet their names are pompously continued in the list, if only a plank be left of the ship: and not a fifth part, of such as are fit for service, can be spared on any one station at one time. The East, and West Indies, Mediterranean, Africa, and other parts over which Britain extends her claim, make large demands upon her navy. From a mixture of prejudice and inattention, we have contracted a false notion respecting the navy of England, and have talked as if we should have the whole of it to encounter at once, and for that reason, supposed that we must have one as large; which not being instantly practicable, have been made use of by a set of disguised tories to discourage our beginning thereon. Nothing can be farther from truth than this; for if America had only a twentieth part of the naval force of Britain, she would be by far an over match for her; because, as we neither have, nor claim any foreign dominion, our whole force would be employed on our own coast, where we should, in the long run, have two to one the advantage of those who had three or four thousand miles to sail over, before they could attack us, and the same distance to return in order to refit and recruit. And although Britain by her fleet, hath a check over our trade to Europe, we have as large a one over her trade to the West Indies, which, by laying in the neighborhood of the Continent, is entirely at its mercy.

Some method might be fallen on to keep up a naval force in time of peace, if we should not judge it necessary to support a constant navy. If premiums were to be given to merchants, to build and employ in their service, ships mounted with twenty, thirty, forty, or fifty guns, (the premiums to be in proportion to the loss of bulk to the merchants) fifty or sixty of those ships, with a few guard ships on constant duty, would keep up a sufficient navy, and that without burdening ourselves with the evil so loudly complained of in England, of suffering their fleet, in time of peace to lie rotting in the docks. To unite the sinews of commerce and defence is sound policy; for when our strength and our riches, play into each other's hand, we need fear no external enemy.

In almost every article of defence we abound. Hemp flourishes even to rankness, so that we need not want cordage. Our iron is superior to that of other countries. Our small arms equal to any in the world. Cannon we can cast at pleasure. Saltpetre and gunpowder we are every day producing. Our knowledge is hourly improving. Resolution is our inherent character, and courage hath never yet forsaken us. Wherefore, what is it that we want? Why is it that we hesitate? From Britain we can expect nothing but ruin. If she is once admitted to the government of America again, this Continent will not be worth living in. Jealousies will be always arising; insurrections will be constantly happening; and who will go forth to quell them? Who will venture his life to reduce his own countrymen to a foreign obedience? The difference between Pennsylvania and Connecticut, respecting some unlocated lands, shows the insignificance of a British government, and fully proves, that nothing but Continental authority can regulate Continental matters.

Another reason why the present time is preferable to all others, is, that the fewer our numbers are, the more land there is yet unoccupied, which instead of being lavished by the king on his worthless dependents, may be hereafter applied, not only to the discharge of the present debt, but to the constant support of government. No nation under heaven hath such an advantage as this.

The infant state of the Colonies, as it is called, so far from being against, is an argument in favor of independence. We are sufficiently numerous, and were we more so, we might be less united. It is a matter worthy of observation, that the more a country is peopled, the smaller their armies are. In military numbers, the ancients far exceeded the moderns: and the reason is evident, for trade being the consequence of population, men become too much absorbed thereby to attend to anything else. Commerce diminishes the spirit, both of patriotism and military defence. And history sufficiently informs us, that the bravest achievements were always accomplished in the non-age of a nation. With the increase of commerce England hath lost its spirit. The city of London, notwithstanding its numbers, submits to continued insults with the patience of a coward. The more men have to lose, the less willing are they to venture. The rich are in general slaves to fear, and submit to courtly power with the trembling duplicity of a spaniel.

Youth is the seed-time of good habits, as well in nations as in individuals. It might be difficult, if not impossible, to form the Continent into one government half a century hence. The vast variety of interests, occasioned by an increase of trade and population, would create confusion. Colony would be against colony. Each being able might scorn each other's assistance: and while the proud and foolish gloried in their little distinctions, the wise would lament that the union had not been formed before. Wherefore, the present time is the true time for establishing it. The intimacy which is contracted in infancy, and the friendship which is formed in misfortune, are, of all others, the most lasting and unalterable. Our present union is marked with both these characters: we are young, and we have been distressed; but our concord hath withstood our troubles, and fixes a memorable area for posterity to glory in.

The present time, likewise, is that peculiar time, which never happens to a nation but once, viz., the time of forming itself into a government. Most nations have let slip the opportunity, and by that means have been compelled to receive laws from their conquerors, instead of making laws for themselves. First, they had a king, and then a form of government; whereas, the articles or charter of government, should be formed first, and men delegated to execute them afterwards: but from the errors of other nations, let us learn wisdom, and lay hold of the present opportunity- to begin government at the right end.

When William the Conqueror subdued England he gave them law at the point of the sword; and until we consent that the seat of government in America, be legally and authoritatively occupied, we shall be in danger of having it filled by some fortunate ruffian, who may treat us in the same manner, and then, where will be our freedom? where our property?

As to religion, I hold it to be the indispensable duty of all government, to protect all conscientious professors thereof, and I know of no other business which government hath to do therewith. Let a man throw aside that narrowness of soul, that selfishness of principle, which the niggards of all professions are so unwilling to part with, and he will be at once delivered of his fears on that head. Suspicion is the companion of mean souls, and the bane of all good society. For myself I fully and conscientiously believe, that it is the will of the Almighty, that there should be diversity of religious opinions among us: It affords a larger field for our Christian kindness. Were we all of one way of thinking, our religious dispositions would want matter for probation; and on this liberal principle, I look on the various denominations among us, to be like children of the same family, differing only, in what is called their Christian names.

Earlier in this work, I threw out a few thoughts on the propriety of a Continental Charter, (for I only presume to offer hints, not plans) and in this place, I take the liberty of rementioning the subject, by observing, that a charter is to be understood as a bond of solemn obligation, which the whole enters into, to support the right of every separate part, whether of religion, personal freedom, or property, A firm bargain and a right reckoning make long friends.

In a former page I likewise mentioned the necessity of a large and equal representation; and there is no political matter which more deserves our attention. A small number of electors, or a small number of representatives, are equally dangerous. But if the number of the representatives be not only small, but unequal, the danger is increased. As an instance of this, I mention the following; when the Associators petition was before the House of Assembly of Pennsylvania; twenty-eight members only were present, all the Bucks County members, being eight, voted against it, and had seven of the Chester members done the same, this whole province had been governed by two counties only, and this danger it is always exposed to. The unwarrantable stretch likewise, which that house made in their last sitting, to gain an undue authority over the delegates of that province, ought to warn the people at large, how they trust power out of their own hands. A set of instructions for the Delegates were put together, which in point of sense and business would have dishonored a school-boy, and after being approved by a few, a very few without doors, were carried into the house, and there passed in behalf of the whole colony; whereas, did the whole colony know, with what ill-will that House hath entered on some necessary public measures, they would not hesitate a moment to think them unworthy of such a trust.

Immediate necessity makes many things convenient, which if continued would grow into oppressions. Expedience and right are different things. When the calamities of America required a consultation, there was no method so ready, or at that time so proper, as to appoint persons from the several Houses of Assembly for that purpose and the wisdom with which they have proceeded hath preserved this continent from ruin. But as it is more than probable that we shall never be without a Congress, every well-wisher to good order, must own, that the mode for choosing members of that body, deserves consideration. And I put it as a question to those, who make a study of mankind, whether representation and election is not too great a power for one and the same body of men to possess? When we are planning for posterity, we ought to remember that virtue is not hereditary.

It is from our enemies that we often gain excellent maxims, and are frequently surprised into reason by their mistakes. Mr. Cornwall (one of the Lords of the Treasury) treated the petition of the New York Assembly with contempt, because that House, he said, consisted but of twenty-six members, which trifling number, he argued, could not with decency be put for the whole. We thank him for his involuntary honesty.*

*Those who would fully understand of what great consequence a large and equal representation is to a state, should read Burgh's political Disquisitions.

To conclude: However strange it may appear to some, or however unwilling they may be to think so, matters not, but many strong and striking reasons may be given, to show, that nothing can settle our affairs so expeditiously as an open and determined declaration for independence. Some of which are:

First. It is the custom of nations, when any two are at war, for some other powers, not engaged in the quarrel, to step in as mediators, and bring about the preliminaries of a peace: but while America calls herself the subject of Great Britain, no power, however well disposed she may be, can offer her mediation. Wherefore, in our present state we may quarrel on for ever.

Secondly. It is unreasonable to suppose, that France or Spain will give us any kind of assistance, if we mean only to make use of that assistance for the purpose of repairing the breach, and strengthening the connection between Britain and America; because, those powers would be sufferers by the consequences.

Thirdly. While we profess ourselves the subjects of Britain, we must, in the eye of foreign nations, be considered as rebels. The precedent is somewhat dangerous to their peace, for men to be in arms under the name of subjects; we on the spot, can solve the paradox: but to unite resistance and subjection, requires an idea much too refined for common understanding.

Fourthly. Were a manifesto to be published, and despatched to foreign courts, setting forth the miseries we have endured, and the peaceable methods we have ineffectually used for redress; declaring, at the same time, that not being able, any longer to live happily or safely under the cruel disposition of the British court, we had been driven to the necessity of breaking off all connection with her; at the same time assuring all such courts of our peaceable disposition towards them, and of our desire of entering into trade with them. Such a memorial would produce more good effects to this Continent, than if a ship were freighted with petitions to Britain.

Under our present denomination of British subjects we can neither be received nor heard abroad: The custom of all courts is against us, and will be so, until, by an independence, we take rank with other nations.

These proceedings may at first appear strange and difficult; but, like all other steps which we have already passed over, will in a little time become familiar and agreeable; and, until an independence is declared, the continent will feel itself like a man who continues putting off some unpleasant business from day to day, yet knows it must be done, hates to set about it, wishes it over, and is continually haunted with the thoughts of its necessity.

## APPENDIX

SINCE the publication of the first edition of this pamphlet, or rather, on the same day on which it came out, the king's speech made its appearance in this city. Had the spirit of prophecy directed the birth of this production, it could not have brought it forth, at a more seasonable juncture, or a more necessary time. The bloody-mindedness of the one, show the necessity of pursuing the doctrine of the other. Men read by way of revenge. And the speech instead of terrifying, prepared a way for the manly principles of independence.

Ceremony, and even, silence, from whatever motive they may arise, have a hurtful tendency, when they give the least degree of countenance to base and wicked performances; wherefore, if this maxim be admitted, it naturally follows, that the king's speech, as being a piece of finished villainy, deserved, and still deserves, a general execration both by the congress and the people. Yet as the domestic tranquility of a nation, depends greatly on the chastity of what may properly be called national manners, it is often better, to pass some things over in silent disdain, than to make use of such new methods of dislike, as might introduce the least innovation, on that guardian of our peace and safety. And perhaps, it is chiefly owing to this prudent delicacy, that the king's speech, hath not before now, suffered a public execution. The speech if it may be called one, is nothing better than a wilful audacious libel against the truth, the common good, and the existence of mankind; and is a formal and pompous method of offering up human sacrifices to the pride of tyrants. But this general massacre of mankind, is one of the privileges, and the certain consequences of kings; for as nature knows them not, they know not her, and although they are beings of our own creating, they know not us, and are become the gods of their creators. The speech hath one good quality, which is, that it is not calculated to deceive, neither can we, even if we would, be deceived by it. Brutality and tyranny appear on the face of it. It leaves us at no loss: And every line convinces, even in the moment of reading, that He, who hunts the woods for prey, the naked and untutored Indian, is less a savage than the king of Britain.

Sir John Dalrymple, the putative father of a whining jesuitical piece, fallaciously called, The address of the people of ENGLAND to the inhabitants of America, hath, perhaps from a vain supposition, that the people here were to be frightened at the pomp and description of a king, given, (though very unwisely on his part) the real character of the present one: "But," says this writer, "if you are inclined to pay compliments to an administration, which we do not complain of," (meaning the Marquis of Rockingham's at the repeal of the Stamp Act) "it is very unfair in you to withhold them from that prince, by whose NOD ALONE they were permitted to do anything." This is toryism with a witness! Here is idolatry even without a mask: And he who can calmly hear, and digest such doctrine, hath forfeited his claim to rationality an apostate from the order of manhood; and ought to be considered- as one, who hath, not only given up the proper dignity of a man, but sunk himself beneath the rank of animals, and contemptibly crawl through the world like a worm.

However, it matters very little now, what the king of England either says or does; he hath wickedly broken through every moral and human obligation, trampled nature and conscience beneath his feet; and by a steady and constitutional spirit of insolence and cruelty, procured for himself an universal hatred. It is now the interest of America to provide for herself. She hath already a large and young family, whom it is more her duty to take care of, than to be granting away her property, to support a power who is become a reproach to the names of men and Christians. Ye, whose office it is to watch over the morals of a nation, of whatsoever sect or denomination ye are of, as well as ye, who are more immediately the guardians of the public liberty, if ye wish to preserve your native country uncontaminated by European corruption, ye must in secret wish a separation But leaving the moral part to private reflection, I shall chiefly confine my farther remarks to the following heads:

First. That it is the interest of America to be separated from Britain. Secondly. Which is the easiest and most practicable plan, reconciliation or independence? with some occasional remarks.

In support of the first, I could, if I judged it proper, produce the opinion of some of the ablest and most experienced men on this continent; and whose sentiments, on that head, are not yet publicly known. It is in reality a self-evident position: For no nation in a state of foreign dependance, limited in its commerce, and cramped and fettered in its legislative powers, can ever arrive at any material eminence. America doth not yet know what opulence is; and although the progress which she hath made stands unparalleled in the history of other nations, it is but childhood, compared with what she would be capable of arriving at, had she, as she ought to have, the legislative powers in her own hands. England is, at this time, proudly coveting what would do her no good, were she to accomplish it; and the Continent hesitating on a matter, which will be her final ruin if neglected. It is the commerce and not the conquest of America, by which England is to be benefited, and that would in a great measure continue, were the countries as independent of each other as France and Spain; because in many articles, neither can go to a better market. But it is the independence of this country on Britain or any other which is now the main and only object worthy of contention, and which, like all other truths discovered by necessity, will appear clearer and stronger every day.

First. Because it will come to that one time or other. Secondly. Because the longer it is delayed the harder it will be to accomplish.

I have frequently amused myself both in public and private companies, with silently remarking the spacious errors of those who speak without reflecting. And among the many which I have heard, the following seems the most general, viz., that had this rupture happened forty or fifty years hence, instead of now, the Continent would have been more able to have shaken off the dependance. To which I reply, that our military ability at this time, arises from the experience gained in the last war, and which in forty or fifty years time, would have been totally extinct. The Continent, would not, by that time, have had a General, or even a military officer left; and we, or those who may succeed us, would have been as ignorant of martial matters as the ancient Indians: And this single position, closely attended to, will unanswerably prove, that the present time is preferable to all others: The argument turns thus- at the conclusion of the last war, we had experience, but wanted numbers; and forty or fifty years hence, we should have numbers, without experience; wherefore, the proper point of time, must be some particular point between the two extremes, in which a sufficiency of the former remains, and a proper increase of the latter is obtained: And that point of time is the present time.

The reader will pardon this digression, as it does not properly come under the head I first set out with, and to which I again return by the following position, viz.:

Should affairs be patched up with Britain, and she to remain the governing and sovereign power of America, (which as matters are now circumstanced, is giving up the point entirely) we shall deprive ourselves of the very means of sinking the debt we have or may contract. The value of the back lands which some of the provinces are clandestinely deprived of, by the unjust extension of the limits of Canada, valued only at five pounds sterling per hundred acres, amount to upwards of twenty-five millions, Pennsylvania currency; and the quit-rents at one penny sterling per acre, to two millions yearly.

It is by the sale of those lands that the debt may be sunk, without burden to any, and the quit-rent reserved thereon, will always lessen, and in time, will wholly support the yearly expense of government. It matters not how long the debt is in paying, so that the lands when sold be applied to the discharge of it, and for the execution of which, the Congress for the time being, will be the continental trustees.

I proceed now to the second head, viz. Which is the earliest and most practicable plan, reconciliation or independence? with some occasional remarks.

He who takes nature for his guide is not easily beaten out of his argument, and on that ground, I answer generally- That INDEPENDENCE being a SINGLE SIMPLE LINE, contained within ourselves; and reconciliation, a matter exceedingly perplexed and complicated, and in which, a treacherous capricious court is to interfere, gives the answer without a doubt.

The present state of America is truly alarming to every man who is capable of reflection. Without law, without government, without any other mode of power than what is founded on, and granted by courtesy. Held together by an unexampled concurrence of sentiment, which is nevertheless subject to change, and which every secret enemy is endeavoring to dissolve. Our present condition, is, legislation without law; wisdom without a plan; a constitution without a name; and, what is strangely astonishing, perfect Independence contending for dependance. The instance is without a precedent; the case never existed before; and who can tell what may be the event? The property of no man is secure in the present unbraced system of things. The mind of the multitude is left at random, and feeling no fixed object before them, they pursue such as fancy or opinion starts. Nothing is criminal; there is no such thing as treason; wherefore, every one thinks himself at liberty to act as he pleases. The tories dared not to have assembled offensively, had they known that their lives, by that act were forfeited to the laws of the state. A line of distinction should be drawn, between English soldiers taken in battle, and inhabitants of America taken in arms. The first are prisoners, but the latter traitors. The one forfeits his liberty the other his head.

Notwithstanding our wisdom, there is a visible feebleness in some of our proceedings which gives encouragement to dissensions. The Continental Belt is too loosely buckled. And if something is not done in time, it will be too late to do any thing, and we shall fall into a state, in which, neither reconciliation nor independence will be practicable. The king and his worthless adherents are got at their old game of dividing the continent, and there are not wanting among us printers, who will be busy spreading specious falsehoods. The artful and hypocritical letter which appeared a few months ago in two of the New York papers, and likewise in two others, is an evidence that there are men who want either judgment or honesty. It is easy getting into holes and corners and talking of reconciliation: But do such men seriously consider, how difficult the task is, and how dangerous it may prove, should the Continent divide thereon. Do they take within their view, all the various orders of men whose situation and circumstances, as well as their own, are to be considered therein. Do they put themselves in the place of the sufferer whose all is already gone, and of the soldier, who hath quitted all for the defence of his country. If their ill judged moderation be suited to their own private situations only, regardless of others, the event will convince them, that "they are reckoning without their Host."

Put us, says some, on the footing we were in the year 1763: To which I answer, the request is not now in the power of Britain to comply with, neither will she propose it; but if it were, and even should be granted, I ask, as a reasonable question, By what means is such a corrupt and faithless court to be kept to its engagements? Another parliament, nay, even the present, may hereafter repeal the obligation, on the pretence of its being violently obtained, or unwisely granted; and in that case, Where is our redress? No going to law with nations; cannon are the barristers of crowns; and the sword, not of justice, but of war, decides the suit. To be on the footing of 1763, it is not sufficient, that the laws only be put on the same state, but, that our circumstances, likewise, be put on the same state; our burnt and destroyed towns repaired or built up, our private losses made good, our public debts (contracted for defence) discharged; otherwise, we shall be millions worse than we were at that enviable period. Such a request had it been complied with a year ago, would have won the heart and soul of the continent- but now it is too late, "the Rubicon is passed."

Besides the taking up arms, merely to enforce the repeal of a pecuniary law, seems as unwarrantable by the divine law, and as repugnant to human feelings, as the taking up arms to enforce obedience thereto. The object, on either side, doth not justify the ways and means; for the lives of men are too valuable to be cast away on such trifles. It is the violence which is done and threatened to our persons; the destruction of our property by an armed force; the invasion of our country by fire and sword, which conscientiously qualifies the use of arms: And the instant, in which such a mode of defence became necessary, all subjection to Britain ought to have ceased; and the independency of America should have been considered, as dating its area from, and published by, the first musket that was fired against her. This line is a line of consistency; neither drawn by caprice, nor extended by ambition; but produced by a chain of events, of which the colonies were not the authors.

I shall conclude these remarks, with the following timely and well intended hints, We ought to reflect, that there are three different ways by which an independency may hereafter be effected; and that one of those three, will one day or other, be the fate of America, viz. By the legal voice of the people in congress; by a military power; or by a mob: It may not always happen that our soldiers are citizens, and the multitude a body of reasonable men; virtue, as I have already remarked, is not hereditary, neither is it perpetual. Should an independency be brought about by the first of those means, we have every opportunity and every encouragement before us, to form the noblest, purest constitution on the face of the earth. We have it in our power to begin the world over again. A situation, similar to the present, hath not happened since the days of Noah until now. The birthday of a new world is at hand, and a race of men perhaps as numerous as all Europe contains, are to receive their portion of freedom from the event of a few months. The reflection is awful- and in this point of view, how trifling, how ridiculous, do the little, paltry cavillings, of a few weak or interested men appear, when weighed against the business of a world.

Should we neglect the present favorable and inviting period, and an independence be hereafter effected by any other means, we must charge the consequence to ourselves, or to those rather, whose narrow and prejudiced souls, are habitually opposing the measure, without either inquiring or reflecting. There are reasons to be given in support of Independence, which men should rather privately think of, than be publicly told of. We ought not now to be debating whether we shall be independent or not, but, anxious to accomplish it on a firm, secure, and honorable basis, and uneasy rather that it is not yet began upon. Every day convinces us of its necessity. Even the tories (if such beings yet remain among us) should, of all men, be the most solicitous to promote it; for, as the appointment of committees at first, protected them from popular rage, so, a wise and well established form of government, will be the only certain means of continuing it securely to them. Wherefore, if they have not virtue enough to be Whigs, they ought to have prudence enough to wish for independence.

In short, independence is the only bond that can tie and keep us together. We shall then see our object, and our ears will be legally shut against the schemes of an intriguing, as well as a cruel enemy. We shall then too, be on a proper footing, to treat with Britain; for there is reason to conclude, that the pride of that court, will be less hurt by treating with the American states for terms of peace, than with those, whom she denominates, "rebellious subjects," for terms of accommodation. It is our delaying it that encourages her to hope for conquest, and our backwardness tends only to prolong the war. As we have, without any good effect therefrom, withheld our trade to obtain a redress of our grievances, let us now try the alternative, by independently redressing them ourselves, and then offering to open the trade. The mercantile and reasonable part of England will be still with us; because, peace with trade, is preferable to war without it. And if this offer be not accepted, other courts may be applied to.

On these grounds I rest the matter. And as no offer hath yet been made to refute the doctrine contained in the former editions of this pamphlet, it is a negative proof, that either the doctrine cannot be refuted, or, that the party in favor of it are too numerous to be opposed. Wherefore, instead of gazing at each other with suspicious or doubtful curiosity, let each of us, hold out to his neighbor the hearty hand of friendship, and unite in drawing a line, which, like an act of oblivion, shall bury in forgetfulness every former dissention. Let the names of Whig and Tory be extinct; and let none other be heard among us, than those of a good citizen, an open and resolute friend, and a virtuous supporter of the RIGHTS of MANKIND and of the FREE AND INDEPENDENT STATES OF AMERICA.

## EPISTLE TO QUAKERS

To the Representatives of the Religious Society of the People called Quakers, or to so many of them as were concerned in publishing a late piece, entitled "THE ANCIENT TESTIMONY and PRINCIPLES of the people called QUAKERS renewed with respect to the KING and GOVERNMENT, and Touching the COMMOTIONS now prevailing in these and other parts of AMERICA, addressed to the PEOPLE IN GENERAL."

THE writer of this is one of those few, who never dishonors religion either by ridiculing, or cavilling at any denomination whatsoever. To God, and not to man, are all men accountable on the score of religion. Wherefore, this epistle is not so properly addressed to you as a religious, but as a political body, dabbling in matters, which the professed quietude of your Principles instruct you not to meddle with.

As you have, without a proper authority for so doing, put yourselves in the place of the whole body of the Quakers, so, the writer of this, in order to be on an equal rank with yourselves, is under the necessity, of putting himself in the place of all those who approve the very writings and principles, against which your testimony is directed: And he hath chosen their singular situation, in order that you might discover in him, that presumption of character which you cannot see in yourselves. For neither he nor you have any claim or title to Political Representation.

When men have departed from the right way, it is no wonder that they stumble and fall. And it is evident from the manner in which ye have managed your testimony, that politics, (as a religious body of men) is not your proper walk; for however well adapted it might appear to you, it is, nevertheless, a jumble of good and bad put unwisely together, and the conclusion drawn therefrom, both unnatural and unjust.

The two first pages, (and the whole doth not make four) we give you credit for, and expect the same civility from you, because the love and desire of peace is not confined to Quakerism, it is the natural, as well as the religious wish of all denominations of men. And on this ground, as men laboring to establish an Independent Constitution of our own, do we exceed all others in our hope, end, and aim. Our plan is peace for ever. We are tired of contention with Britain, and can see no real end to it but in a final separation. We act consistently, because for the sake of introducing an endless and uninterrupted peace, do we bear the evils and burdens of the present day. We are endeavoring, and will steadily continue to endeavor, to separate and dissolve a connection which hath already filled our land with blood; and which, while the name of it remains, will be the fatal cause of future mischiefs to both countries.

We fight neither for revenge nor conquest; neither from pride nor passion; we are not insulting the world with our fleets and armies, nor ravaging the globe for plunder. Beneath the shade of our own vines are we attacked; in our own houses, and on our own lands, is the violence committed against us. We view our enemies in the characters of highwaymen and housebreakers, and having no defence for ourselves in the civil law; are obliged to punish them by the military one, and apply the sword, in the very case, where you have before now, applied the halter. Perhaps we feel for the ruined and insulted sufferers in all and every part of the continent, and with a degree of tenderness which hath not yet made its way into some of your bosoms. But be ye sure that ye mistake not the cause and ground of your Testimony. Call not coldness of soul, religion; nor put the bigot in the place of the Christian.

O ye partial ministers of your own acknowledged principles! If the bearing arms be sinful, the first going to war must be more so, by all the difference between wilful attack and unavoidable defence.

Wherefore, if ye really preach from conscience, and mean not to make a political hobby-horse of your religion, convince the world thereof, by proclaiming your doctrine to our enemies, for they likewise bear ARMS. Give us proof of your sincerity by publishing it at St. James's, to the commanders in chief at Boston, to the admirals and captains who are practically ravaging our coasts, and to all the murdering miscreants who are acting in authority under HIM whom ye profess to serve. Had ye the honest soul of Barclay* ye would preach repentance to your king; Ye would tell the royal tyrant of his sins, and warn him of eternal ruin. Ye would not spend your partial invectives against the injured and the insulted only, but like faithful ministers, would cry aloud and spare none. Say not that ye are persecuted, neither endeavor to make us the authors of that reproach, which, ye are bringing upon yourselves; for we testify unto all men, that we do not complain against you because ye are Quakers, but because ye pretend to be and are NOT Quakers.

*"Thou hast tasted of prosperity and adversity; thou knowest what it is to be banished thy native country, to be overruled as well as to rule, and set upon the throne; and being oppressed thou hast reason to know now hateful the oppressor is both to God and man. If after all these warnings and advertisements, thou dost not turn unto the Lord with all thy heart, but forget him who remembered thee in thy distress, and give up thyself to follow lust and vanity, surely great will be thy condemnation. Against which snare, as well as the temptation of those who may or do feed thee, and prompt thee to evil, the most excellent and prevalent remedy will be, to apply thyself to that light of Christ which shineth in thy conscience and which neither can, nor will flatter thee, nor suffer thee to be at ease in thy sins."- Barclay's Address to Charles II.

Alas! it seems by the particular tendency of some part of your Testimony, and other parts of your conduct, as if all sin was reduced to, and comprehended in the act of bearing arms, and that by the people only. Ye appear to us, to have mistaken party for conscience, because the general tenor of your actions wants uniformity: And it is exceedingly difficult to us to give credit to many of your pretended scruples; because we see them made by the same men, who, in the very instant that they are exclaiming against the mammon of this world, are nevertheless, hunting after it with a step as steady as Time, and an appetite as keen as Death.

The quotation which ye have made from Proverbs, in the third page of your testimony, that, "when a man's ways please the Lord, he maketh even his enemies to be at peace with him;" is very unwisely chosen on your part; because it amounts to a proof, that the king's ways (whom ye are so desirous of supporting) do not please the Lord, otherwise, his reign would be in peace.

I now proceed to the latter part of your testimony, and that, for which all the foregoing seems only an introduction, viz:

"It hath ever been our judgment and principle, since we were called to profess the light of Christ Jesus, manifested in our consciences unto this day, that the setting up and putting down kings and governments, is God's peculiar prerogative; for causes best known to himself: And that it is not our business to have any hand or contrivance therein; nor to be busy-bodies above our station, much less to plot and contrive the ruin, or overturn any of them, but to pray for the king, and safety of our nation, and good of all men: that we may live a peaceable and quiet life, in all goodliness and honesty; under the government which God is pleased to set over us." If these are really your principles why do ye not abide by them? Why do ye not leave that, which ye call God's work, to be managed by himself? These very principles instruct you to wait with patience and humility, for the event of all public measures, and to receive that event as the divine will towards you. Wherefore, what occasion is there for your political Testimony if you fully believe what it contains? And the very publishing it proves, that either, ye do not believe what ye profess, or have not virtue enough to practice what ye believe.

The principles of Quakerism have a direct tendency to make a man the quiet and inoffensive subject of any, and every government which is set over him. And if the setting up and putting down of kings and governments is God's peculiar prerogative, he most certainly will not be robbed thereof by us; wherefore, the principle itself leads you to approve of every thing, which ever happened, or may happen to kings as being his work. Oliver Cromwell thanks you. Charles, then, died not by the hands of man; and should the present proud imitator of him, come to the same untimely end, the writers and publishers of the Testimony, are bound by the doctrine it contains, to applaud the fact. Kings are not taken away by miracles, neither are changes in governments brought about by any other means than such as are common and human; and such as we are now using. Even the dispersing of the Jews, though foretold by our Savior, was effected by arms. Wherefore, as ye refuse to be the means on one side, ye ought not to be meddlers on the other; but to wait the issue in silence; and unless you can produce divine authority, to prove, that the Almighty who hath created and placed this new world, at the greatest distance it could possibly stand, east and west, from every part of the old, doth, nevertheless, disapprove of its being independent of the corrupt and abandoned court of Britain; unless I say, ye can show this, how can ye, on the ground of your principles, justify the exciting and stirring up of the people "firmly to unite in the abhorrence of all such writings, and measures, as evidence a desire and design to break off the happy connection we have hitherto enjoyed, with the kingdom of Great Britain, and our just and necessary subordination to the king, and those who are lawfully placed in authority under him." What a slap in the face is here! the men, who, in the very paragraph before, have quietly and passively resigned up the ordering, altering, and disposal of kings and governments, into the hands of God, are now recalling their principles, and putting in for a share of the business. Is it possible, that the conclusion, which is here justly quoted, can any ways follow from the doctrine laid down? The inconsistency is too glaring not to be seen; the absurdity too great not to be laughed at; and such as could only have been made by those, whose understandings were darkened by the narrow and crabby spirit of a despairing political party; for ye are not to be considered as the whole body of the Quakers but only as a factional and fractional part thereof.

Here ends the examination of your testimony; (which I call upon no man to abhor, as ye have done, but only to read and judge of fairly;) to which I subjoin the following remark; "That the setting up and putting down of kings," most certainly mean, the making him a king, who is yet not so, and the making him no king who is already one. And pray what hath this to do in the present case? We neither mean to set up nor to put down, neither to make nor to unmake, but to have nothing to do with them. Wherefore your testimony in whatever light it is viewed serves only to dishonor your judgment, and for many other reasons had better have been let alone than published.

First. Because it tends to the decrease and reproach of religion whatever, and is of the utmost danger to society, to make it a party in political disputes. Secondly. Because it exhibits a body of men, numbers of whom disavow the publishing political testimonies, as being concerned therein and approvers thereof. Thirdly. Because it hath a tendency to undo that continental harmony and friendship which yourselves by your late liberal and charitable donations hath lent a hand to establish; and the preservation of which, is of the utmost consequence to us all.

And here, without anger or resentment I bid you farewell. Sincerely wishing, that as men and Christians, ye may always fully and uninterruptedly enjoy every civil and religious right; and be, in your turn, the means of securing it to others; but that the example which ye have unwisely set, of mingling religion with politics, may be disavowed and reprobated by every inhabitant of America.

**-THE END-**
*Source: Common Sense, by Thomas Paine, printed by W. and T. Bradford, Philadelphia, 1791.*

# Appendix B: Declaration of Independence

*Here is the complete text of the Declaration of Independence.*
*The original spelling and capitalization have been retained.*

*(Adopted by Congress on July 4, 1776)*

The Unanimous Declaration
of the Thirteen United States of America

When, in the course of human events, it becomes necessary for one people to dissolve the political bands which have connected them with another, and to assume among the powers of the earth, the separate and equal station to which the laws of nature and of nature's God entitle them, a decent respect to the opinions of mankind requires that they should declare the causes which impel them to the separation.

We hold these truths to be self-evident, that all men are created equal, that they are endowed by their Creator with certain unalienable rights, that among these are life, liberty and the pursuit of happiness. That to secure these rights, governments are instituted among men, deriving their just powers from the consent of the governed. That whenever any form of government becomes destructive to these ends, it is the right of the people to alter or to abolish it, and to institute new government, laying its foundation on such principles and organizing its powers in such form, as to them shall seem most likely to effect their safety and happiness. Prudence, indeed, will dictate that governments long established should not be changed for light and transient causes; and accordingly all experience hath shown that mankind are more disposed to suffer, while evils are sufferable, than to right themselves by abolishing the forms to which they are accustomed. But when a long train of abuses and usurpations, pursuing invariably the same object evinces a design to reduce them under absolute despotism, it is their right, it is their duty, to throw off such government, and to provide new guards for their future security. --Such has been the patient sufferance of these colonies; and such is now the necessity which constrains them to alter their former systems of government. The history of the present King of Great Britain is a history of repeated injuries and usurpations, all having in direct object the establishment of an absolute tyranny over these states. To prove this, let facts be submitted to a candid world.

He has refused his assent to laws, the most wholesome and necessary for the public good.

He has forbidden his governors to pass laws of immediate and pressing importance, unless suspended in their operation till his assent should be obtained; and when so suspended, he has utterly neglected to attend to them.

He has refused to pass other laws for the accommodation of large districts of people, unless those people would relinquish the right of representation in the legislature, a right inestimable to them and formidable to tyrants only.

He has called together legislative bodies at places unusual, uncomfortable, and distant from the depository of their public records, for the sole purpose of fatiguing them into compliance with his measures.

He has dissolved representative houses repeatedly, for opposing with manly firmness his invasions on the rights of the people.

He has refused for a long time, after such dissolutions, to cause others to be elected; whereby the legislative powers, incapable of annihilation, have returned to the people at large for their exercise; the state remaining in the meantime exposed to all the dangers of invasion from without, and convulsions within.

He has endeavored to prevent the population of these states; for that purpose obstructing the laws for naturalization of foreigners; refusing to pass others to encourage their migration hither, and raising the conditions of new appropriations of lands.

He has obstructed the administration of justice, by refusing his assent to laws for establishing judiciary powers.

He has made judges dependent on his will alone, for the tenure of their offices, and the amount and payment of their salaries.

He has erected a multitude of new offices, and sent hither swarms of officers to harass our people, and eat out their substance.

He has kept among us, in times of peace, standing armies without the consent of our legislature.

He has affected to render the military independent of and superior to civil power.

He has combined with others to subject us to a jurisdiction foreign to our constitution, and unacknowledged by our laws; giving his assent to their acts of pretended legislation:

For quartering large bodies of armed troops among us:

For protecting them, by mock trial, from punishment for any murders which they should commit on the inhabitants of these states:

For cutting off our trade with all parts of the world:

For imposing taxes on us without our consent:

For depriving us in many cases, of the benefits of trial by jury:

For transporting us beyond seas to be tried for pretended offenses:

For abolishing the free system of English laws in a neighboring province, establishing therein an arbitrary government, and enlarging its boundaries so as to render it at once an example and fit instrument for introducing the same absolute rule in these colonies:

For taking away our charters, abolishing our most valuable laws, and altering fundamentally the forms of our governments:

For suspending our own legislatures, and declaring themselves invested with power to legislate for us in all cases whatsoever.

He has abdicated government here, by declaring us out of his protection and waging war against us.

He has plundered our seas, ravaged our coasts, burned our towns, and destroyed the lives of our people.

He is at this time transporting large armies of foreign mercenaries to complete the works of death, desolation and tyranny, already begun with circumstances of cruelty and perfidy scarcely paralleled in the most barbarous ages, and totally unworthy the head of a civilized nation.

He has constrained our fellow citizens taken captive on the high seas to bear arms against their country, to become the executioners of their friends and brethren, or to fall themselves by their hands.

He has excited domestic insurrections amongst us, and has endeavored to bring on the inhabitants of our frontiers, the merciless Indian savages, whose known rule of warfare, is undistinguished destruction of all ages, sexes and conditions.

In every stage of these oppressions we have petitioned for redress in the most humble terms: our repeated petitions have been answered only by repeated injury. A prince, whose character is thus marked by every act which may define a tyrant, is unfit to be the ruler of a free people.

Nor have we been wanting in attention to our British brethren. We have warned them from time to time of attempts by their legislature to extend an unwarrantable jurisdiction over us. We have reminded them of the circumstances of our emigration and settlement here. We have appealed to their native justice and magnanimity, and we have conjured them by the ties of our common kindred to disavow these usurpations, which, would inevitably interrupt our connections and correspondence. They too have been deaf to the voice of justice and of consanguinity. We must, therefore, acquiesce in the necessity, which denounces our separation, and hold them, as we hold the rest of mankind, enemies in war, in peace friends.

We, therefore, the representatives of the United States of America, in General Congress, assembled, appealing to the Supreme Judge of the world for the rectitude of our intentions, do, in the name, and by the authority of the good people of these colonies, solemnly publish and declare, that these united colonies are, and of right ought to be free and independent states; that they are absolved from all allegiance to the British Crown, and that all political connection between them and the state of Great Britain, is and ought to be totally dissolved; and that as free and independent states, they have full power to levy war, conclude peace, contract alliances, establish commerce, and to do all other acts and things which independent states may of right do. And for the support of this declaration, with a firm reliance on the protection of Divine Providence, we mutually pledge to each other our lives, our fortunes and our sacred honor.

New Hampshire: Josiah Bartlett, William Whipple, Matthew Thornton

Massachusetts: John Hancock, Samual Adams, John Adams, Robert Treat Paine, Elbridge Gerry

Rhode Island: Stephen Hopkins, William Ellery

Connecticut: Roger Sherman, Samuel Huntington, William Williams, Oliver Wolcott

New York: William Floyd, Philip Livingston, Francis Lewis, Lewis Morris

New Jersey: Richard Stockton, John Witherspoon, Francis Hopkinson, John Hart, Abraham Clark

Pennsylvania: Robert Morris, Benjamin Rush, Benjamin Franklin, John Morton, George Clymer, James Smith, George Taylor, James Wilson, George Ross

Delaware: Caesar Rodney, George Read, Thomas McKean

Maryland: Samuel Chase, William Paca, Thomas Stone, Charles Carroll of Carrollton

Virginia: George Wythe, Richard Henry Lee, Thomas Jefferson, Benjamin Harrison, Thomas Nelson, Jr., Francis Lightfoot Lee, Carter Braxton

North Carolina: William Hooper, Joseph Hewes, John Penn

South Carolina: Edward Rutledge, Thomas Heyward, Jr., Thomas Lynch, Jr., Arthur Middleton

Georgia: Button Gwinnett, Lyman Hall, George Walton

Source: The Pennsylvania Packet, July 8, 1776

# Appendix C: U.S. Constitution & Amendments

## The Constitution of the United States of America

**WE, the PEOPLE of the UNITED STATES,** in order to form a more perfect union, establish justice, ensure domestic tranquility, provide for the common defence, promote the general welfare, and secure the blessings of liberty to ourselves and our posterity, do ordain and establish this Constitution for the United States of America.

### *ARTICLE I.*

*Sect.* 1. ALL legislative powers, herein granted, shall be vested in a Congress of the United States, which shall consist of a Senate and House of Representatives.

*Sect.* 2. The House of Representatives shall be composed of Members chosen every second year by all the people of the several States, and the Electors in each State shall have the qualifications requisite for Electors of the most numerous branch of the State Legislature.

No person shall be a Representative who shall not have attained to the age of twenty-five years, and been seven years a citizen of the United States, and who shall not, when elected, be an inhabitant of that State in which he shall be chosen.

Representatives and direct taxes shall be apportioned among the several States which may be included within this Union, according to the respective numbers, which shall be determined by adding to the whole number of free persons, including those bound to service for a term of years, and excluding Indians not taxed, three fifths of all other persons. The actual enumeration shall be made within three years after the first meeting of the Congress of the United States, and within every subsequent term of ten years, in such manner as they shall by law direct. The number of Representatives shall not exceed one for every thirty thousand, but each State shall have at least one Representative; and until such enumeration shall be made, the State of New-Hampshire shall be entitled to choose three, Massachusetts eight, Rhode-Island and Providence Plantation one, Connecticut five, New-York six, New-Jersey four, Pennsylvania eight, Delaware one, Maryland six, Virginia ten, North-Carolina five, South-Carolina five, and Georgia three.

When vacancies happen in the Representation from any State, the Executive authority thereof shall issue writs of election to fill such vacancies.

The House of Representatives shall choose their Speaker and other officers, and shall have the sole power of impeachment.

*Sect.* 3. The Senate of the United States shall be composed of two Senators from each State, chosen by the Legislature thereof, for six years; and each Senator shall have one vote.

Immediately after they shall be assembled in consequence of the first election, they shall be divided as equally as may be into three classes. The seats of the Senators of the first class shall be vacated at the expiration of the second year, of the second class at the expiration of the fourth year, and of the third class at the expiration of the sixth year; so that one third may be chosen every second year; and if vacancies happen, by resignation or otherwise, during the recess of the Legislature of any State, the Executive thereof may make temporary appointments until the next meeting of the Legislature, which shall then fill such vacancies.

No person shall be a Senator who shall not have attained to the age of thirty years, and been nine years a citizen of the United States, and who shall not, when elected, be an inhabitant of that State for which he shall be chosen.

The Vice-President of the United States shall be President of the Senate, but shall have no vote, unless they be equally divided. The Senate shall choose their other officers, and also a President pro tempore, in a the absence of the Vice-President, or when he shall exercise the office of President of the United States.

The Senate shall have the sole power to try all impeachments. When sitting for that purpose, they shall by on oath or affirmation. When the President of the United State is tried, the Chief Justice shall preside; and no person shall be convicted without the concurrence of two thirds of the members present.

Judgment, in cases of impeachment, shall not extend further than to removal from office, and disqualification to hold and enjoy any office of honour, trust or profit, under the United States; but the party convicted shall nevertheless be liable and subject to indictment, trial, judgment and punishment, according to law.

*Sect.* 4. The times, places and manner, of holding elections for Senators and Representatives, shall be prescribed in each State by the Legislature thereof; but the Congress may at any time, by law, make or alter such regulations, except as to the place of choosing Senators.

The Congress shall assemble at least once in every year, and such meeting shall be on the first Monday in December, unless they shall by law appoint a different day.

*Sect.* 5. Each House shall be the judge of the elections, returns and qualification, of its own members, and a majority of each shall constitute a quorum to do business; but a smaller number may adjourn from day to day, and may be authorized to compel the attendance of absent members, in such manner, and under such penalties, as each House may provide.

Each House may determine the rules of its proceedings, punish its members for disorderly behavior, and, with the concurrence of two thirds, expel a member.

Each House shall keep a journal of its proceedings, and from time to time publish the same, excepting such parts as may in their judgment require secresy; and the yeas and nays of the members of either House on any question shall, at the desire of one fifth of those present, be entered on the journal.

Neither House, during the session of Congress, shall, without the consent of the other, adjourn for more than three days, nor to any other place than that in which the two Houses shall be sitting.

*Sect.* 6. The Senators and Representatives shall receive a compensation for their services, to be ascertained by law, and paid out of the treasury of the United States. They shall in all cases, except treason, felony and breach of peace, be privileged from arrest during their attendance at the session of their respective Houses, and in going to and returning from the same; and for any speech or debate in either House, they shall not be questioned in any other place.

No Senator or Representative shall, during the time for which he was elected, be appointed to any civil office under the authority of the United States, which shall have been created, or the emoluments whereof shall have been encreased, during such time; and no person holding any officer under the United States shall be a member of either House, during his continuance in office.

*Sect.* 7. All bills for raising revenue shall originate in the House of Representatives; but the Senate may propose or concur with amendments, as on other bills.

Every bill which shall have passed the House of Representatives and the Senates shall, before it become a law, be presented to the President of the United States; if he approve; he shall sign it; but if not, he shall return it, with his objections, to that House in which it shall have originated, who shall enter the objections at large on their journal, and proceed to reconsider it. If after such reconsideration two thirds of that House shall agree to pass the bill, it shall be sent, together with the objections, to the other House, by which it shall likewise be reconsidered, and if approved by two thirds of that House, it shall become a law. But in all such cases the votes of both Houses shall be determined by yeas and nays, and the names of the persons voting for and against the bill shall be entered on the journal of each House respectively. If any bill shall not be returned by the President within ten days (Sundays excepted) after it shall have been presented to him, the same shall be a law in like manner as if he had signed it, unless the Congress by their adjournment prevent its return, in which case it shall not be a law.

Every order, resolution or vote, to which the concurrence of the Senate and House of Representatives may be necessary (except on a question of adjournment) shall be presented to the President of the United States; and before the same shall take effect, shall be approved by him, or being disapproved by him, shall be re-passed by two thirds of the Senate and House of Representatives, according to the rules and limitations prescribed in the case of a bill.

*Sect.* 8. The Congress shall have power To lay and collect taxes, duties, imposts and excises, to pay the debts and provide for the common defence and general welfare of the United States; but all duties; imposts and excises, shall be uniform throughout the United States;

To borrow money on the credit of the United States;

To regulate commerce with foreign nations, and among the several States, and with the Indian tribes;

To establish an uniform rule of naturalization, and uniform laws on the subject of bankruptcies, throughout the United States;

To coin money, regulate the value thereof, and of foreign coin, and fix the standard of weights and measures;

To provide for the punishment of counterfeiting the securities and current coin of the United States;

To establish post-offices and post-roads;

To promote the progress of science and useful arts, by securing for limited times to authors and inventors the exclusive right to their respective writings and discoveries;

To constitute tribunals inferior to the Supreme Court;

To define and punish piracies and felonies committed on the high seas and offences against the law of nations;

To declare war, grant letters of marque and reprisal, and make rules concerning captures on land and water;

To raise and support armies, but no appropriation of money to that use shall be for a longer term than two years;

To provide and maintain a navy;

To make rules for the government and regulation of the land and naval forces;

To provide for calling forth the militia to execute the laws of the Union, suppress insurrections, and repel invasions;

To provide for organizing, arming and disciplining the militia, and for governing such part of them as may be employed in the service of the United States, reserving to the States respectively the appointment of the officers, and the authority of training the militia according to the discipline prescribed by Congress;

To exercise exclusive legislation, in all cases whatsoever, over such district (not exceeding ten miles square) as may, by cession of particular States, and the acceptance of Congress, become the seat of the government of the United States, and to exercise like authority over all places purchased by the consent of the Legislature of the State in which the same shall be, for the erection of forts, magazines, arsenals, dock-yards, and other needful buildings;--and,

To make all laws which shall be necessary and proper for carrying into execution the foregoing powers, and all other powers vested by this Constitution in the government of the United States, or in any department or officer thereof.

*Sect.* 9. The migration or importation of such persons as any of the States now existing shall think proper to admit, shall not be prohibited by the Congress prior to the year one thousand eight hundred and eight; but a tax or duty may be imposed on such importation, not exceeding ten dollars for each person.

The privilege of the writ of habeas corpus shall not be suspended, unless when in cases of rebellion or invasion the public safety may require it.

No bill of attainder, or ex post facto law, shall be passed.

No capitation or other direct tax shall be laid, unless in proportion to the sensus or enumeration herein before directed to be taken.

No tax or duty shall be laid on articles exported from any State. No preference shall be given by any regulation of commerce or revenue to the ports of one State over those of another: Nor shall vessels bound to or from one State, be obliged to enter, clear, or pay duties, in another.

No money shall be drawn from the treasury, but in consequence of appropriations made by law; and a regular statement and account of the receipts and expenditures of all public money shall be published from time to time.

No title of nobility shall be granted by the United States: And no person holding any office of profit or trust under them shall, without the consent of the Congress, accept of any present, emolument, office or title, or any kind whatever from any King, Prince, or foreign State.

*Sect.* 10. No State shall enter into any treaty, alliance or confederation; grant letters of marque and reprisal; coin money; emit bills of credit; make any thing but gold and silver coin a tender in payment of debts; pass any bill of attainder, ex post facto law, or law impairing the obligation of contracts, or grant any title of nobility.

No State shall, without the consent of Congress, lay any imposts or duties on imports or exports, except what may be absolutely necessary for executing its inspection laws; and the new produce of all duties and imposts, laid by any State, on imports or exports, shall be for the use of the treasury of the United States; and all such laws shall be subject to the revision and controul of the Congress. No State shall, without the consent of Congress, lay any duty of tonnage, keep troops or ships of war in time of peace, enter into any agreement or compact with another State, or with a foreign power, or engage in war, unless actually invaded, or in such imminent danger as will not admit of delay.

## ARTICLE II.

*Sec.* 1. The executive power shall be vested in a President of the United States of America. He shall hold his office during the term of four years, and, together with the Vice-President, chosen for the same term, be elected as follows.

Each State shall appoint, in such manner as the Legislature thereof may direct, a number of Electors, equal to the whole number of Senators and Representatives to which the State may be entitled in the Congress; but no Senator or Representative, or person holding an office of trust or profit under the United States, shall be appointed an Elector.

The Electors shall meet in their respective States, and vote by ballot for two persons, of whom one at least shall not be an inhabitant of the same state with themselves. And they shall make a list of all the persons voted for, and of the number of votes for each; which list they shall sign and certify, and transmit sealed to the seat of the government of the United States, directed to the President of the Senate. The President of the Senate shall, in the presence of the Senate and House of Representatives, open all the certificates, and the votes shall then be counted. The person having the greatest number of votes shall be the President, if such number be a majority of the whole number of Electors appointed; and if there be more than one who have such majority, and have an equal number of votes, then the House of Representatives shall immediately choose by ballot one of them for President; and if no person have a majority, then from the five highest on the list the said House shall in like manner choose a President. But in choosing the President the votes shall be taken by States, the representation from each State having one vote; a quorum for this purpose shall consist of a member or members from two thirds of the States, and a majority of all the States shall be necessary to a choice. In every case, after the choice of the President, the person having the greatest number of votes of the Electors, shall be the Vice-President. But if there should remain two or more who have equal votes, the Senate shall choose from them by ballot the Vice-President.

The Congress may determine the time of choosing the Electors, and the day on which they shall give their votes; which day shall be the same throughout the United States.

No person, except a natural born citizen, or a citizen of the United States at the time of the adoption of this Constitution, shall be eligible to the office of President; neither shall any person be eligible to that office, who shall not have attained to the age of thirty-five years, and been fourteen years a resident within the United States.

In case of the removal of the President from office, or of his death, resignation, or inability to discharge the powers and duties of the said office, the same shall devolve on the Vice-President; and the Congress may by law provide for the case of removal, death, resignation, or inability, both of the President and Vice-President, declaring what officer shall then act as President, and such officer shall act accordingly, until the disability be removed, or a President shall be elected.

The President shall, at stated times, receive for his services a compensation, which shall neither be increased nor diminished during the period for which he shall have been elected, and he shall not receive within that period any other emolument from the United States, or any of them.

Before he enter on the execution of his office, he shall take the following oath or affirmation:

"I do solemnly swear (or affirm) that I will faithfully execute the office of President of the United States; and will, to the best of my ability, preserve, protect and defend, the Constitution of the United States."

*Sect.* 2. The President shall be Commander in Chief of the army and navy of the United States, and of the militia of the several states, when called into the actual service of the United States; he may require the opinion, in writing, of the principal officer in each of the executive departments, upon any subject relating to the duties of their respective offices, and he shall have power to grant reprieves and pardons for offences against the United States, except in cases of impeachment.

He shall have power, by and with the advice and consent of the Senate, to make treaties, provided two thirds of the Senators present concur; and he shall nominate, and by and with the advice and consent of the Senate shall appoint Ambassadors, other public Ministers, and Consuls, Judges of the Supreme Court, and all other offices of the United States, whose appointments are not herein otherwise provided for, and which shall be established by law. But the Congress may by law vest the appointment of such inferior officers as they think proper in the President alone, in the courts of law, or in the heads of departments.

The President shall have power to fill up all vacancies that may happen during the recess of the Senate, by granting commissions, which shall expire at the end of their next session.

*Sect.* 3. He shall from time to time give to the Congress information of the state of the Union, and recommend to their consideration such measures as he shall judge necessary and expedient; he may, on extraordinary occasions, convene both Houses, or either of them, and in case of disagreement between them, with respect to the time of adjournment, he may adjourn them to such time as he shall think proper; he shall receive Ambassadors and other public Ministers; he shall take care that the laws be faithfully executed, and shall commission all the officers of the United States.

*Sect.* 4. The President, Vice-President, and all civil officers of the United States, shall be removed from office, on impeachment for and conviction of treason, bribery, or other high crimes and misdemeanors.

## ARTICLE III.

*Sect.* 1. The judicial power of the United States shall be vested in one Supreme Court, and in such Inferior Courts as the Congress may from time to time ordain and establish. The Judges, both of the supreme and Inferior Courts, shall hold their offices during good behaviour; and shall, at stated times, receive for their services a compensation, which shall not be diminished during their continuance in office.

*Sect.* 2. The judicial power shall extend to all cases in law and equity, arising under this Constitution, the laws of the United States, and treaties made, or which shall be made, under their authority; to all cases affecting Ambassadors, other public Ministers, and Consuls; to all cases of admiralty and maritime jurisdiction; to controversies to which the United States shall be a party; to controversies between two or more States, between a State and citizen of another State, between citizens of different States, between citizens of the same State claiming lands under grants of different States, and between a State, or the citizens thereof, and foreign States, citizens or subjects.

In all cases affecting Ambassadors, other public Ministers and consuls, and those in which a State shall be party, the Supreme Court shall have original jurisdiction. In all the other cases before mentioned, the Supreme Court shall have appellate jurisdiction, both as to law and fact, with such exceptions and under such regulations as the Congress shall make.

The trial of all crimes, except in cases of impeachment, shall be by jury; and such trial shall be held in the State where the said crimes shall have been committed; but when not committed within any State, the trial shall be at such place or places as the Congress may by law have directed.

*Sect.* 3. Treason, against the United States, shall consist only in levying war against them, or in adhering to their enemies, giving them aid and comfort. No person shall be convicted of treason, unless on the testimony of two witnesses to the same overt act, or on consession in open court.

The Congress shall have power to declare the punishment of treason, but no attainder of treason shall work corruption of blood, or forfeiture, except during the life of the person attainted.

## *ARTICLE IV.*

*Sect.* 1. Full faith and credit shall be given in each State to the public acts, records and judicial proceedings, of every other State. And the Congress may by general laws prescribe the manner in which such acts, records and proceedings, shall be proved, and the effect thereof.

*Sect.* 2. The citizens of each State shall be entitled to all privileges and immunities of citizens in the several states.

A person, charged in any State with treason, felony, or other crime, who shall flee from justice, and be found in another State, shall, on demand of the executive authority of the State from which he fled, be delivered up, to be removed to the State having jurisdiction of the crime.

No person, held to service or labour in one State, under the laws thereof, escaping into another, shall, in consequence of any law or regulation therein, be discharged from such service or labour; but shall be delivered up, on claim of the party to whom such service or labour may be due.

*Sect.* 3. New States may be admitted by the Congress into this Union; but no new State shall be formed to erected within the jurisdiction of any other State; nor any State be formed by the junction of two or more States, or parts of States, without the consent of the Legislatures of the States concerned, as well as of the Congress.

The Congress shall have power to dispose of an make all needful rules and regulations, respecting the territory or other property belonging to the United States; and nothing in this Constitution shall be so construed, as to prejudice any claims of the United States, or of any particular State.

*Sect.* 4. The United States shall guarantee, to every State in this Union, a republican form of government, and shall protect each of them against invasion; and, on application of the Legislature, or of the Executive, (when the Legislature cannot be convened) against domestic violence.

## ARTICLE V.

The Congress, whenever two thirds of both Houses shall deem it necessary, shall propose amendments to this Constitution; or, on the application of the Legislatures of two thirds of the several States, shall call a Convention, for proposing amendments; which, in either case, shall be valid, to all intents and purposes, as part of this Constitution, when ratified by the Legislature of three fourths of the several States, or by conventions in three fourths thereof, as the one or the other mode of ratification may be proposed by the Congress: Provided, that no amendment which may be made prior to the year one thousand eight hundred and eight shall in any manner affect the first and fourth clauses, in the ninth section of the first article; and that no State, without its consent, shall be deprived of its equal suffrage in the Senate.

## ARTICLE VI.

All debts contracted, and engagements entered into, before the adoption of this Constitution, shall be as valid against the United States under this Constitution, as under the Confederation.

This Constitution, and the laws of the United States which shall be made in pursuance thereof, and all treaties made, or which shall be made, under the authority of the United States, shall be the supreme law of the land; and the Judges in every State, shall be bound thereby; any thing in the constitution or laws of any State to the contrary notwithstanding.

The Senators and Representatives before mentioned, and the members of the several State Legislatures, and all executive and judicial officers, both of the United States and of the several States, shall be bound by oath or affirmation to support this Constitution; but no religious test shall ever be required as a qualification to any office, or public trust, under the United States.

## ARTICLE VII.

The ratification of the Conventions of Nine States shall be sufficient for the establishment of this constitution, between the States so ratifying the same.

## *[Signatories, Resolutions & Orders]*

*Done in Convention, by the unanimous consent of the States present, the seventeenth day of September, in the year of our Lord one thousand seven hundred and eighty-seven, and of the Independence of the United States of America the twelfth. In witness whereof, we have hereunto subscribed our names.*

GEORGE WASHINGTON, President, (and Deputy from Virginia.

*New-Hampshire.* John Langdon, Nicholas Gilman.

*Massachusetts.* Nathaniel Gorham, Rufus King.

*Connecticut.* William Samuel Johnson, Roger Sherman.

*New-York.* Alexander Hamilton.

*New-Jersey.* William Livingston, David Brearley, William Paterson, Jonathan Dayton.

*Pennsylvania.* Benjamin Franklin, Thomas Mifflin, Robert Morris, George Clymer, Thomas Fitzsimons, Jared Ingersoll, James Wilson, Gouverneur Morris.

*Delaware.* George Read, Gunning Bedford, jun. John Dickenson, Richard Bassett, Jacob Broom.

*Maryland.* James McHenry, Daniel of St. Tho. Jenifer, Daniel Carrol.

*Virginia.* John Blair, James Madison, jun.

*North-Carolina.* William Blount, Richard Dobbs Spaight, Hugh Williamson.

*South-Carolina.* John Rutledge, Charles Cotesworth Pinckney, Charles Pinckney, Pierce Butler.

*Georgia.* William Few, Abraham Baldwin.

Attest,..........**WILLIAM JACKSON,** Secretary.

**IN CONVENTION, Monday, September 17th, 1787.**
**PRESENT,**

The States of New-Hampshire, Massachusetts, Connecticut, Mr. *Hamilton* from New-York, New-Jersey, Pennsylvania, Delaware, Maryland, Virginia, North-Carolina, South-Carolina, and Georgia.

*Resolved,*

**THAT** the preceding Constitution be laid before the United States in Congress assembled, and that it is the opinion of this Convention, that it should afterwards be submitted to a Convention of Delegates, chosen in each State by the People thereof, under the recommendation of its Legislature, for their assent and ratification; and that each Convention assenting to and ratifying the same, should give notice thereof to the United States in Congress assembled.

*Resolved,* That it is the opinion of this Convention, That as soon as the Conventions of Nine States shall have ratified this Constitution, the United States in Congress assembled should fix a day on which Electors should be appointed by the States which shall have ratified the same, and a day on which the Electors should assemble to vote for the President, and the time and place for commencing proceedings under this Constitution: That after such publication the Electors should be appointed, and the Senators and Representatives elected: That the Electors should meet on the day fixed for the election of the President, and should transmit their votes, certified, signed, sealed and directed, as the Constitution requires, to the Secretary of the United States in congress assembled: That the Senators and Representatives should convene at the time and place assigned: That the Senators should appoint a President of the Senate, for the sole purpose of receiving, opening and counting the votes for President; and that, after he shall be chose, the Congress, together with the President, should without delay proceed to execute this Constitution.

*By the unanimous order of the Convention,*
GEORGE WASHINGTON, President.
..........WILLIAM JACKSON, Sec'ry.

**In Convention, Sept 17, 1787.**
**SIR,**

*WE have now the honour to submit to the consideration of the United States in Congress in Congress assembled, that Constitution which has appeared to us the most adviseable.*

*The friends of our country have long seen and desired, that the power of making war, peace and treaties, that of levying money and regulating commerce, and the correspondent executive and judicial authorities, should be fully and effectually vested in the general government of the Union; but the impropriety of delegating such extensive trust to one body of men is evident.--Hence results the necessity of a different organization.*

*It is obviously impracticable, in the federal government of these States, to secure all rights of independent sovereignty to each, and yet provide for the interest and safety of all. Individuals entering into society must give up a share of liberty to preserve the rest. The magnitude of the sacrifice must depend as well on situation and circumstance, as on the object to be obtained. It is at all times difficult to draw with precision the line between those rights which must be surrendered, and those which may be reserved, and on the present occasion this difficulty was increased by a difference among the several states as to their situation, extent, habits and particular interests.*

*In all our deliberations on this subject, we kept steadily in our view that which appears to us the greatest interest of every true American, the consolidation of our Union, in which are involved our prosperity, felicity, safety, perhaps our national existence. This important consideration, seriously and deeply impressed on our minds, led each State in the Convention to be less rigid on points of inferior magnitude, than might have been otherwise expected; and thus the constitution, which we now present, is the result of a spirit of amity, and of that mutual deference and concession which the peculiarity of our political situation rendered indispensible.*

*That it will meet the full and entire approbation of every State is not perhaps to be expected, but each will doubtless consider, that had her interests been alone consulted, the consequences might have been particularly disagreeable or injurious to others; that it is liable to as few exceptions as could reasonably have been expected, we hope and believe; that it may promote the lasting welfare of that country so dear to us all, and secure her freedom and happiness, is our most ardent wish.*

*With great respect, we have the honour to be, Sir, your Excellency's most obedient and humble Servants,*
**GEORGE WASHINGTON,** *President.*
*By unanimous Order of the Convention.*
His Excellency the President of Congress.
**UNITED STATES in Congress Assembled.**
*Friday, September 28, 1787.*

Present, New-Hampshire, Massachusetts, Connecticut, New-York, New-Jersey, Pennsylvania, Delaware, Virginia, North-Carolina, South-Carolina and Georgia, and from Maryland Mr. Ross. Congress having received the report of the Convention lately assembled in Philadelphia,

*Resolved, unanimously,* That the said report, with the resolutions and letter accompanying the same, be transmitted to the several Legislatures, in order to be submitted to a Convention of Delegates, chosen in each State by the People thereof, in conformity to the resolves of the Convention made and provided in that case.
**CHARLES THOMSON,** *Sec'ry.*

State of Rhode-Island and Providence Plantations.
*In* **GENERAL ASSEMBLY,** *October Session, 1787.*

**IT** is Voted and Resolved, That the Report of the Convention, lately held at Philadelphia, proposing a new Constitution for the United States of America, be printed as soon as may be: That the following Number of Copies be sent to the several Town-Clerks in the State, to be distributed among the Inhabitants, that the Freemen may have an Opportunity of forming their Sentiments of the said proposed Constitution,*to wit:* For Newport 10, Portsmouth 25, Middletown 15, New-Shoreham 15, Jamestown 16, Tiverton 40, Little-Compton 36, Providence 10, Smithfield 75, Scituate 55, Foster 55, Glocester 60, Cumberland 40, Cranston 50, Johnston 30, North-Providence 20, Westerly 31, North-Kingstown 50, South-Kingstown 100, Charlestown 25, Richmond 25, Exeter 31, Hopkinton 30, Bristol 20, Warren 10, Barrington 10, Warwick 56, East-Greenwich 25, West-Greenwich 22, and Coventry 30.

*A true Copy:*
*Witness,* **HENRY WARD,** *Sec'ry.*
**PROVIDENCE: Printed by JOHN CARTER.**

## The Amendments To The Constitution Of The United States

The following are the Amendments to the Constitution. The first ten Amendments collectively are commonly known as the Bill of Rights.

### *Amendment 1 - Freedom of Religion, Press, Expression.* (Ratified 12/15/1791)

Congress shall make no law respecting an establishment of religion, or prohibiting the free exercise thereof; or abridging the freedom of speech, or of the press; or the right of the people peaceably to assemble, and to petition the Government for a redress of grievances.

### *Amendment 2 - Right to Bear Arms.* (Ratified 12/15/1791)

A well regulated Militia, being necessary to the security of a free State, the right of the people to keep and bear Arms, shall not be infringed.

### *Amendment 3 - Quartering of Soldiers.* (Ratified 12/15/1791)

No Soldier shall, in time of peace be quartered in any house, without the consent of the Owner, nor in time of war, but in a manner to be prescribed by law.

### *Amendment 4 - Search and Seizure.* (Ratified 12/15/1791)

The right of the people to be secure in their persons, houses, papers, and effects, against unreasonable searches and seizures, shall not be violated, and no Warrants shall issue, but upon probable cause, supported by Oath or affirmation, and particularly describing the place to be searched, and the persons or things to be seized.

### Amendment 5 - Trial and Punishment, Compensation for Takings. (Ratified 12/15/1791)

No person shall be held to answer for a capital, or otherwise infamous crime, unless on a presentment or indictment of a Grand Jury, except in cases arising in the land or naval forces, or in the Militia, when in actual service in time of War or public danger; nor shall any person be subject for the same offense to be twice put in jeopardy of life or limb; nor shall be compelled in any criminal case to be a witness against himself, nor be deprived of life, liberty, or property, without due process of law; nor shall private property be taken for public use, without just compensation.

### Amendment 6 - Right to Speedy Trial, Confrontation of Witnesses. (Ratified 12/15/1791)

In all criminal prosecutions, the accused shall enjoy the right to a speedy and public trial, by an impartial jury of the State and district wherein the crime shall have been committed, which district shall have been previously ascertained by law, and to be informed of the nature and cause of the accusation; to be confronted with the witnesses against him; to have compulsory process for obtaining witnesses in his favor, and to have the Assistance of Counsel for his defence.

### Amendment 7 - Trial by Jury in Civil Cases. (Ratified 12/15/1791)

In Suits at common law, where the value in controversy shall exceed twenty dollars, the right of trial by jury shall be preserved, and no fact tried by a jury, shall be otherwise re-examined in any Court of the United States, than according to the rules of the common law.

### Amendment 8 - Cruel and Unusual Punishment. (Ratified 12/15/1791)

Excessive bail shall not be required, nor excessive fines imposed, nor cruel and unusual punishments inflicted.

### Amendment 9 - Construction of Constitution. (Ratified 12/15/1791)

The enumeration in the Constitution, of certain rights, shall not be construed to deny or disparage others retained by the people.

### Amendment 10 - Powers of the States and People.

(Ratified 12/15/1791)

The powers not delegated to the United States by the Constitution, nor prohibited by it to the States, are reserved to the States respectively, or to the people.

### Amendment 11 - Judicial Limits. (Ratified 2/7/1795)

The Judicial power of the United States shall not be construed to extend to any suit in law or equity, commenced or prosecuted against one of the United States by Citizens of another State, or by Citizens or Subjects of any Foreign State.

### Amendment 12 - Choosing the President, Vice-President. (Ratified 6/15/1804)

The Electors shall meet in their respective states, and vote by ballot for President and Vice-President, one of whom, at least, shall not be an inhabitant of the same state with themselves; they shall name in their ballots the person voted for as President, and in distinct ballots the person voted for as Vice-President, and they shall make distinct lists of all persons voted for as President, and of all persons voted for as Vice-President and of the number of votes for each, which lists they shall sign and certify, and transmit sealed to the seat of the government of the United States, directed to the President of the Senate;

The President of the Senate shall, in the presence of the Senate and House of Representatives, open all the certificates and the votes shall then be counted;

The person having the greatest Number of votes for President, shall be the President, if such number be a majority of the whole number of Electors appointed; and if no person have such majority, then from the persons having the highest numbers not exceeding three on the list of those voted for as President, the House of Representatives shall choose immediately, by ballot, the President. But in choosing the President, the votes shall be taken by states, the representation from each state having one vote; a quorum for this purpose shall consist of a member or members from two-thirds of the states, and a majority of all the states shall be necessary to a choice. And if the House of Representatives shall not choose a President whenever the right of choice shall devolve upon them, before the fourth day of March next following, then the Vice-President shall act as President, as in the case of the death or other constitutional disability of the President.

The person having the greatest number of votes as Vice-President, shall be the Vice-President, if such number be a majority of the whole number of Electors appointed, and if no person have a majority, then from the two highest numbers on the list, the Senate shall choose the Vice-President; a quorum for the purpose shall consist of two-thirds of the whole number of Senators, and a majority of the whole number shall be necessary to a choice. But no person constitutionally ineligible to the office of President shall be eligible to that of Vice-President of the United States.

### *Amendment 13 - Slavery Abolished.* (Ratified 12/6/1865)

1. Neither slavery nor involuntary servitude, except as a punishment for crime whereof the party shall have been duly convicted, shall exist within the United States, or any place subject to their jurisdiction.

2. Congress shall have power to enforce this article by appropriate legislation.

### *Amendment 14 - Citizenship Rights.* (Ratified 7/9/1868)

1. All persons born or naturalized in the United States, and subject to the jurisdiction thereof, are citizens of the United States and of the State wherein they reside. No State shall make or enforce any law which shall abridge the privileges or immunities of citizens of the United States; nor shall any State deprive any person of life, liberty, or property, without due process of law; nor deny to any person within its jurisdiction the equal protection of the laws.

2. Representatives shall be apportioned among the several States according to their respective numbers, counting the whole number of persons in each State, excluding Indians not taxed. But when the right to vote at any election for the choice of electors for President and Vice-President of the United States, Representatives in Congress, the Executive and Judicial officers of a State, or the members of the Legislature thereof, is denied to any of the male inhabitants of such State, being twenty-one years of age, and citizens of the United States, or in any way abridged, except for participation in rebellion, or other crime, the basis of representation therein shall be reduced in the proportion which the number of such male citizens shall bear to the whole number of male citizens twenty-one years of age in such State.

3. No person shall be a Senator or Representative in Congress, or elector of President and Vice-President, or hold any office, civil or military, under the United States, or under any State, who, having previously taken an oath, as a member of Congress, or as an officer of the United States, or as a member of any State legislature, or as an executive or judicial officer of any State, to support the Constitution of the United States, shall have engaged in insurrection or rebellion against the same, or given aid or comfort to the enemies thereof. But Congress may by a vote of two-thirds of each House, remove such disability.

4. The validity of the public debt of the United States, authorized by law, including debts incurred for payment of pensions and bounties for services in suppressing insurrection or rebellion, shall not be questioned. But neither the United States nor any State shall assume or pay any debt or obligation incurred in aid of insurrection or rebellion against the United States, or any claim for the loss or emancipation of any slave; but all such debts, obligations and claims shall be held illegal and void.

5. The Congress shall have power to enforce, by appropriate legislation, the provisions of this article.

### Amendment 15 - Race No Bar to Vote. (Ratified 2/3/1870)

1. The right of citizens of the United States to vote shall not be denied or abridged by the United States or by any State on account of race, color, or previous condition of servitude.

2. The Congress shall have power to enforce this article by appropriate legislation.

### Amendment 16 - Status of Income Tax Clarified.

(Ratified 2/3/1913) *[Author's Note: Taxing "income" is contrary to our Founding Father's principles and therefore this Amendment needs to be repealed & replaced with a 10% Federal Sales Tax!]*

The Congress shall have power to lay and collect taxes on incomes, from whatever source derived, without apportionment among the several States, and without regard to any census or enumeration.

### Amendment 17 - Senators Elected by Popular Vote. (Ratified 4/8/1913)

The Senate of the United States shall be composed of two Senators from each State, elected by the people thereof, for six years; and each Senator shall have one vote. The electors in each State shall have the qualifications requisite for electors of the most numerous branch of the State legislatures.

When vacancies happen in the representation of any State in the Senate, the executive authority of such State shall issue writs of election to fill such vacancies: Provided, That the legislature of any State may empower the executive thereof to make temporary appointments until the people fill the vacancies by election as the legislature may direct.

This amendment shall not be so construed as to affect the election or term of any Senator chosen before it becomes valid as part of the Constitution.

### Amendment 18 - Liquor Abolished. (Ratified 1/16/1919. Repealed by Amendment 21, 12/5/1933)

1. After one year from the ratification of this article the manufacture, sale, or transportation of intoxicating liquors within, the importation thereof into, or the exportation thereof from the United States and all territory subject to the jurisdiction thereof for beverage purposes is hereby prohibited.

2. The Congress and the several States shall have concurrent power to enforce this article by appropriate legislation.

3. This article shall be inoperative unless it shall have been ratified as an amendment to the Constitution by the legislatures of the several States, as provided in the Constitution, within seven years from the date of the submission hereof to the States by the Congress.

### *Amendment 19 - Women's Suffrage.* (Ratified 8/18/1920)

The right of citizens of the United States to vote shall not be denied or abridged by the United States or by any State on account of sex.

Congress shall have power to enforce this article by appropriate legislation.

### *Amendment 20 - Presidential, Congressional Terms.* (Ratified 1/23/1933)

1. The terms of the President and Vice President shall end at noon on the 20th day of January, and the terms of Senators and Representatives at noon on the 3d day of January, of the years in which such terms would have ended if this article had not been ratified; and the terms of their successors shall then begin.

2. The Congress shall assemble at least once in every year, and such meeting shall begin at noon on the 3d day of January, unless they shall by law appoint a different day.

3. If, at the time fixed for the beginning of the term of the President, the President elect shall have died, the Vice President elect shall become President. If a President shall not have been chosen before the time fixed for the beginning of his term, or if the President elect shall have failed to qualify, then the Vice President elect shall act as President until a President shall have qualified; and the Congress may by law provide for the case wherein neither a President elect nor a Vice President elect shall have qualified, declaring who shall then act as President, or the manner in which one who is to act shall be selected, and such person shall act accordingly until a President or Vice President shall have qualified.

4. The Congress may by law provide for the case of the death of any of the persons from whom the House of Representatives may choose a President whenever the right of choice shall have devolved upon them, and for the case of the death of any of the persons from whom the Senate may choose a Vice President whenever the right of choice shall have devolved upon them.

5. Sections 1 and 2 shall take effect on the 15th day of October following the ratification of this article.

6. This article shall be inoperative unless it shall have been ratified as an amendment to the Constitution by the legislatures of three-fourths of the several States within seven years from the date of its submission.

## Amendment 21 - Amendment 18 Repealed.

(Ratified 12/5/1933)

1. The eighteenth article of amendment to the Constitution of the United States is hereby repealed.

2. The transportation or importation into any State, Territory, or possession of the United States for delivery or use therein of intoxicating liquors, in violation of the laws thereof, is hereby prohibited.

3. The article shall be inoperative unless it shall have been ratified as an amendment to the Constitution by conventions in the several States, as provided in the Constitution, within seven years from the date of the submission hereof to the States by the Congress.

## Amendment 22 - Presidential Term Limits. (Ratified 2/27/1951)

1. No person shall be elected to the office of the President more than twice, and no person who has held the office of President, or acted as President, for more than two years of a term to which some other person was elected President shall be elected to the office of the President more than once. But this Article shall not apply to any person holding the office of President, when this Article was proposed by the Congress, and shall not prevent any person who may be holding the office of President, or acting as President, during the term within which this Article becomes operative from holding the office of President or acting as President during the remainder of such term.

2. This article shall be inoperative unless it shall have been ratified as an amendment to the Constitution by the legislatures of three-fourths of the several States within seven years from the date of its submission to the States by the Congress.

### Amendment 23 - Presidential Vote for District of Columbia. (Ratified 3/29/1961)

1. The District constituting the seat of Government of the United States shall appoint in such manner as the Congress may direct: A number of electors of President and Vice President equal to the whole number of Senators and Representatives in Congress to which the District would be entitled if it were a State, but in no event more than the least populous State; they shall be in addition to those appointed by the States, but they shall be considered, for the purposes of the election of President and Vice President, to be electors appointed by a State; and they shall meet in the District and perform such duties as provided by the twelfth article of amendment.

2. The Congress shall have power to enforce this article by appropriate legislation.

### Amendment 24 - Poll Tax Barred. (Ratified 1/23/1964)

1. The right of citizens of the United States to vote in any primary or other election for President or Vice President, for electors for President or Vice President, or for Senator or Representative in Congress, shall not be denied or abridged by the United States or any State by reason of failure to pay any poll tax or other tax.

2. The Congress shall have power to enforce this article by appropriate legislation.

## *Amendment 25 - Presidential Disability and*

## *Succession.* (Ratified 2/10/1967)

1. In case of the removal of the President from office or of his death or resignation, the Vice President shall become President.

2. Whenever there is a vacancy in the office of the Vice President, the President shall nominate a Vice President who shall take office upon confirmation by a majority vote of both Houses of Congress.

3. Whenever the President transmits to the President pro tempore of the Senate and the Speaker of the House of Representatives his written declaration that he is unable to discharge the powers and duties of his office, and until he transmits to them a written declaration to the contrary, such powers and duties shall be discharged by the Vice President as Acting President.

4. Whenever the Vice President and a majority of either the principal officers of the executive departments or of such other body as Congress may by law provide, transmit to the President pro tempore of the Senate and the Speaker of the House of Representatives their written declaration that the President is unable to discharge the powers and duties of his office, the Vice President shall immediately assume the powers and duties of the office as Acting President.

Thereafter, when the President transmits to the President pro tempore of the Senate and the Speaker of the House of Representatives his written declaration that no inability exists, he shall resume the powers and duties of his office unless the Vice President and a majority of either the principal officers of the executive department or of such other body as Congress may by law provide, transmit within four days to the President pro tempore of the Senate and the Speaker of the House of Representatives their written declaration that the President is unable to discharge the powers and duties of his office. Thereupon Congress shall decide the issue, assembling within forty eight hours for that purpose if not in session. If the Congress, within twenty one days after receipt of the latter written declaration, or, if Congress is not in session, within twenty one days after Congress is required to assemble, determines by two thirds vote of both Houses that the President is unable to discharge the powers and duties of his office, the Vice President shall continue to discharge the same as Acting President; otherwise, the President shall resume the powers and duties of his office.

### *Amendment 26 - Voting Age Set to 18 Years.*

(Ratified 7/1/1971)

1. The right of citizens of the United States, who are eighteen years of age or older, to vote shall not be denied or abridged by the United States or by any State on account of age.

2. The Congress shall have power to enforce this article by appropriate legislation.

### *Amendment 27 - Limiting Changes to*

### *Congressional Pay.* (Ratified 5/7/1992)

No law, varying the compensation for the services of the Senators and Representatives, shall take effect, until an election of Representatives shall have intervened.

www.ingramcontent.com/pod-product-compliance
Lightning Source LLC
Chambersburg PA
CBHW072344290526
45794CB00001B/9